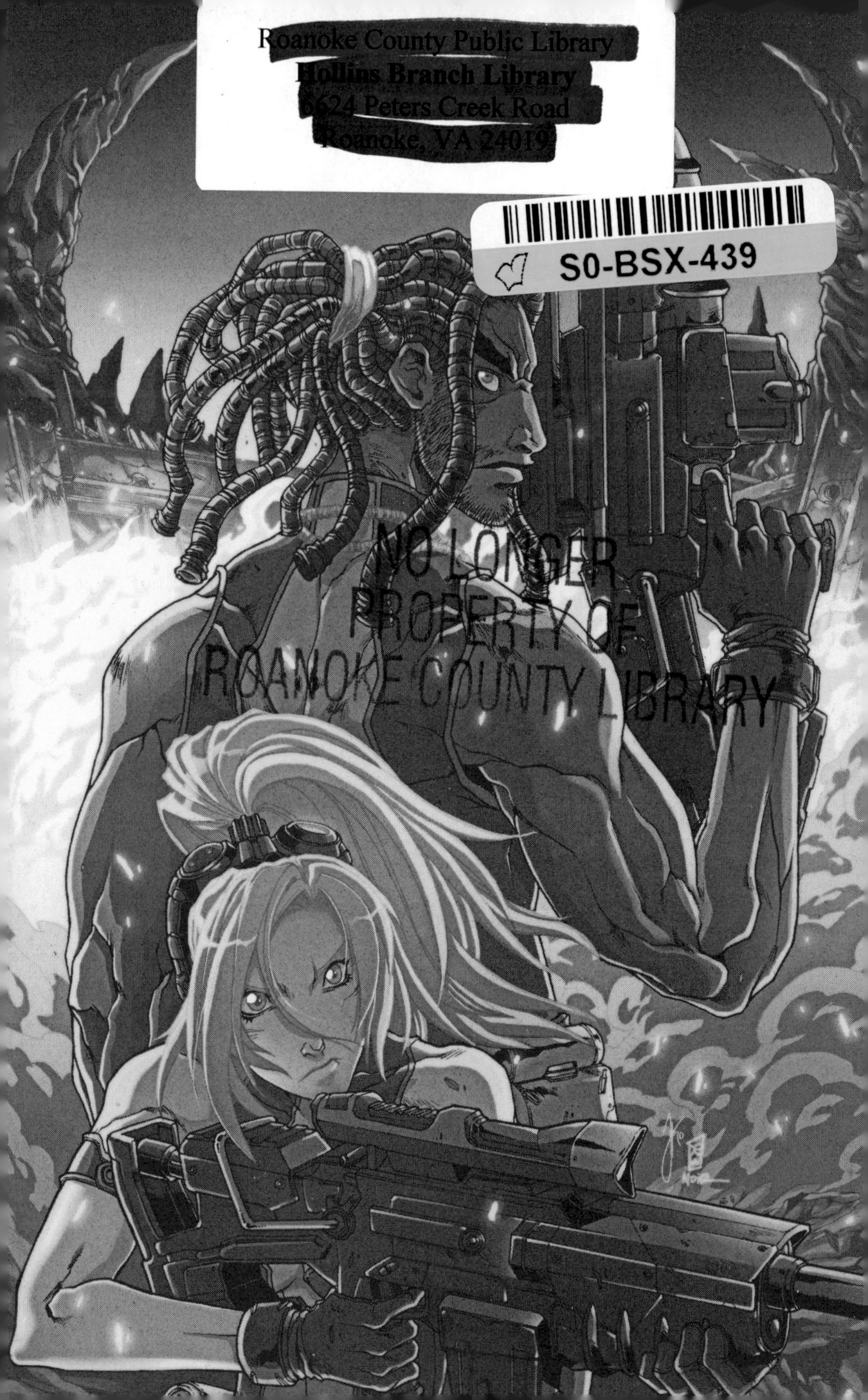

# StarCraft: Ghost Academy Vol. 2

Story by: David Gerrold

Art by: Fernando Heinz Furukawa

Contributing Editor - Troy Lewter
Layout, Lettering & Retouch Artist - Michael Paolilli
Creative Consultant - Michael Paolilli
Cover Designer - Louis Csontos & Roderick Pio-Roda
Cover Artist - Fernando Heinz Furukawa
Cover Colors - Rocio Zucchi

Editor - Hope Donovan
Print Production Manager - Lucas Rivera
Managing Editor - Vy Nguyen
Senior Designer - Louis Csontos
Art Director - Al-Insan Lashley
Director of Sales and Manufacturing - Allyson De Simone
Associate Publisher - Marco F. Pavia
President and C.O.O. - John Parker
C.E.O. and Chief Creative Officer - Stu Levy

BLIZZARD ENTERTAINMENT

Senior Vice President, Creative Development - Chris Metzen
Director, Creative Development - Jeff Donais
Lead Developer, Licensed Products - Mike Hummel
Publishing Lead, Creative Development - Micky Neilson
Senior Story Developer - James Waugh
Art Director - Glenn Rane
Licensing Manager - Jason Bischoff
Historian - Evelyn Fredericksen
Additional Development - Samwise Didier, Cameron Dayton and Tommy Newcomer

A TOKYOPOP Manga

TOKYOPOP and are trademarks or registered trademarks of TOKYOPOP Inc.

TOKYOPOP Inc.
5900 Wilshire Blvd. Suite 2000
Los Angeles, CA 90036

E-mail: info@TOKYOPOP.com
Come visit us online at www.TOKYOPOP.com

ISBN: 978-1-4278-1613-9

First TOKYOPOP printing: August 2010

10 9 8 7 6 5 4 3 2 1

Printed in the USA

# STARCRAFT
## GHOST ACADEMY
### VOLUME 2

STORY BY:

DAVID GERROLD

ART BY:

FERNANDO HEINZ FURUKAWA

TOKYOPOP

HAMBURG // LONDON // LOS ANGELES // TOKYO

# The Administrative Office of the Ghost Academy

Dear Ghost Academy trainees,

Recently, at the Ghost Academy we all call home, you may have noticed some "shake-ups." Aal Cistler, son of Arcturus Mengsk's finance minister, joined your ranks briefly before being dismissed as part of a disciplinary action.

But not all the "re-shuffling" has been negative! Take pride in your fellow trainees' recent success stories: Trainee Nova Terra of Team Blue has been promoted to third class; and her teammate, longtime trainee Delta Emblock, has been promoted to fourth class. Congratulations, Team Blue leader Gabriel Tosh!

Take pride in your training. Your preceptors have prepared excellent indoctrinations to mold you into highly-skilled top defenders of the Dominion. Invisible, invincible, and PROUD!

All the Best,

*Superintendent Sarco Angelini*

# StarCraft Ghost Academy

## CONTENTS



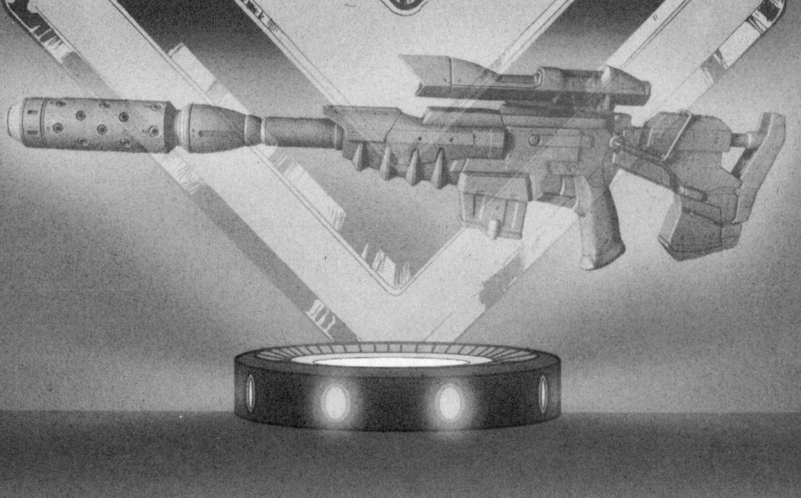

# PROLOGUE

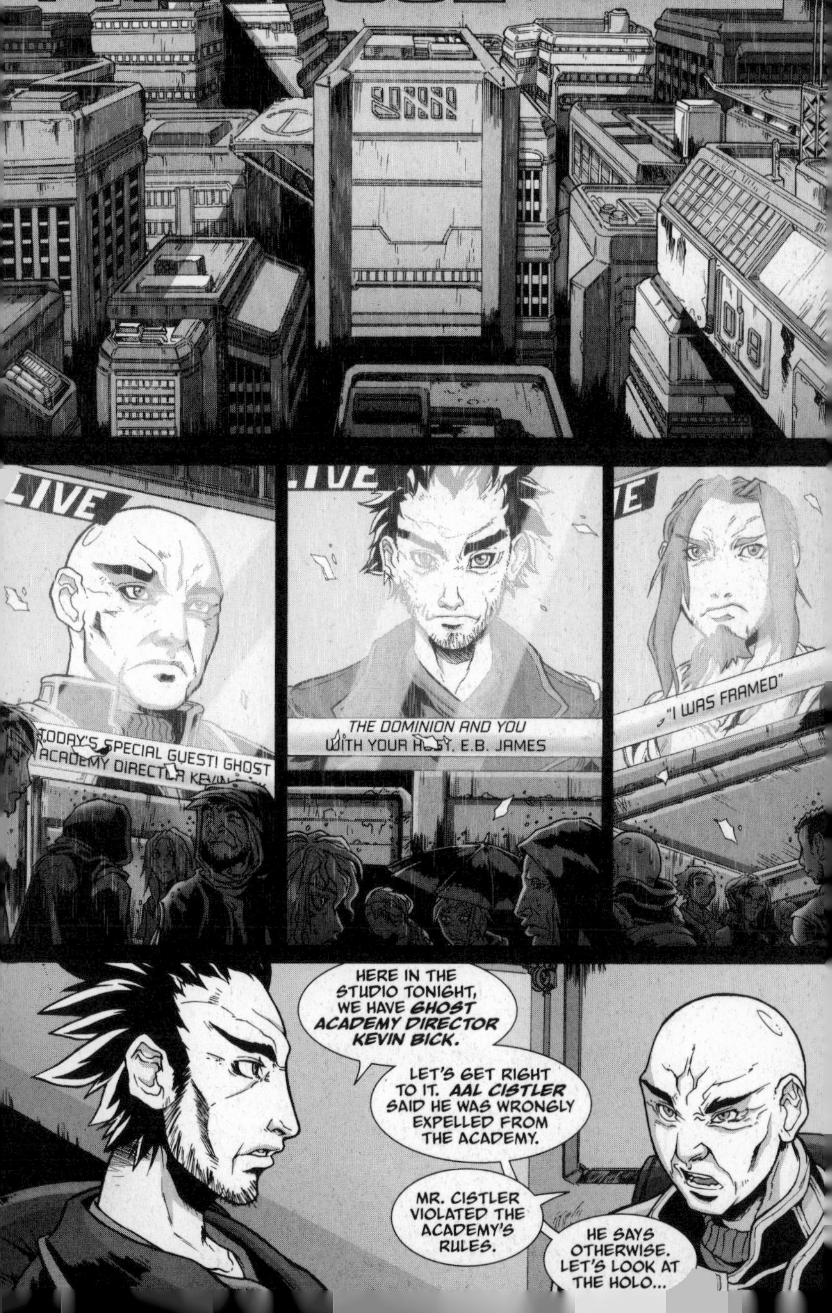
LIVE
TODAY'S SPECIAL GUEST! GHOST ACADEMY DIRECTOR
THE DOMINION AND YOU
WITH YOUR HOST, E.B. JAMES
"I WAS FRAMED"
HERE IN THE STUDIO TONIGHT, WE HAVE GHOST ACADEMY DIRECTOR KEVIN BICK.
LET'S GET RIGHT TO IT. AAL CISTLER SAID HE WAS WRONGLY EXPELLED FROM THE ACADEMY.
MR. CISTLER VIOLATED THE ACADEMY'S RULES.
HE SAYS OTHERWISE. LET'S LOOK AT THE HOLO...

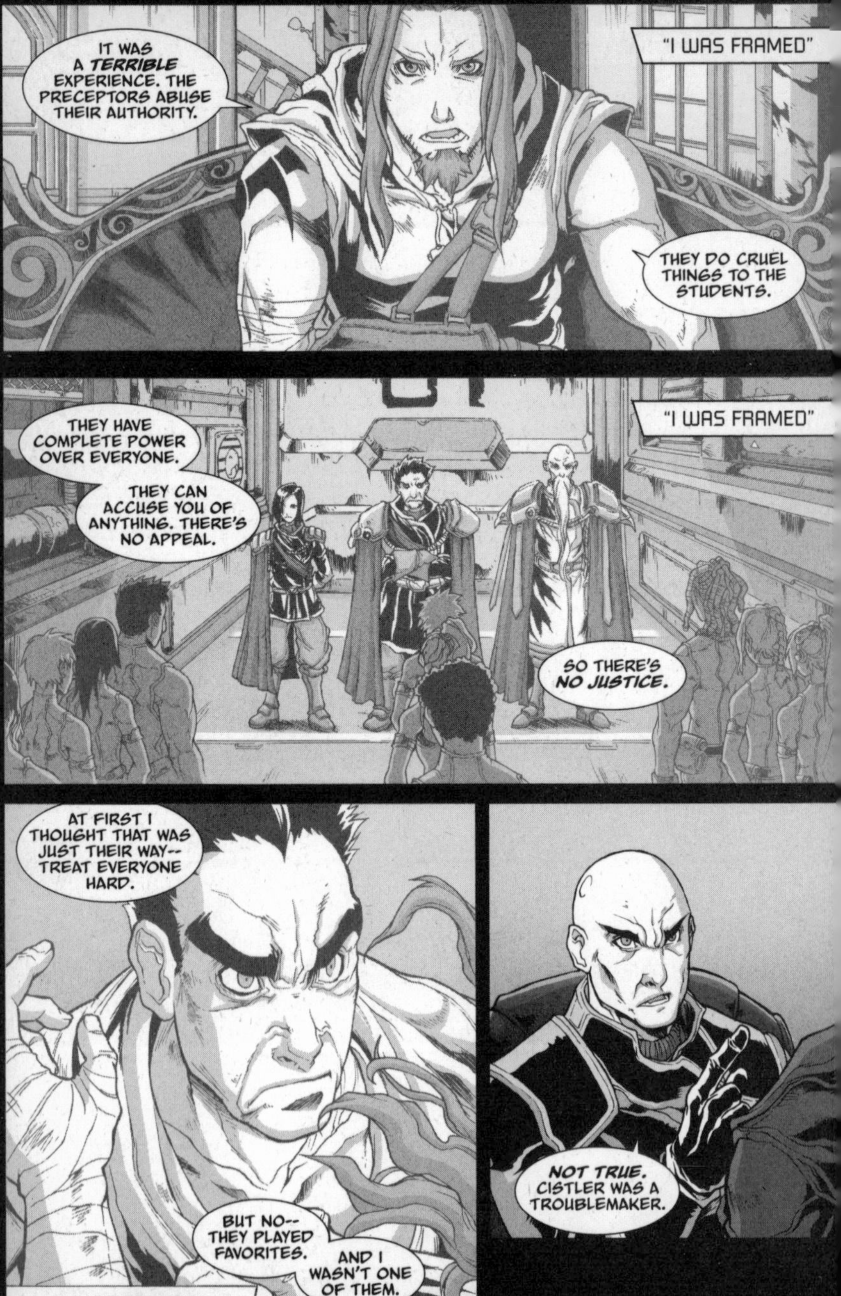
"I WAS FRAMED"
IT WAS A *TERRIBLE* EXPERIENCE. THE PRECEPTORS ABUSE THEIR AUTHORITY.
THEY DO CRUEL THINGS TO THE STUDENTS.
"I WAS FRAMED"
THEY HAVE COMPLETE POWER OVER EVERYONE.
THEY CAN ACCUSE YOU OF ANYTHING. THERE'S NO APPEAL.
SO THERE'S *NO JUSTICE*.
AT FIRST I THOUGHT THAT WAS JUST THEIR WAY-- TREAT EVERYONE HARD.
BUT NO-- THEY PLAYED FAVORITES.
AND I WASN'T ONE OF THEM.
"I WAS FRAMED"
*NOT TRUE.* CISTLER WAS A TROUBLEMAKER.

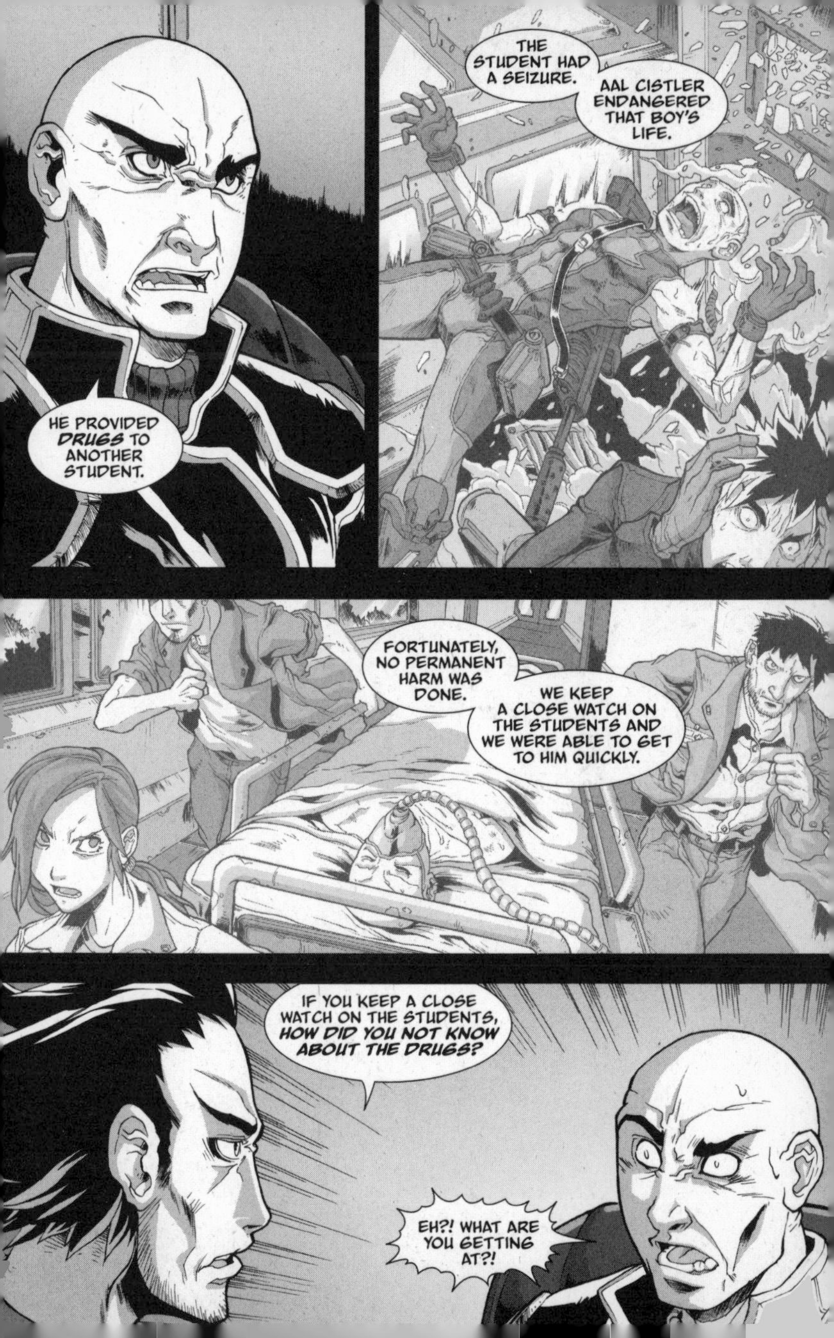
HE PROVIDED *DRUGS* TO ANOTHER STUDENT.
THE STUDENT HAD A SEIZURE.
AAL CISTLER ENDANGERED THAT BOY'S LIFE.
FORTUNATELY, NO PERMANENT HARM WAS DONE.
WE KEEP A CLOSE WATCH ON THE STUDENTS AND WE WERE ABLE TO GET TO HIM QUICKLY.
IF YOU KEEP A CLOSE WATCH ON THE STUDENTS, *HOW DID YOU NOT KNOW ABOUT THE DRUGS?*
EH?! WHAT ARE YOU GETTING AT?!

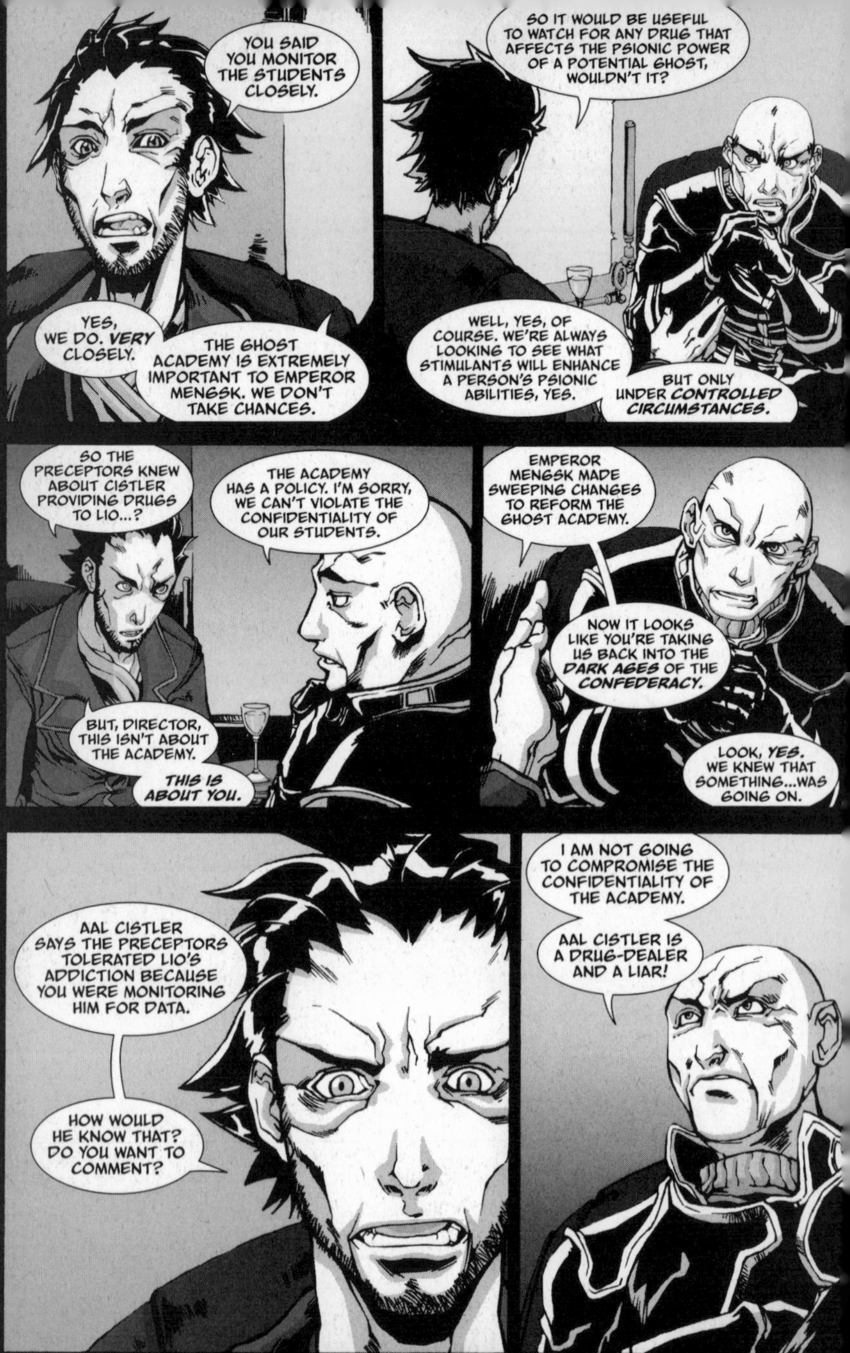
YOU SAID YOU MONITOR THE STUDENTS CLOSELY.
YES, WE DO. VERY CLOSELY.
THE GHOST ACADEMY IS EXTREMELY IMPORTANT TO EMPEROR MENGSK. WE DON'T TAKE CHANCES.
SO IT WOULD BE USEFUL TO WATCH FOR ANY DRUG THAT AFFECTS THE PSIONIC POWER OF A POTENTIAL GHOST, WOULDN'T IT?
WELL, YES, OF COURSE. WE'RE ALWAYS LOOKING TO SEE WHAT STIMULANTS WILL ENHANCE A PERSON'S PSIONIC ABILITIES, YES.
BUT ONLY UNDER CONTROLLED CIRCUMSTANCES.
SO THE PRECEPTORS KNEW ABOUT CISTLER PROVIDING DRUGS TO LIO...?
THE ACADEMY HAS A POLICY. I'M SORRY, WE CAN'T VIOLATE THE CONFIDENTIALITY OF OUR STUDENTS.
BUT, DIRECTOR, THIS ISN'T ABOUT THE ACADEMY.
THIS IS ABOUT YOU.
EMPEROR MENGSK MADE SWEEPING CHANGES TO REFORM THE GHOST ACADEMY.
NOW IT LOOKS LIKE YOU'RE TAKING US BACK INTO THE DARK AGES OF THE CONFEDERACY.
LOOK, YES. WE KNEW THAT SOMETHING...WAS GOING ON.
AAL CISTLER SAYS THE PRECEPTORS TOLERATED LIO'S ADDICTION BECAUSE YOU WERE MONITORING HIM FOR DATA.
HOW WOULD HE KNOW THAT? DO YOU WANT TO COMMENT?
I AM NOT GOING TO COMPROMISE THE CONFIDENTIALITY OF THE ACADEMY.
AAL CISTLER IS A DRUG-DEALER AND A LIAR!

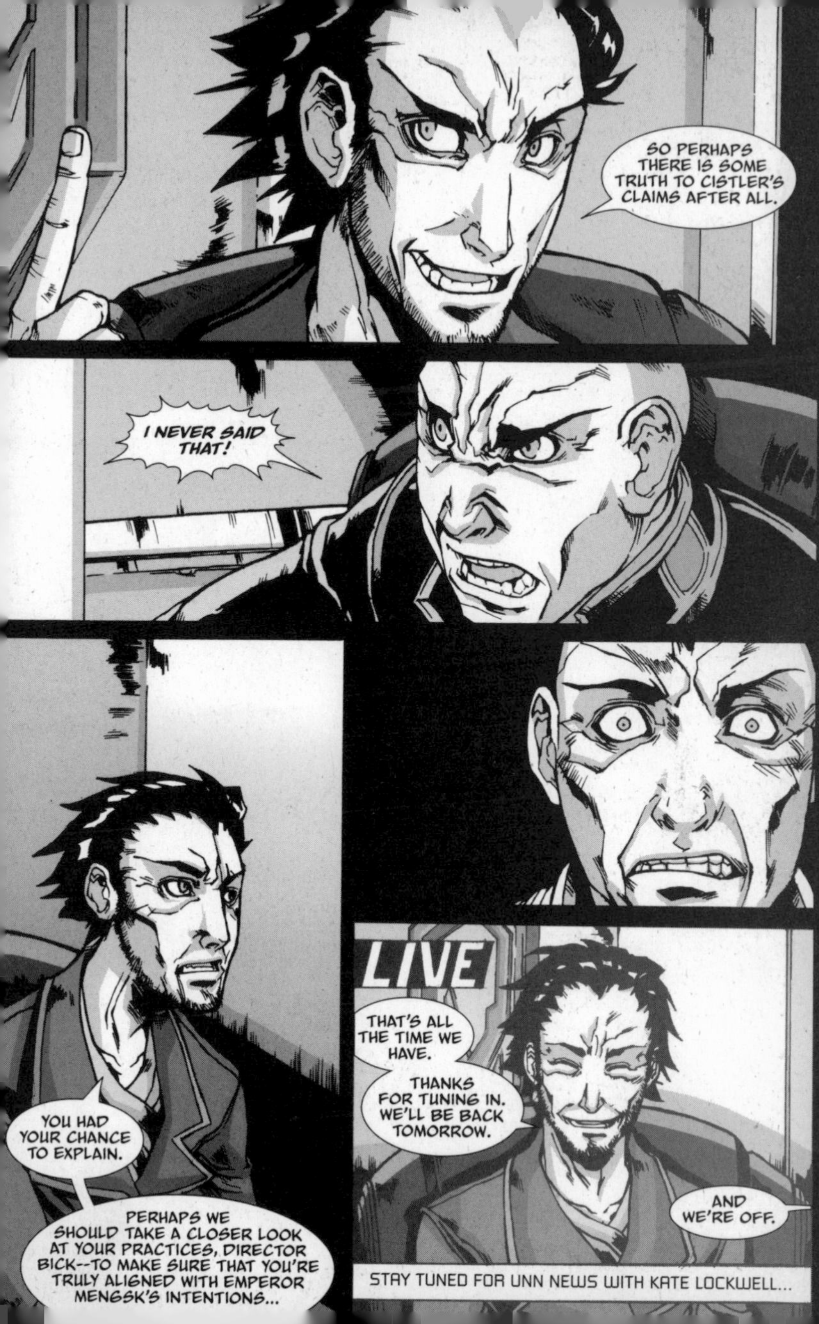
SO PERHAPS THERE IS SOME TRUTH TO CISTLER'S CLAIMS AFTER ALL.
I NEVER SAID THAT!
YOU HAD YOUR CHANCE TO EXPLAIN.
PERHAPS WE SHOULD TAKE A CLOSER LOOK AT YOUR PRACTICES, DIRECTOR BICK--TO MAKE SURE THAT YOU'RE TRULY ALIGNED WITH EMPEROR MENGSK'S INTENTIONS...
LIVE
THAT'S ALL THE TIME WE HAVE.
THANKS FOR TUNING IN. WE'LL BE BACK TOMORROW.
AND WE'RE OFF.
STAY TUNED FOR UNN NEWS WITH KATE LOCKWELL...

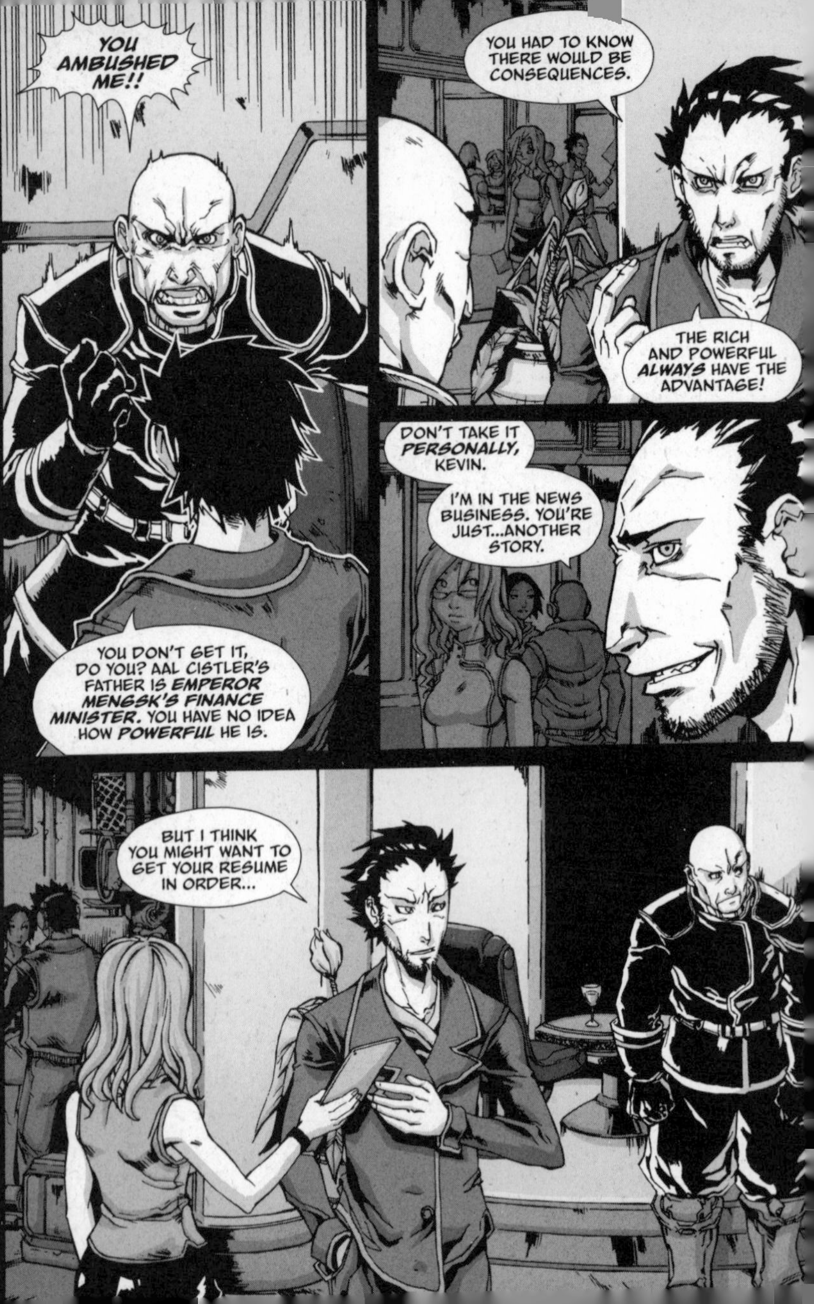
YOU AMBUSHED ME!!
YOU DON'T GET IT, DO YOU? AAL CISTLER'S FATHER IS EMPEROR MENGSK'S FINANCE MINISTER. YOU HAVE NO IDEA HOW POWERFUL HE IS.
YOU HAD TO KNOW THERE WOULD BE CONSEQUENCES.
THE RICH AND POWERFUL ALWAYS HAVE THE ADVANTAGE!
DON'T TAKE IT PERSONALLY, KEVIN.
I'M IN THE NEWS BUSINESS. YOU'RE JUST...ANOTHER STORY.
BUT I THINK YOU MIGHT WANT TO GET YOUR RESUME IN ORDER...

# CHAPTER 1
## MIND GAMES

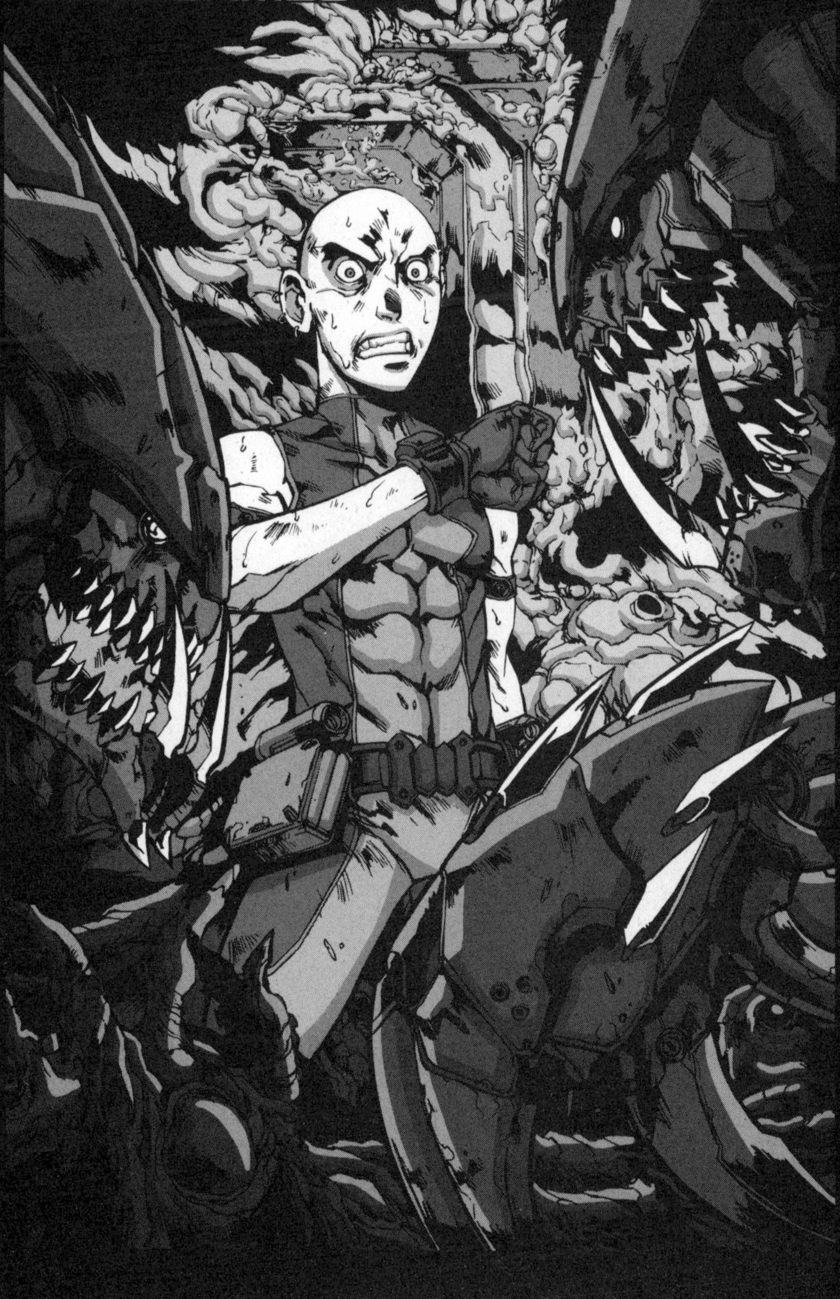

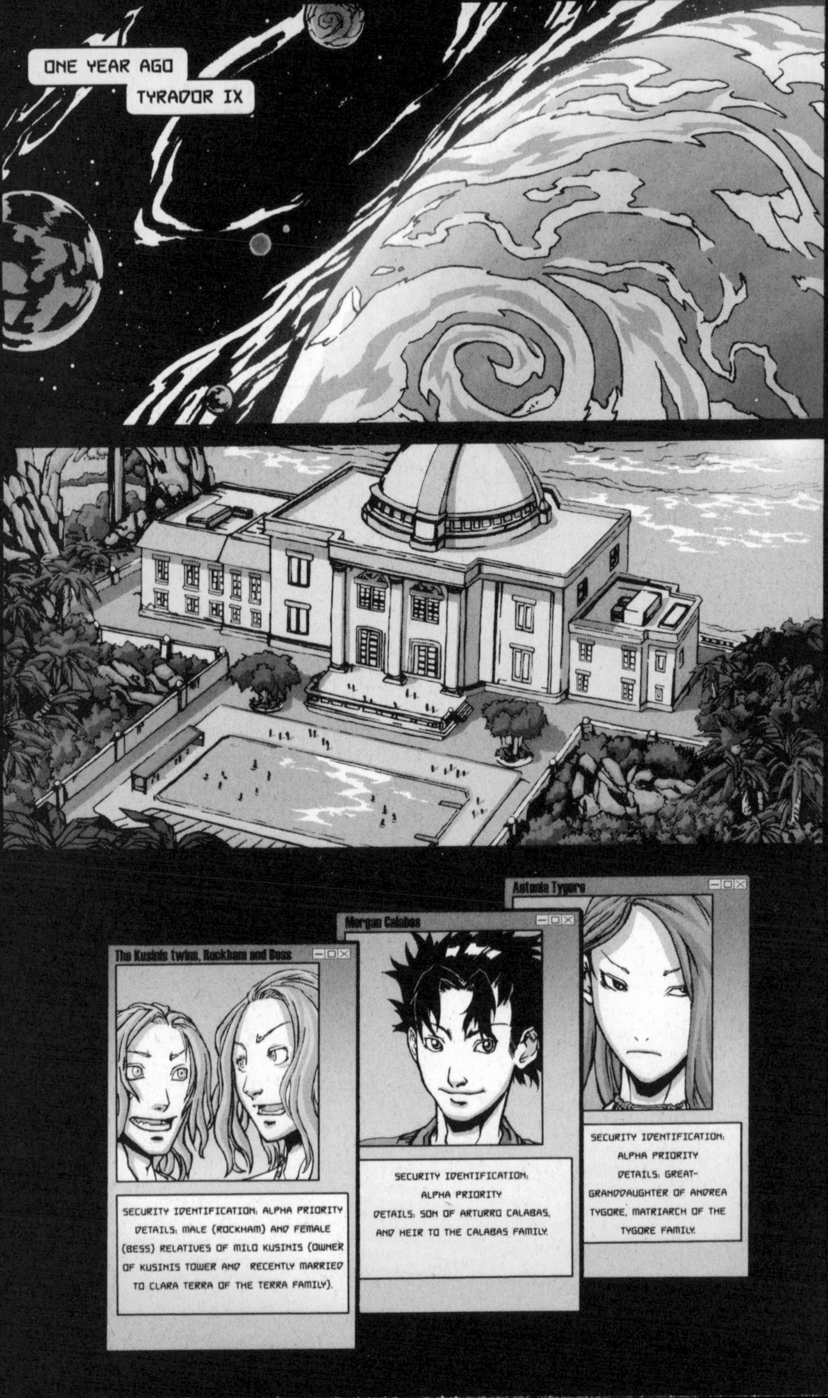
ONE YEAR AGO
TYRADOR IX
The Kusinis twins, Rockham and Bess
SECURITY IDENTIFICATION: ALPHA PRIORITY
DETAILS: MALE (ROCKHAM) AND FEMALE (BESS) RELATIVES OF MILO KUSINIS (OWNER OF KUSINIS TOWER AND RECENTLY MARRIED TO CLARA TERRA OF THE TERRA FAMILY).
Morgan Calabas
SECURITY IDENTIFICATION:
ALPHA PRIORITY
DETAILS: SON OF ARTURRO CALABAS, AND HEIR TO THE CALABAS FAMILY.
Antonia Tygore
SECURITY IDENTIFICATION:
ALPHA PRIORITY
DETAILS: GREAT-GRANDDAUGHTER OF ANDREA TYGORE, MATRIARCH OF THE TYGORE FAMILY.

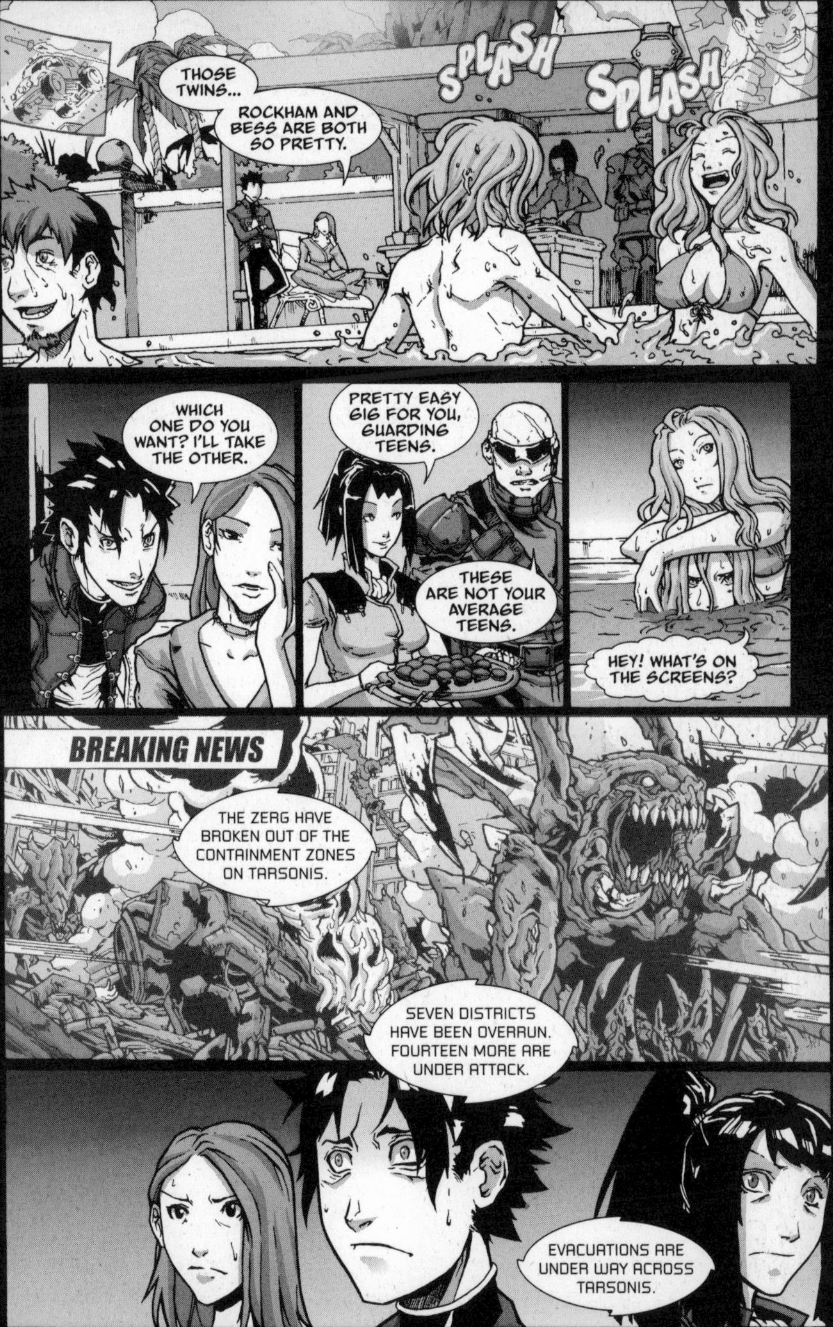
THOSE TWINS...
ROCKHAM AND BESS ARE BOTH SO PRETTY.
SPLASH
SPLASH
WHICH ONE DO YOU WANT? I'LL TAKE THE OTHER.
PRETTY EASY GIG FOR YOU, GUARDING TEENS.
THESE ARE NOT YOUR AVERAGE TEENS.
HEY! WHAT'S ON THE SCREENS?
BREAKING NEWS
THE ZERG HAVE BROKEN OUT OF THE CONTAINMENT ZONES ON TARSONIS.
SEVEN DISTRICTS HAVE BEEN OVERRUN. FOURTEEN MORE ARE UNDER ATTACK.
EVACUATIONS ARE UNDER WAY ACROSS TARSONIS.

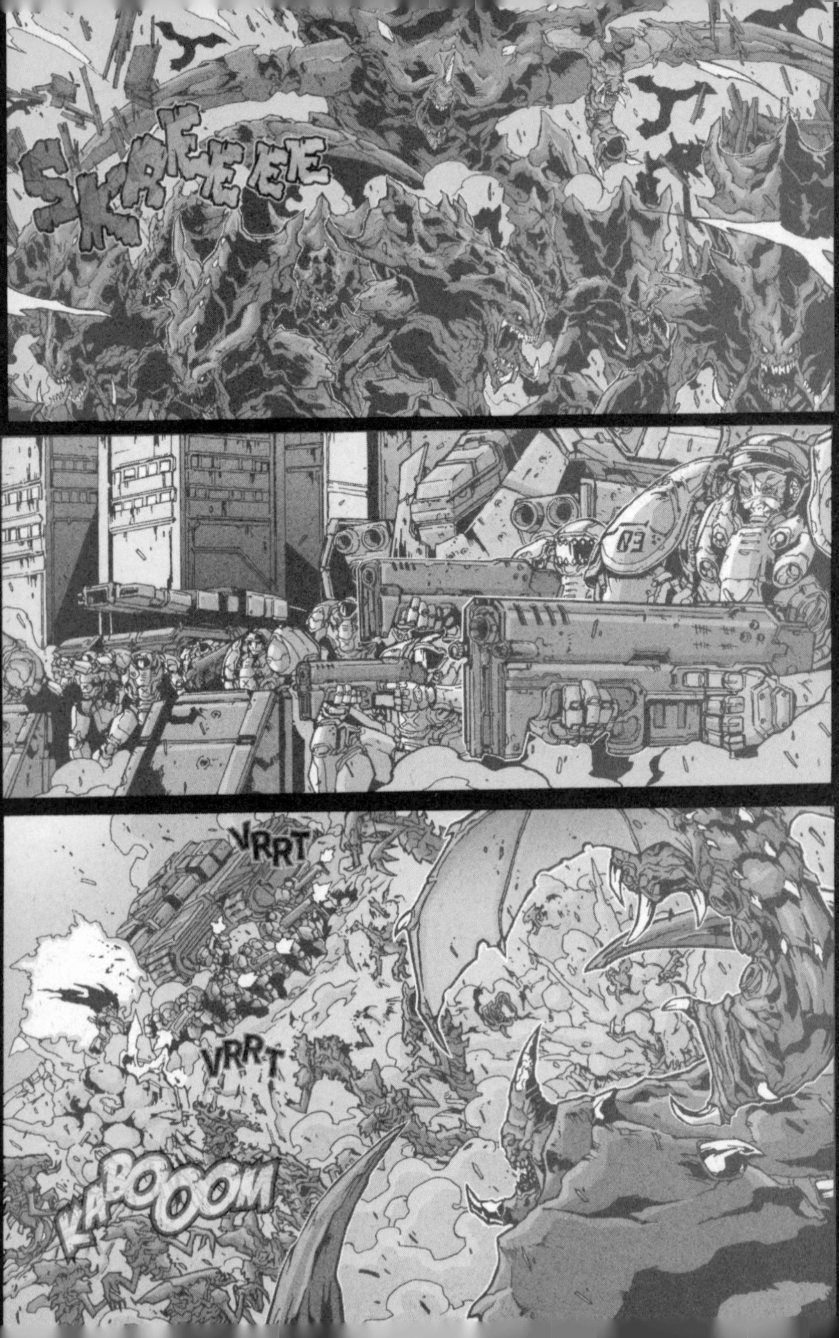
SKREEEE
VRRT
VRRT
KABOOOM

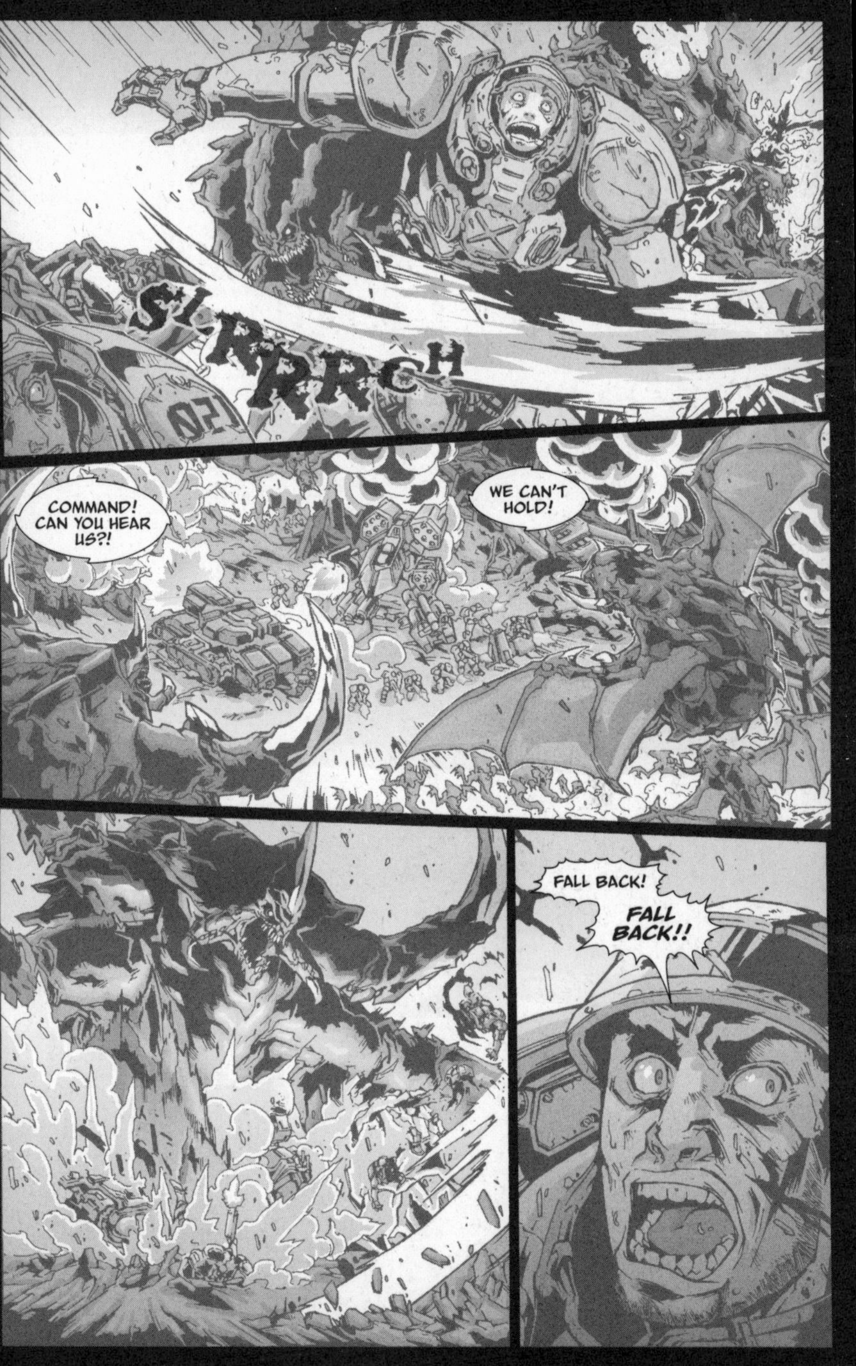
SLRRRCH
COMMAND! CAN YOU HEAR US?!
WE CAN'T HOLD!
FALL BACK!
FALL BACK!!

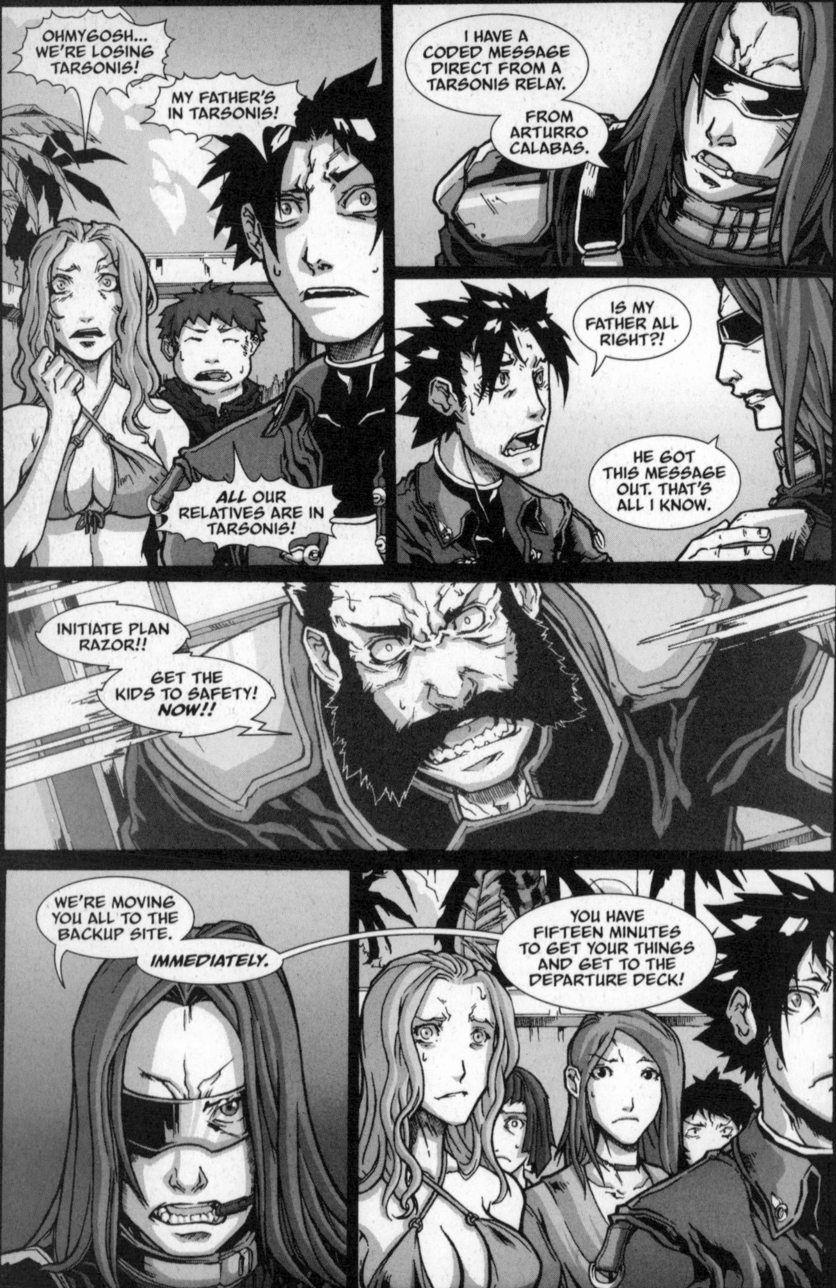
OHMYGOSH... WE'RE LOSING TARSONIS!
MY FATHER'S IN TARSONIS!
ALL OUR RELATIVES ARE IN TARSONIS!
I HAVE A CODED MESSAGE DIRECT FROM A TARSONIS RELAY.
FROM ARTURRO CALABAS.
IS MY FATHER ALL RIGHT?!
HE GOT THIS MESSAGE OUT. THAT'S ALL I KNOW.
INITIATE PLAN RAZOR!!
GET THE KIDS TO SAFETY! NOW!!
WE'RE MOVING YOU ALL TO THE BACKUP SITE.
IMMEDIATELY.
YOU HAVE FIFTEEN MINUTES TO GET YOUR THINGS AND GET TO THE DEPARTURE DECK!

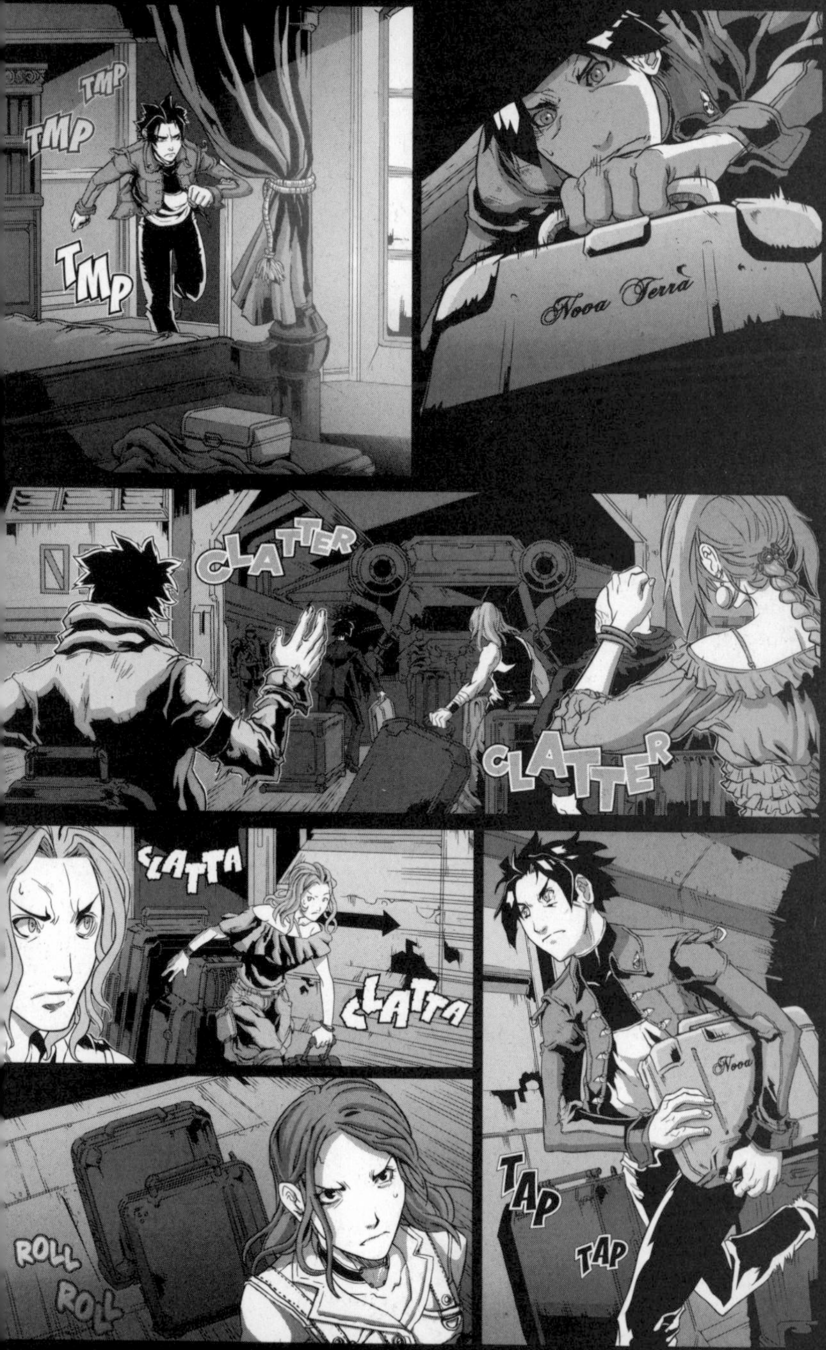
TMP
TMP
TMP
Nooa Terra
CLATTER
CLATTER
CLATTA
CLATTA
Nooa
TAP
TAP
ROLL
ROLL

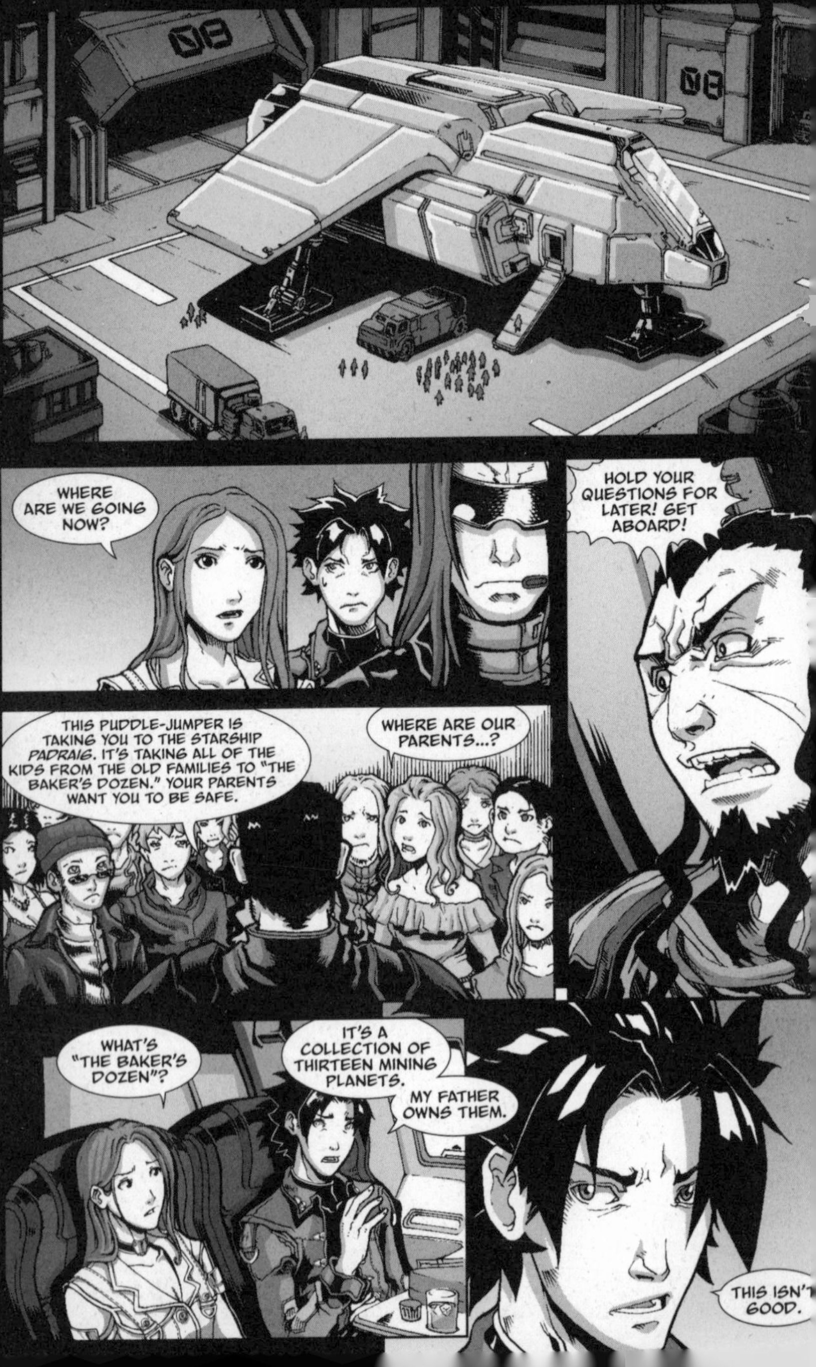
08
08
WHERE ARE WE GOING NOW?
HOLD YOUR QUESTIONS FOR LATER! GET ABOARD!
THIS PUDDLE-JUMPER IS TAKING YOU TO THE STARSHIP *PADRAIG*. IT'S TAKING ALL OF THE KIDS FROM THE OLD FAMILIES TO "THE BAKER'S DOZEN." YOUR PARENTS WANT YOU TO BE SAFE.
WHERE ARE OUR PARENTS...?
WHAT'S "THE BAKER'S DOZEN"?
IT'S A COLLECTION OF THIRTEEN MINING PLANETS.
MY FATHER OWNS THEM.
THIS ISN'T GOOD.

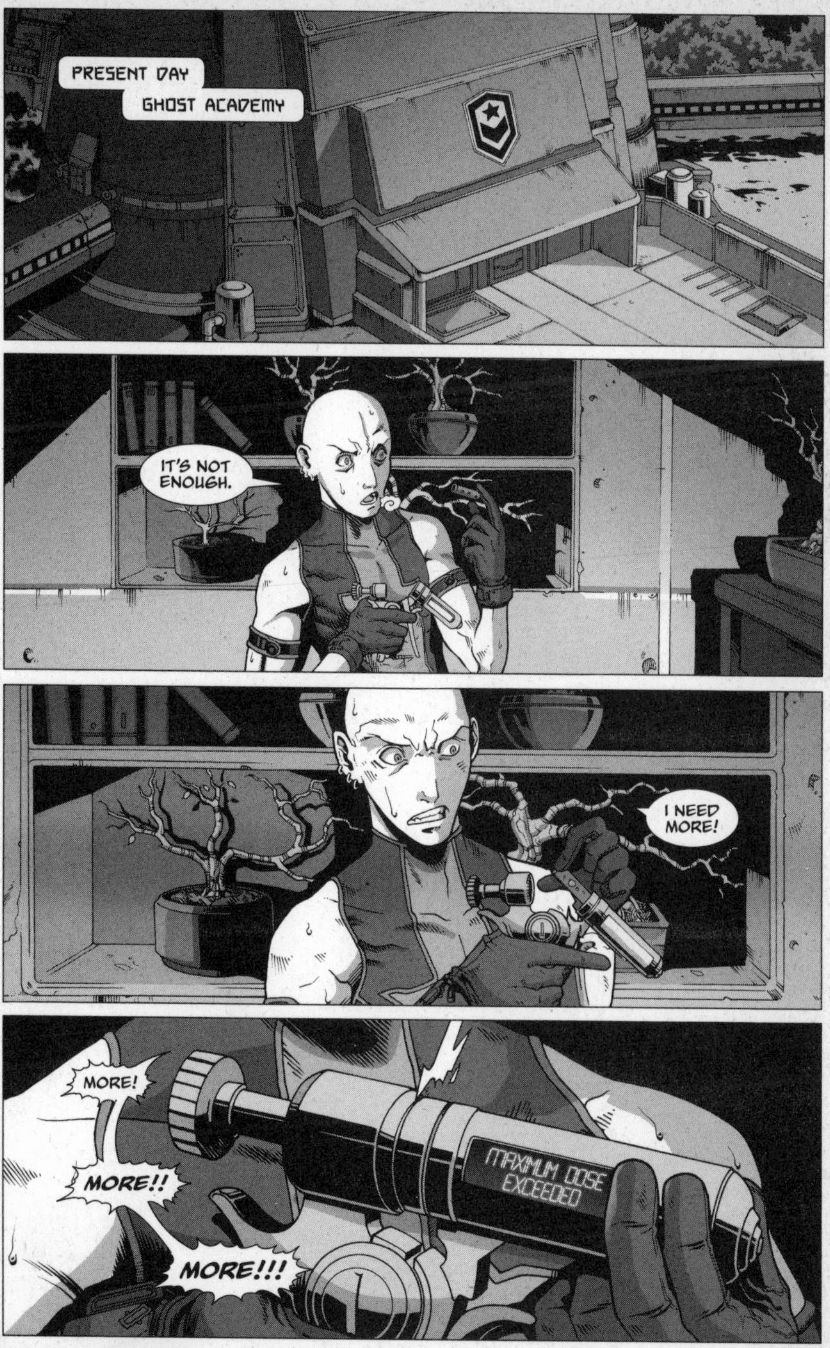
PRESENT DAY
GHOST ACADEMY
IT'S NOT ENOUGH.
I NEED MORE!
MORE!
MORE!!
MORE!!!
MAXIMUM DOSE EXCEEDED

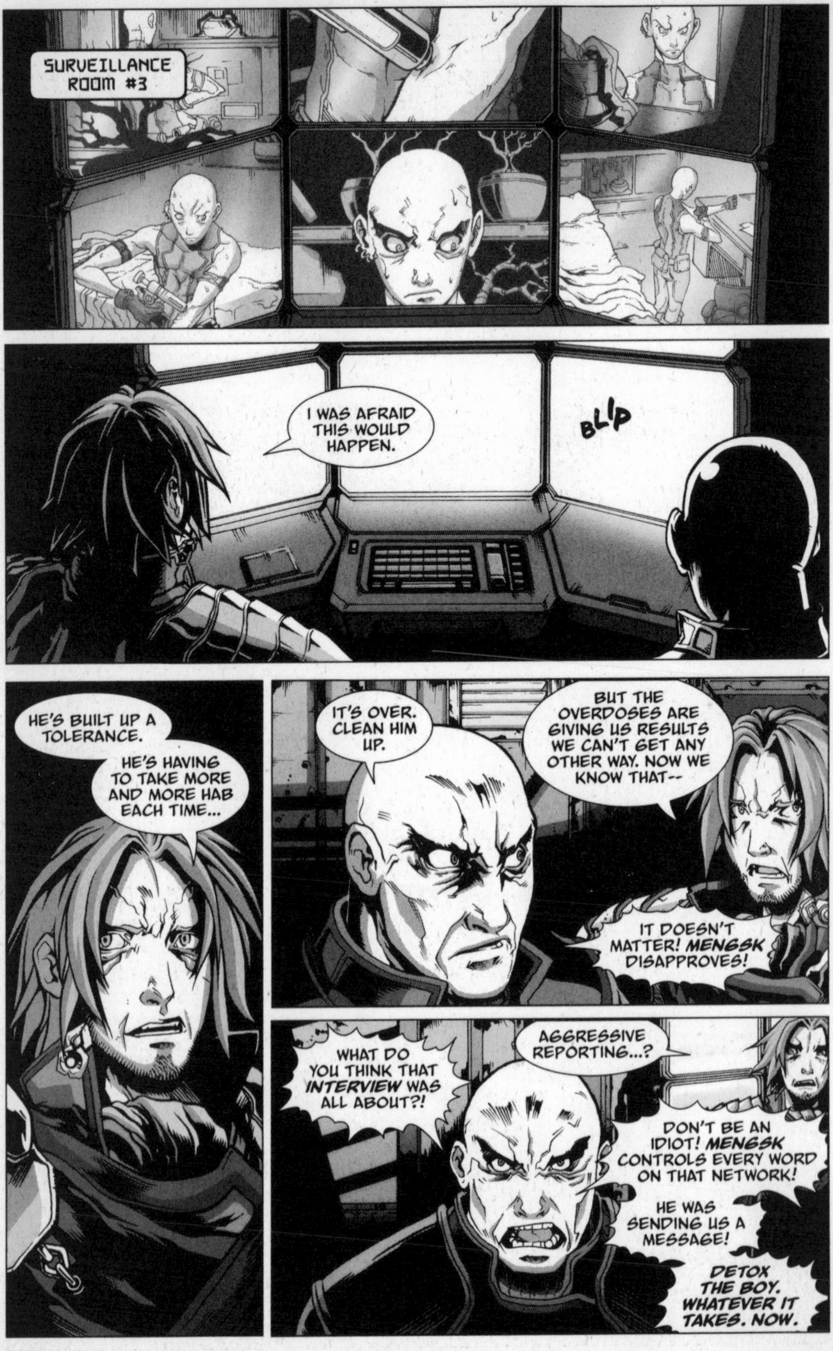

SURVEILLANCE ROOM #3
I WAS AFRAID THIS WOULD HAPPEN.
BLIP
HE'S BUILT UP A TOLERANCE.
HE'S HAVING TO TAKE MORE AND MORE HAB EACH TIME...
IT'S OVER. CLEAN HIM UP.
BUT THE OVERDOSES ARE GIVING US RESULTS WE CAN'T GET ANY OTHER WAY. NOW WE KNOW THAT--
IT DOESN'T MATTER! MENGSK DISAPPROVES!
AGGRESSIVE REPORTING...?
WHAT DO YOU THINK THAT INTERVIEW WAS ALL ABOUT?!
DON'T BE AN IDIOT! MENGSK CONTROLS EVERY WORD ON THAT NETWORK!
HE WAS SENDING US A MESSAGE!
DETOX THE BOY. WHATEVER IT TAKES. NOW.

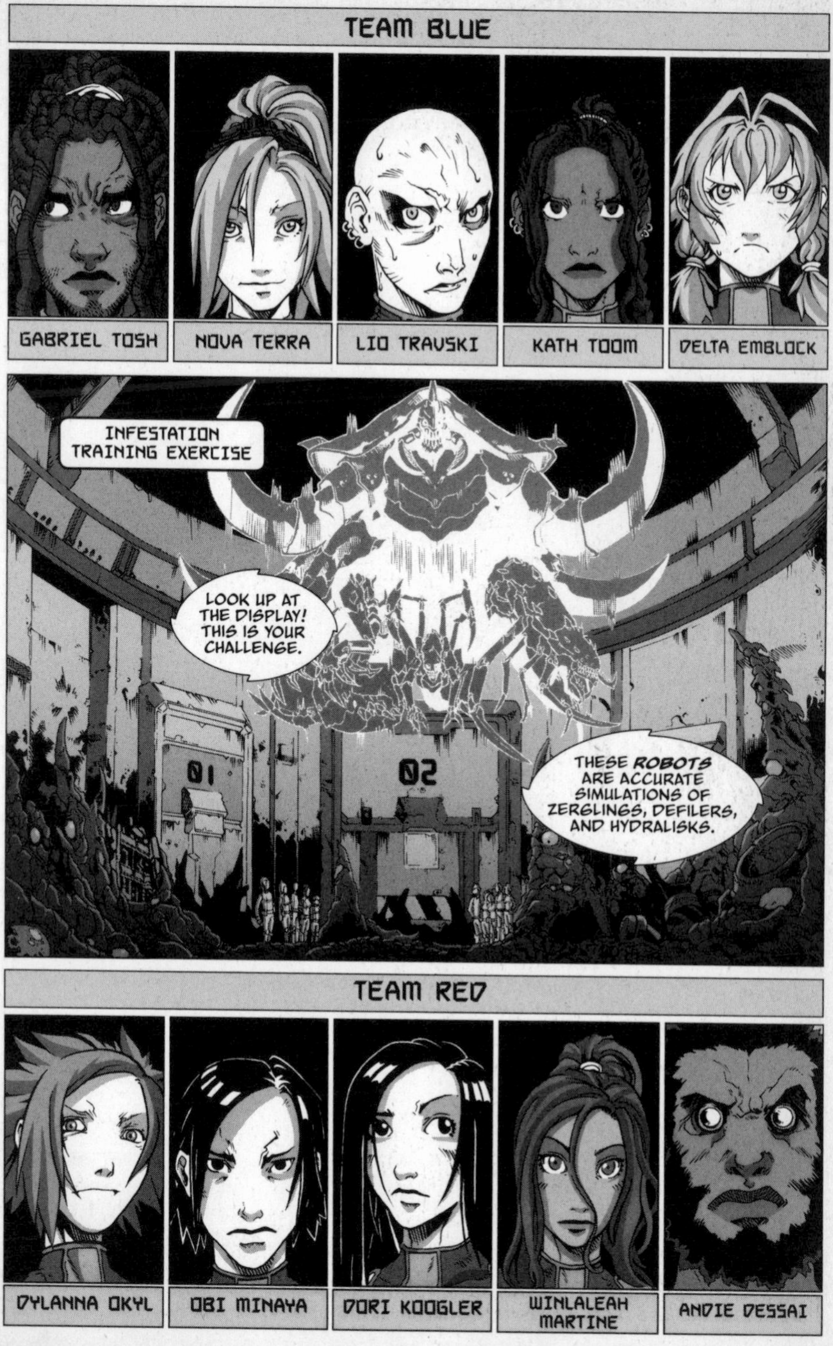
TEAM BLUE
GABRIEL TOSH
NOVA TERRA
LIO TRAVSKI
KATH TOOM
DELTA EMBLOCK
INFESTATION TRAINING EXERCISE
LOOK UP AT THE DISPLAY! THIS IS YOUR CHALLENGE.
01
02
THESE *ROBOTS* ARE ACCURATE SIMULATIONS OF ZERGLINGS, DEFILERS, AND HYDRALISKS.
TEAM RED
DYLANNA OKYL
OBI MINAYA
DORI KOOGLER
WINLALEAH MARTINE
ANDIE DESSAI

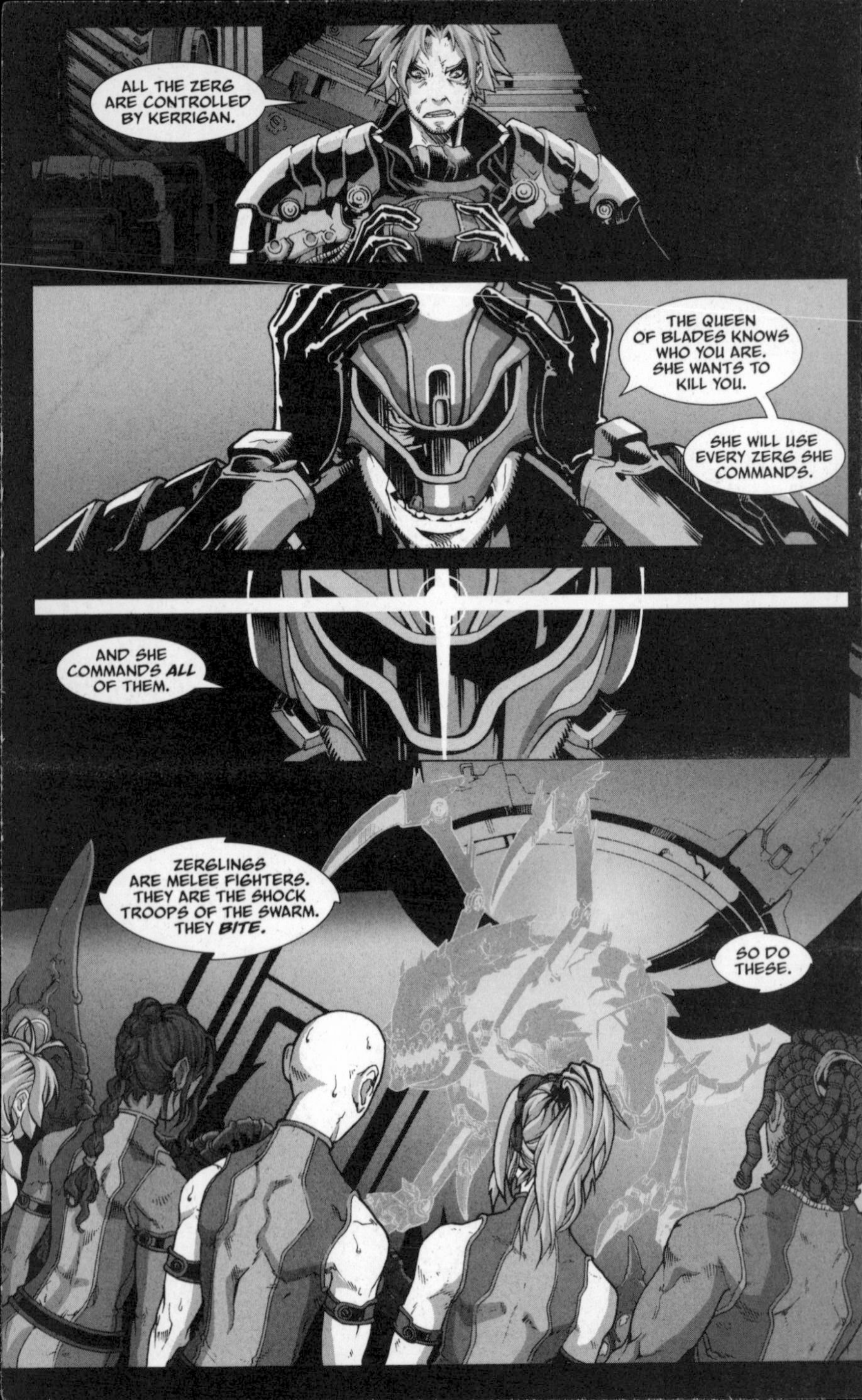
ALL THE ZERG ARE CONTROLLED BY KERRIGAN.
THE QUEEN OF BLADES KNOWS WHO YOU ARE. SHE WANTS TO KILL YOU.
SHE WILL USE EVERY ZERG SHE COMMANDS.
AND SHE COMMANDS *ALL* OF THEM.
ZERGLINGS ARE MELEE FIGHTERS. THEY ARE THE SHOCK TROOPS OF THE SWARM. THEY *BITE*.
SO DO THESE.

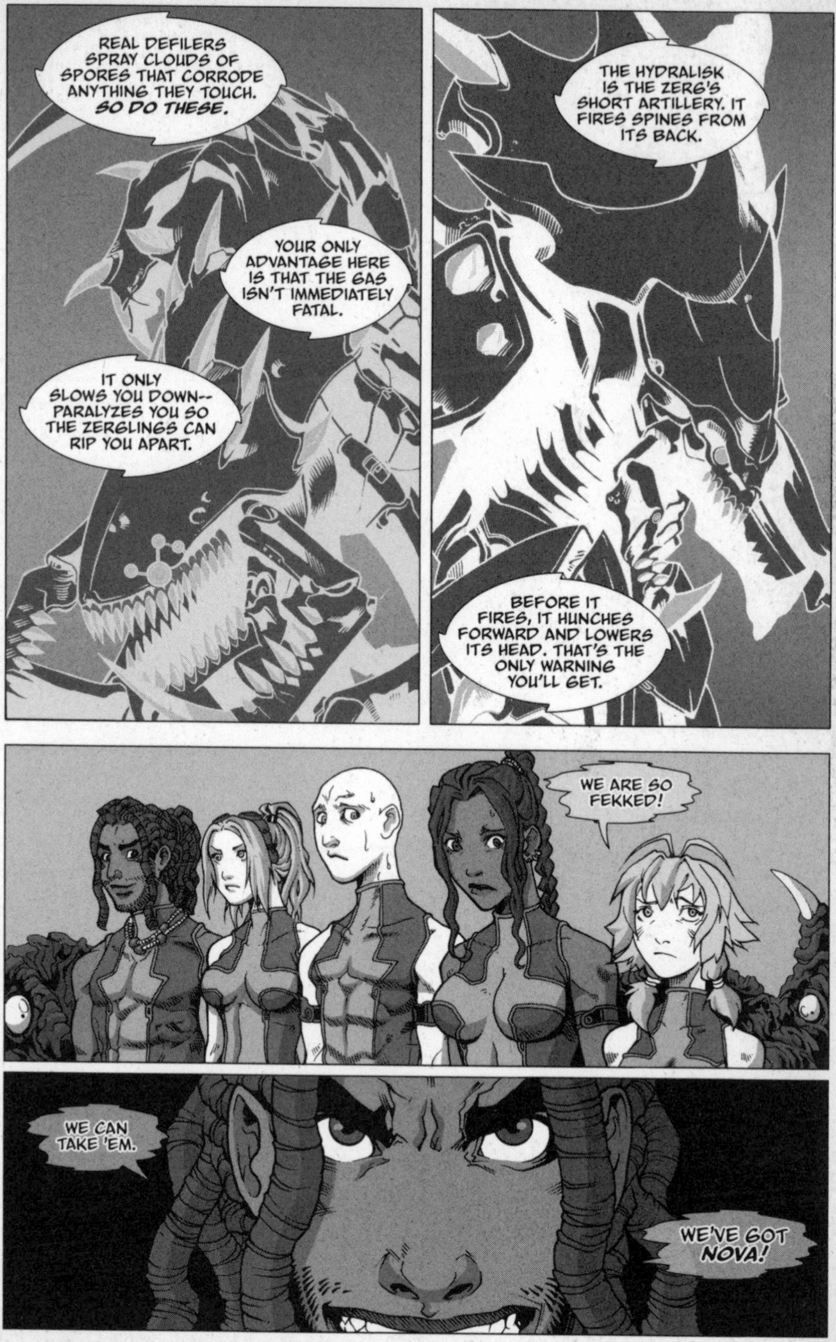
REAL DEFILERS SPRAY CLOUDS OF SPORES THAT CORRODE ANYTHING THEY TOUCH. SO DO THESE.
YOUR ONLY ADVANTAGE HERE IS THAT THE GAS ISN'T IMMEDIATELY FATAL.
IT ONLY SLOWS YOU DOWN--PARALYZES YOU SO THE ZERGLINGS CAN RIP YOU APART.
THE HYDRALISK IS THE ZERG'S SHORT ARTILLERY. IT FIRES SPINES FROM ITS BACK.
BEFORE IT FIRES, IT HUNCHES FORWARD AND LOWERS ITS HEAD. THAT'S THE ONLY WARNING YOU'LL GET.
WE ARE SO FEKKED!
WE CAN TAKE 'EM.
WE'VE GOT NOVA!

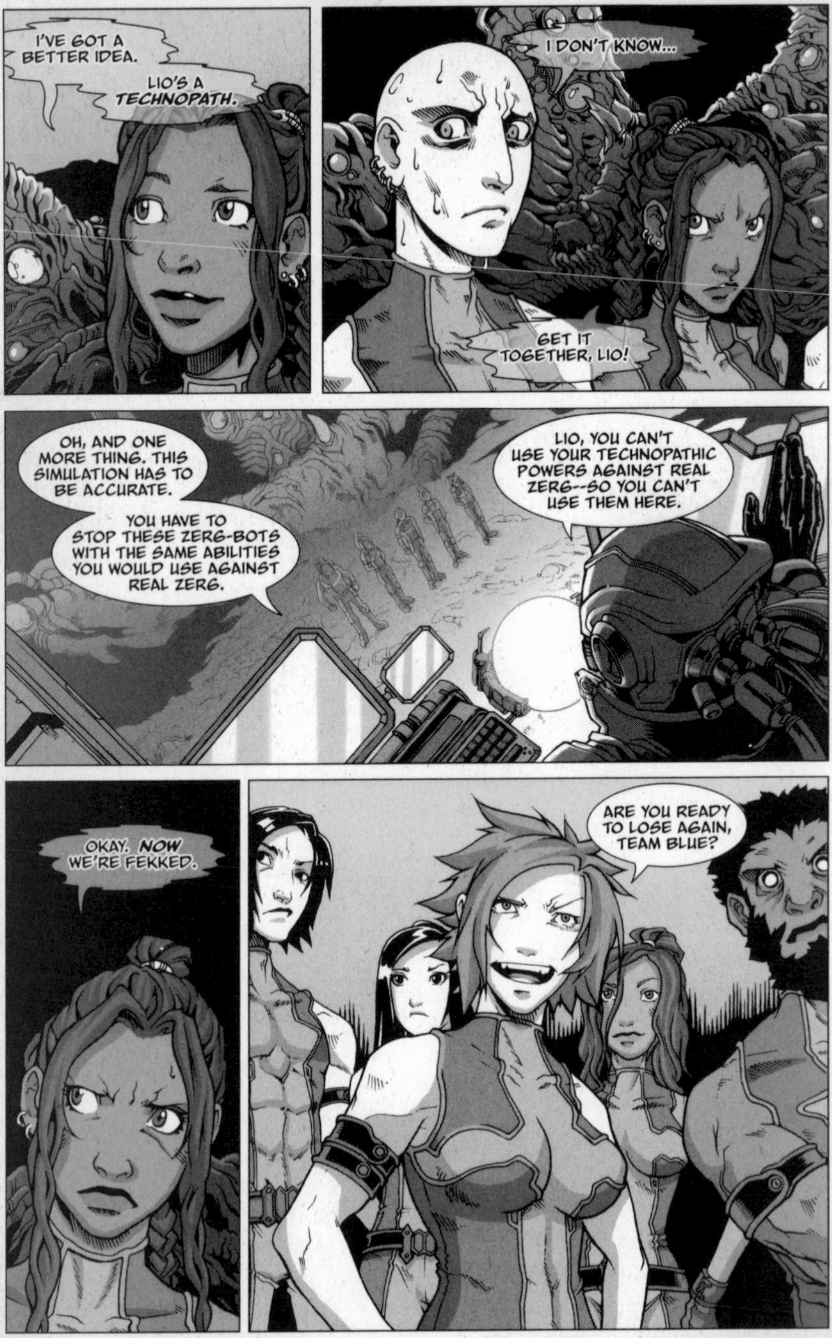
I'VE GOT A BETTER IDEA.
LIO'S A *TECHNOPATH.*
I DON'T KNOW...
GET IT TOGETHER, LIO!
OH, AND ONE MORE THING. THIS SIMULATION HAS TO BE ACCURATE.
YOU HAVE TO STOP THESE ZERG-BOTS WITH THE SAME ABILITIES YOU WOULD USE AGAINST REAL ZERG.
LIO, YOU CAN'T USE YOUR TECHNOPATHIC POWERS AGAINST REAL ZERG--SO YOU CAN'T USE THEM HERE.
OKAY. *NOW* WE'RE FEKKED.
ARE YOU READY TO LOSE AGAIN, TEAM BLUE?

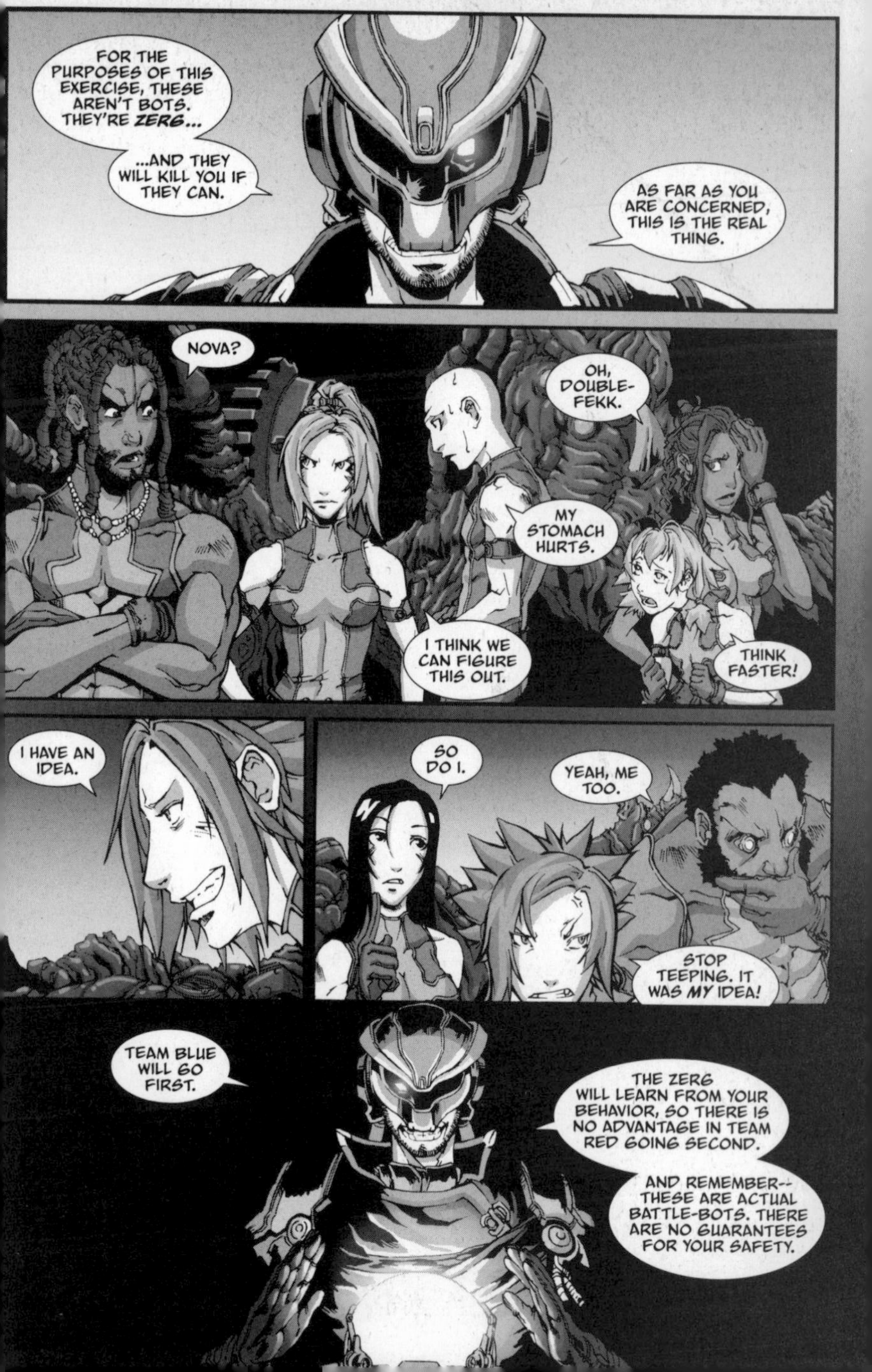
FOR THE PURPOSES OF THIS EXERCISE, THESE AREN'T BOTS. THEY'RE *ZERG*...
...AND THEY WILL KILL YOU IF THEY CAN.
AS FAR AS YOU ARE CONCERNED, THIS IS THE REAL THING.
NOVA?
OH, DOUBLE-FEKK.
MY STOMACH HURTS.
I THINK WE CAN FIGURE THIS OUT.
THINK FASTER!
I HAVE AN IDEA.
SO DO I.
YEAH, ME TOO.
STOP TEEPING. IT WAS *MY* IDEA!
TEAM BLUE WILL GO FIRST.
THE ZERG WILL LEARN FROM YOUR BEHAVIOR, SO THERE IS NO ADVANTAGE IN TEAM RED GOING SECOND.
AND REMEMBER-- THESE ARE ACTUAL BATTLE-BOTS. THERE ARE NO GUARANTEES FOR YOUR SAFETY.

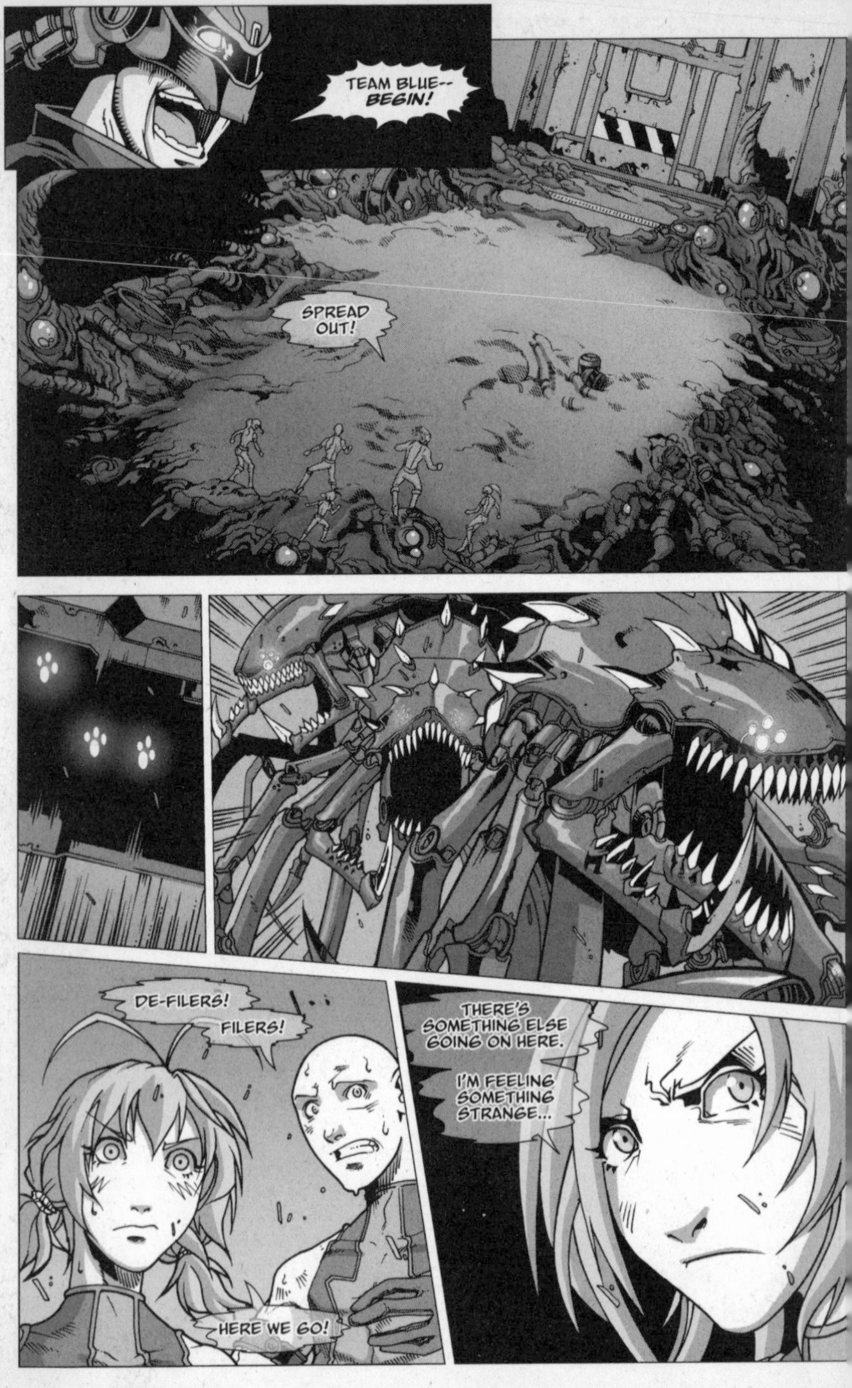
TEAM BLUE--
BEGIN!
SPREAD OUT!
DE-FILERS!
FILERS!
HERE WE GO!
THERE'S SOMETHING ELSE GOING ON HERE.
I'M FEELING SOMETHING STRANGE...

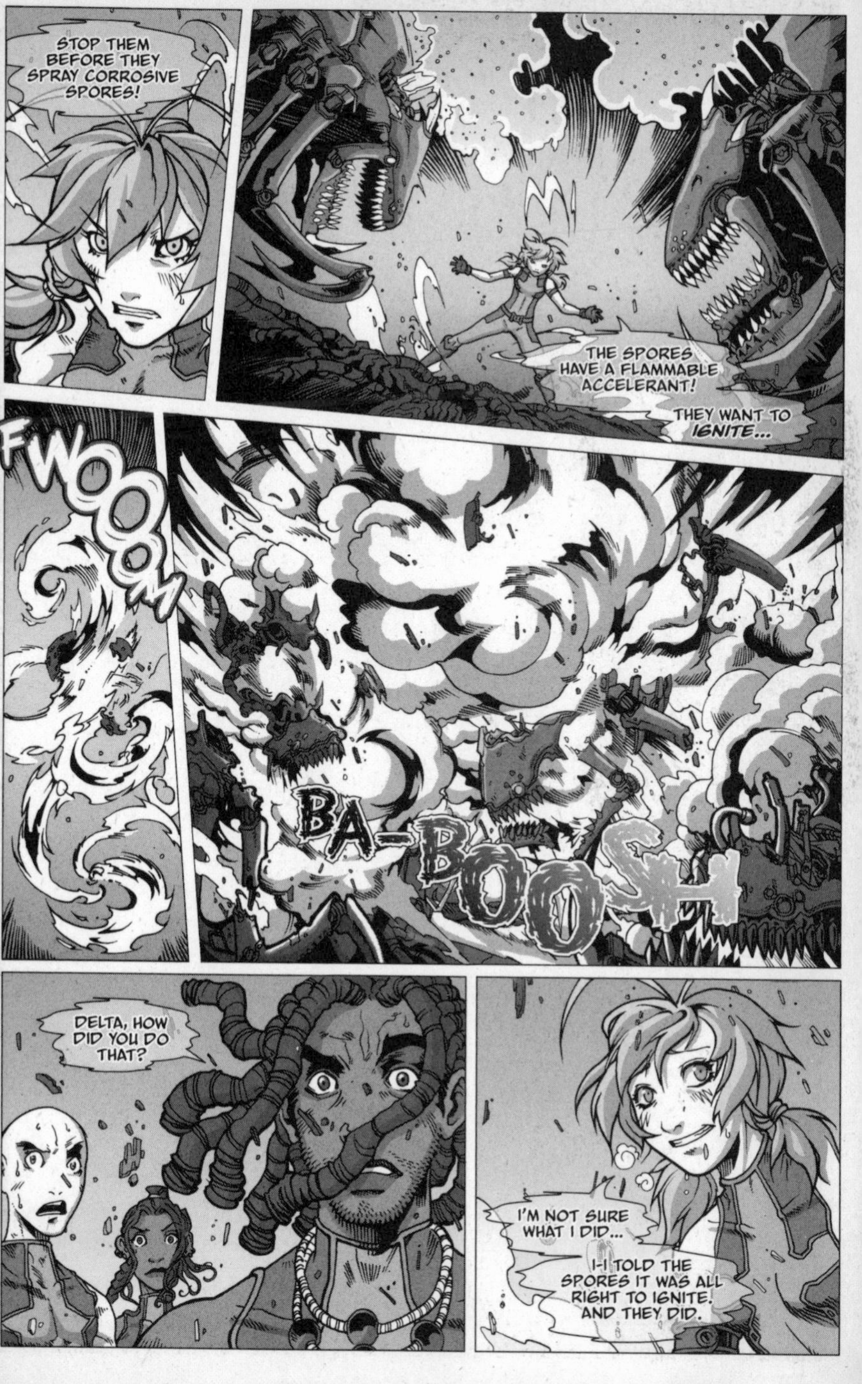
STOP THEM BEFORE THEY SPRAY CORROSIVE SPORES!
THE SPORES HAVE A FLAMMABLE ACCELERANT!
THEY WANT TO IGNITE...
FWOOOM
BA-BOOSH
DELTA, HOW DID YOU DO THAT?
I'M NOT SURE WHAT I DID...
I-I TOLD THE SPORES IT WAS ALL RIGHT TO IGNITE. AND THEY DID.

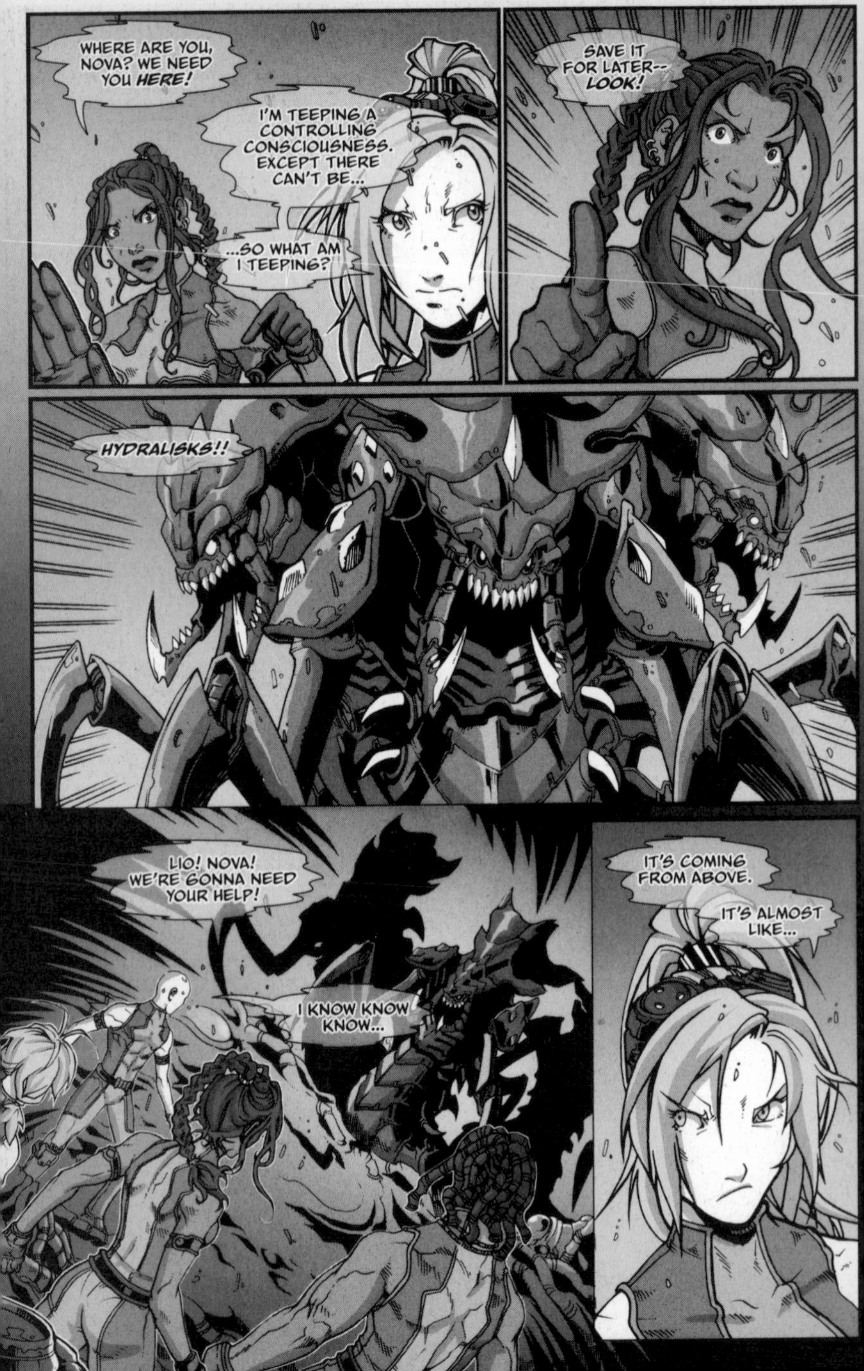
WHERE ARE YOU, NOVA? WE NEED YOU *HERE!*
I'M TEEPING A CONTROLLING CONSCIOUSNESS. EXCEPT THERE CAN'T BE...
...SO WHAT AM I TEEPING?
SAVE IT FOR LATER-- *LOOK!*
*HYDRALISKS!!*
LIO! NOVA! WE'RE GONNA NEED YOUR HELP!
I KNOW KNOW KNOW...
IT'S COMING FROM ABOVE.
IT'S ALMOST LIKE...

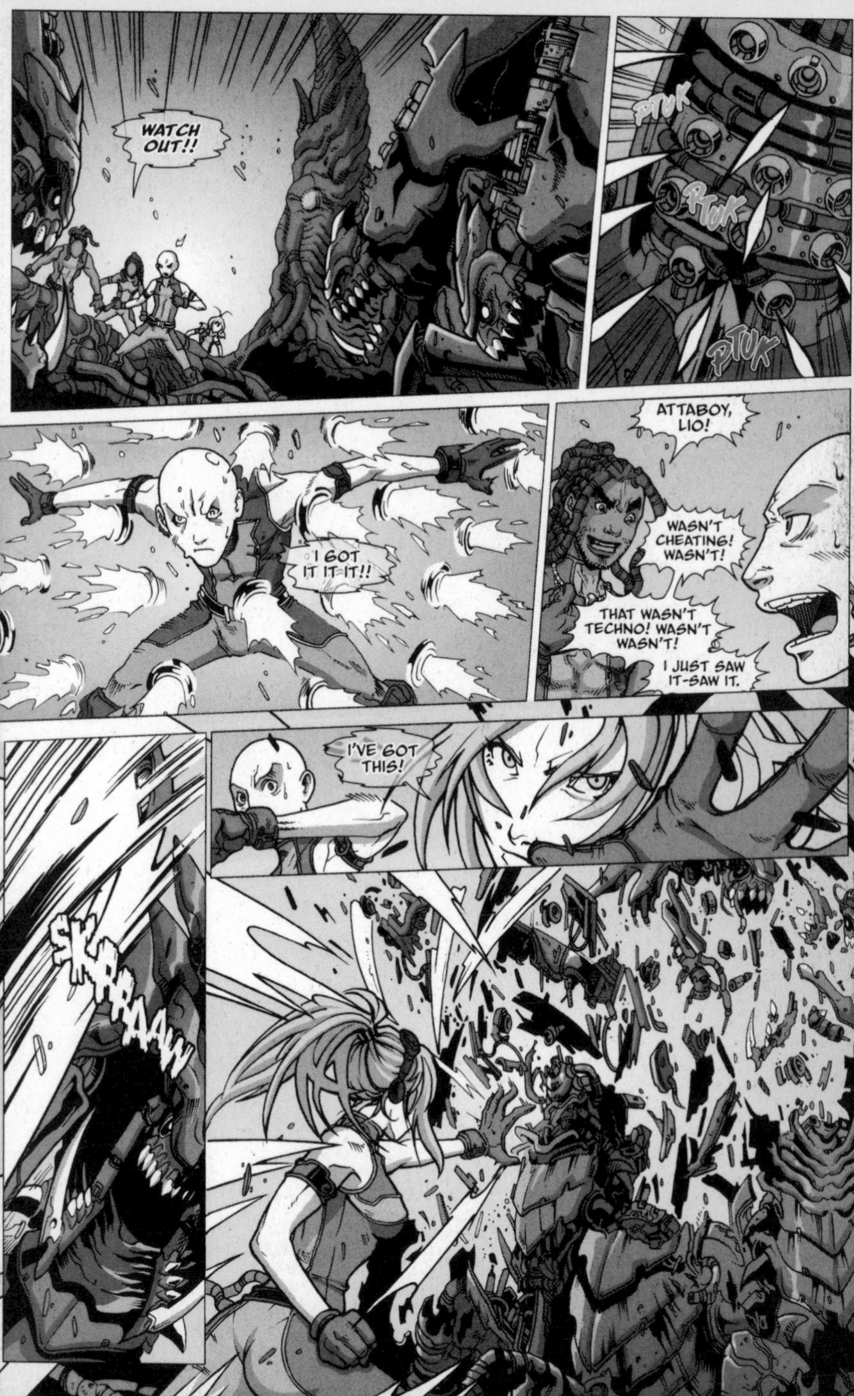
WATCH OUT!!
PTUK
PTUK
PTUK
I GOT IT IT IT!!
ATTABOY, LIO!
WASN'T CHEATING! WASN'T!
THAT WASN'T TECHNO! WASN'T WASN'T!
I JUST SAW IT-SAW IT.
I'VE GOT THIS!
SKRRAAAW

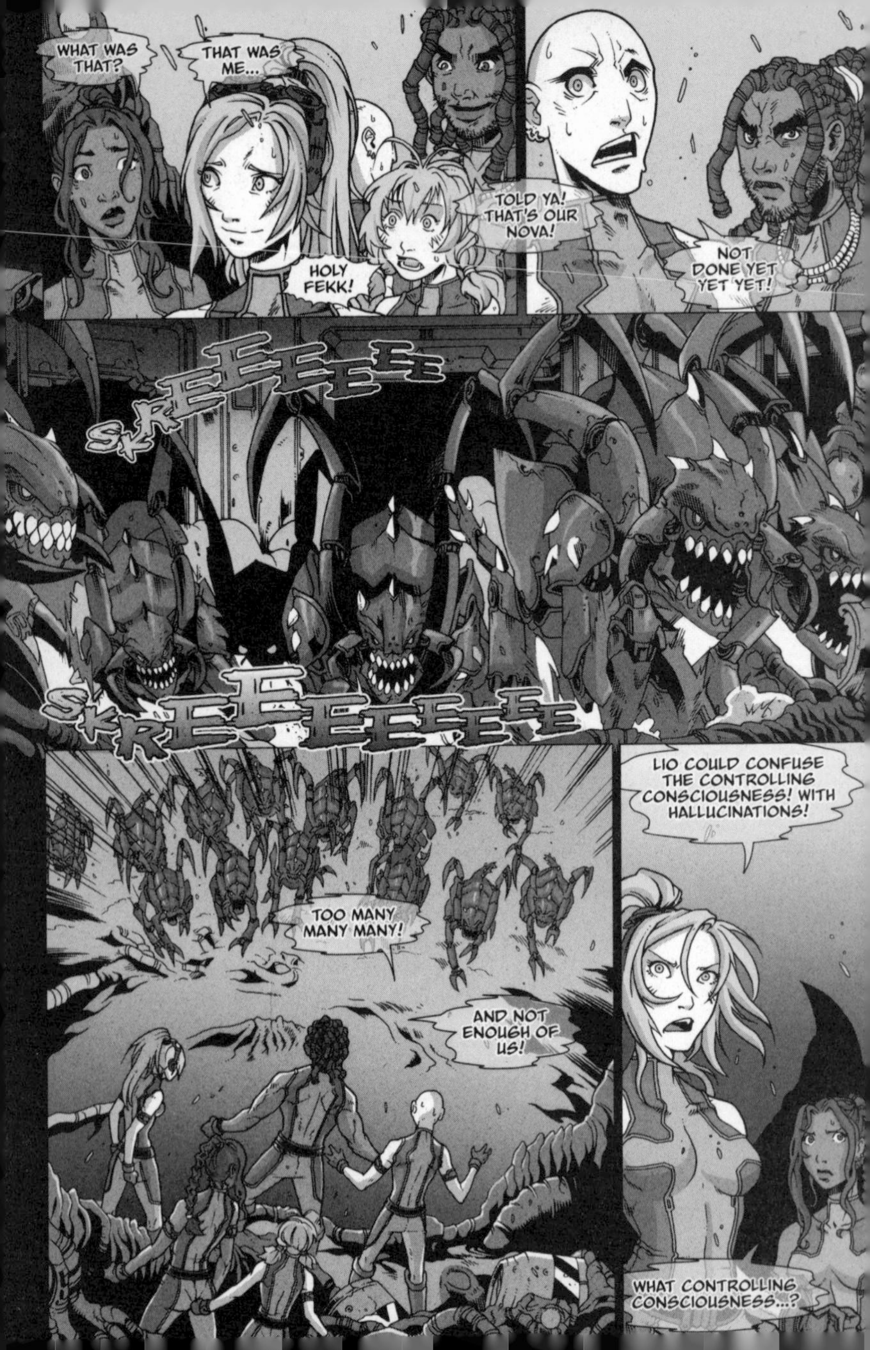
WHAT WAS THAT?
THAT WAS ME...
HOLY FEKK!
TOLD YA! THAT'S OUR NOVA!
NOT DONE YET YET YET!
SKREEEEEEE
SKREEEEEEEEEE
TOO MANY MANY MANY!
AND NOT ENOUGH OF US!
LIO COULD CONFUSE THE CONTROLLING CONSCIOUSNESS! WITH HALLUCINATIONS!
WHAT CONTROLLING CONSCIOUSNESS...?

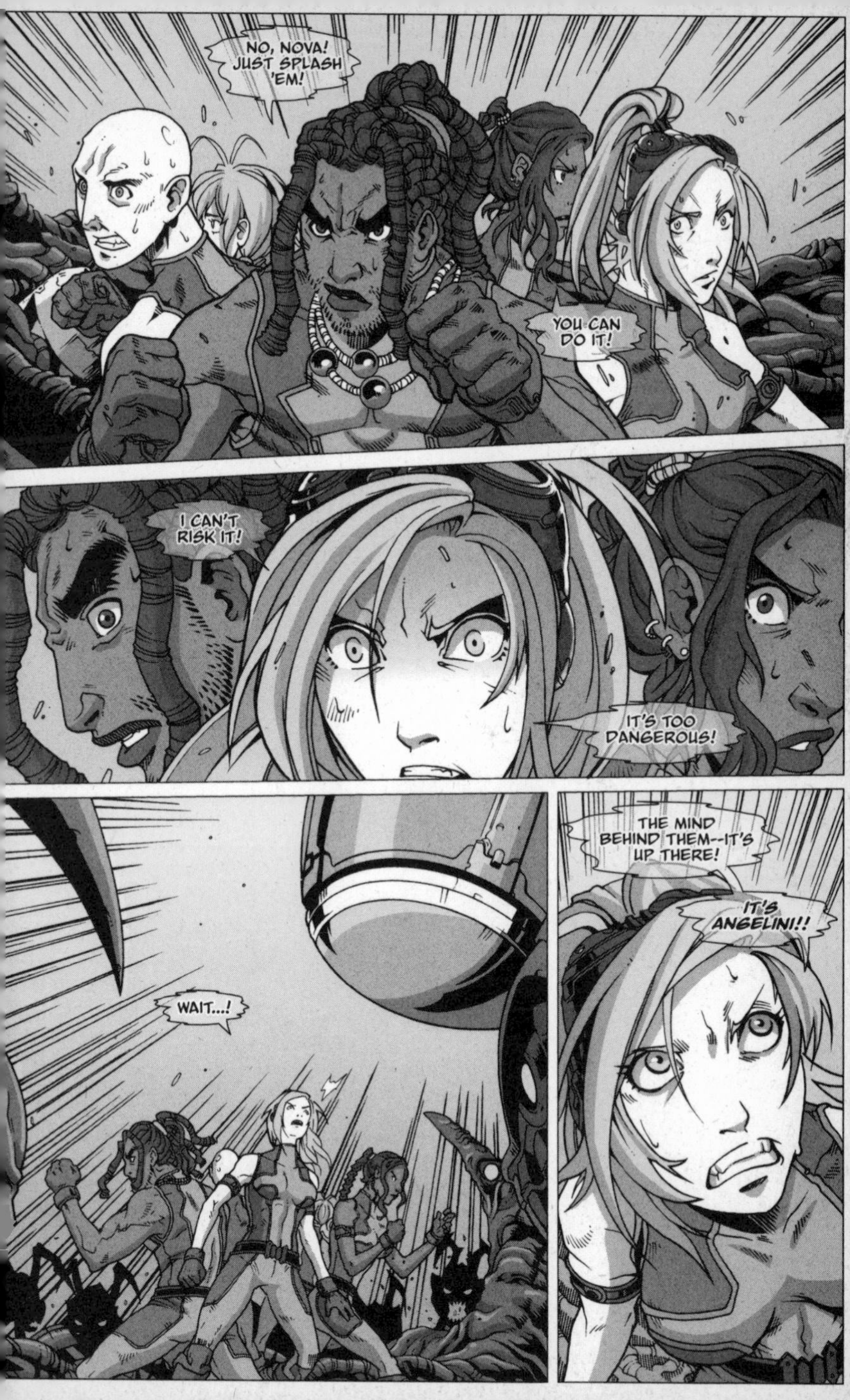
NO, NOVA! JUST SPLASH 'EM!
YOU CAN DO IT!
I CAN'T RISK IT!
IT'S TOO DANGEROUS!
WAIT...!
THE MIND BEHIND THEM--IT'S UP THERE!
IT'S ANGELINI!!

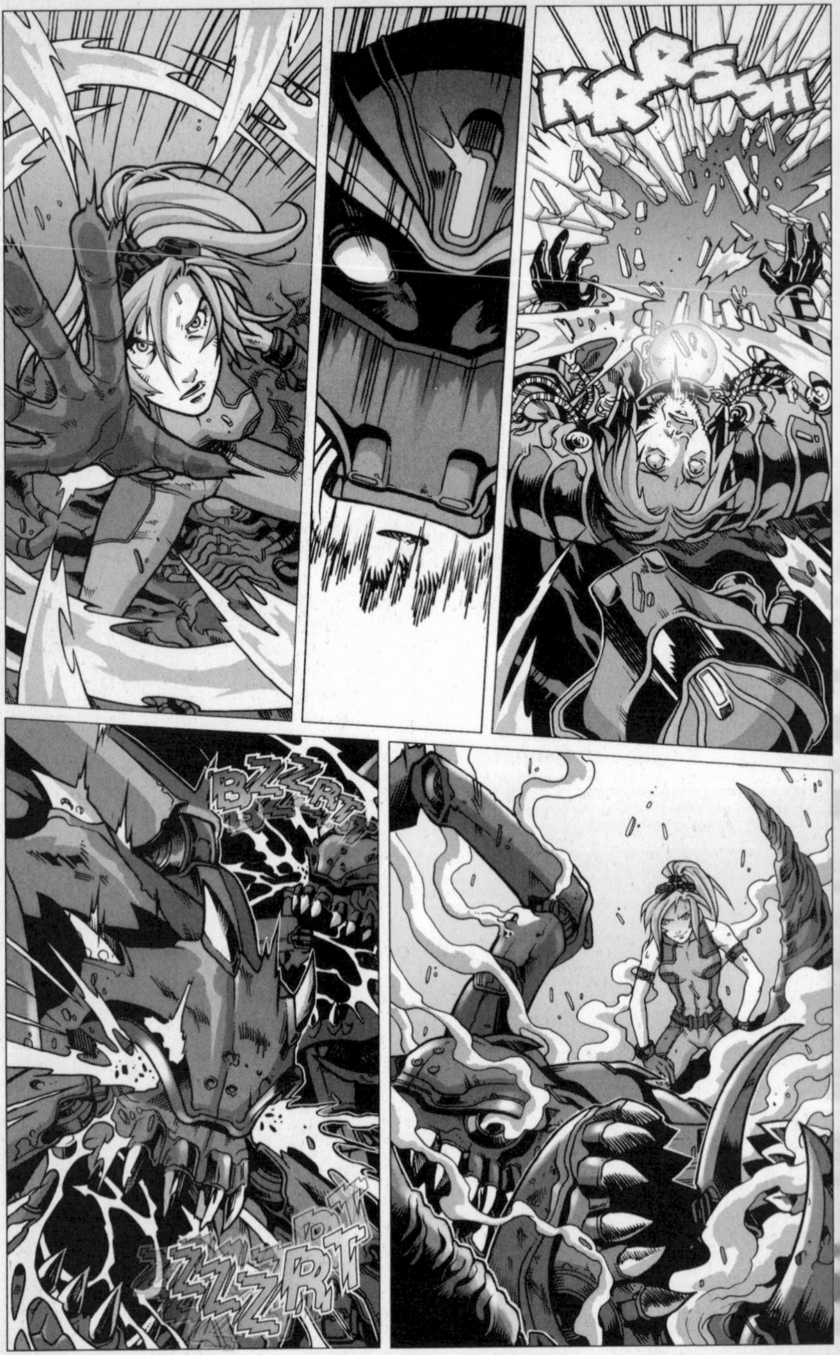
KRASH
BZZZRT
ZZZZRT

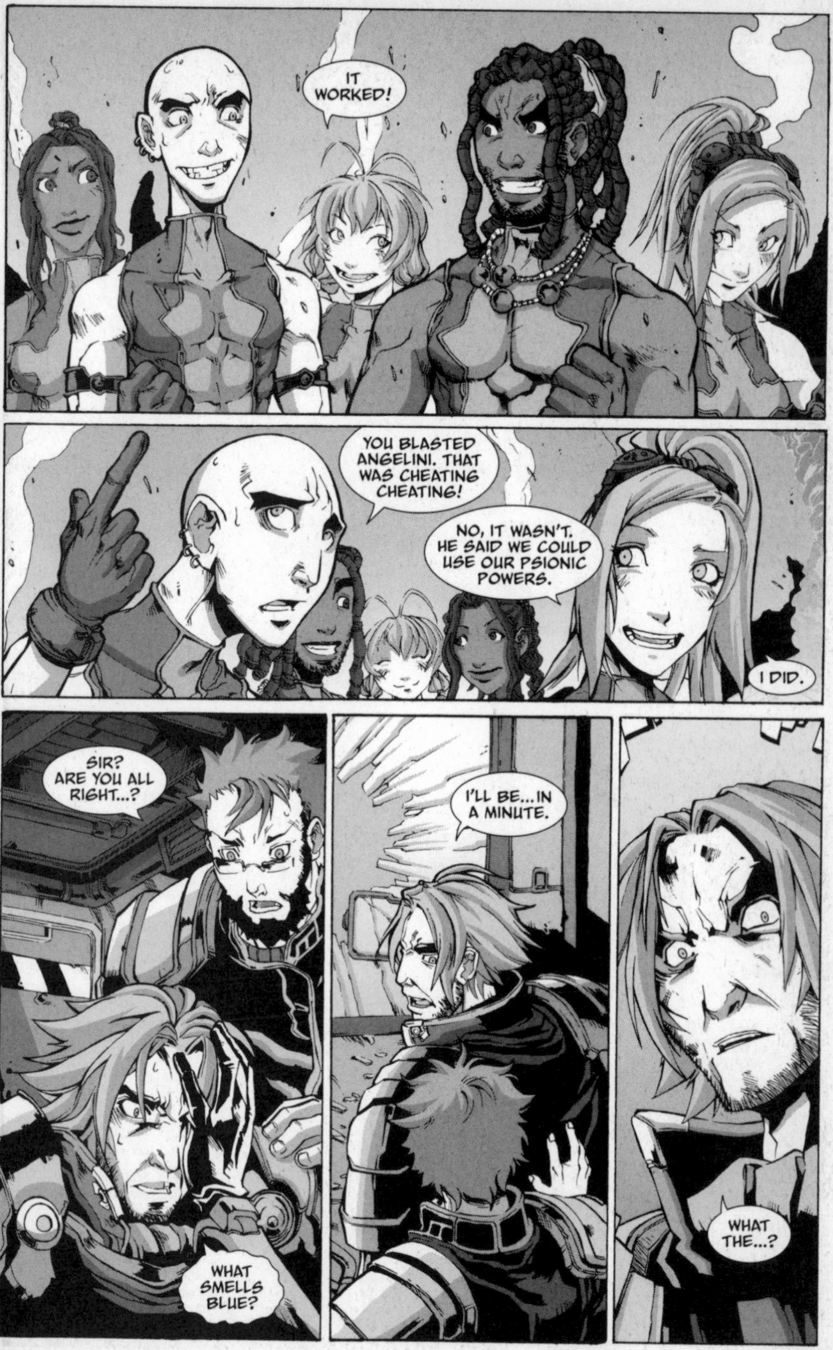
IT WORKED!
YOU BLASTED ANGELINI. THAT WAS CHEATING CHEATING!
NO, IT WASN'T. HE SAID WE COULD USE OUR PSIONIC POWERS.
I DID.
SIR? ARE YOU ALL RIGHT...?
WHAT SMELLS BLUE?
I'LL BE...IN A MINUTE.
WHAT THE...?

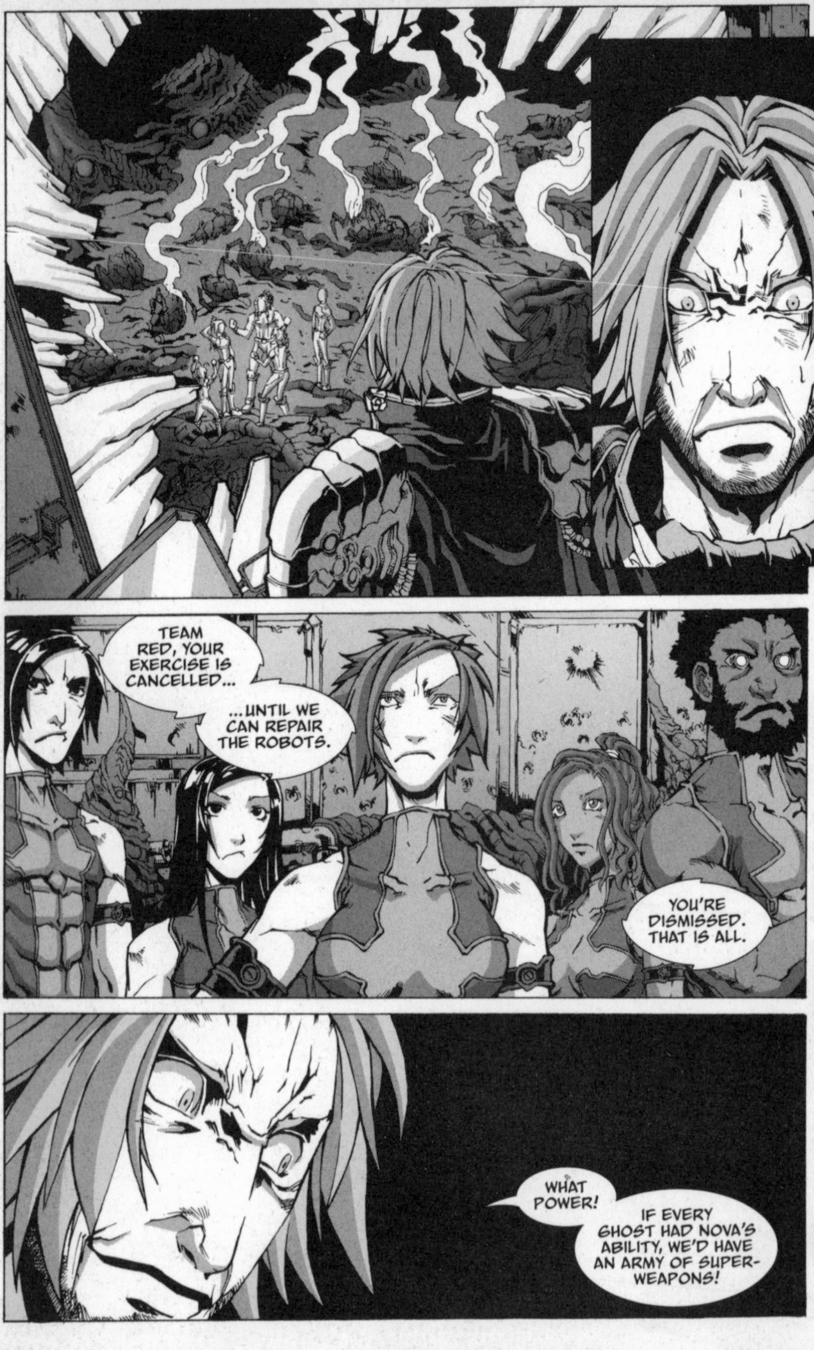
TEAM RED, YOUR EXERCISE IS CANCELLED...
...UNTIL WE CAN REPAIR THE ROBOTS.
YOU'RE DISMISSED. THAT IS ALL.
WHAT POWER!
IF EVERY GHOST HAD NOVA'S ABILITY, WE'D HAVE AN ARMY OF SUPER-WEAPONS!

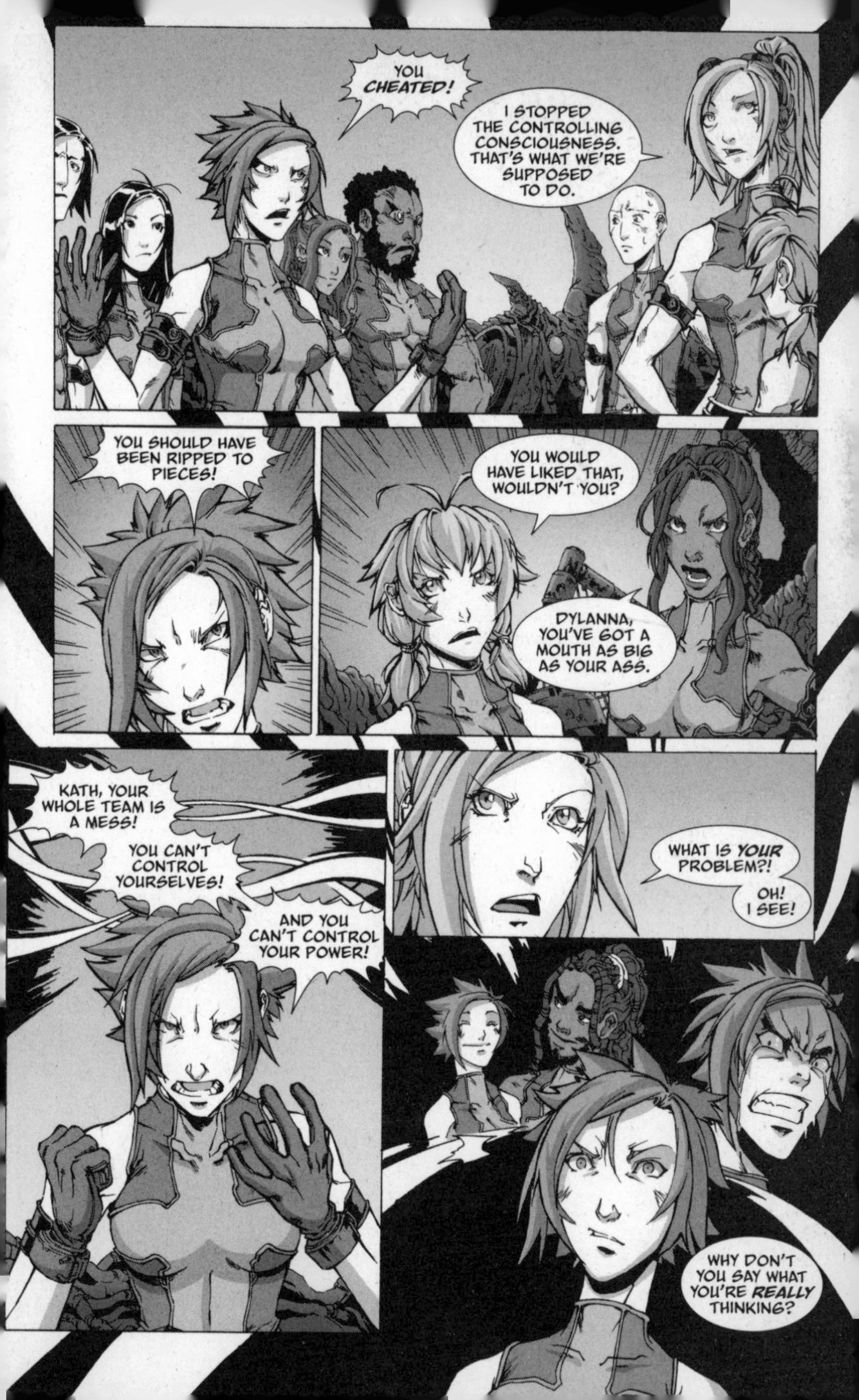
YOU CHEATED!
I STOPPED THE CONTROLLING CONSCIOUSNESS. THAT'S WHAT WE'RE SUPPOSED TO DO.
YOU SHOULD HAVE BEEN RIPPED TO PIECES!
YOU WOULD HAVE LIKED THAT, WOULDN'T YOU?
DYLANNA, YOU'VE GOT A MOUTH AS BIG AS YOUR ASS.
KATH, YOUR WHOLE TEAM IS A MESS!
YOU CAN'T CONTROL YOURSELVES!
AND YOU CAN'T CONTROL YOUR POWER!
WHAT IS YOUR PROBLEM?!
OH! I SEE!
WHY DON'T YOU SAY WHAT YOU'RE REALLY THINKING?

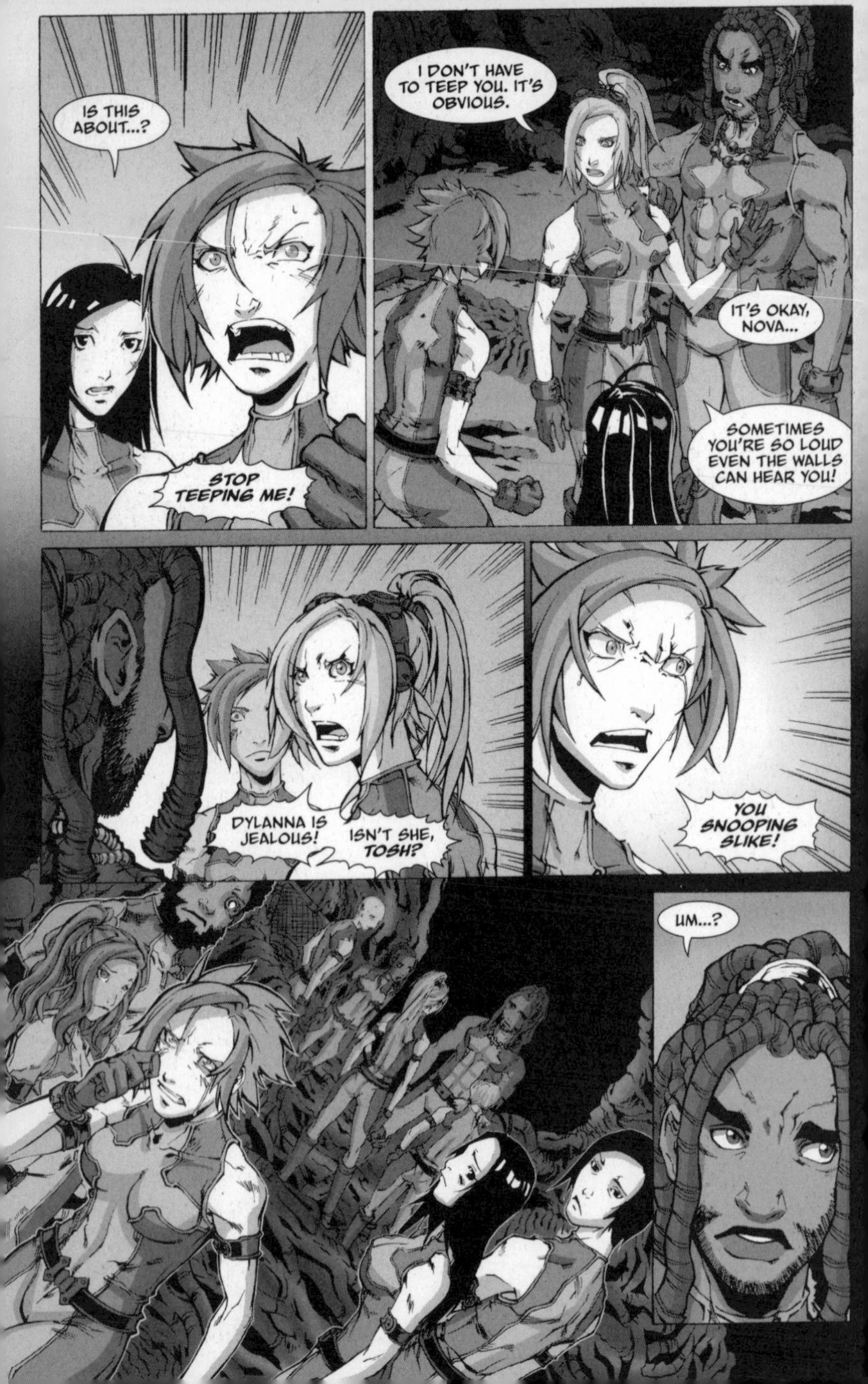
IS THIS ABOUT...?
STOP TEEPING ME!
I DON'T HAVE TO TEEP YOU. IT'S OBVIOUS.
IT'S OKAY, NOVA...
SOMETIMES YOU'RE SO LOUD EVEN THE WALLS CAN HEAR YOU!
DYLANNA IS JEALOUS!
ISN'T SHE, TOSH?
YOU SNOOPING SLIKE!
UM...?

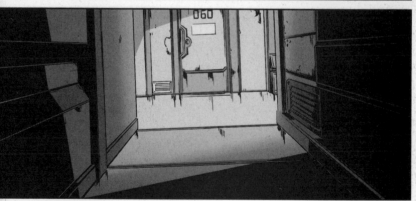

Lio's Room
Don't Knock, Don't Enter
Just Go Away

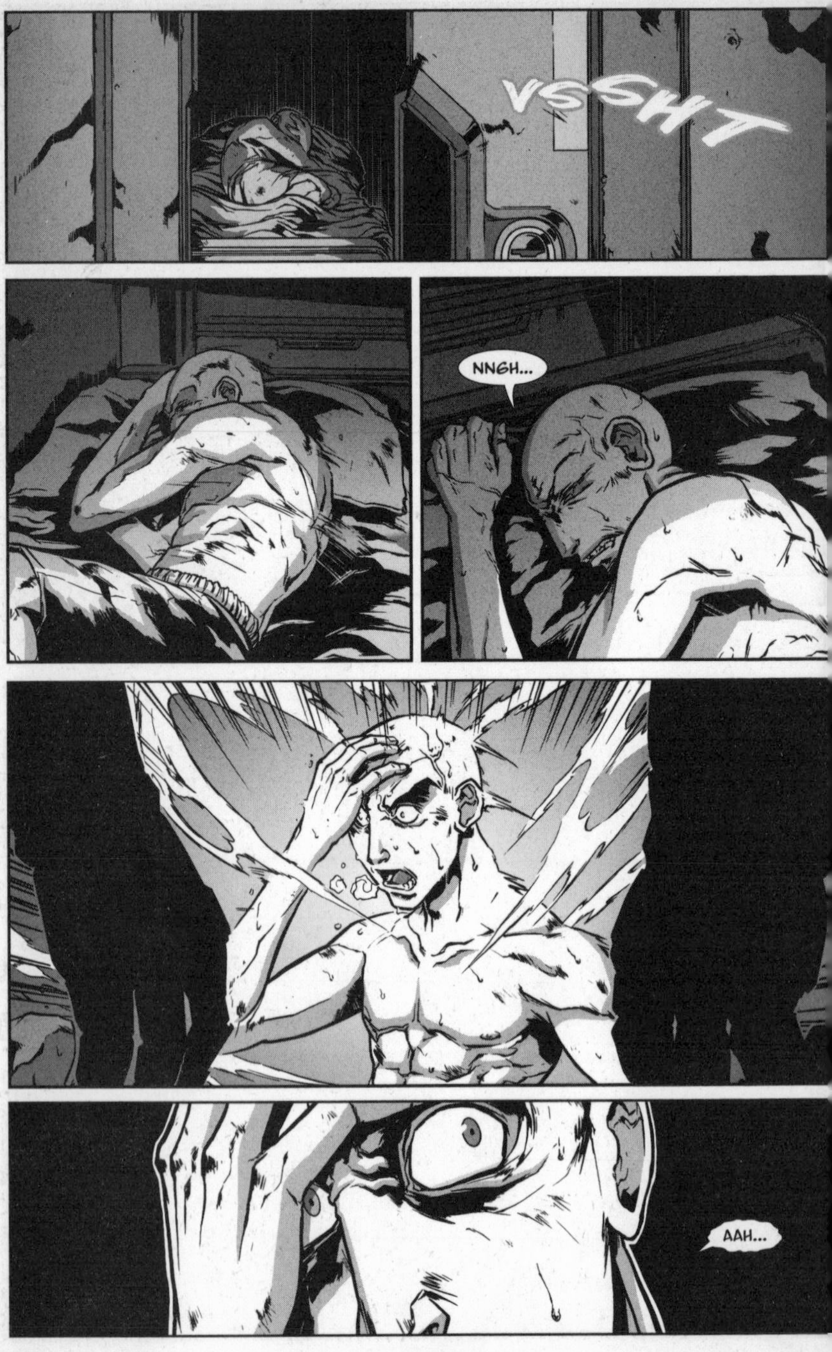
VSSHT
NNGH...
AAH...

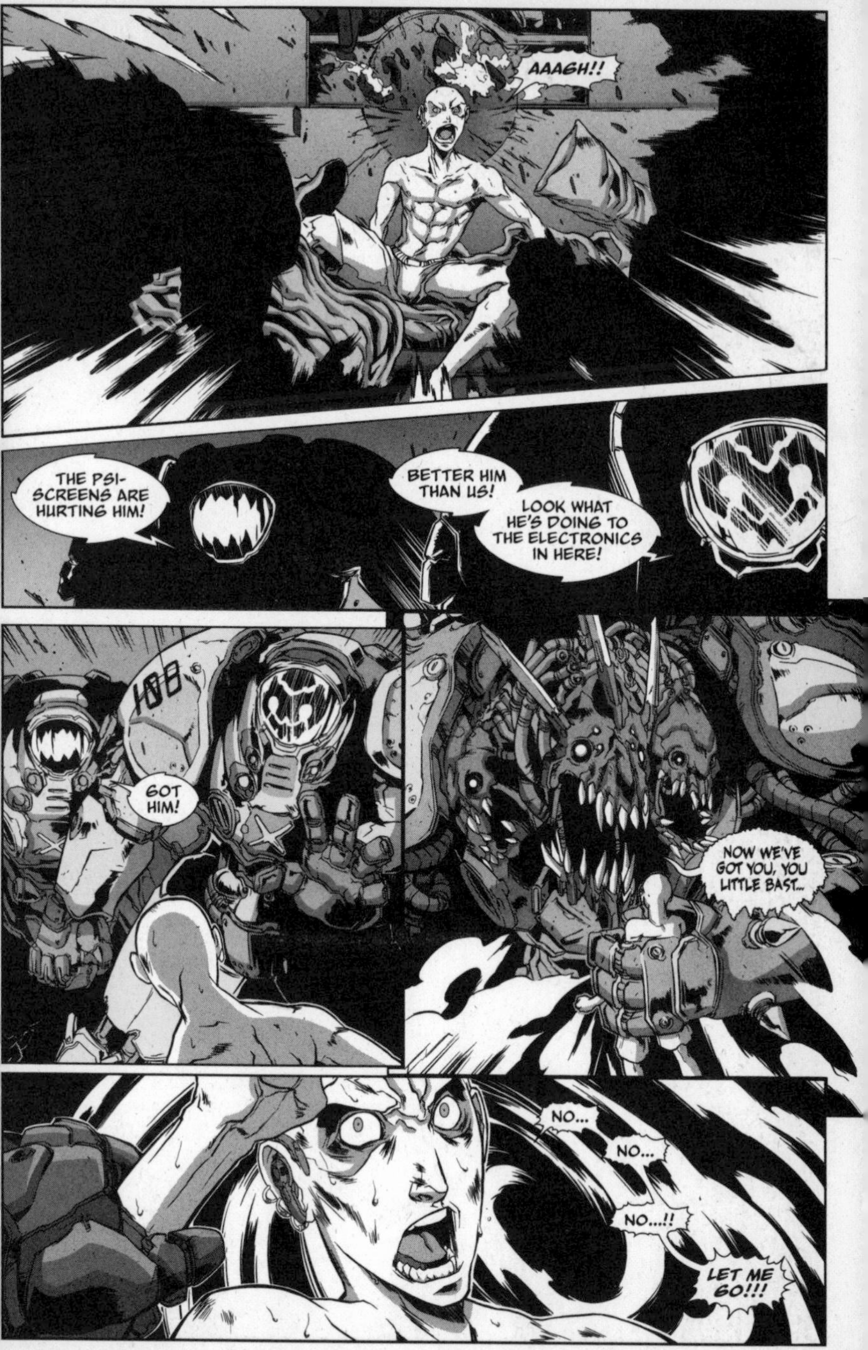
AAAGH!!
THE PSI-SCREENS ARE HURTING HIM!
BETTER HIM THAN US!
LOOK WHAT HE'S DOING TO THE ELECTRONICS IN HERE!
108
GOT HIM!
NOW WE'VE GOT YOU, YOU LITTLE BAST...
NO...
NO...
NO...!!
LET ME GO!!!

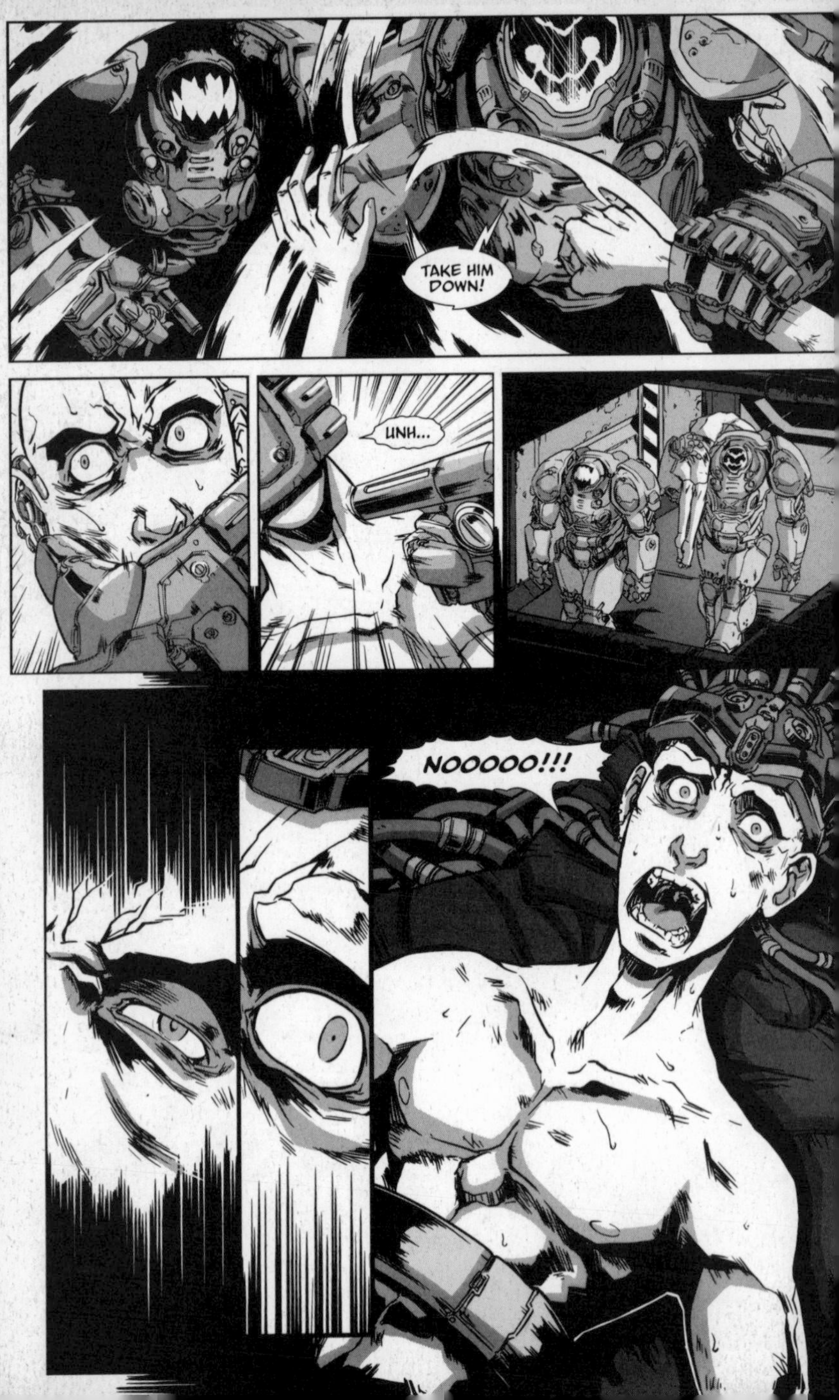
TAKE HIM DOWN!
UNH...
NOOOOO!!!

# CHAPTER 2
## SHADOWS BEFORE THEM

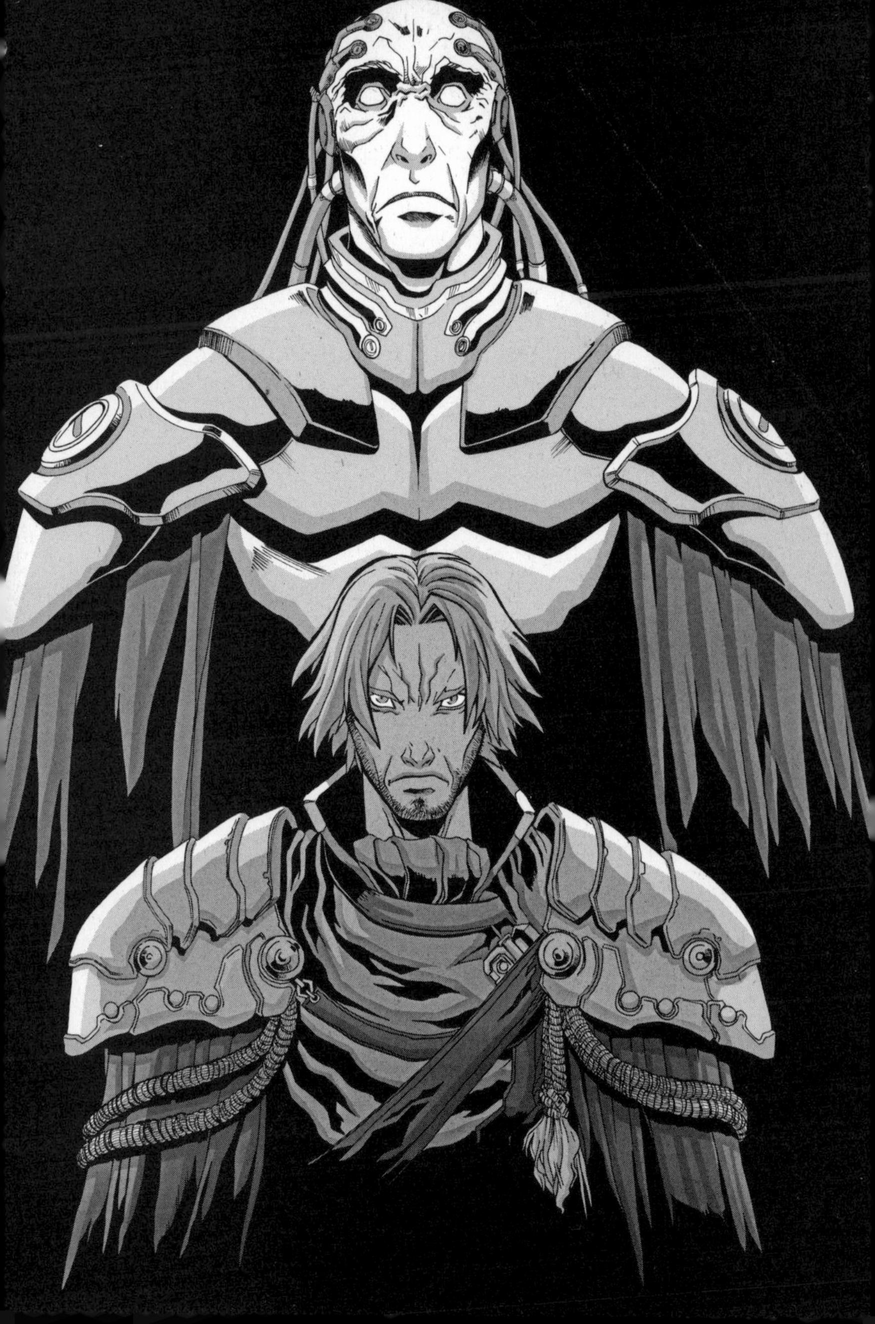

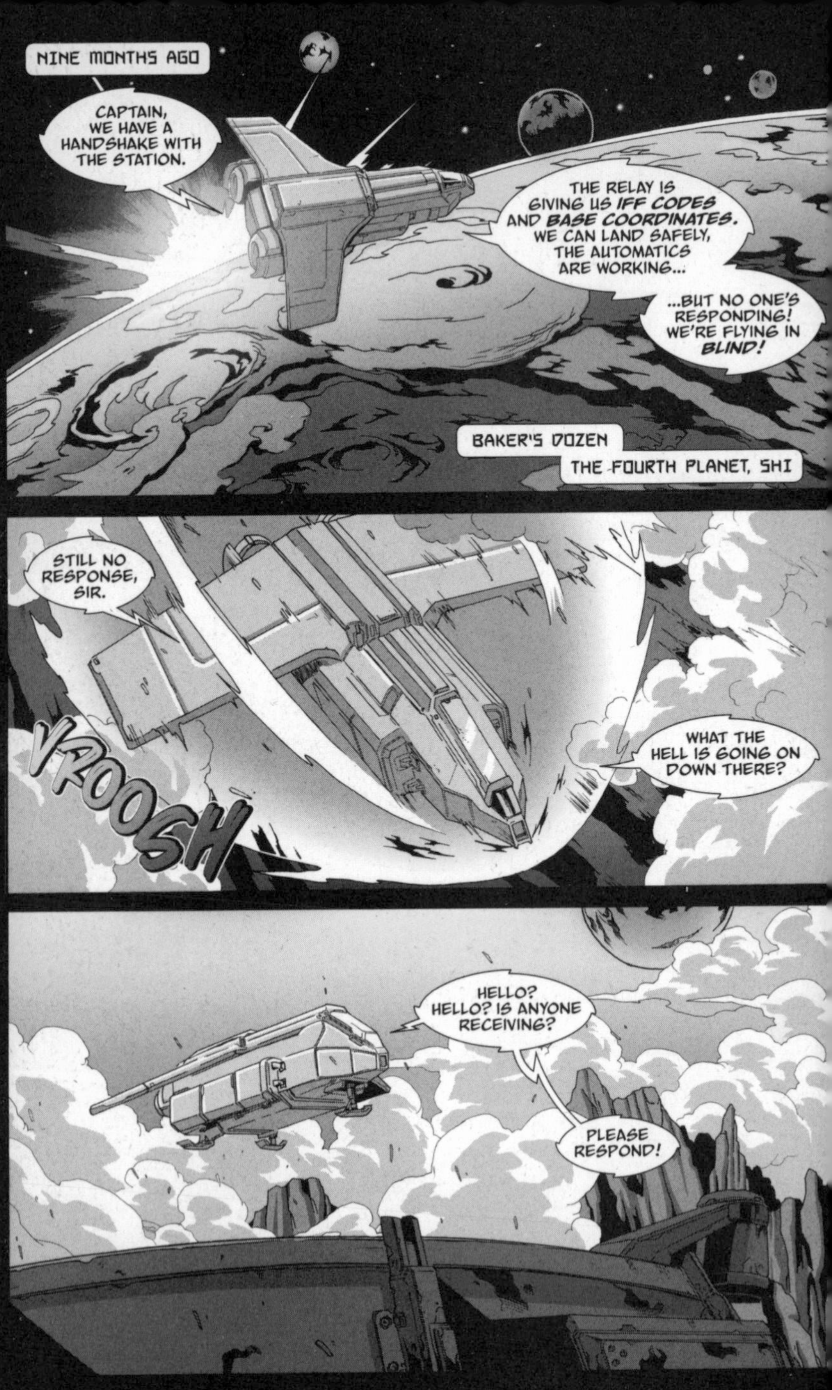
NINE MONTHS AGO
CAPTAIN, WE HAVE A HANDSHAKE WITH THE STATION.
THE RELAY IS GIVING US IFF CODES AND BASE COORDINATES. WE CAN LAND SAFELY, THE AUTOMATICS ARE WORKING...
...BUT NO ONE'S RESPONDING! WE'RE FLYING IN BLIND!
BAKER'S DOZEN
THE FOURTH PLANET, SHI
STILL NO RESPONSE, SIR.
VROOSH
WHAT THE HELL IS GOING ON DOWN THERE?
HELLO? HELLO? IS ANYONE RECEIVING?
PLEASE RESPOND!

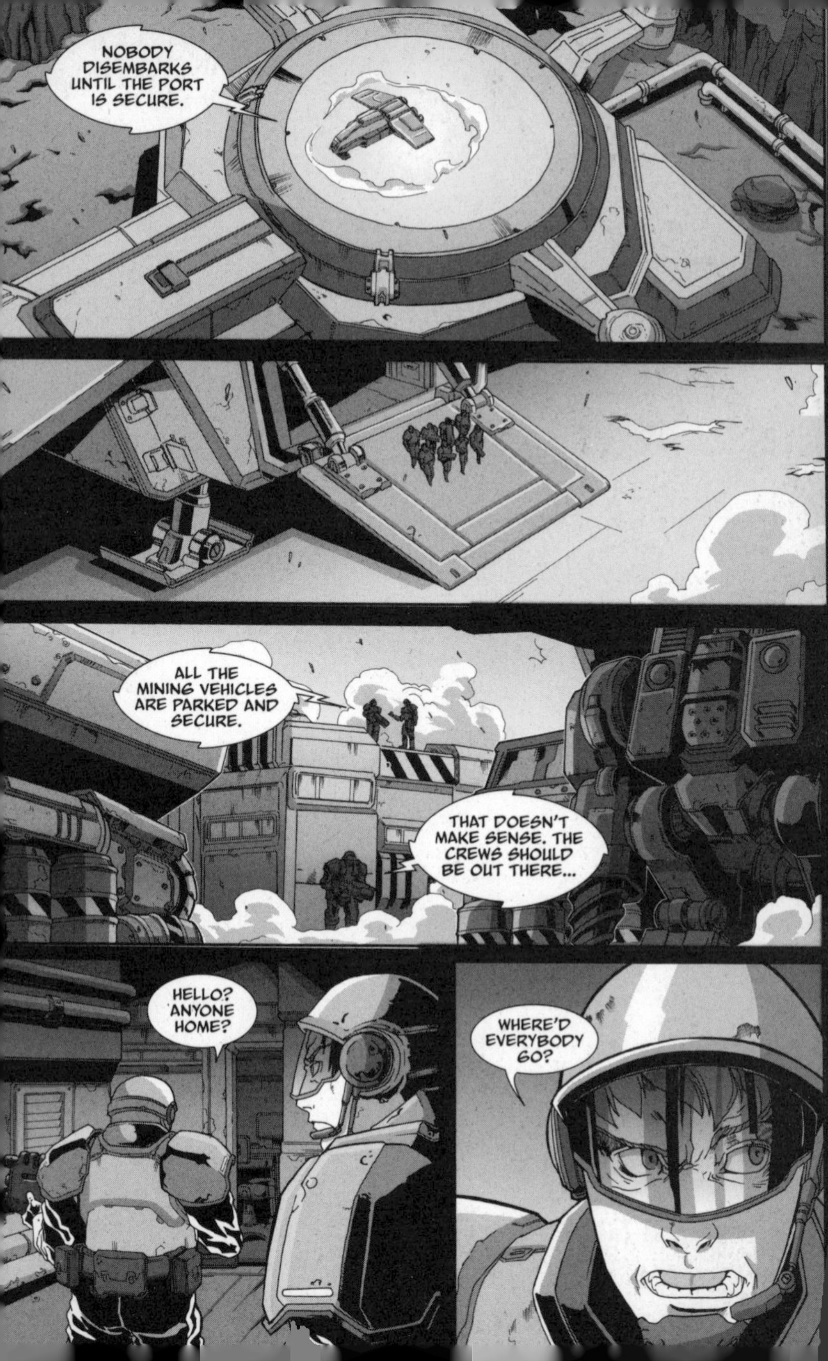
NOBODY DISEMBARKS UNTIL THE PORT IS SECURE.
ALL THE MINING VEHICLES ARE PARKED AND SECURE.
THAT DOESN'T MAKE SENSE. THE CREWS SHOULD BE OUT THERE...
HELLO? ANYONE HOME?
WHERE'D EVERYBODY GO?

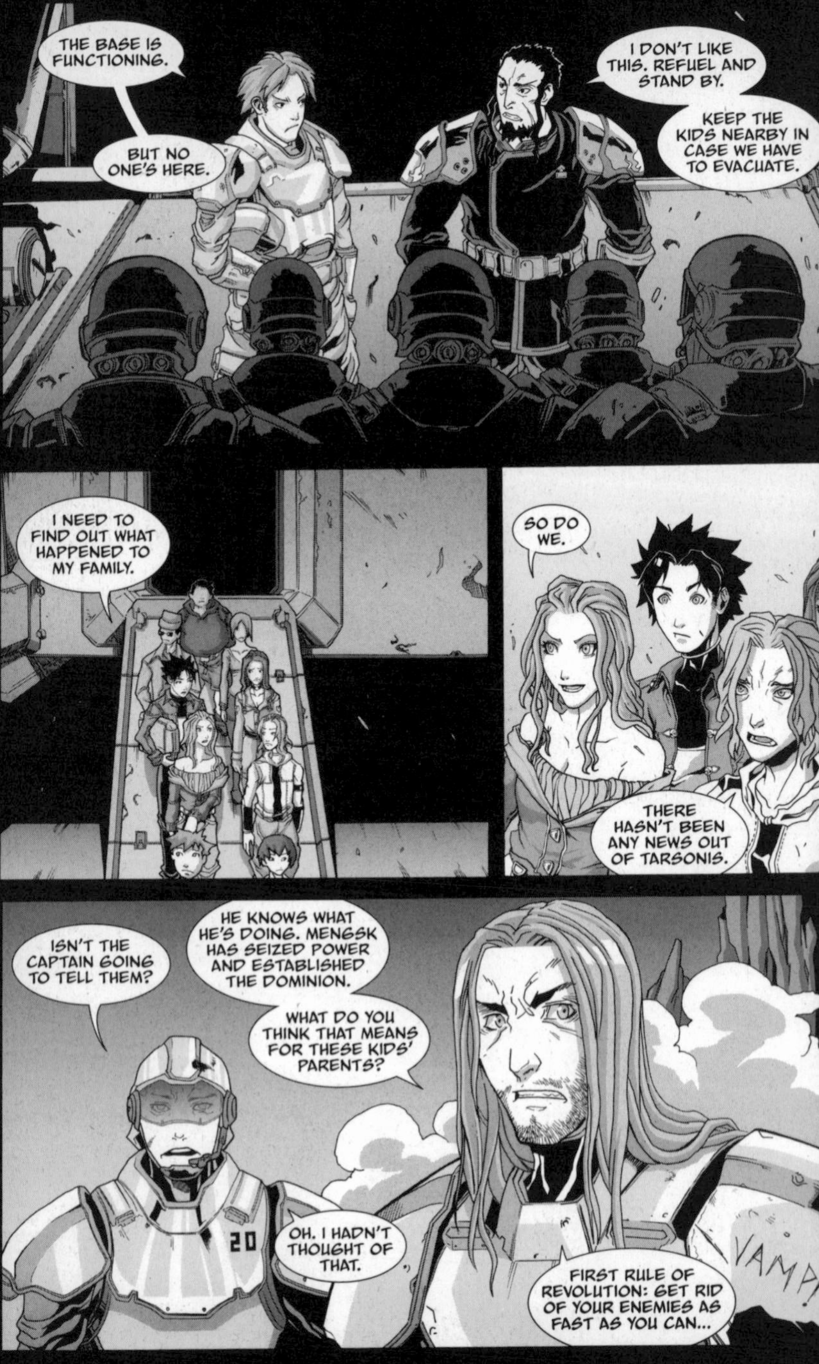
THE BASE IS FUNCTIONING.
BUT NO ONE'S HERE.
I DON'T LIKE THIS. REFUEL AND STAND BY.
KEEP THE KIDS NEARBY IN CASE WE HAVE TO EVACUATE.
I NEED TO FIND OUT WHAT HAPPENED TO MY FAMILY.
SO DO WE.
THERE HASN'T BEEN ANY NEWS OUT OF TARSONIS.
ISN'T THE CAPTAIN GOING TO TELL THEM?
HE KNOWS WHAT HE'S DOING. MENGSK HAS SEIZED POWER AND ESTABLISHED THE DOMINION.
WHAT DO YOU THINK THAT MEANS FOR THESE KIDS' PARENTS?
20
OH. I HADN'T THOUGHT OF THAT.
FIRST RULE OF REVOLUTION: GET RID OF YOUR ENEMIES AS FAST AS YOU CAN...
VAMP!

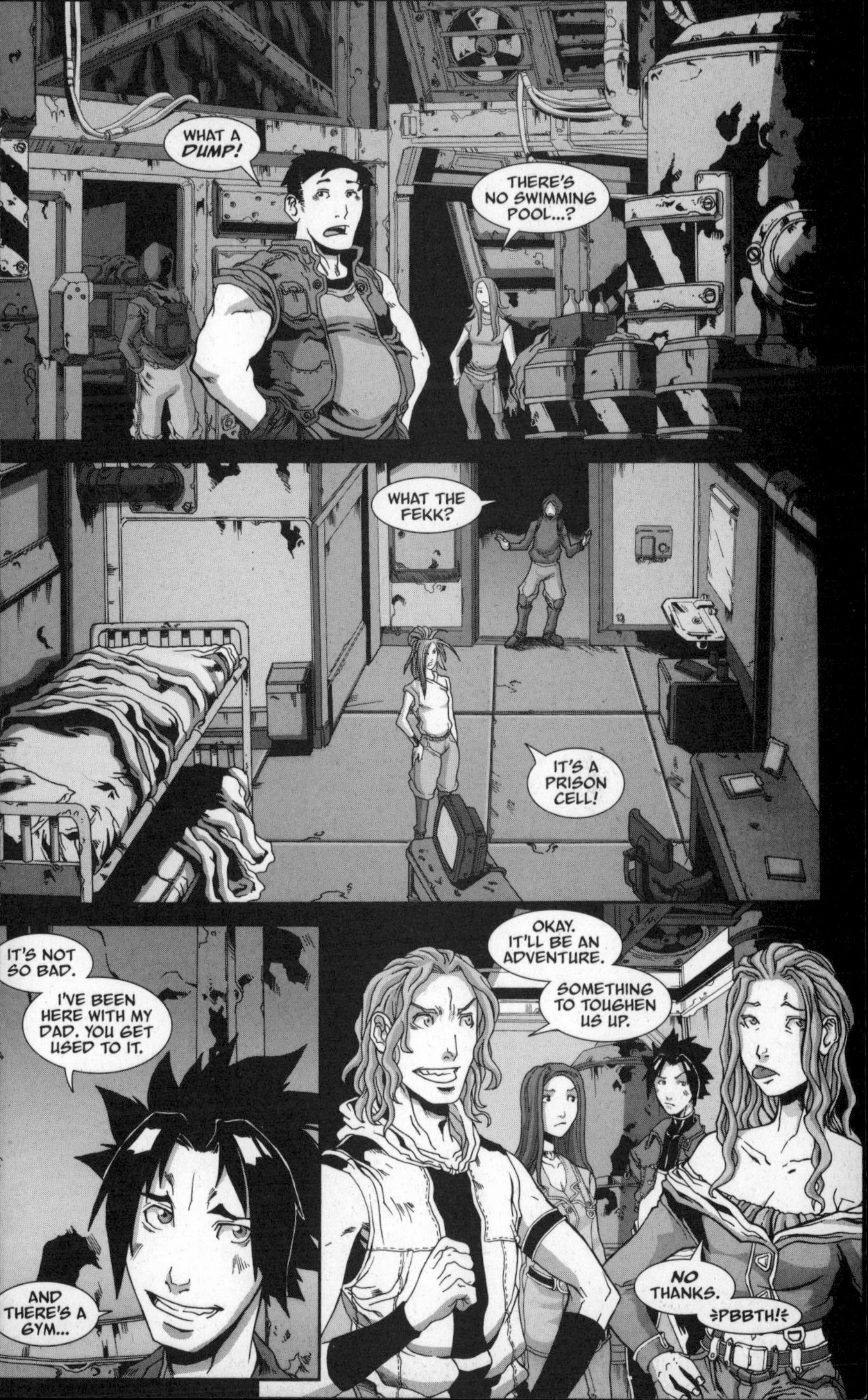
WHAT A DUMP!
THERE'S NO SWIMMING POOL...?
WHAT THE FEKK?
IT'S A PRISON CELL!
IT'S NOT SO BAD.
I'VE BEEN HERE WITH MY DAD. YOU GET USED TO IT.
AND THERE'S A GYM...
OKAY. IT'LL BE AN ADVENTURE.
SOMETHING TO TOUGHEN US UP.
NO THANKS.
PBBTH!

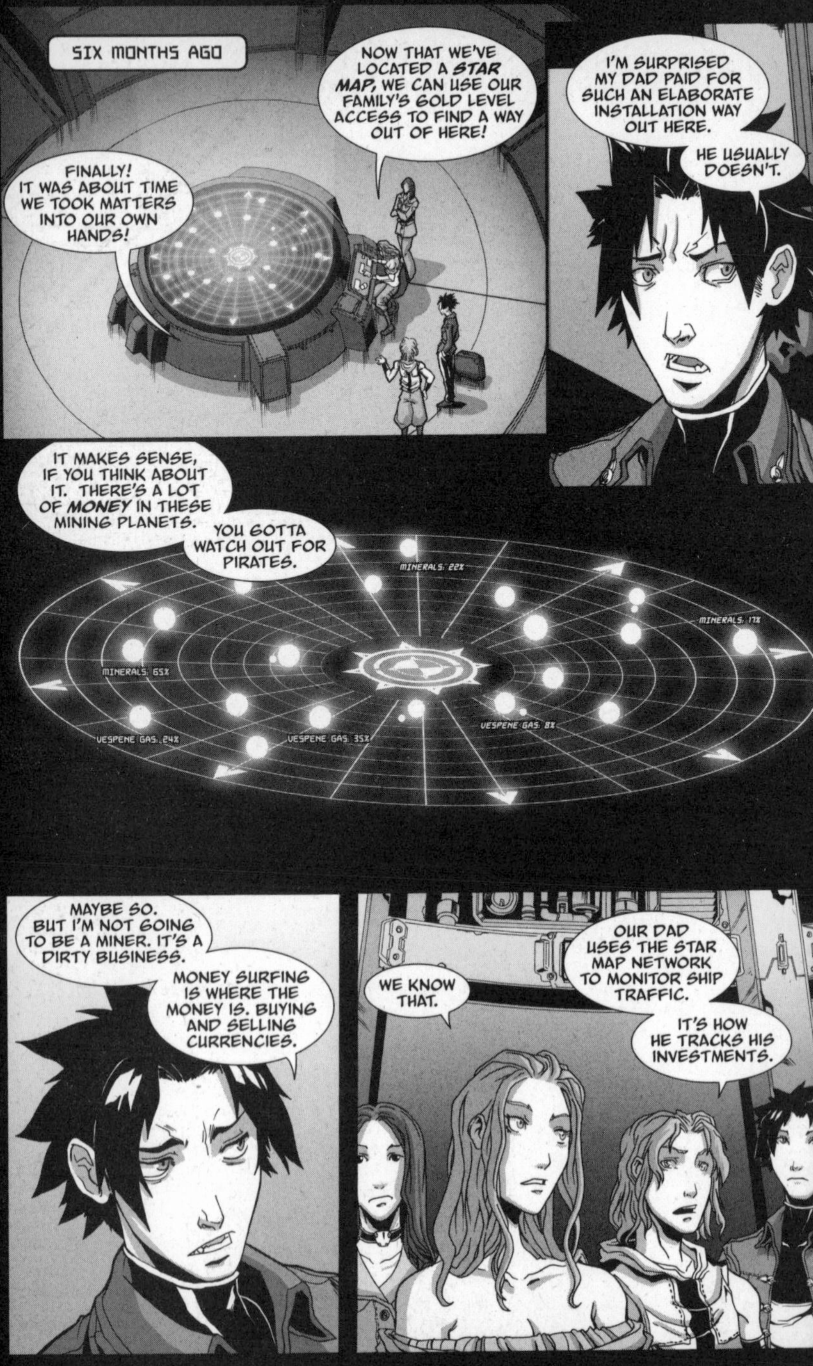
SIX MONTHS AGO
NOW THAT WE'VE LOCATED A *STAR MAP,* WE CAN USE OUR FAMILY'S GOLD LEVEL ACCESS TO FIND A WAY OUT OF HERE!
FINALLY! IT WAS ABOUT TIME WE TOOK MATTERS INTO OUR OWN HANDS!
I'M SURPRISED MY DAD PAID FOR SUCH AN ELABORATE INSTALLATION WAY OUT HERE.
HE USUALLY DOESN'T.
IT MAKES SENSE, IF YOU THINK ABOUT IT. THERE'S A LOT OF *MONEY* IN THESE MINING PLANETS.
YOU GOTTA WATCH OUT FOR PIRATES.
MINERALS: 22%
MINERALS: 17%
MINERALS: 65%
VESPENE GAS: 8%
VESPENE GAS: 24%
VESPENE GAS: 35%
MAYBE SO. BUT I'M NOT GOING TO BE A MINER. IT'S A DIRTY BUSINESS.
MONEY SURFING IS WHERE THE MONEY IS. BUYING AND SELLING CURRENCIES.
WE KNOW THAT.
OUR DAD USES THE STAR MAP NETWORK TO MONITOR SHIP TRAFFIC.
IT'S HOW HE TRACKS HIS INVESTMENTS.

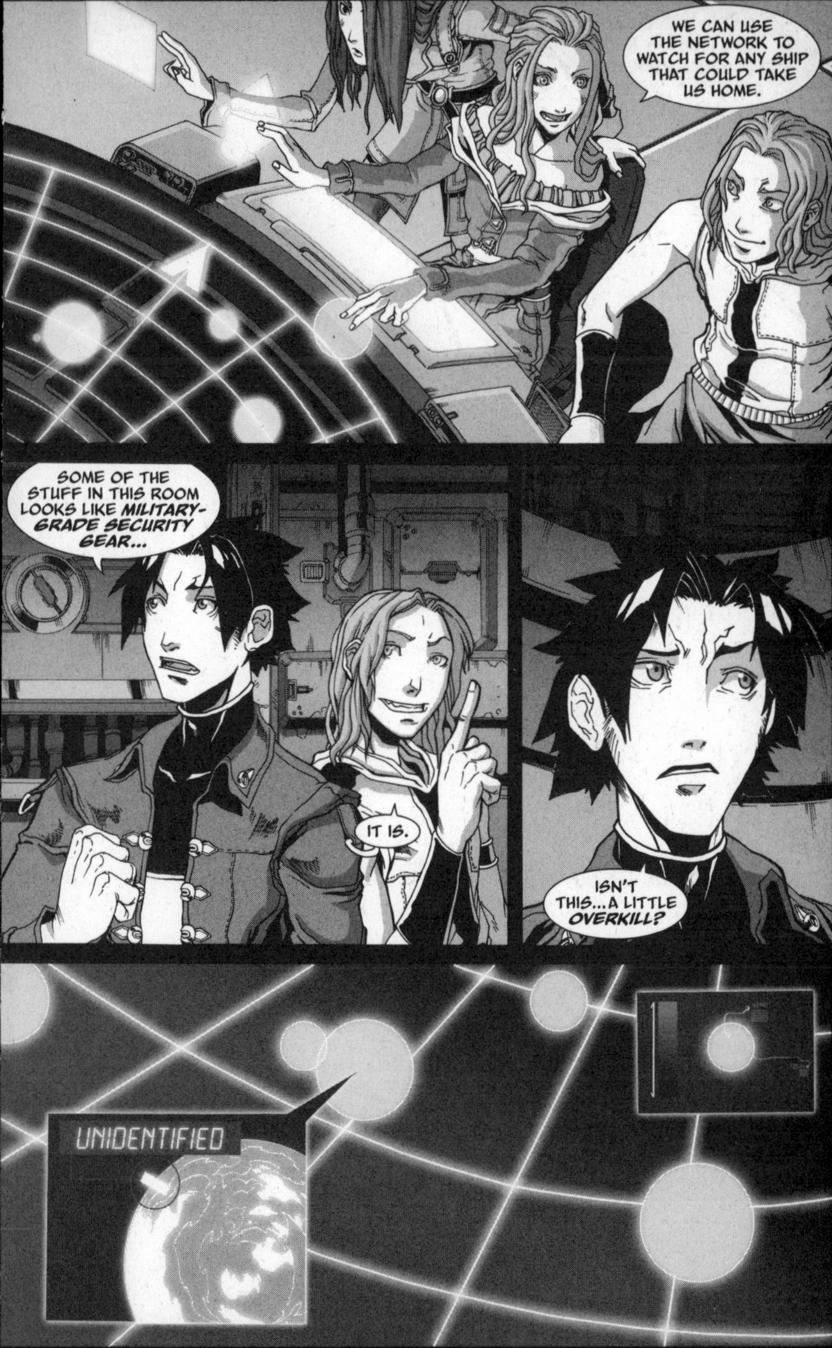
WE CAN USE THE NETWORK TO WATCH FOR ANY SHIP THAT COULD TAKE US HOME.
SOME OF THE STUFF IN THIS ROOM LOOKS LIKE MILITARY-GRADE SECURITY GEAR...
IT IS.
ISN'T THIS...A LITTLE OVERKILL?
UNIDENTIFIED

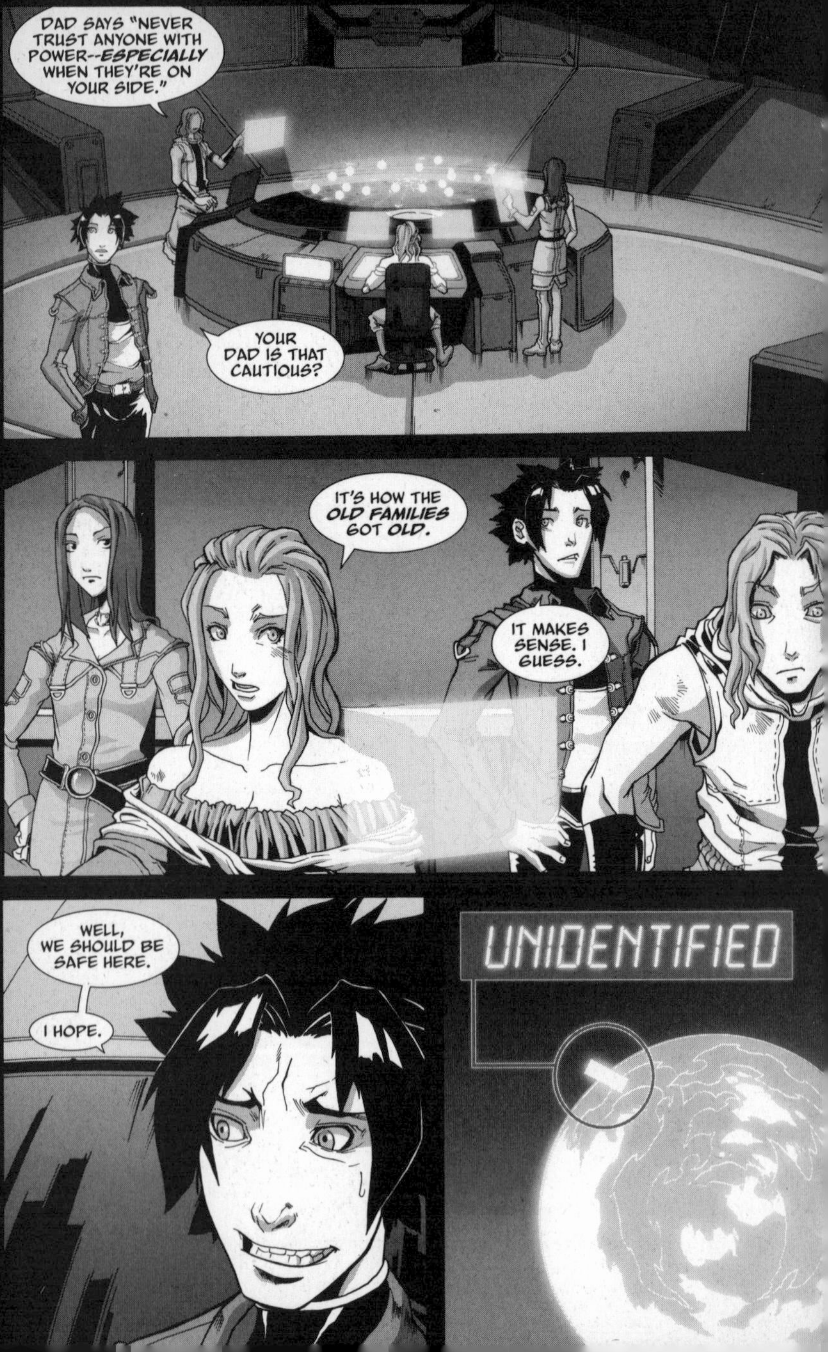
DAD SAYS "NEVER TRUST ANYONE WITH POWER--ESPECIALLY WHEN THEY'RE ON YOUR SIDE."
YOUR DAD IS THAT CAUTIOUS?
IT'S HOW THE OLD FAMILIES GOT OLD.
IT MAKES SENSE. I GUESS.
WELL, WE SHOULD BE SAFE HERE.
I HOPE.
UNIDENTIFIED

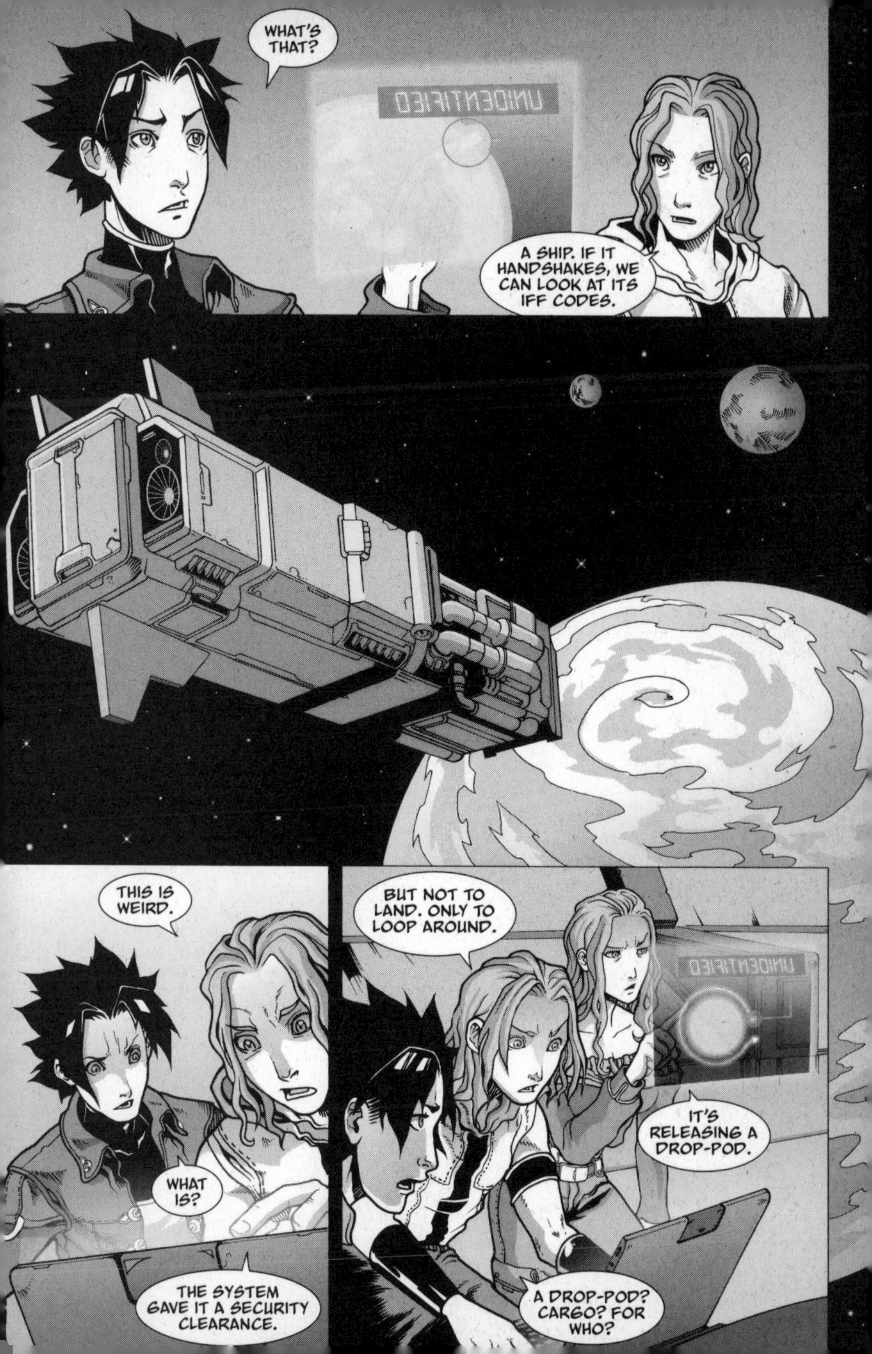
WHAT'S THAT?
A SHIP. IF IT HANDSHAKES, WE CAN LOOK AT ITS IFF CODES.
THIS IS WEIRD.
WHAT IS?
THE SYSTEM GAVE IT A SECURITY CLEARANCE.
BUT NOT TO LAND. ONLY TO LOOP AROUND.
IT'S RELEASING A DROP-POD.
A DROP-POD? CARGO? FOR WHO?

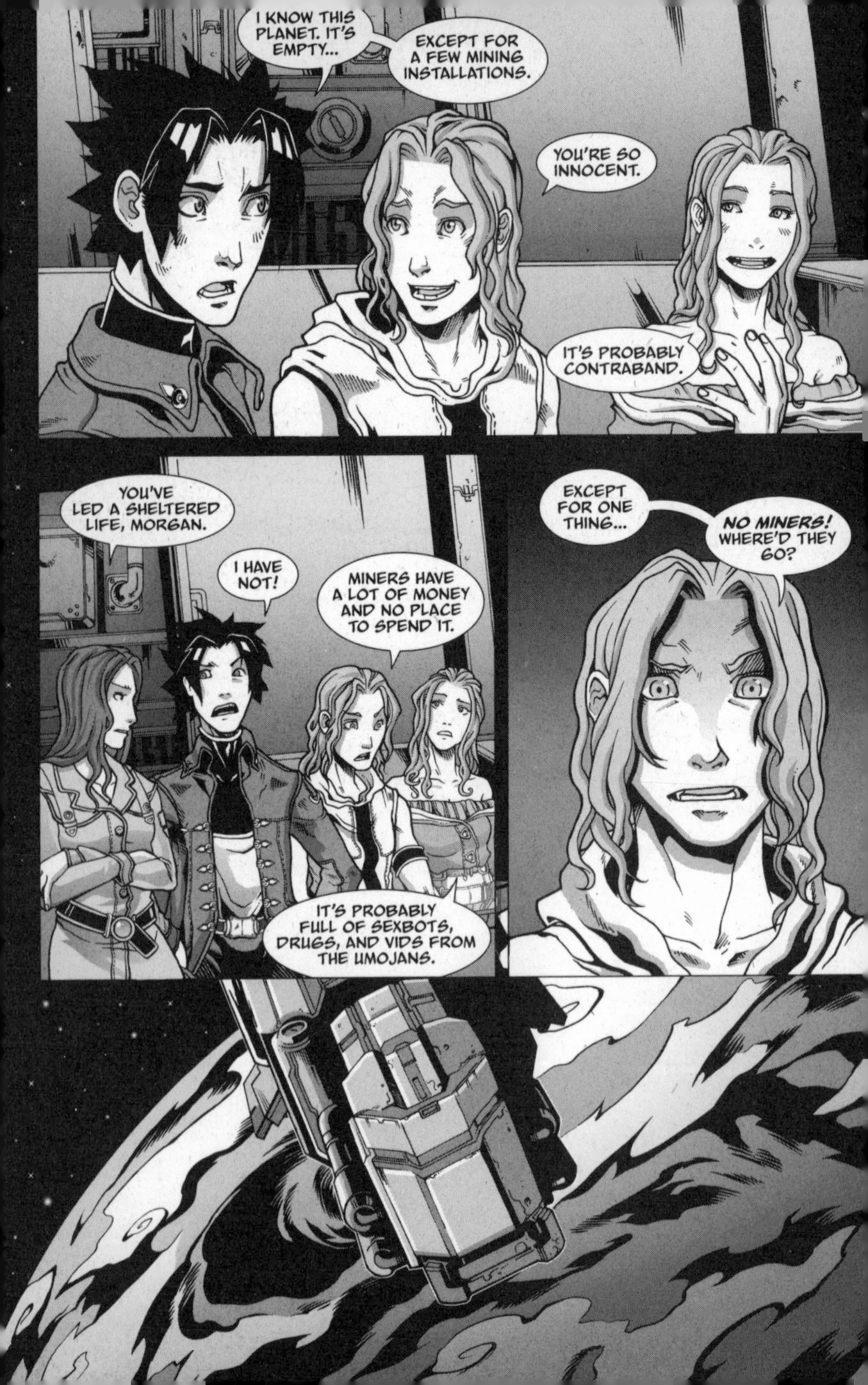
I KNOW THIS PLANET. IT'S EMPTY...
EXCEPT FOR A FEW MINING INSTALLATIONS.
YOU'RE SO INNOCENT.
IT'S PROBABLY CONTRABAND.
YOU'VE LED A SHELTERED LIFE, MORGAN.
I HAVE NOT!
MINERS HAVE A LOT OF MONEY AND NO PLACE TO SPEND IT.
IT'S PROBABLY FULL OF SEXBOTS, DRUGS, AND VIDS FROM THE UMOJANS.
EXCEPT FOR ONE THING...
NO MINERS! WHERE'D THEY GO?

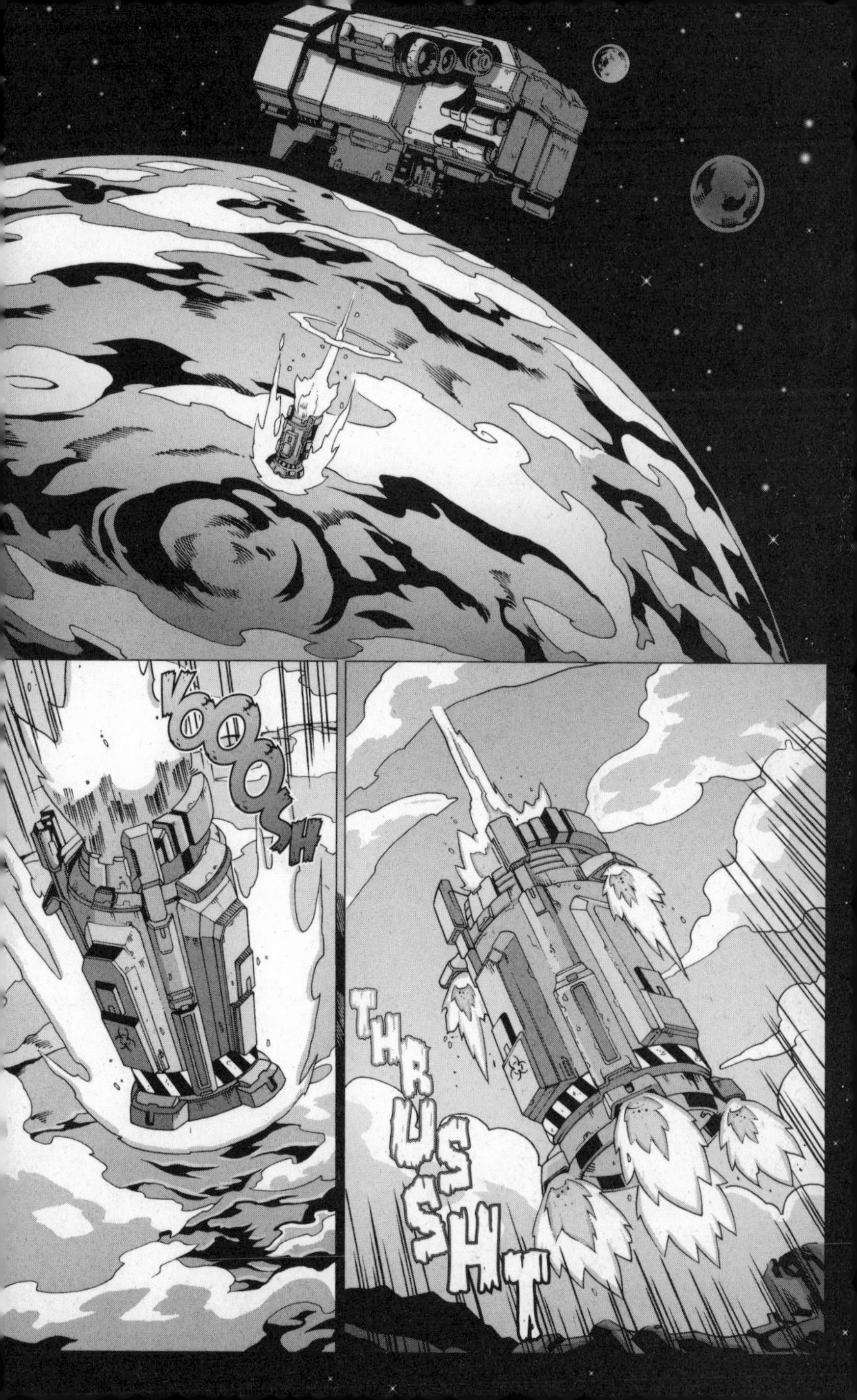
VOOOSH
THRUSSHT

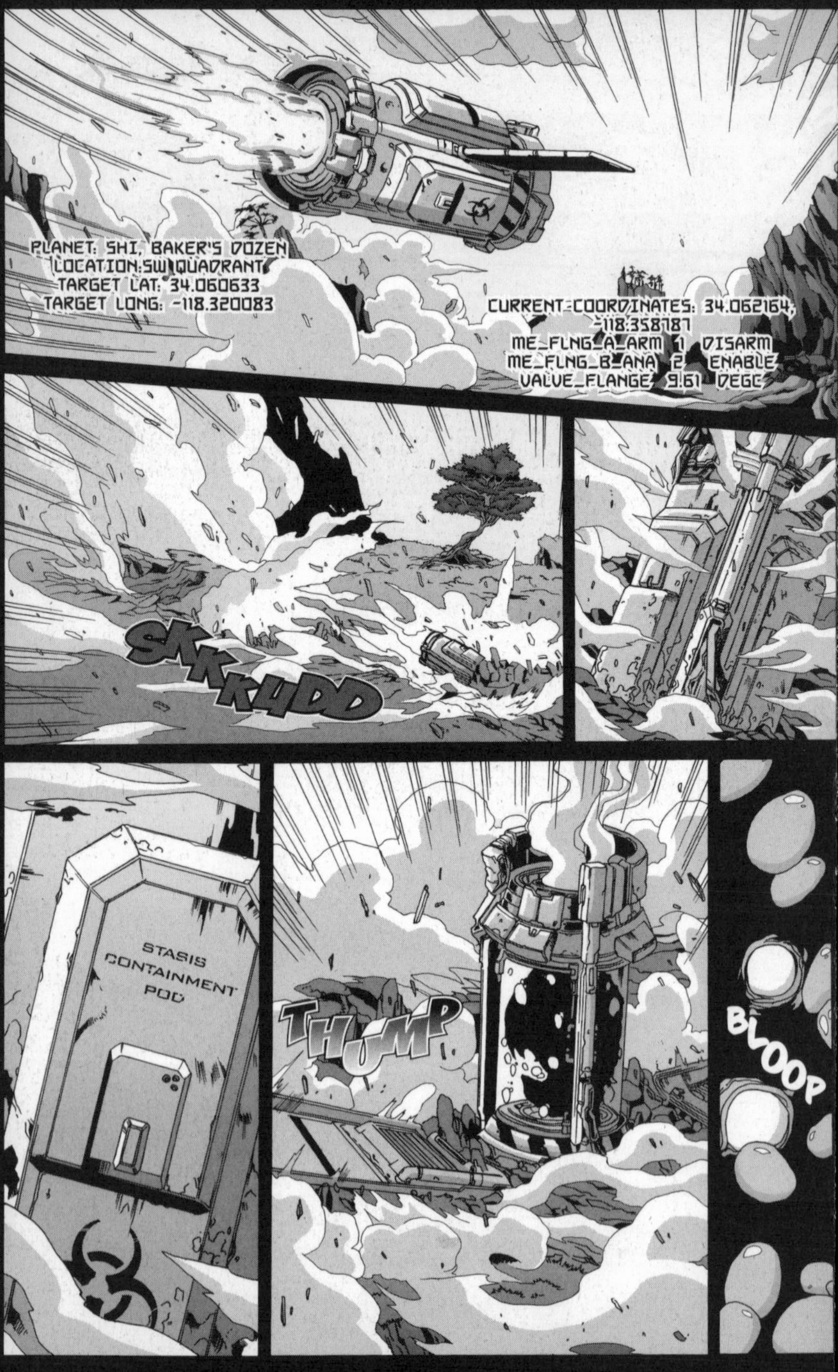
PLANET: SHI, BAKER'S DOZEN
LOCATION: SW QUADRANT
TARGET LAT: 34.060633
TARGET LONG: -118.320083
CURRENT COORDINATES: 34.062164, -118.358787
ME_FLNG_A_ARM 1 DISARM
ME_FLNG_B_ANA 2 ENABLE
VALVE_FLANGE 9.61 DEGC
SKKKUDD
STASIS CONTAINMENT POD
THUMP
BLOOP

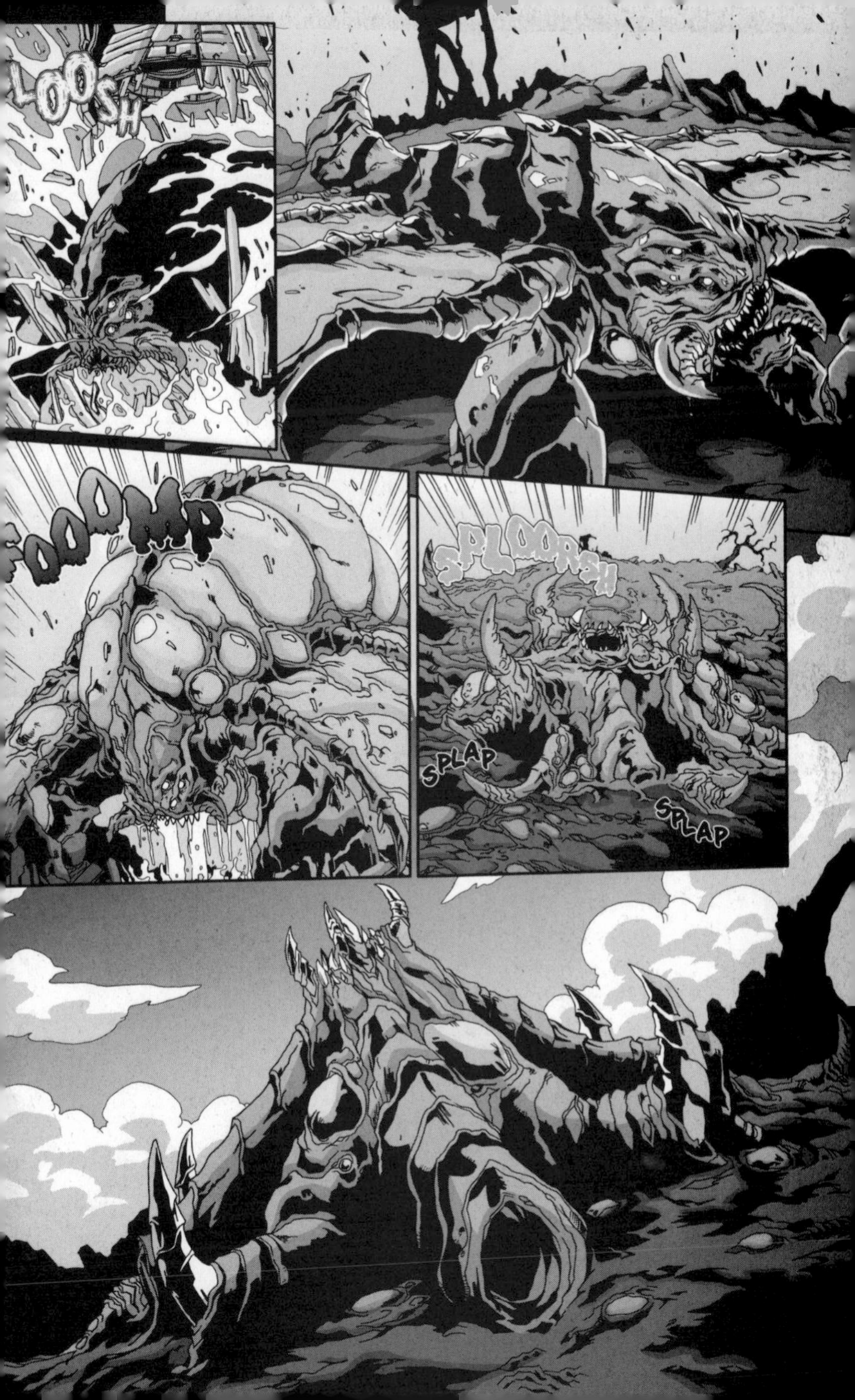
LOOSH
FOOOMP
SPLOORSH
SPLAP
SPLAP

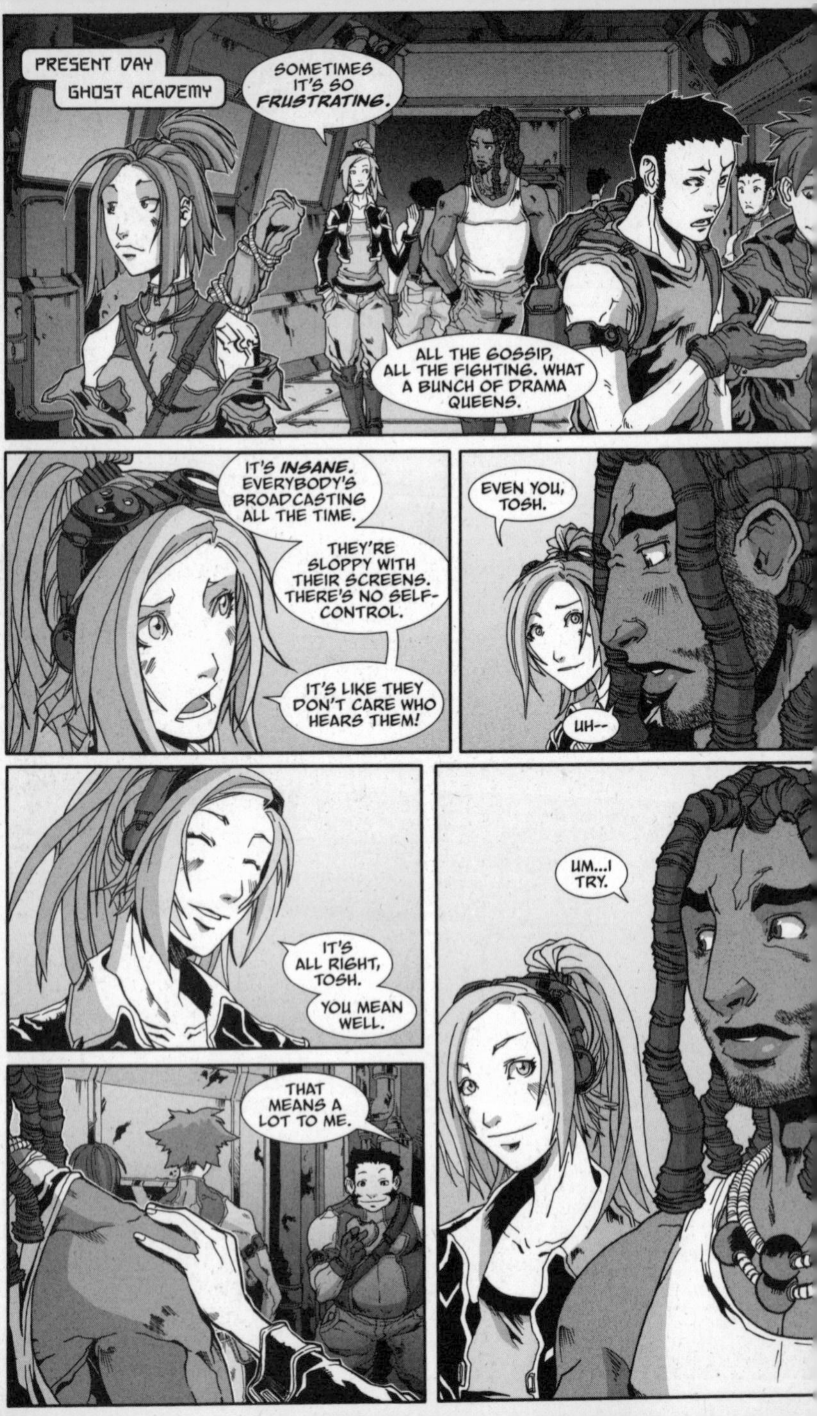
PRESENT DAY
GHOST ACADEMY
SOMETIMES IT'S SO FRUSTRATING.
ALL THE GOSSIP, ALL THE FIGHTING. WHAT A BUNCH OF DRAMA QUEENS.
IT'S INSANE. EVERYBODY'S BROADCASTING ALL THE TIME.
THEY'RE SLOPPY WITH THEIR SCREENS. THERE'S NO SELF-CONTROL.
IT'S LIKE THEY DON'T CARE WHO HEARS THEM!
EVEN YOU, TOSH.
UH--
IT'S ALL RIGHT, TOSH.
YOU MEAN WELL.
UM...I TRY.
THAT MEANS A LOT TO ME.

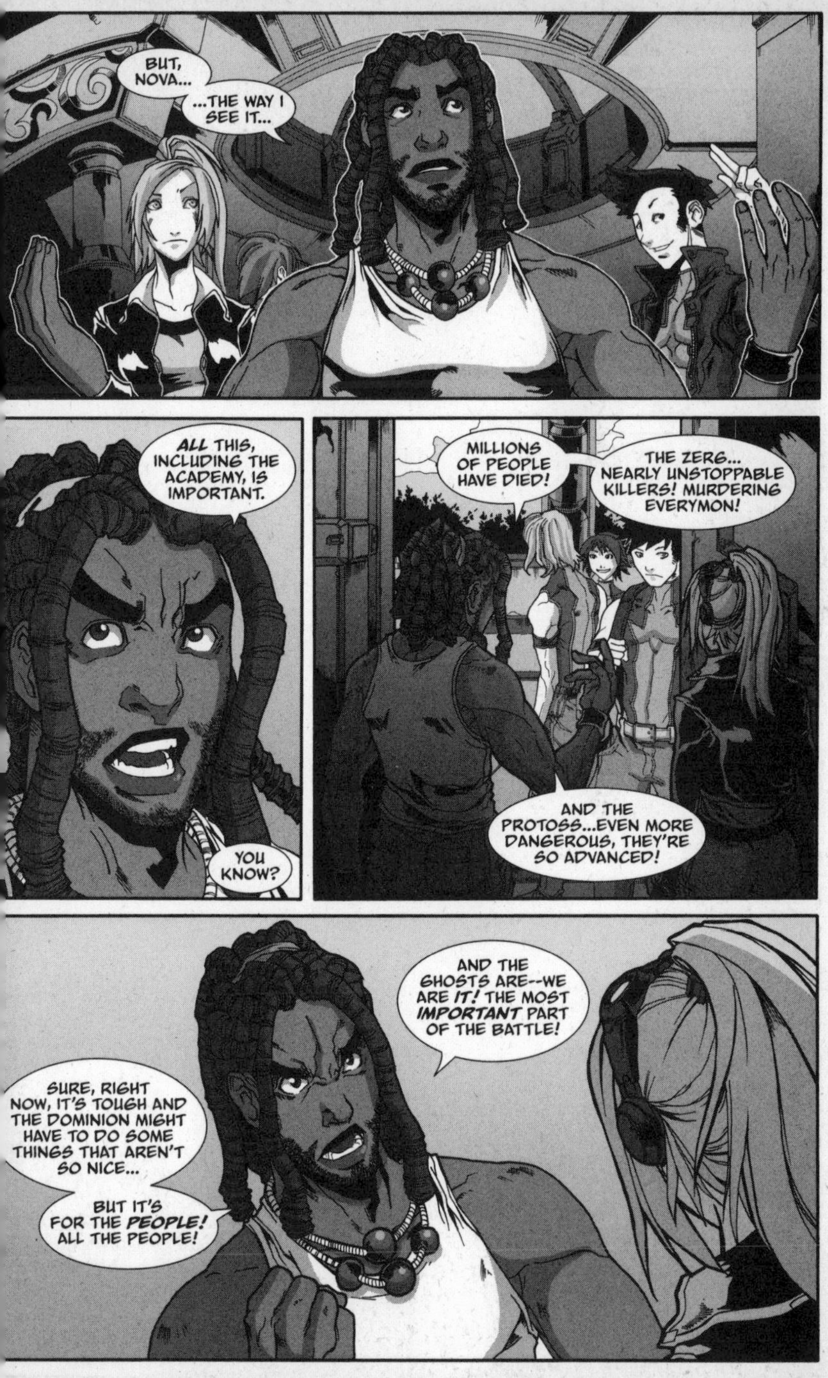
BUT, NOVA...
...THE WAY I SEE IT...
ALL THIS, INCLUDING THE ACADEMY, IS IMPORTANT.
YOU KNOW?
MILLIONS OF PEOPLE HAVE DIED!
THE ZERG... NEARLY UNSTOPPABLE KILLERS! MURDERING EVERYMON!
AND THE PROTOSS...EVEN MORE DANGEROUS, THEY'RE SO ADVANCED!
AND THE GHOSTS ARE--WE ARE IT! THE MOST IMPORTANT PART OF THE BATTLE!
SURE, RIGHT NOW, IT'S TOUGH AND THE DOMINION MIGHT HAVE TO DO SOME THINGS THAT AREN'T SO NICE...
BUT IT'S FOR THE PEOPLE! ALL THE PEOPLE!

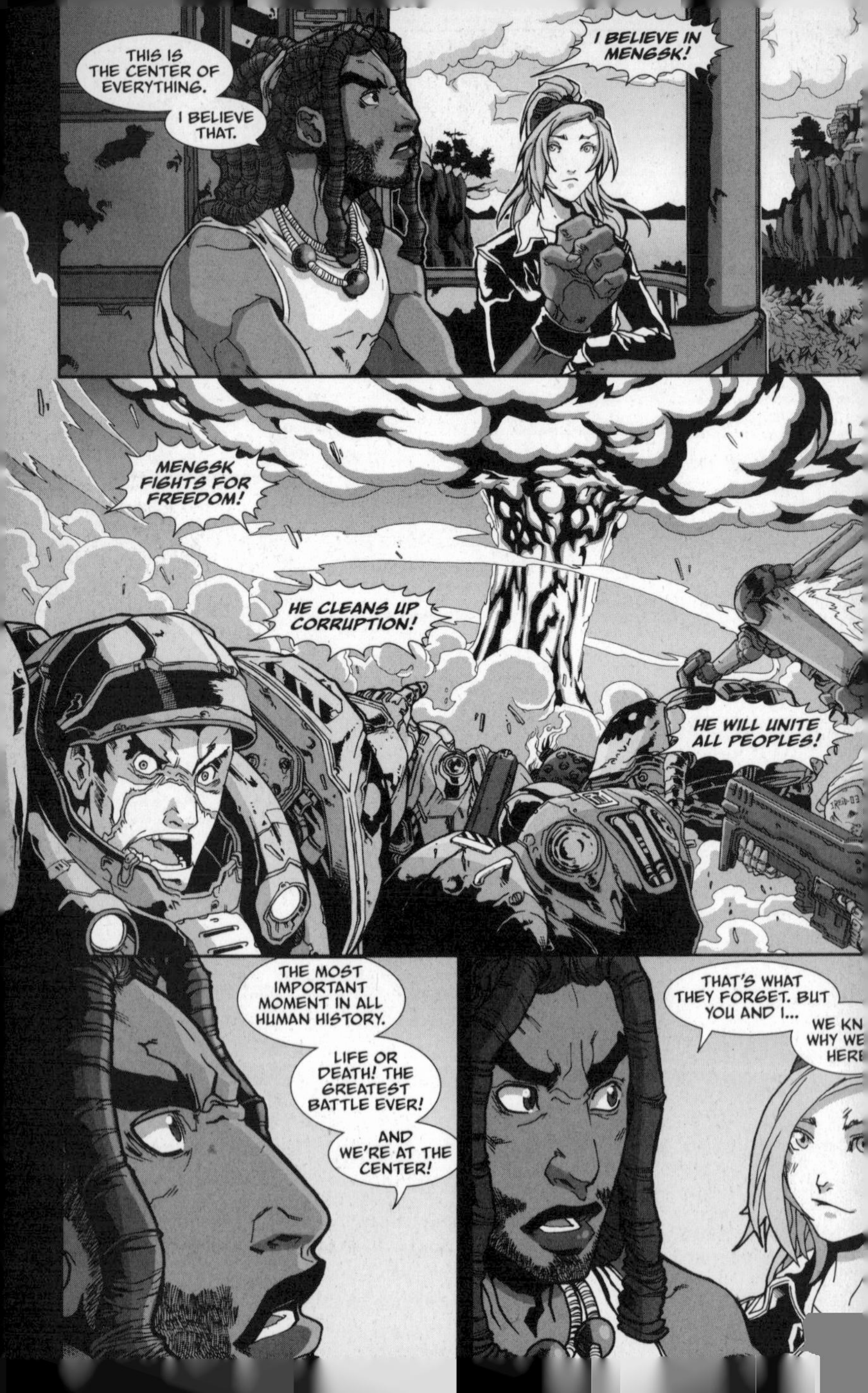
THIS IS THE CENTER OF EVERYTHING.
I BELIEVE THAT.
I BELIEVE IN MENGSK!
MENGSK FIGHTS FOR FREEDOM!
HE CLEANS UP CORRUPTION!
HE WILL UNITE ALL PEOPLES!
THE MOST IMPORTANT MOMENT IN ALL HUMAN HISTORY.
LIFE OR DEATH! THE GREATEST BATTLE EVER!
AND WE'RE AT THE CENTER!
THAT'S WHAT THEY FORGET. BUT YOU AND I...

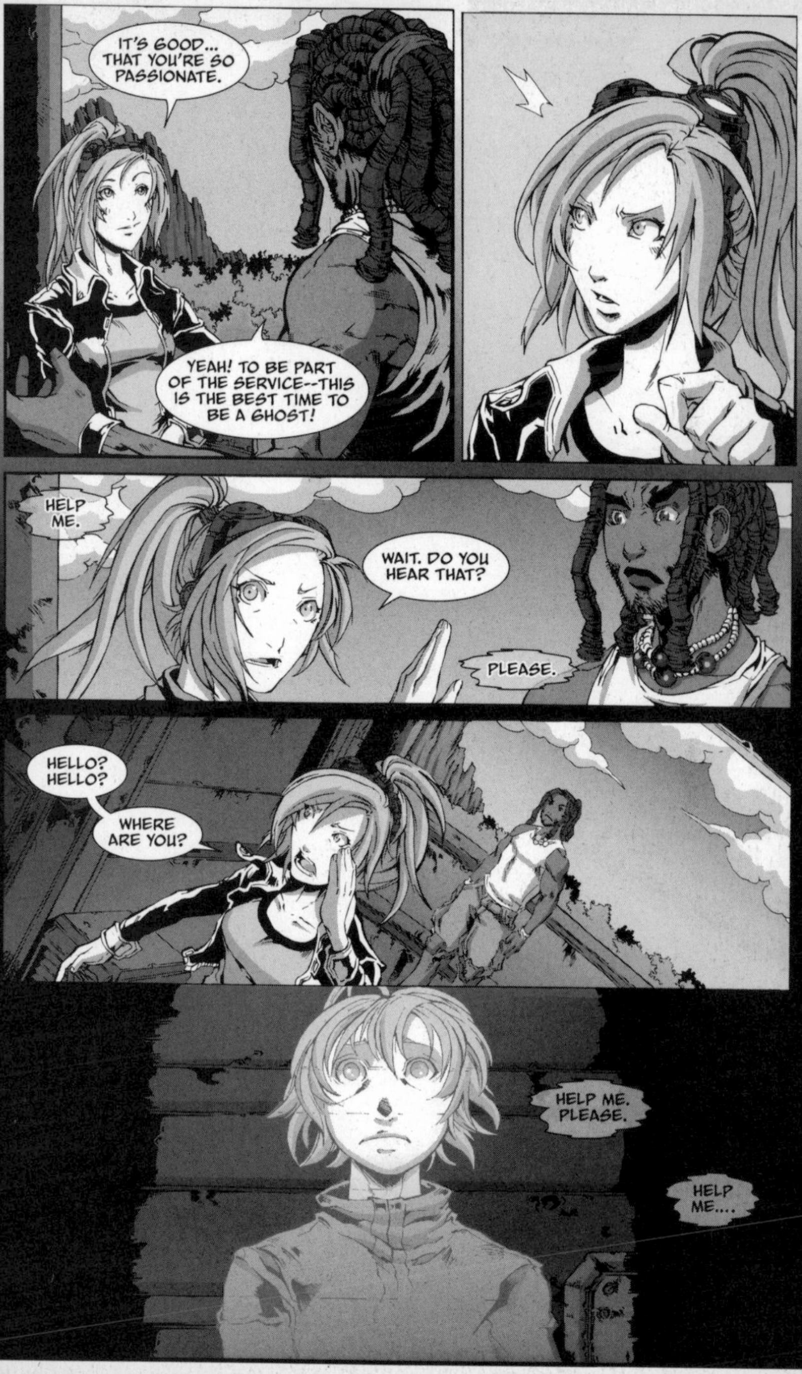
IT'S GOOD... THAT YOU'RE SO PASSIONATE.
YEAH! TO BE PART OF THE SERVICE--THIS IS THE BEST TIME TO BE A GHOST!
HELP ME.
WAIT. DO YOU HEAR THAT?
PLEASE.
HELLO? HELLO?
WHERE ARE YOU?
HELP ME. PLEASE.
HELP ME....

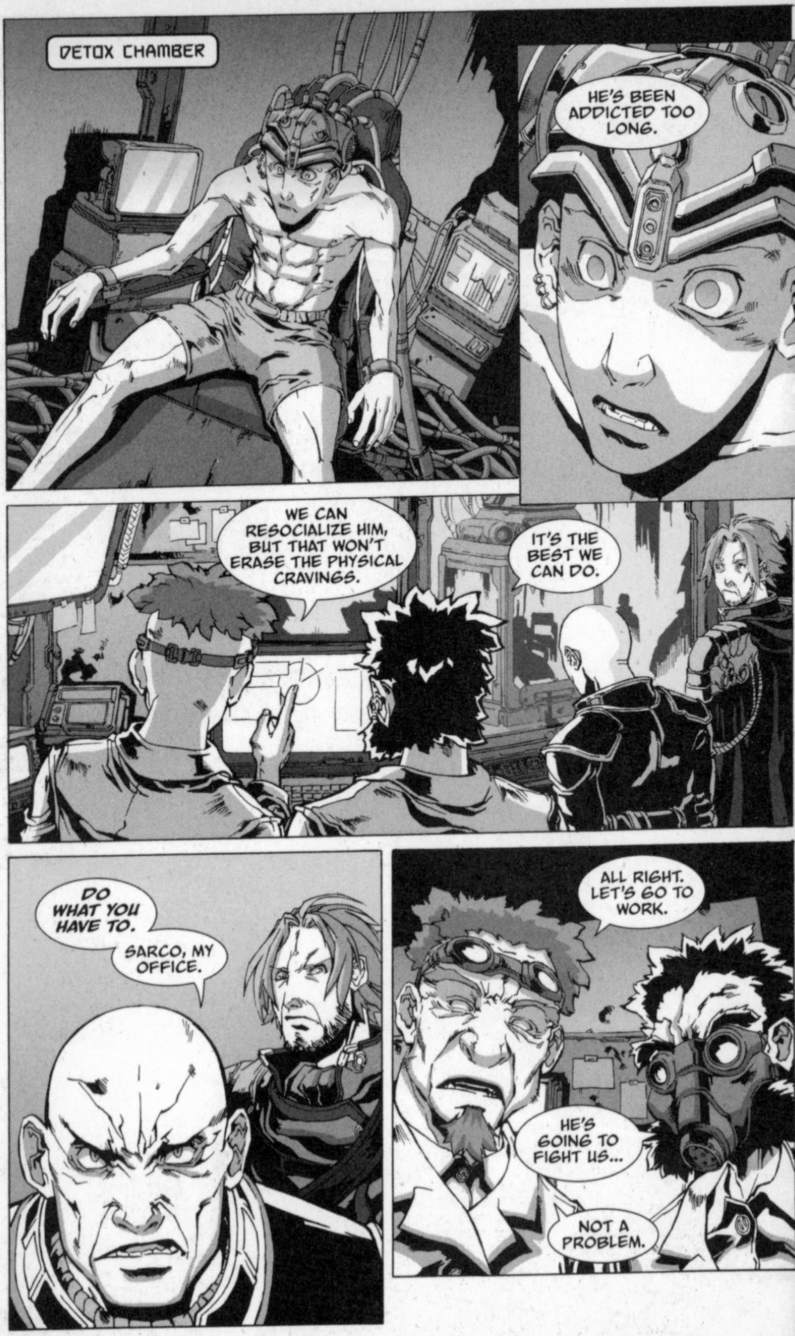
DETOX CHAMBER
HE'S BEEN ADDICTED TOO LONG.
WE CAN RESOCIALIZE HIM, BUT THAT WON'T ERASE THE PHYSICAL CRAVINGS.
IT'S THE BEST WE CAN DO.
DO WHAT YOU HAVE TO.
SARCO, MY OFFICE.
ALL RIGHT. LET'S GO TO WORK.
HE'S GOING TO FIGHT US...
NOT A PROBLEM.

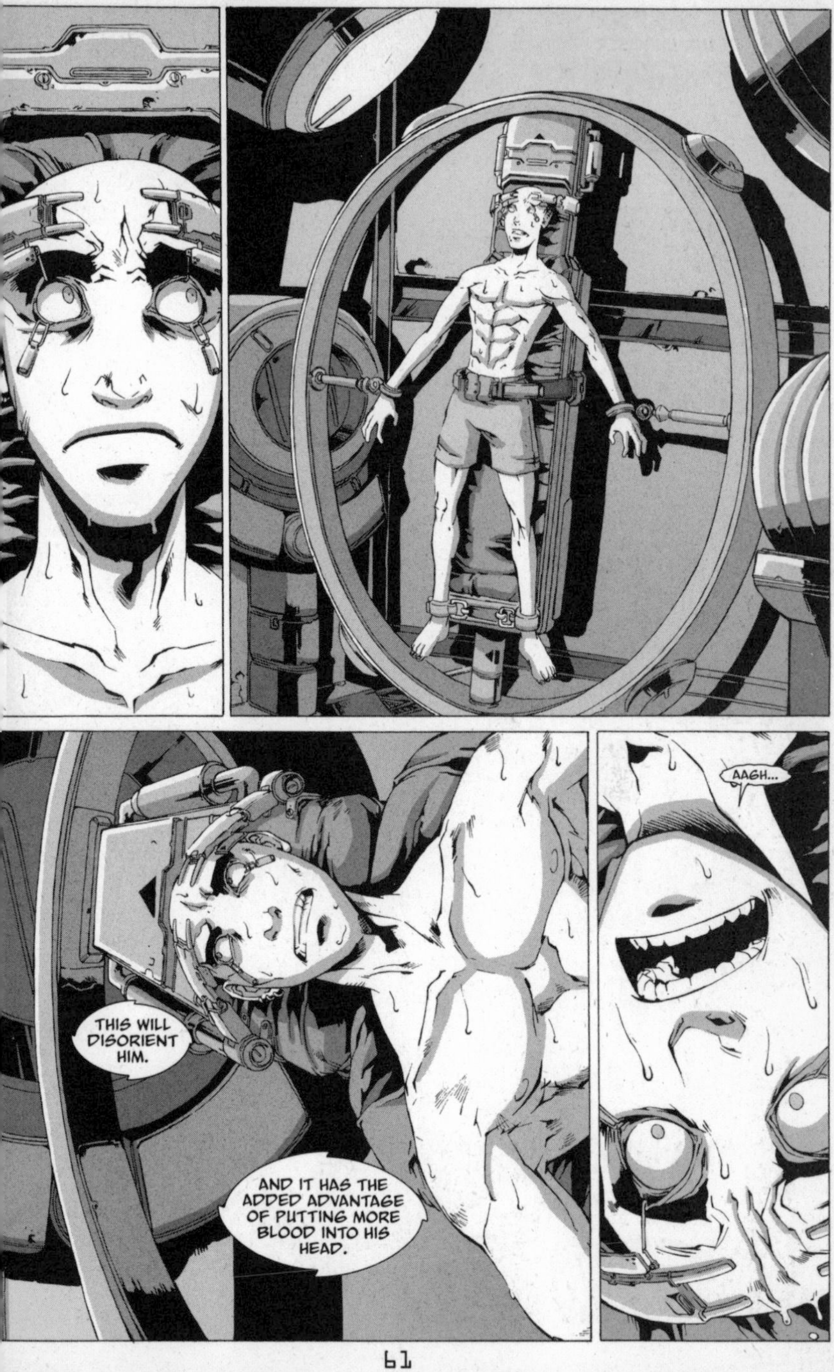
THIS WILL DISORIENT HIM.
AND IT HAS THE ADDED ADVANTAGE OF PUTTING MORE BLOOD INTO HIS HEAD.
AAGH...

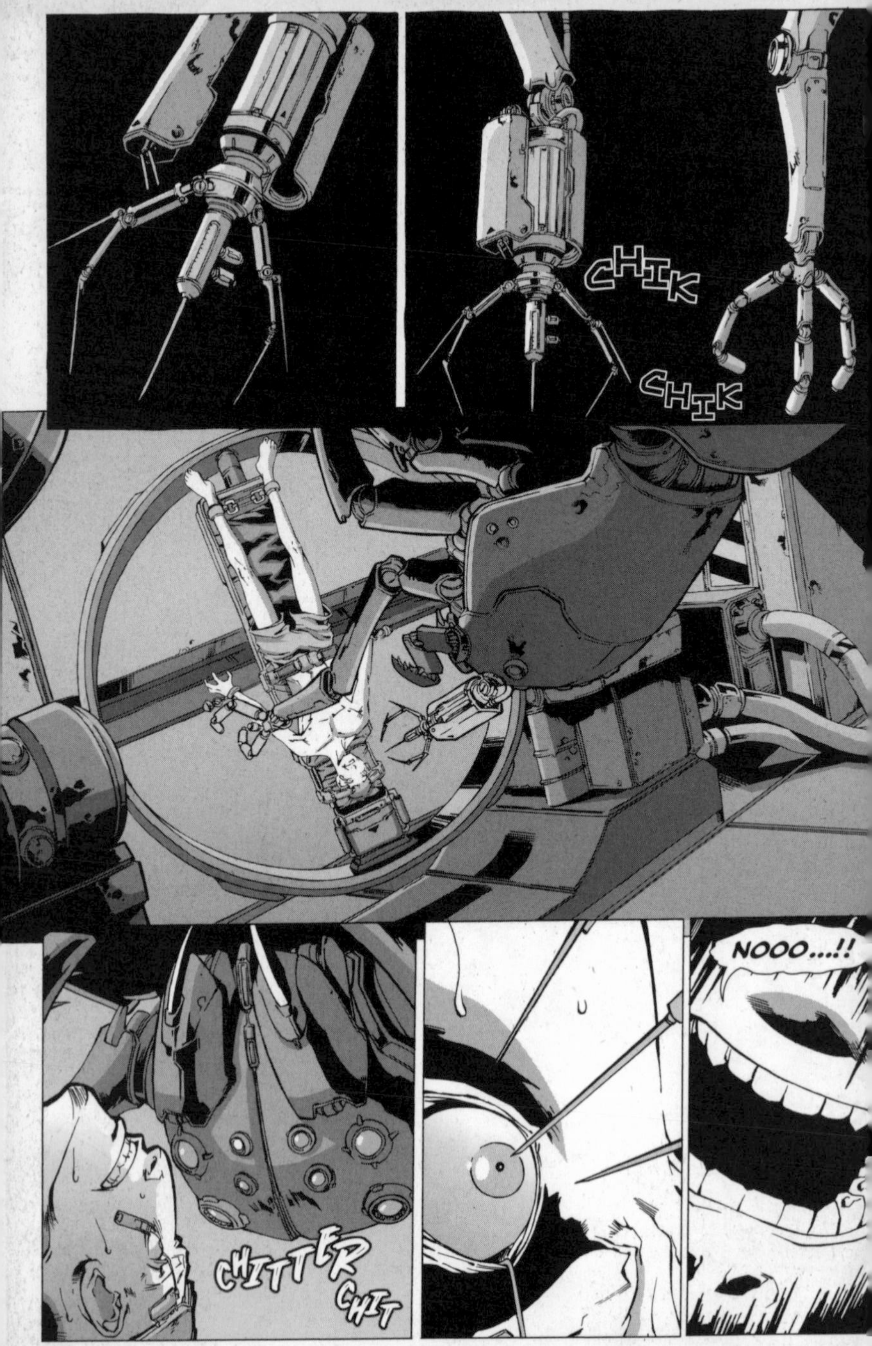
CHIK
CHIK
CHITTER
CHIT
NOOO...!!

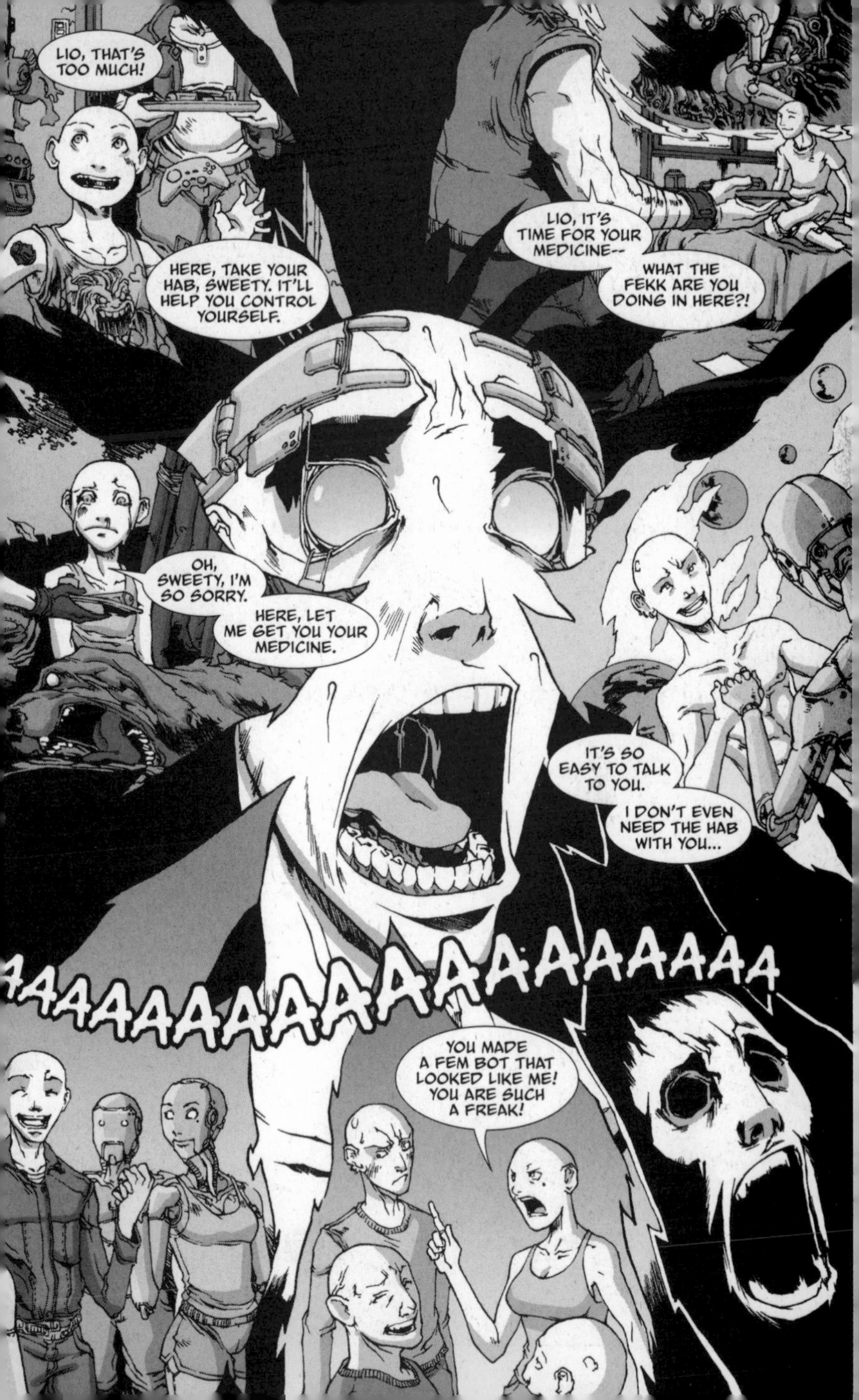
LIO, THAT'S TOO MUCH!
HERE, TAKE YOUR HAB, SWEETY. IT'LL HELP YOU CONTROL YOURSELF.
LIO, IT'S TIME FOR YOUR MEDICINE--
WHAT THE FEKK ARE YOU DOING IN HERE?!
OH, SWEETY, I'M SO SORRY.
HERE, LET ME GET YOU YOUR MEDICINE.
IT'S SO EASY TO TALK TO YOU.
I DON'T EVEN NEED THE HAB WITH YOU...
AAAAAAAAAAAAAAAAAAA
YOU MADE A FEM BOT THAT LOOKED LIKE ME! YOU ARE SUCH A FREAK!

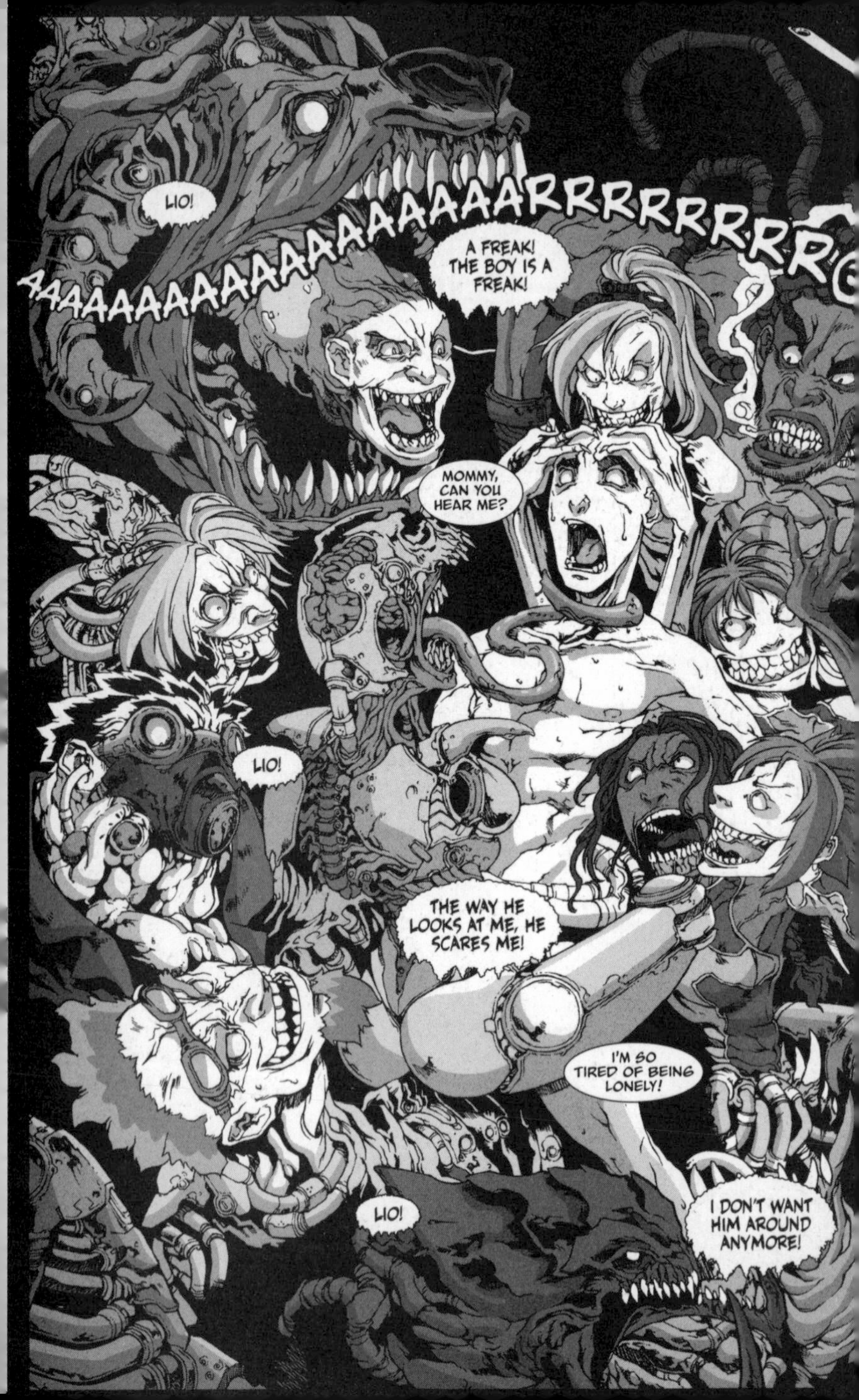
LIO!
AAAAAAAAAAAAAAAAAAAAARRRRRRRRRRG
A FREAK! THE BOY IS A FREAK!
MOMMY, CAN YOU HEAR ME?
LIO!
THE WAY HE LOOKS AT ME, HE SCARES ME!
I'M SO TIRED OF BEING LONELY!
LIO!
I DON'T WANT HIM AROUND ANYMORE!

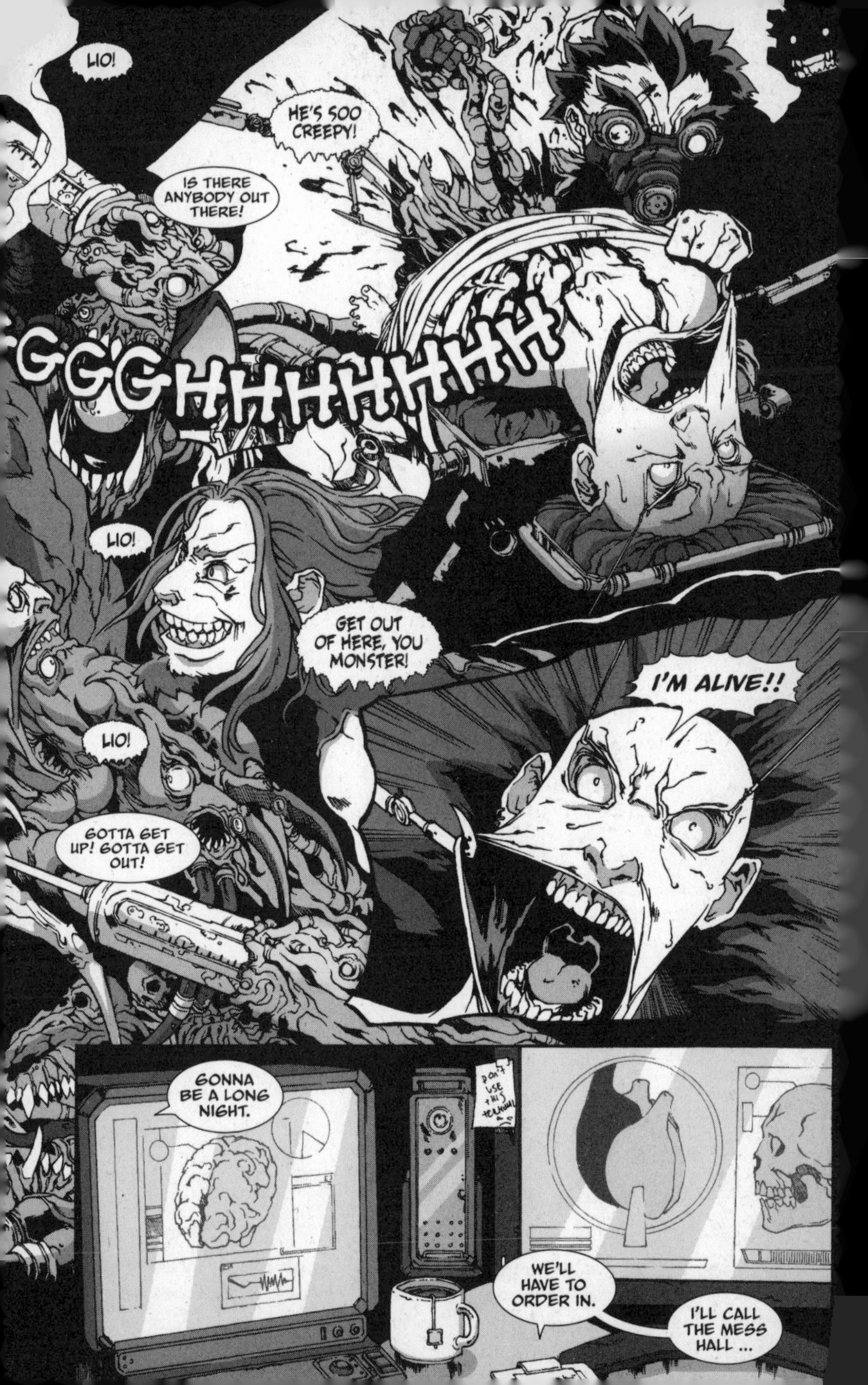
LIO!
HE'S SOO CREEPY!
IS THERE ANYBODY OUT THERE!
GGGHHHHHHHH
LIO!
GET OUT OF HERE, YOU MONSTER!
I'M ALIVE!!
LIO!
GOTTA GET UP! GOTTA GET OUT!
GONNA BE A LONG NIGHT.
DON'T USE THIS TERMINAL
WE'LL HAVE TO ORDER IN.
I'LL CALL THE MESS HALL ...

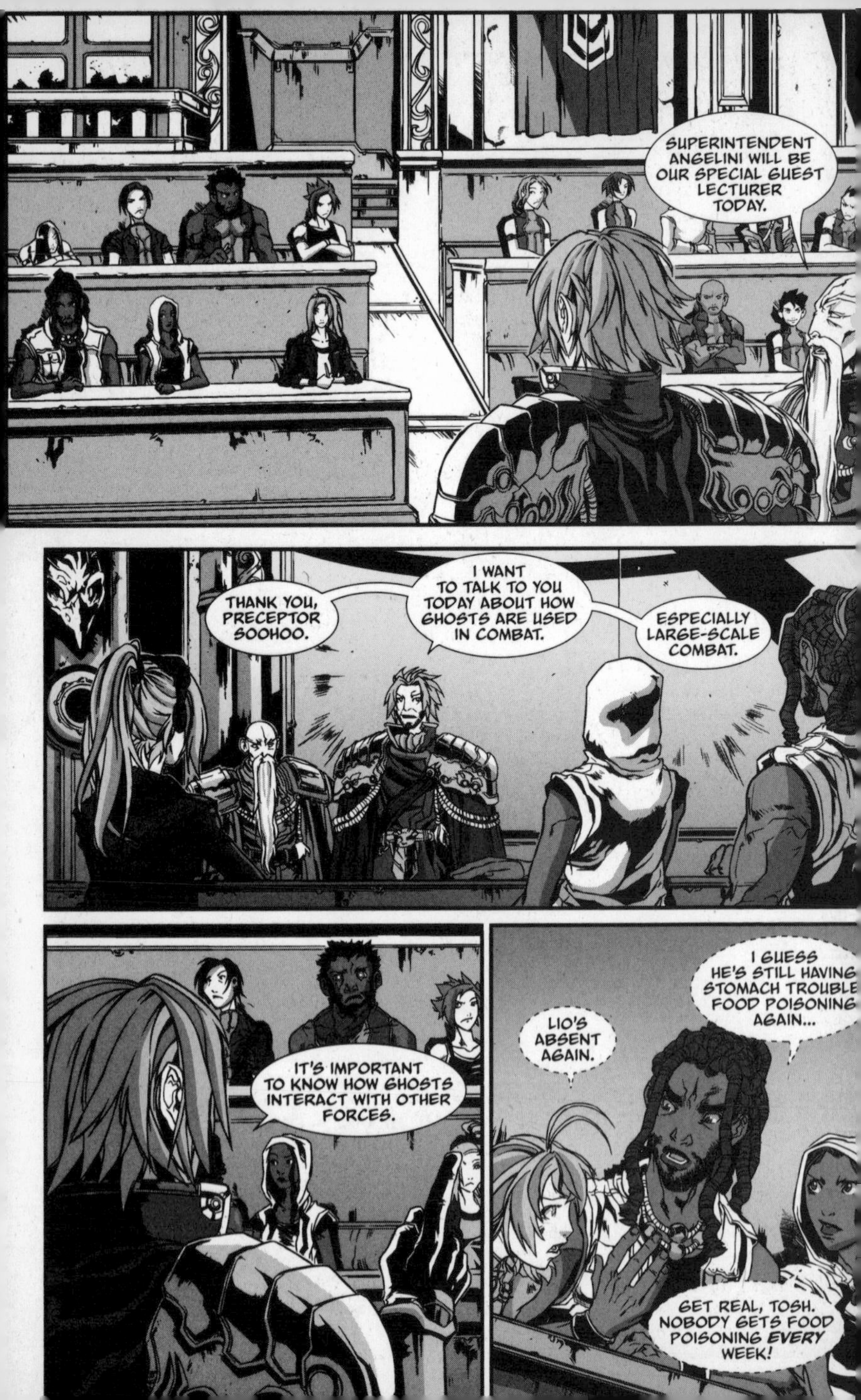
SUPERINTENDENT ANGELINI WILL BE OUR SPECIAL GUEST LECTURER TODAY.
THANK YOU, PRECEPTOR SOOHOO.
I WANT TO TALK TO YOU TODAY ABOUT HOW GHOSTS ARE USED IN COMBAT.
ESPECIALLY LARGE-SCALE COMBAT.
IT'S IMPORTANT TO KNOW HOW GHOSTS INTERACT WITH OTHER FORCES.
LIO'S ABSENT AGAIN.
I GUESS HE'S STILL HAVING STOMACH TROUBLE FOOD POISONING AGAIN...
GET REAL, TOSH. NOBODY GETS FOOD POISONING EVERY WEEK!

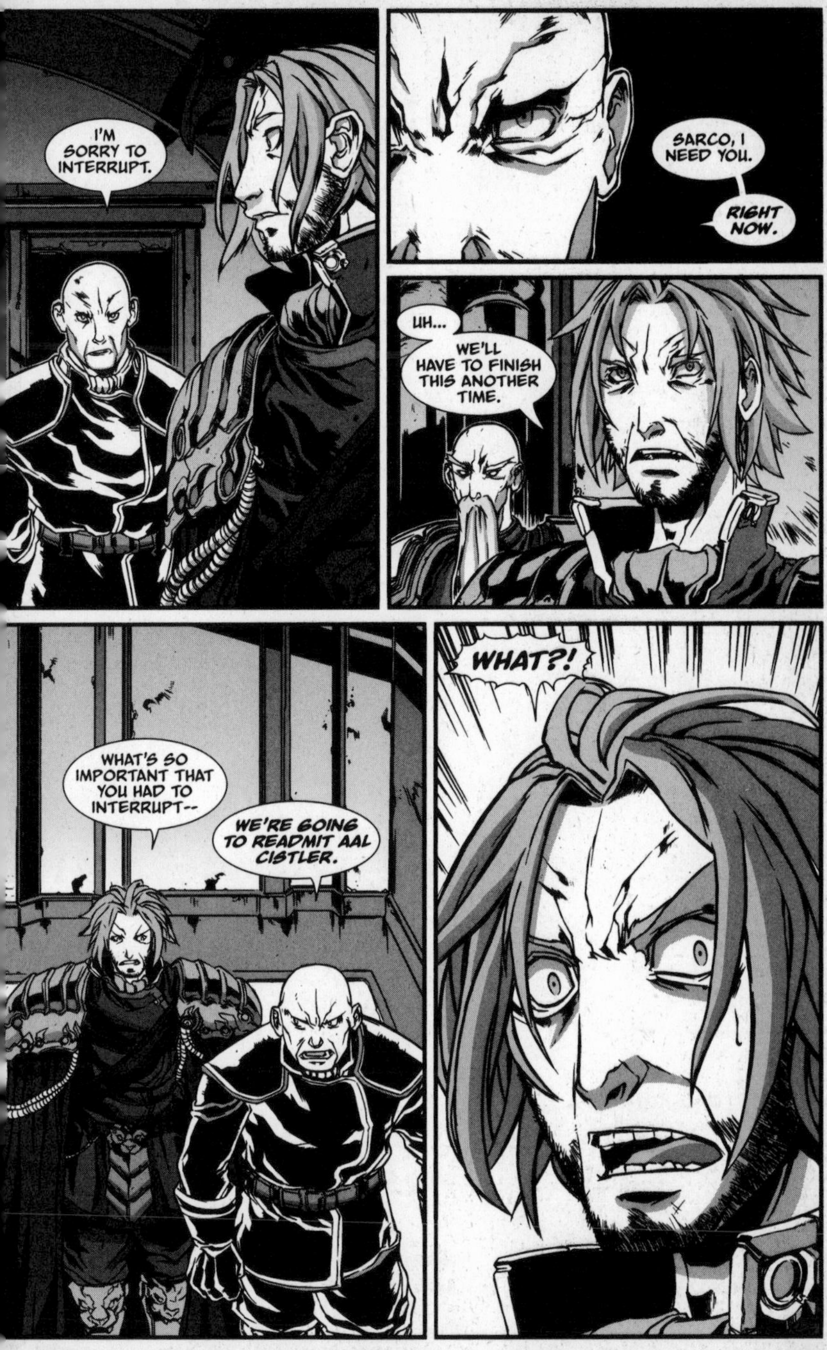
I'M SORRY TO INTERRUPT.
SARCO, I NEED YOU.
RIGHT NOW.
UH...
WE'LL HAVE TO FINISH THIS ANOTHER TIME.
WHAT'S SO IMPORTANT THAT YOU HAD TO INTERRUPT--
WE'RE GOING TO READMIT AAL CISTLER.
WHAT?!

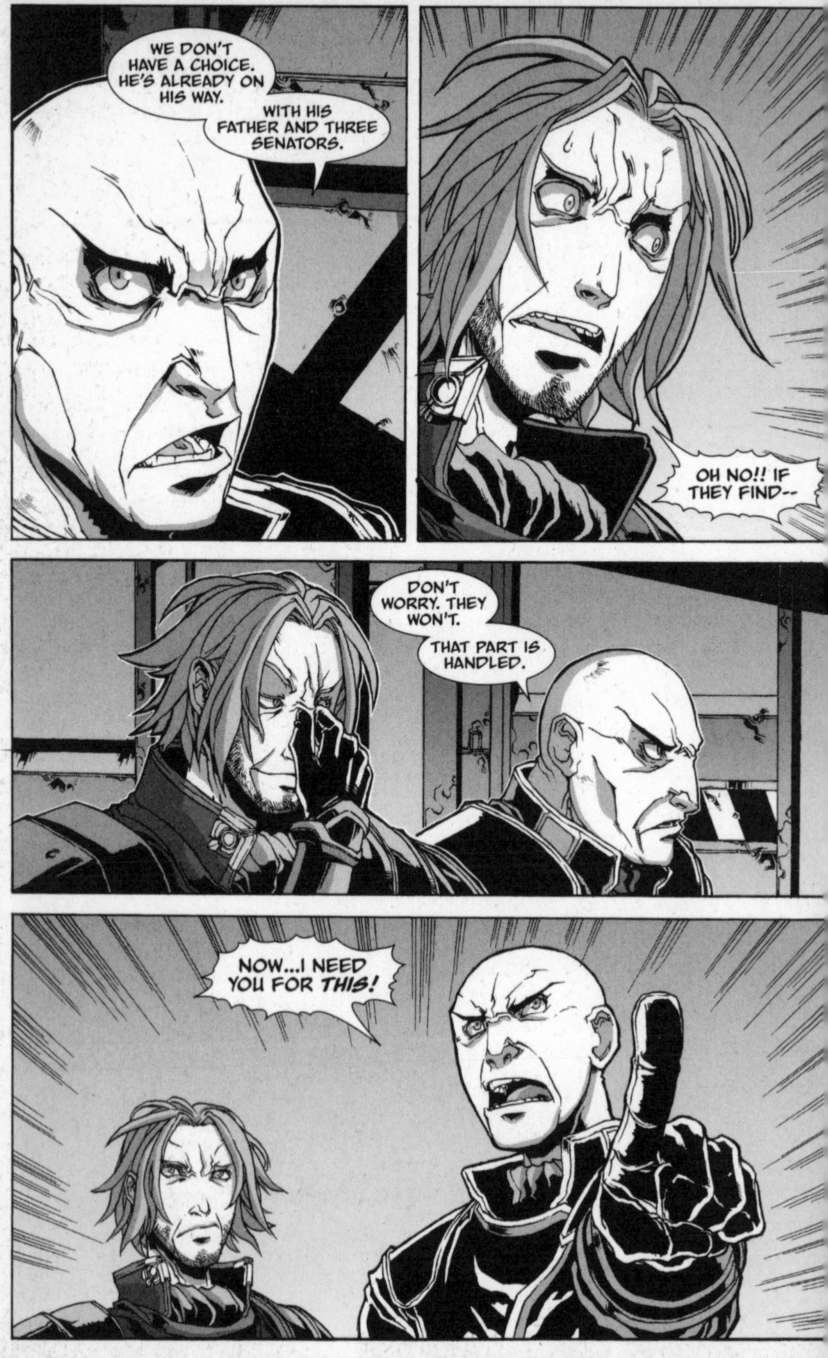

WE DON'T HAVE A CHOICE. HE'S ALREADY ON HIS WAY.
WITH HIS FATHER AND THREE SENATORS.
OH NO!! IF THEY FIND--
DON'T WORRY. THEY WON'T.
THAT PART IS HANDLED.
NOW...I NEED YOU FOR THIS!

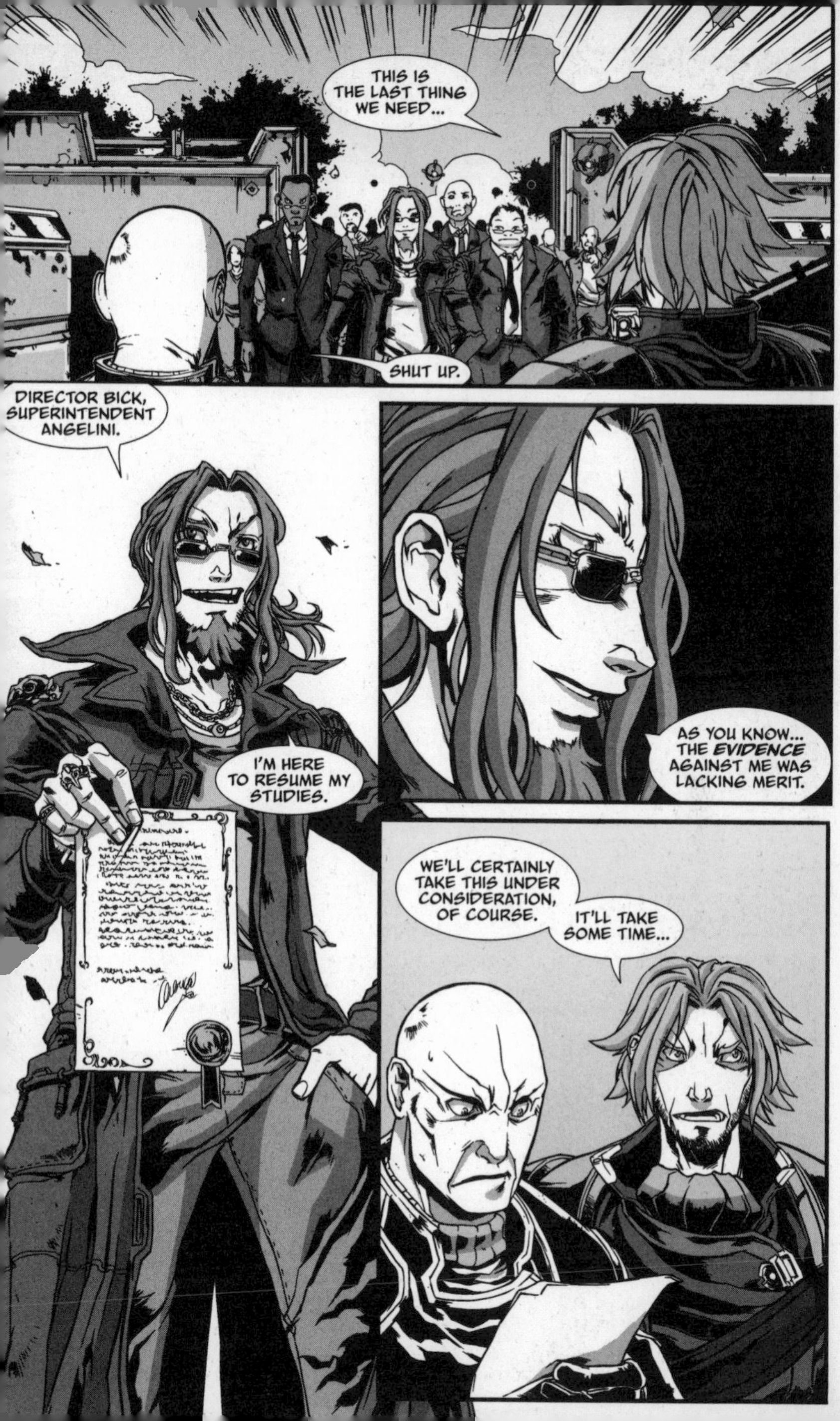
THIS IS THE LAST THING WE NEED...
SHUT UP.
DIRECTOR BICK, SUPERINTENDENT ANGELINI.
I'M HERE TO RESUME MY STUDIES.
AS YOU KNOW... THE *EVIDENCE* AGAINST ME WAS LACKING MERIT.
WE'LL CERTAINLY TAKE THIS UNDER CONSIDERATION, OF COURSE.
IT'LL TAKE SOME TIME...

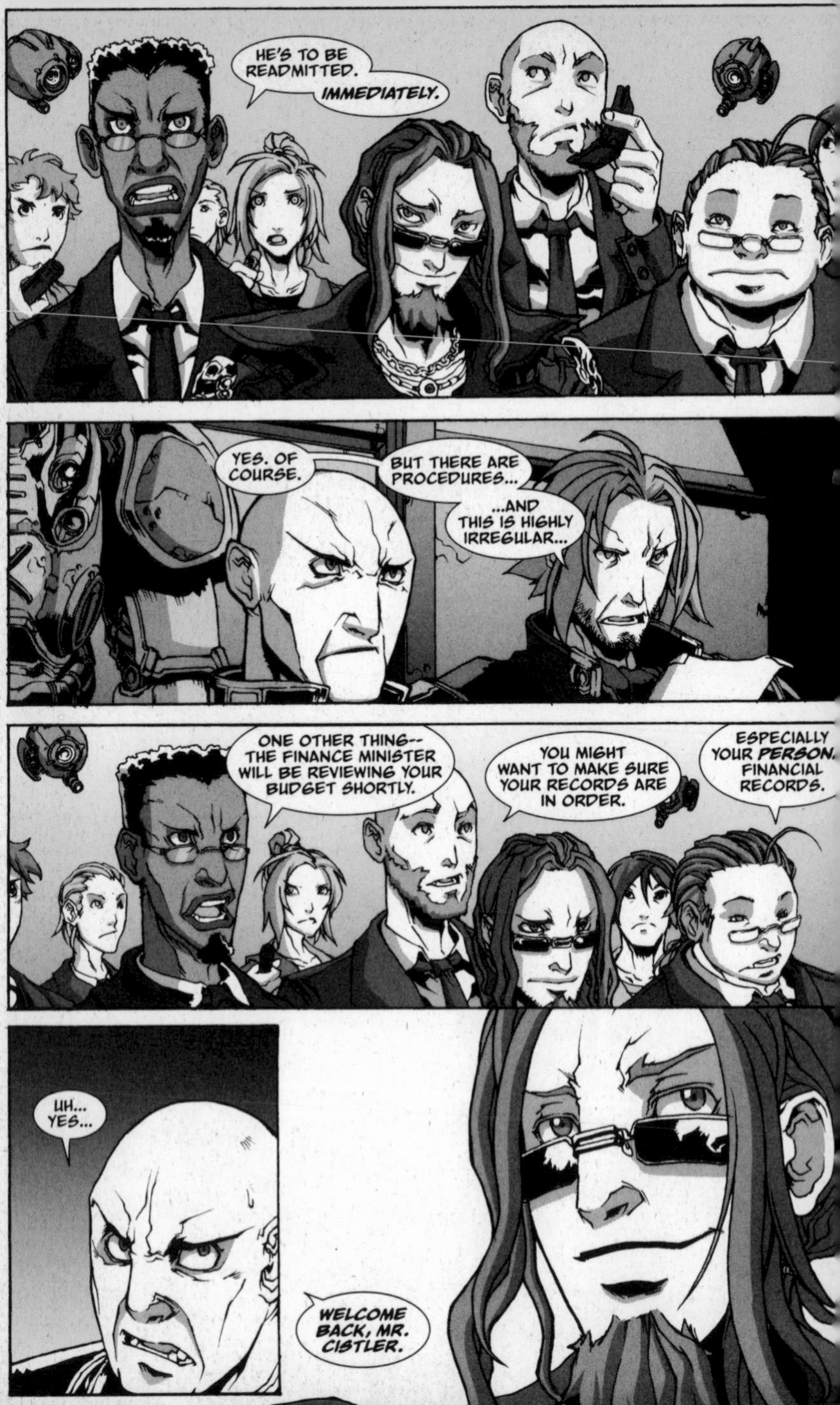
HE'S TO BE READMITTED.
IMMEDIATELY.
YES. OF COURSE.
BUT THERE ARE PROCEDURES...
...AND THIS IS HIGHLY IRREGULAR...
ONE OTHER THING-- THE FINANCE MINISTER WILL BE REVIEWING YOUR BUDGET SHORTLY.
YOU MIGHT WANT TO MAKE SURE YOUR RECORDS ARE IN ORDER.
ESPECIALLY YOUR PERSON. FINANCIAL RECORDS.
UH... YES...
WELCOME BACK, MR. CISTLER.

# CHAPTER 3

## IN THE DEADLANDS

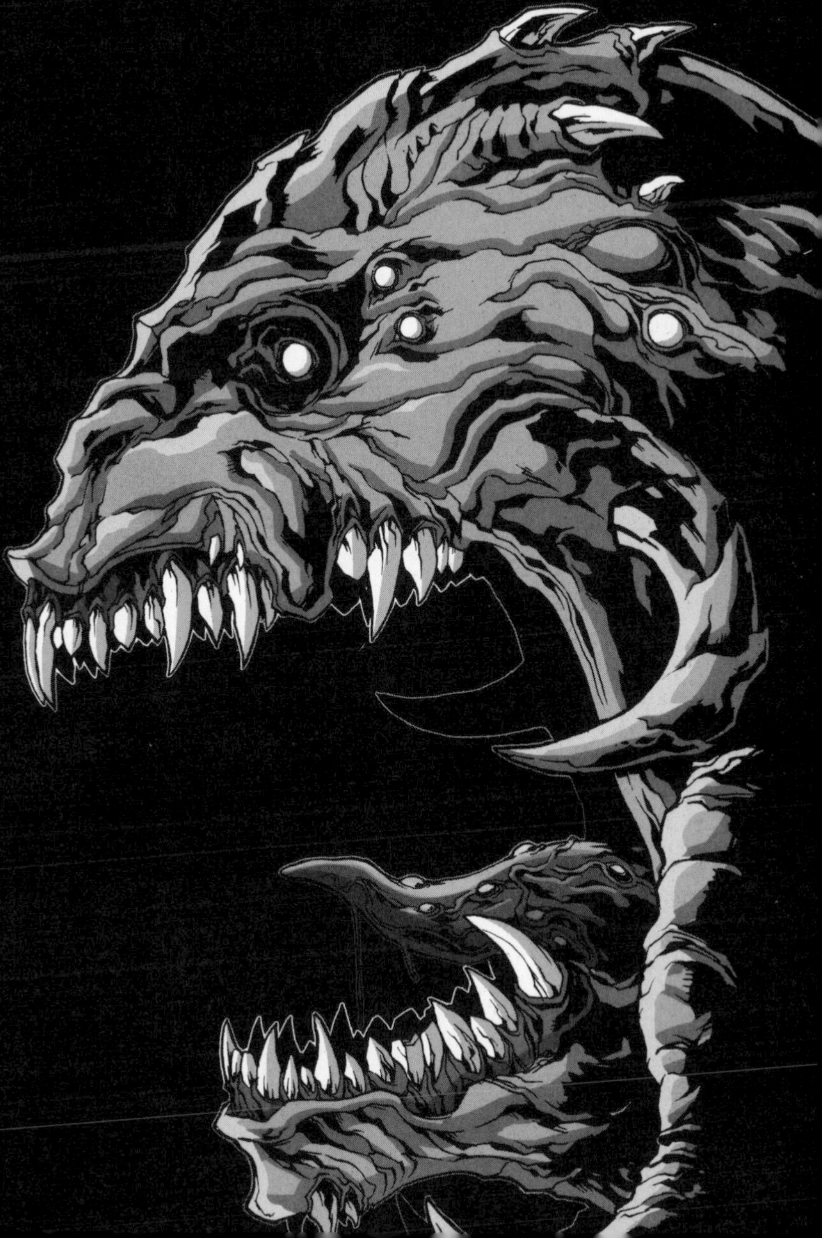

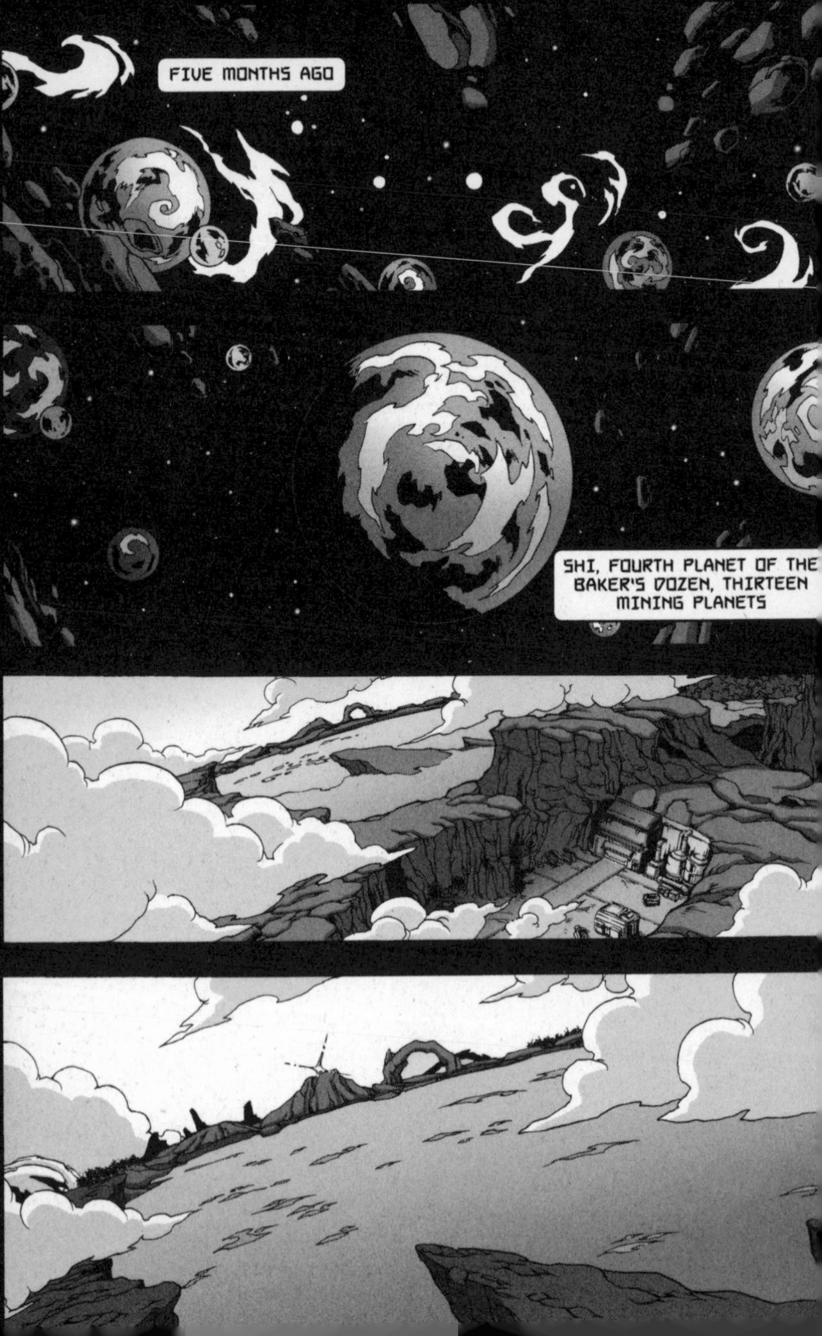
FIVE MONTHS AGO
SHI, FOURTH PLANET OF THE BAKER'S DOZEN, THIRTEEN MINING PLANETS

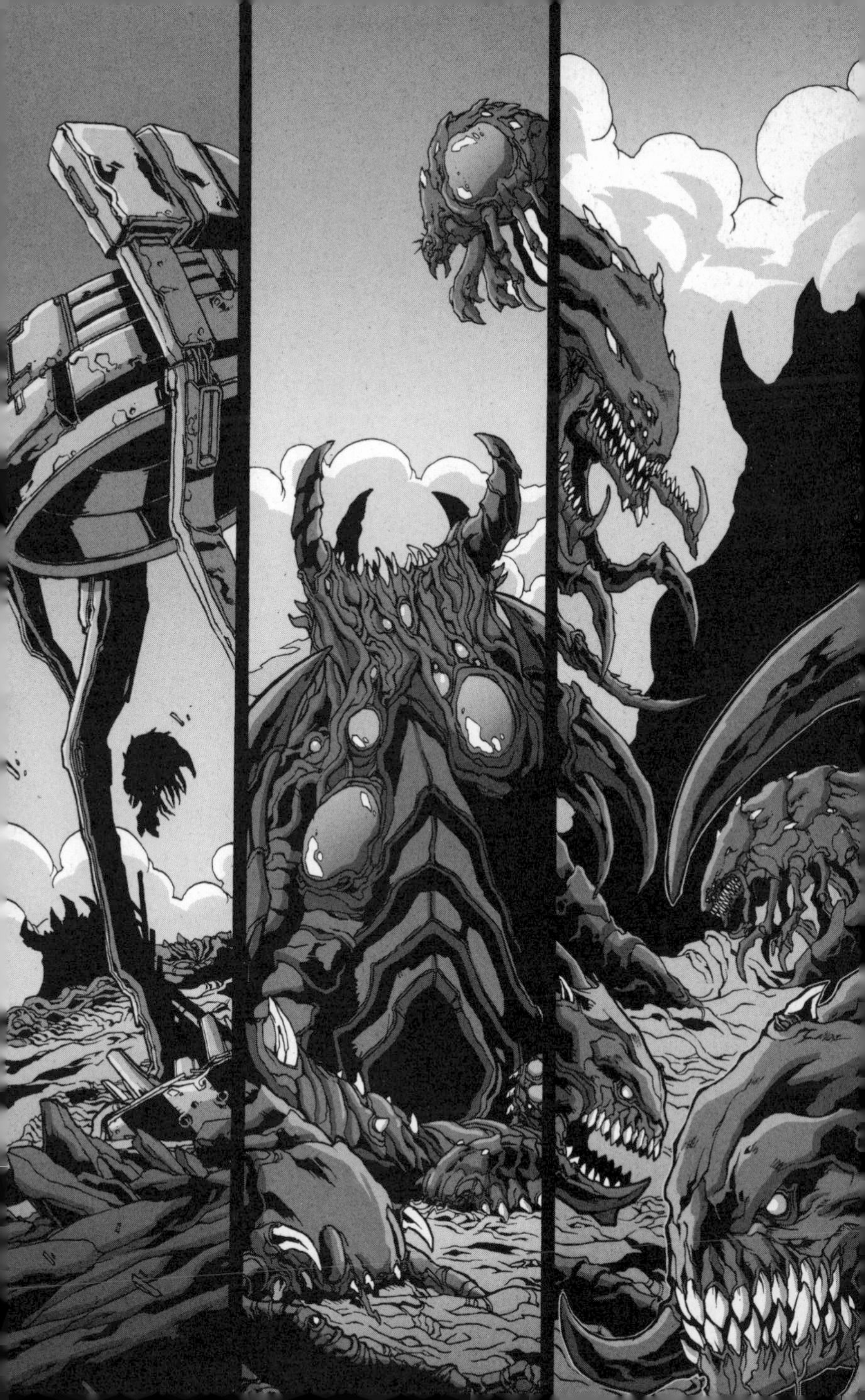

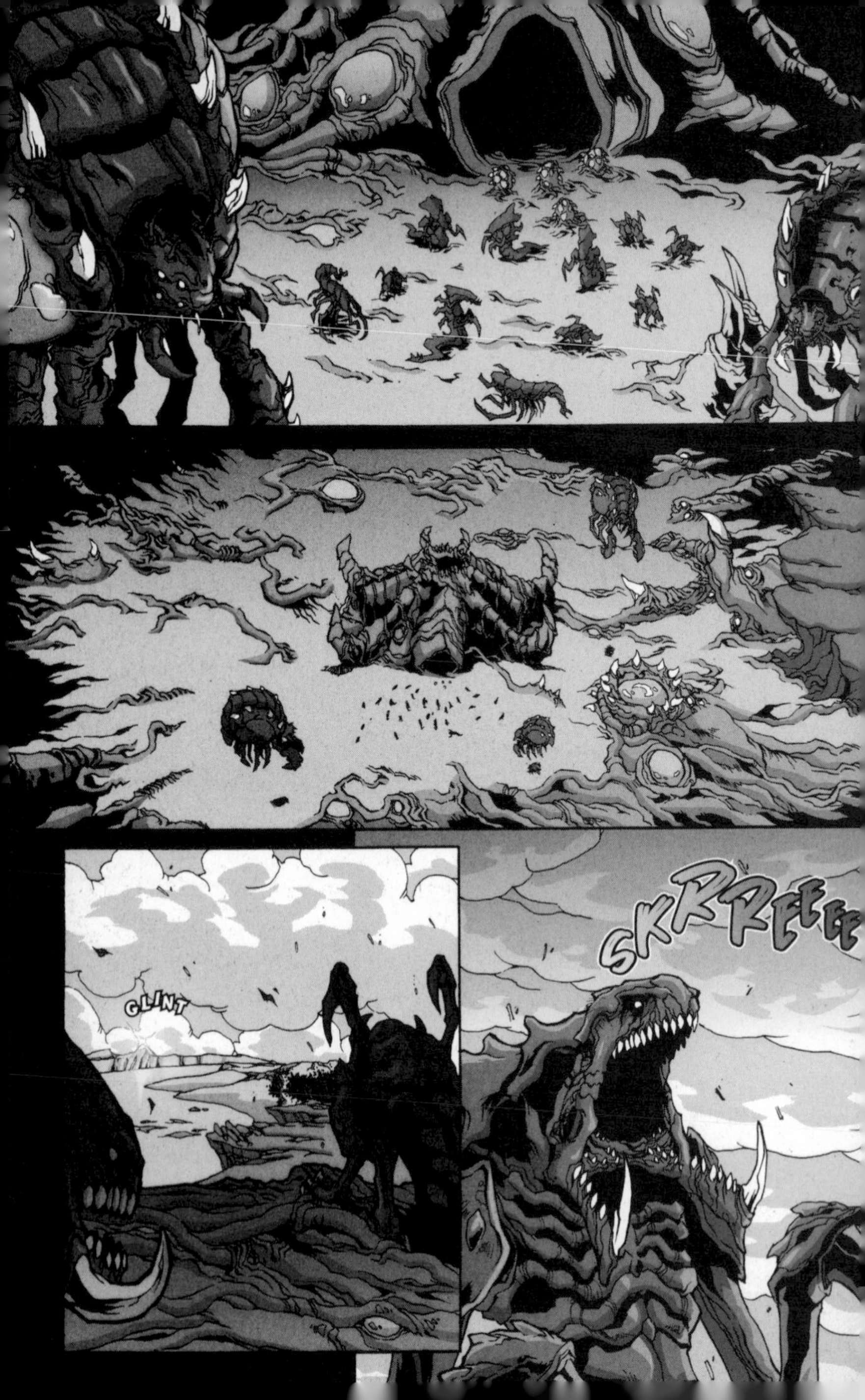
GLINT
SKRREEEE

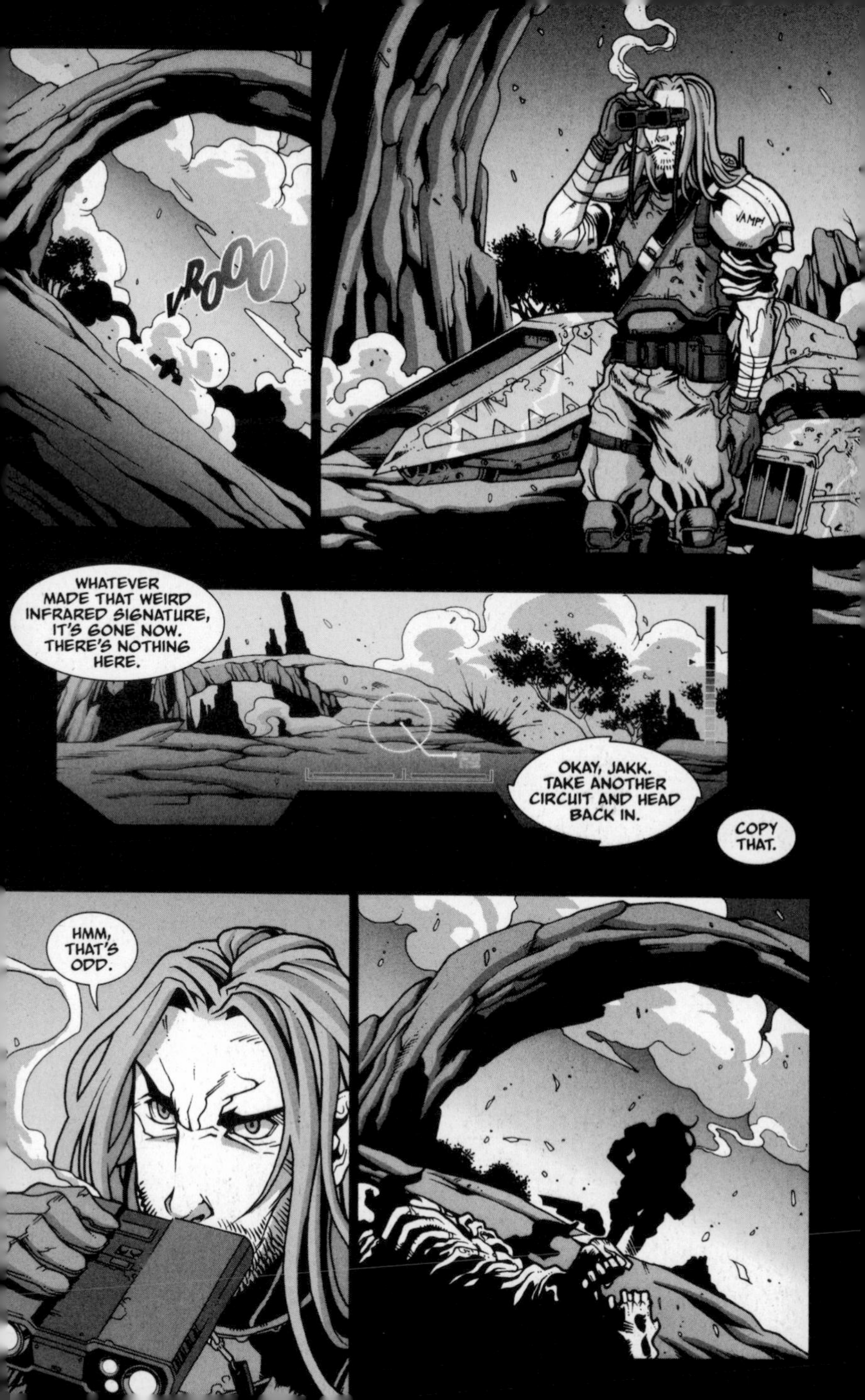
VROOO
VAMP!
WHATEVER MADE THAT WEIRD INFRARED SIGNATURE, IT'S GONE NOW. THERE'S NOTHING HERE.
OKAY, JAKK. TAKE ANOTHER CIRCUIT AND HEAD BACK IN.
COPY THAT.
HMM, THAT'S ODD.

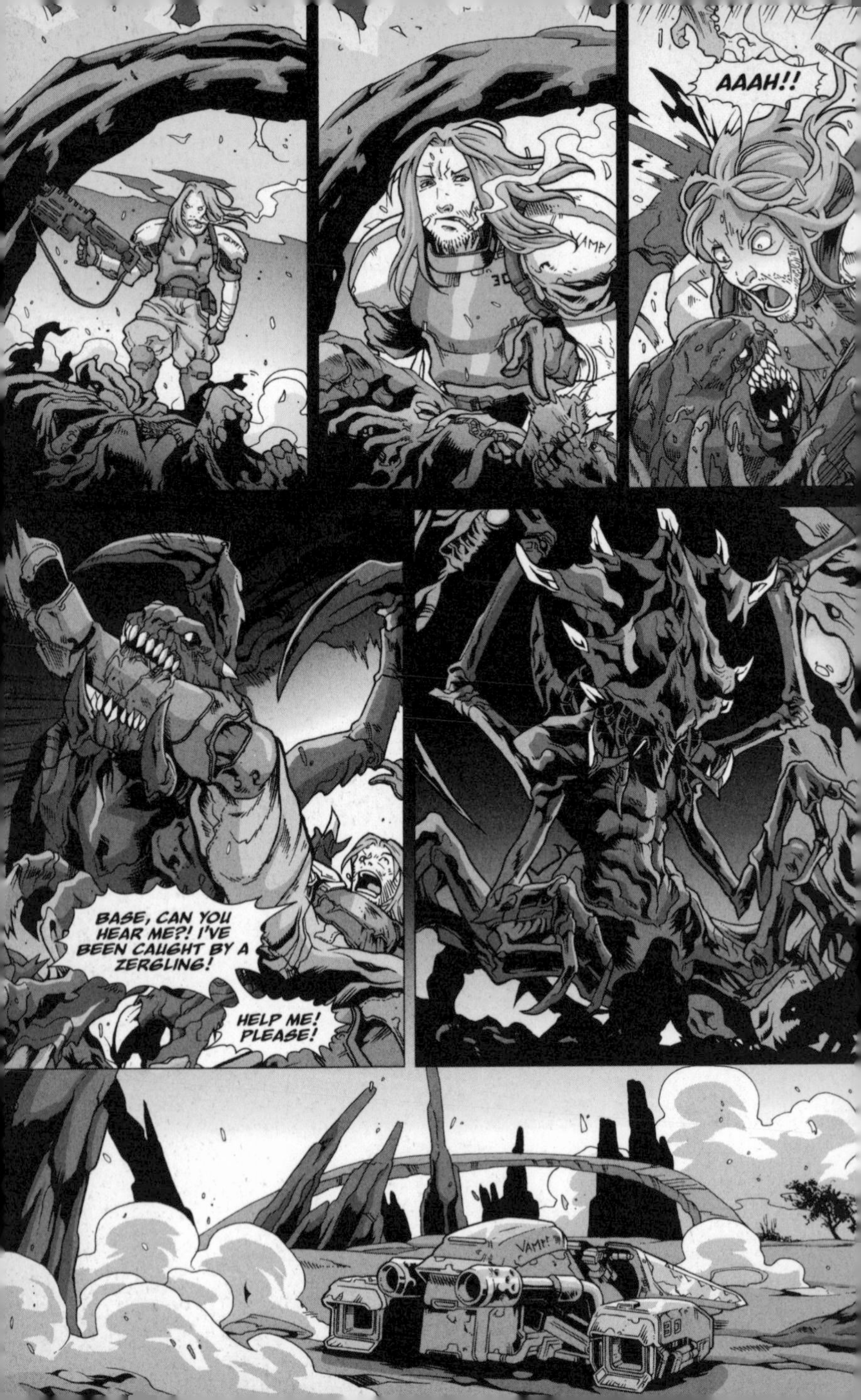
AAAH!!
VAMP!
BASE, CAN YOU HEAR ME?! I'VE BEEN CAUGHT BY A ZERGLING!
HELP ME! PLEASE!
VAMP!

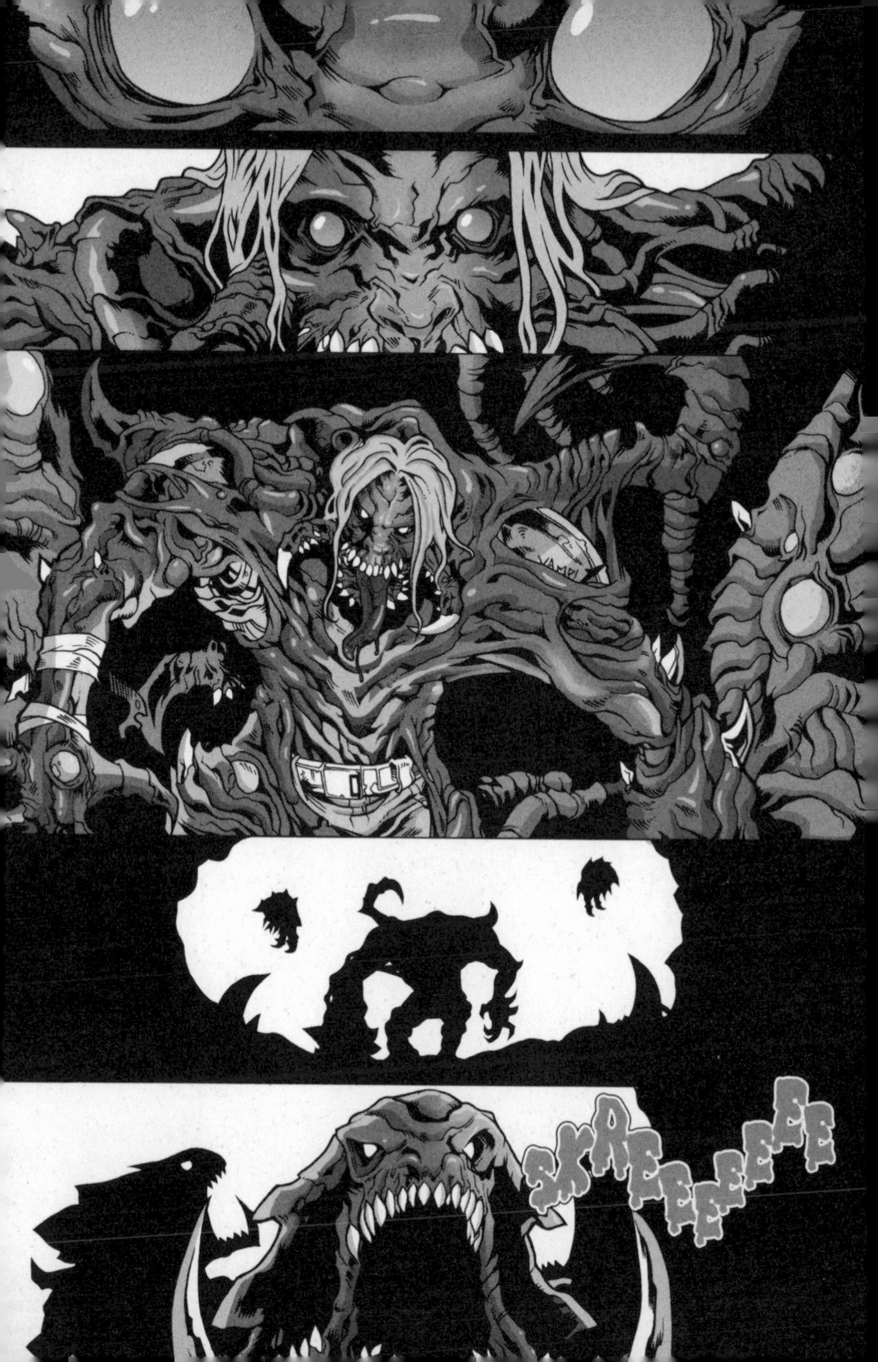
SKREEEEEEE

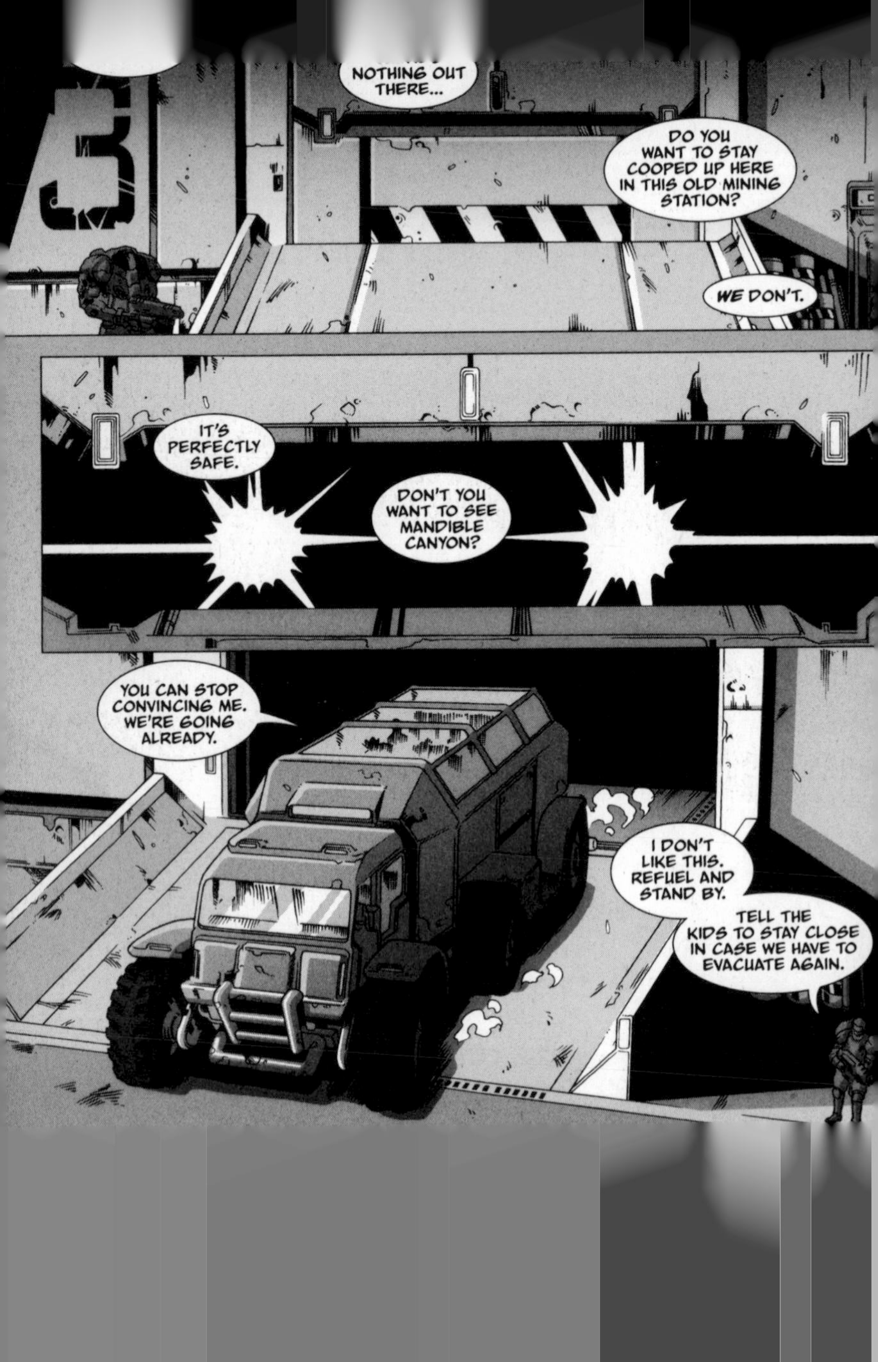
NOTHING OUT THERE...
DO YOU WANT TO STAY COOPED UP HERE IN THIS OLD MINING STATION?
WE DON'T.
IT'S PERFECTLY SAFE.
DON'T YOU WANT TO SEE MANDIBLE CANYON?
YOU CAN STOP CONVINCING ME. WE'RE GOING ALREADY.
I DON'T LIKE THIS. REFUEL AND STAND BY.
TELL THE KIDS TO STAY CLOSE IN CASE WE HAVE TO EVACUATE AGAIN.

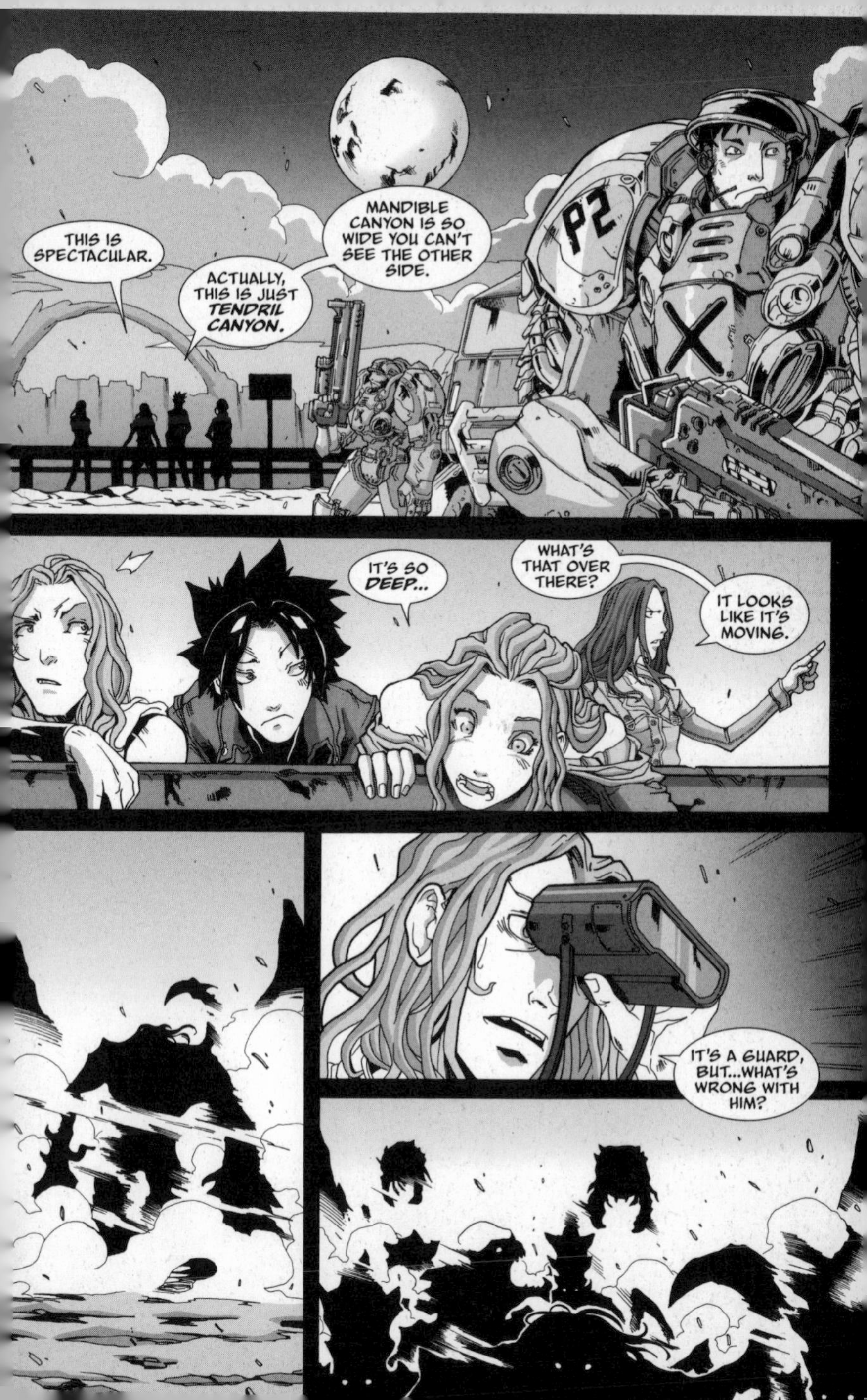
THIS IS SPECTACULAR.
ACTUALLY, THIS IS JUST TENDRIL CANYON.
MANDIBLE CANYON IS SO WIDE YOU CAN'T SEE THE OTHER SIDE.
P2
IT'S SO DEEP...
WHAT'S THAT OVER THERE?
IT LOOKS LIKE IT'S MOVING.
IT'S A GUARD, BUT...WHAT'S WRONG WITH HIM?

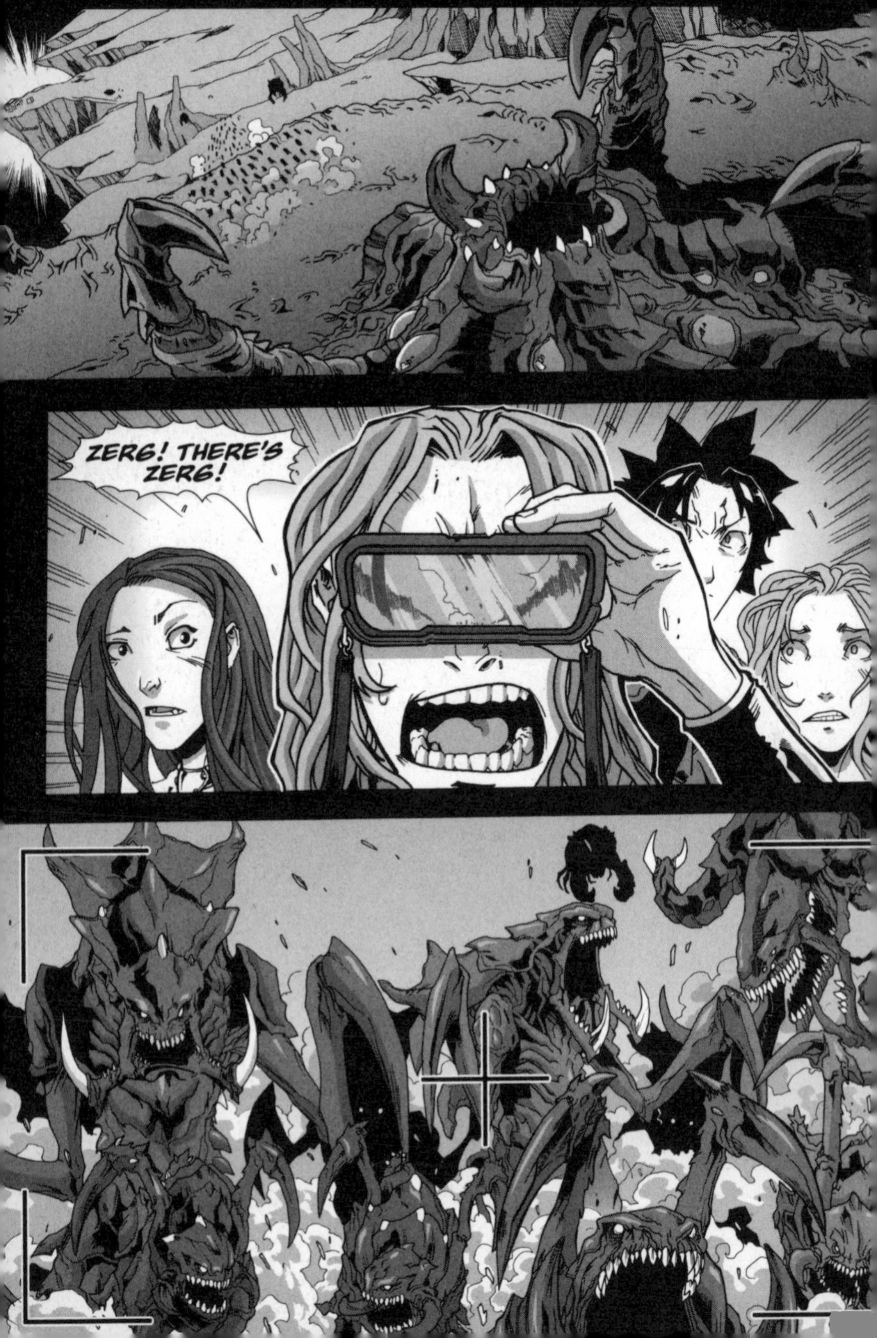
ZERG! THERE'S ZERG!

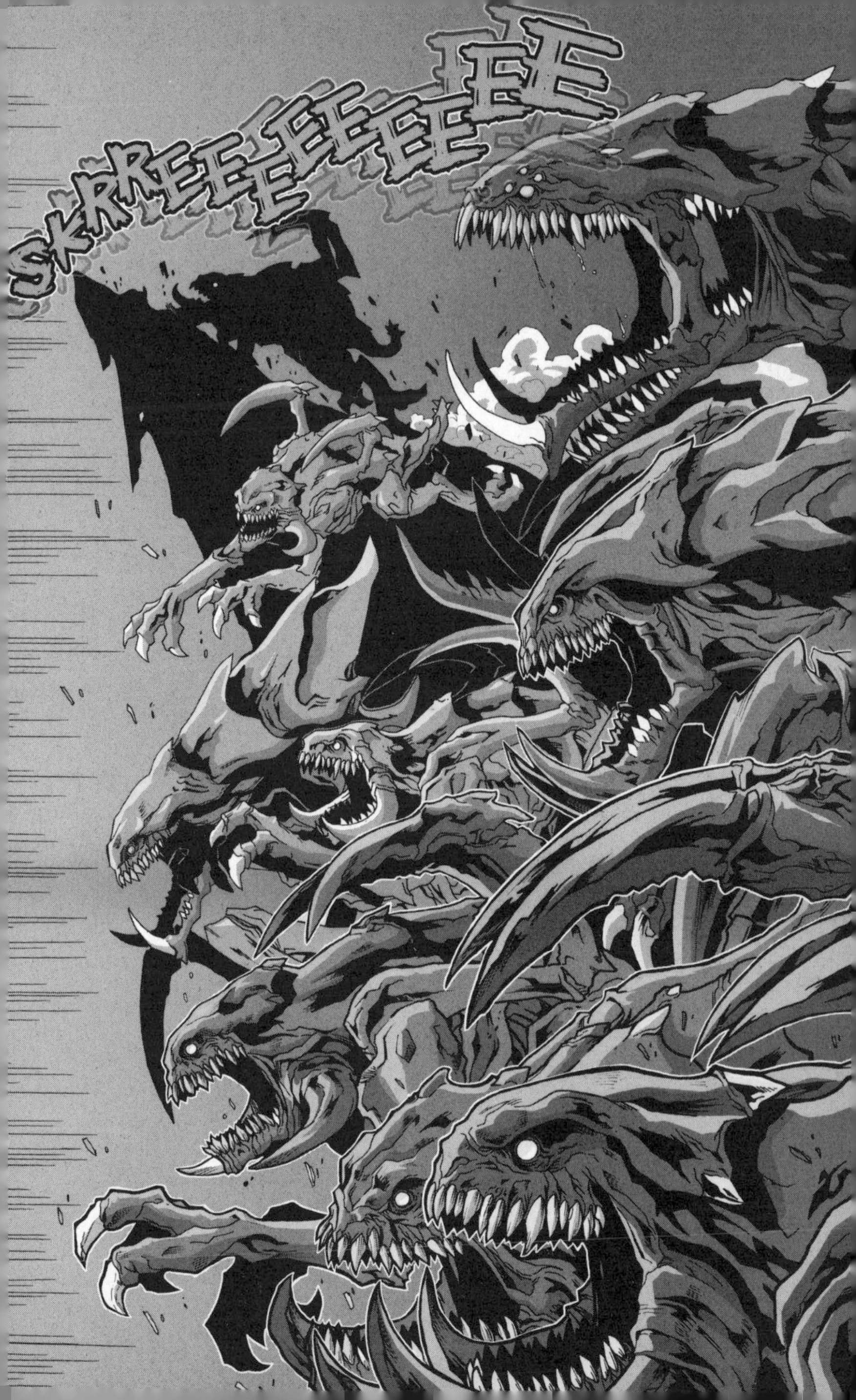
SKREEEEEEEEEEEE

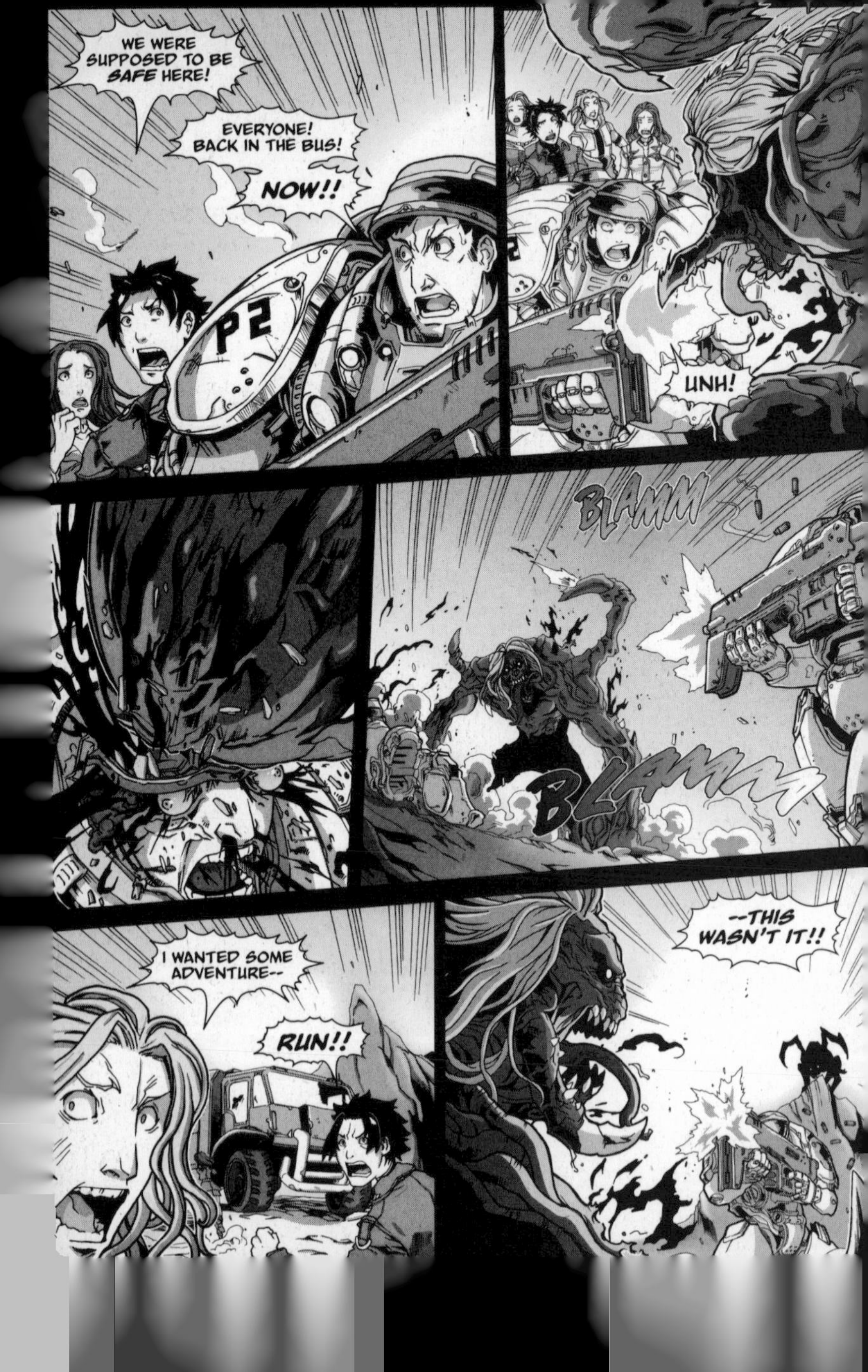

WE WERE SUPPOSED TO BE SAFE HERE!
EVERYONE! BACK IN THE BUS!
NOW!!
UNH!
BLAMM
BLAMMM
I WANTED SOME ADVENTURE--
--THIS WASN'T IT!!
RUN!!

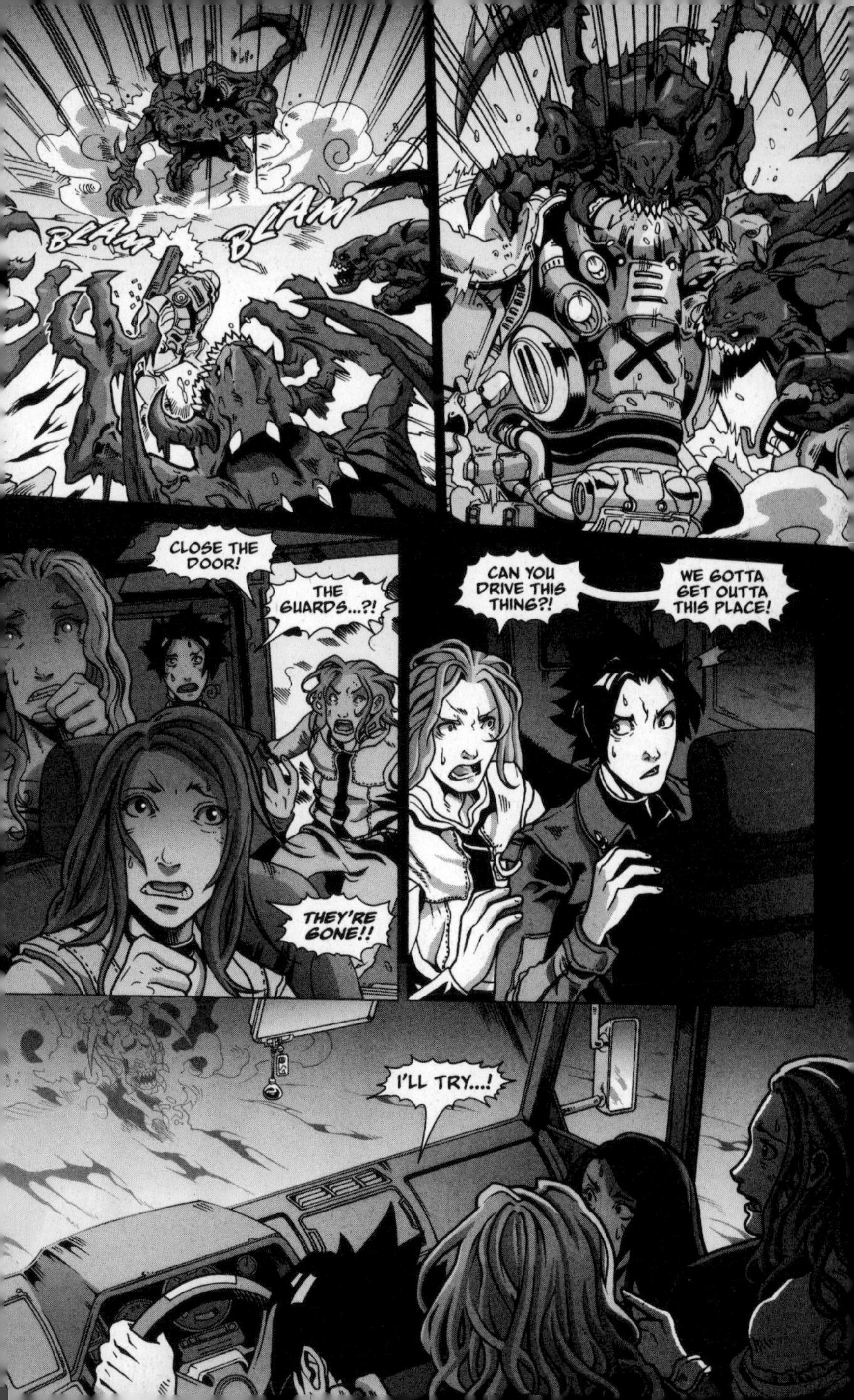
BLAM
BLAM
CLOSE THE DOOR!
THE GUARDS...?!
THEY'RE GONE!!
CAN YOU DRIVE THIS THING?!
WE GOTTA GET OUTTA THIS PLACE!
I'LL TRY...!

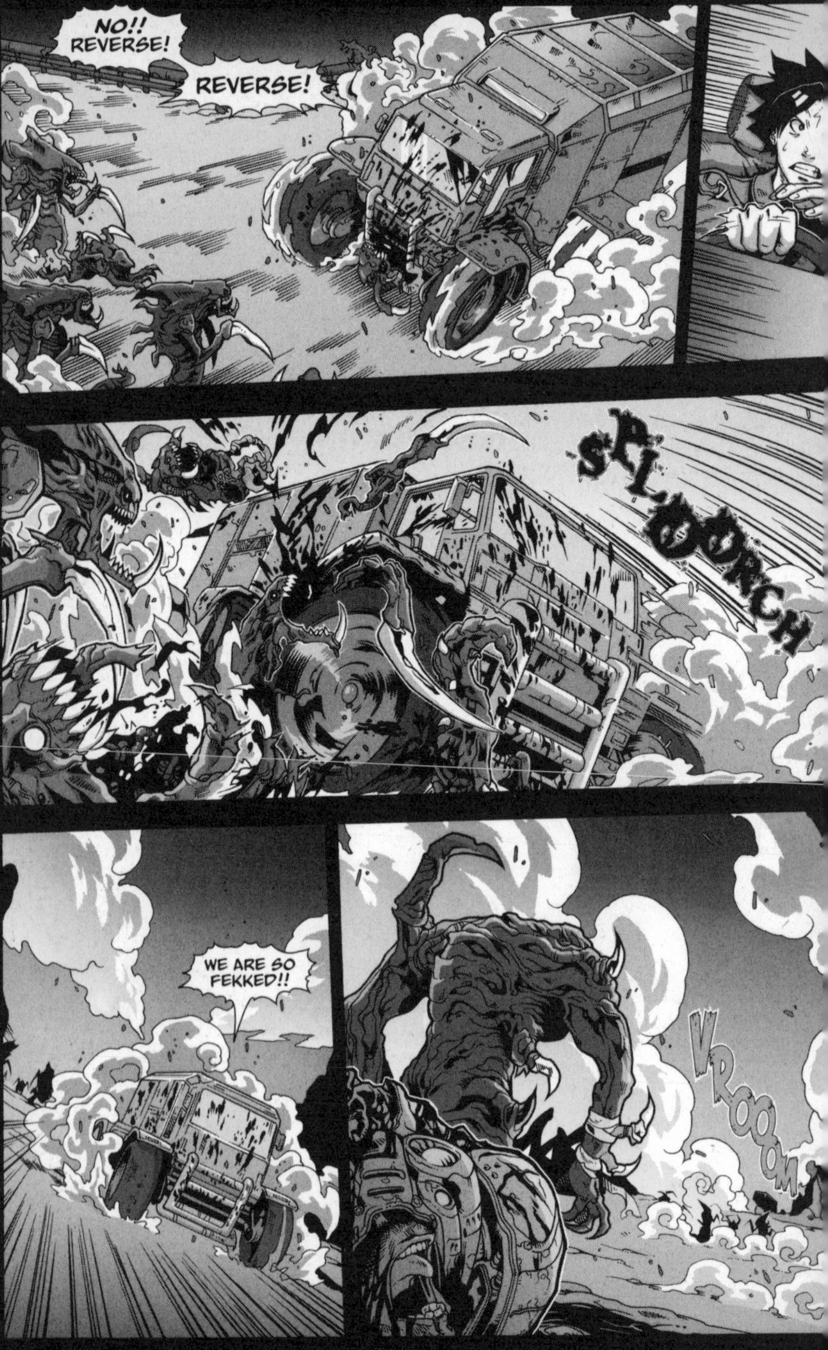
NO!! REVERSE!
REVERSE!
SPLOORCH
WE ARE SO FEKKED!!
VROOOM

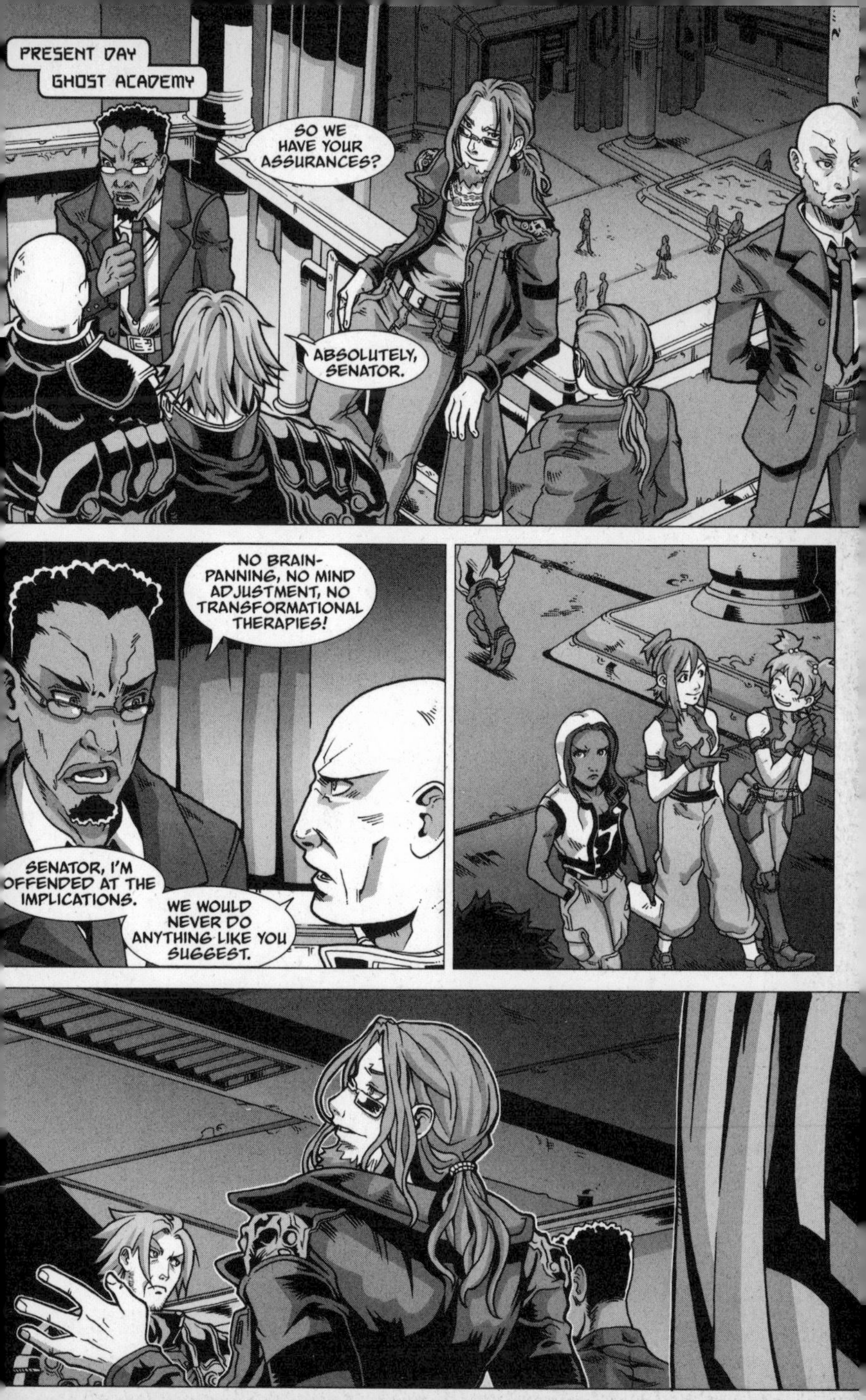
PRESENT DAY
GHOST ACADEMY
SO WE HAVE YOUR ASSURANCES?
ABSOLUTELY, SENATOR.
NO BRAIN-PANNING, NO MIND ADJUSTMENT, NO TRANSFORMATIONAL THERAPIES!
SENATOR, I'M OFFENDED AT THE IMPLICATIONS.
WE WOULD NEVER DO ANYTHING LIKE YOU SUGGEST.

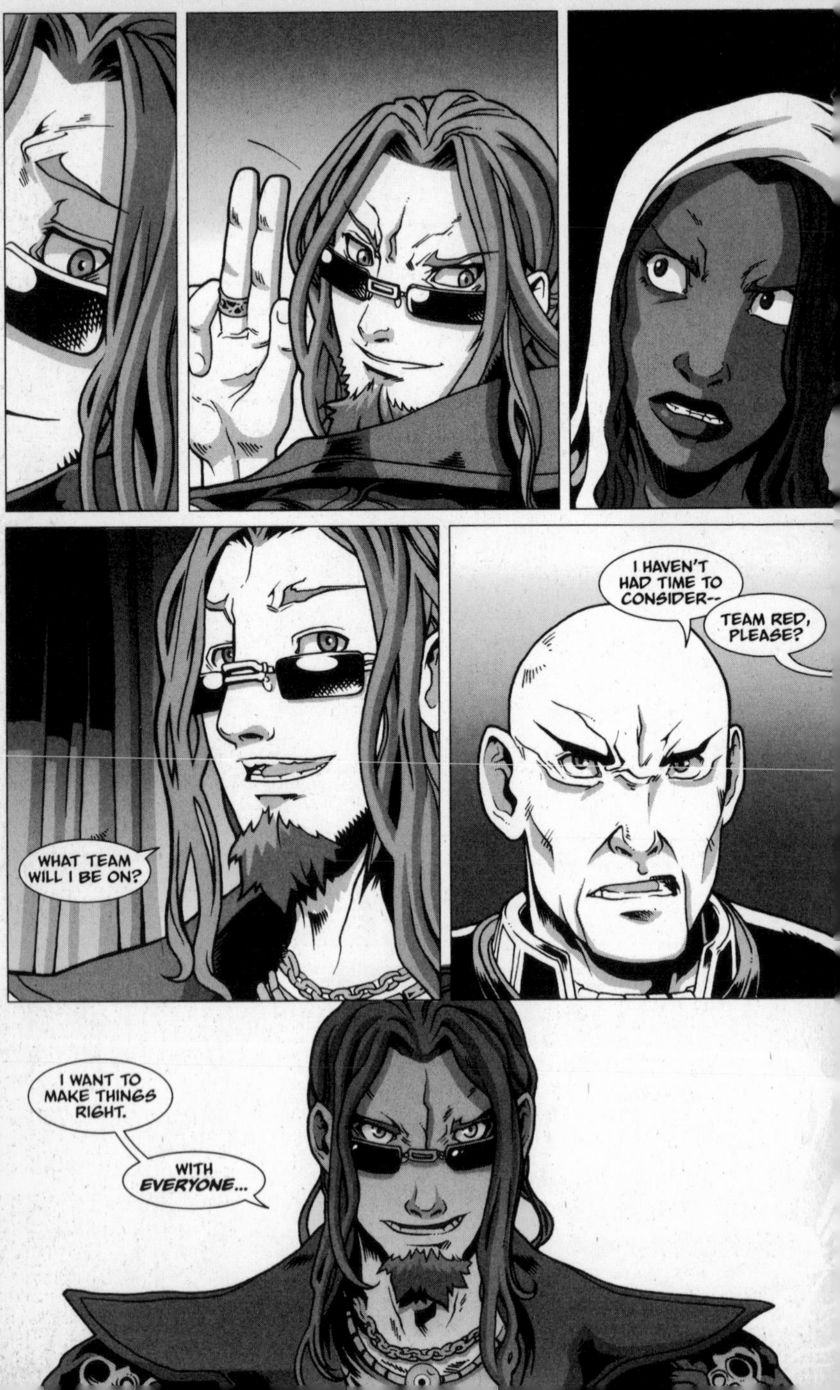
WHAT TEAM WILL I BE ON?
I HAVEN'T HAD TIME TO CONSIDER--
TEAM RED, PLEASE?
I WANT TO MAKE THINGS RIGHT.
WITH *EVERYONE*...

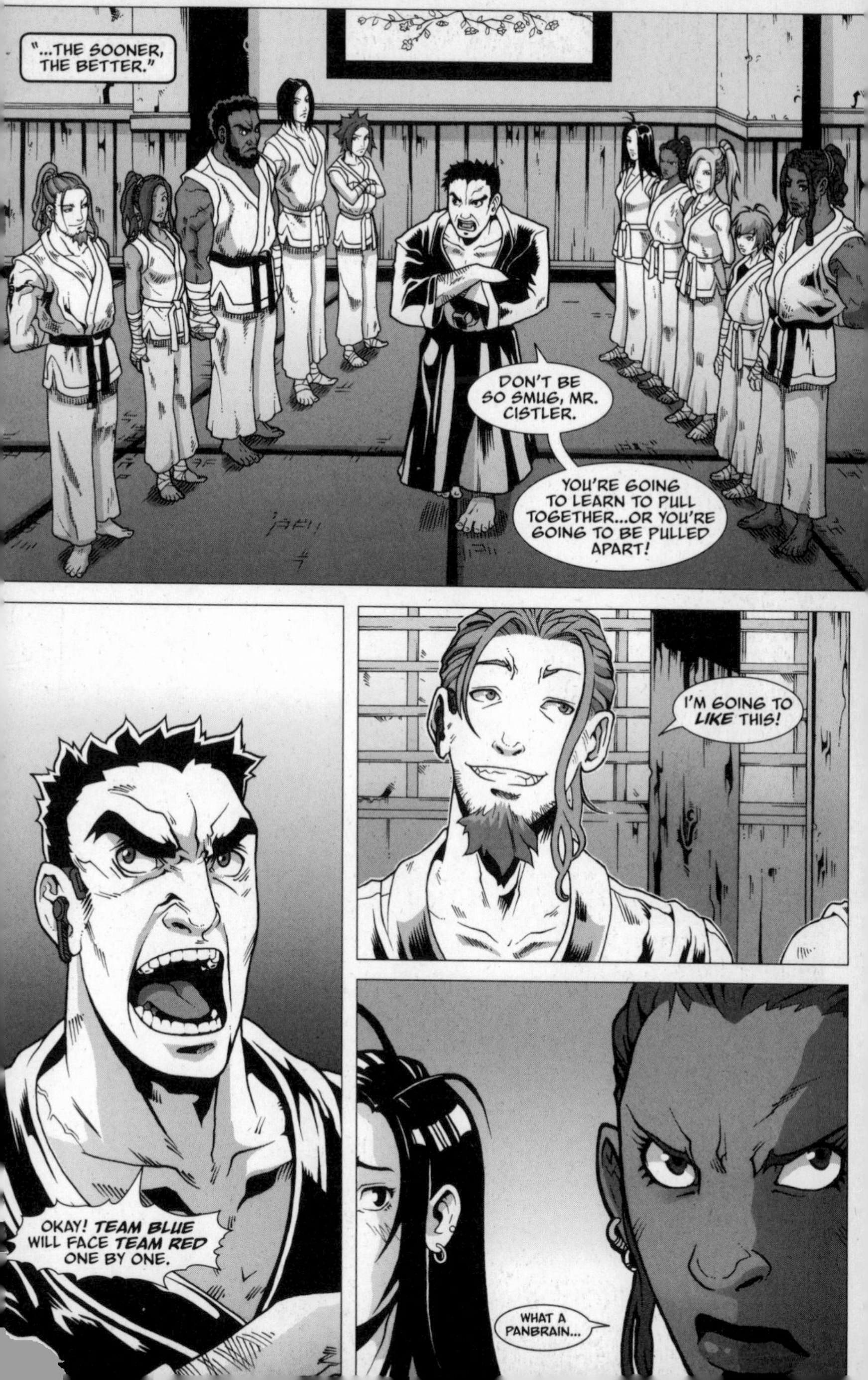
"...THE SOONER, THE BETTER."
DON'T BE SO SMUG, MR. CISTLER.
YOU'RE GOING TO LEARN TO PULL TOGETHER...OR YOU'RE GOING TO BE PULLED APART!
I'M GOING TO *LIKE* THIS!
OKAY! *TEAM BLUE* WILL FACE *TEAM RED* ONE BY ONE.
WHAT A PANBRAIN...

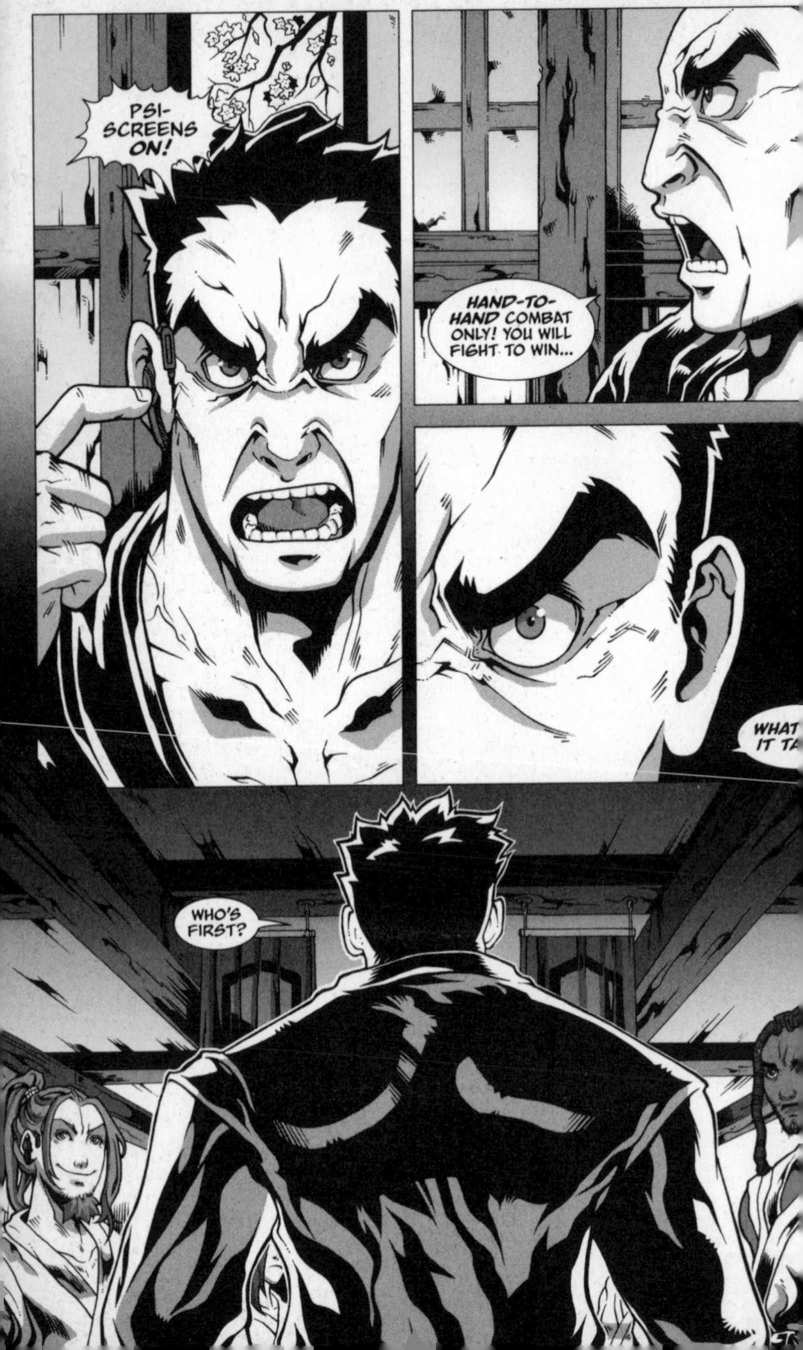
PSI-SCREENS ON!
HAND-TO-HAND COMBAT ONLY! YOU WILL FIGHT TO WIN...
WHO'S FIRST?

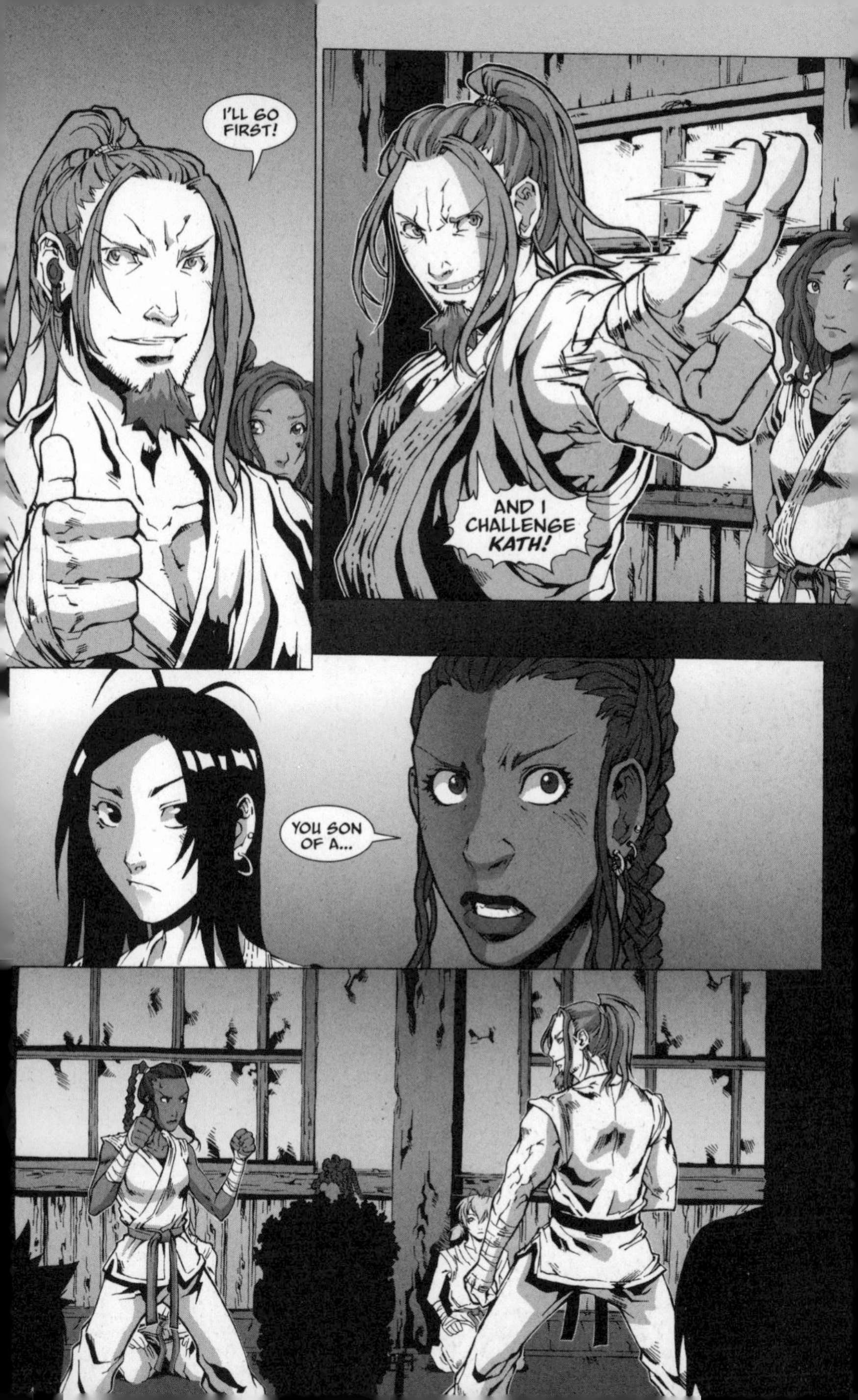
I'LL GO FIRST!
AND I CHALLENGE KATH!
YOU SON OF A...

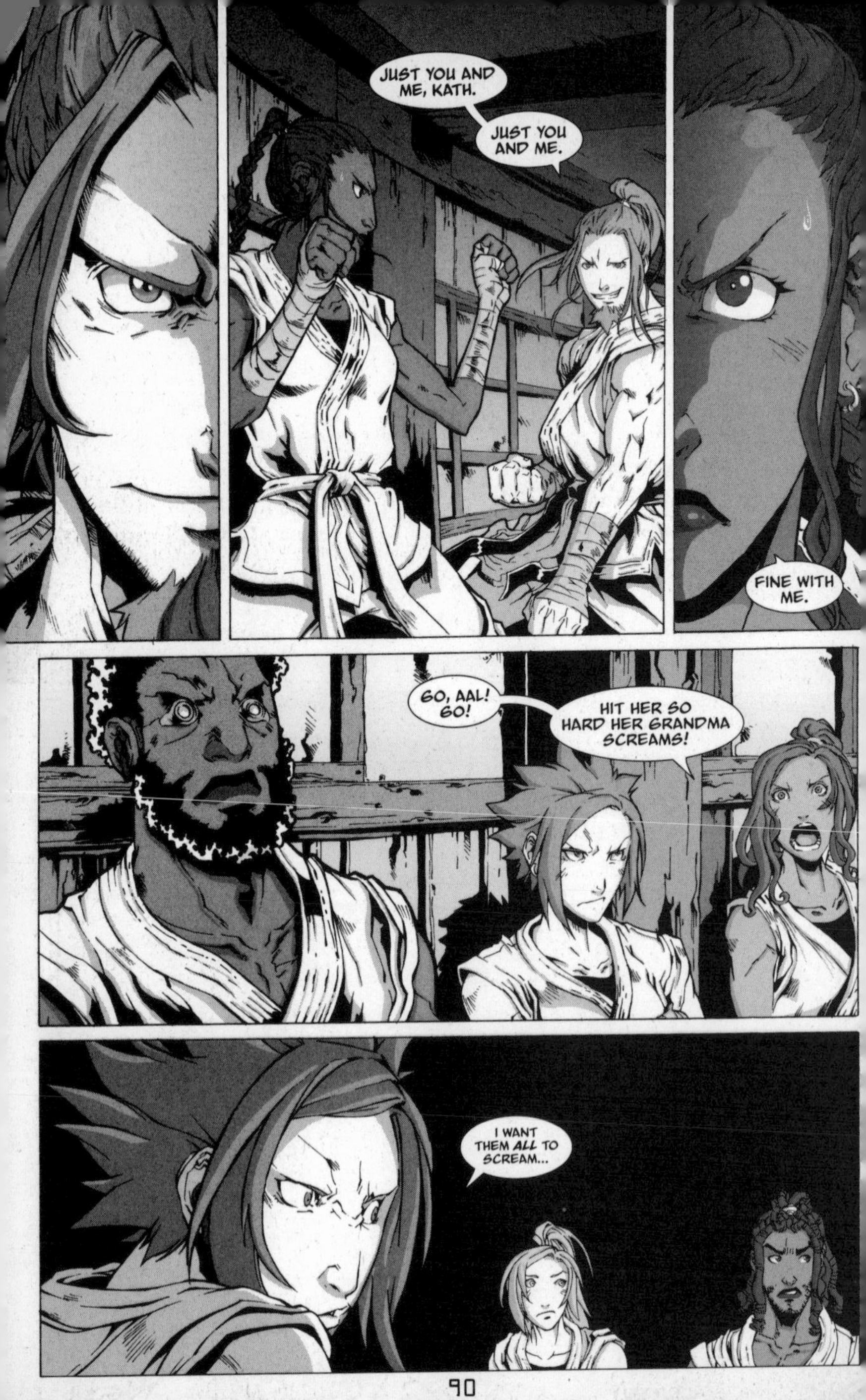

JUST YOU AND ME, KATH.
JUST YOU AND ME.
FINE WITH ME.
GO, AAL! GO!
HIT HER SO HARD HER GRANDMA SCREAMS!
I WANT THEM ALL TO SCREAM...

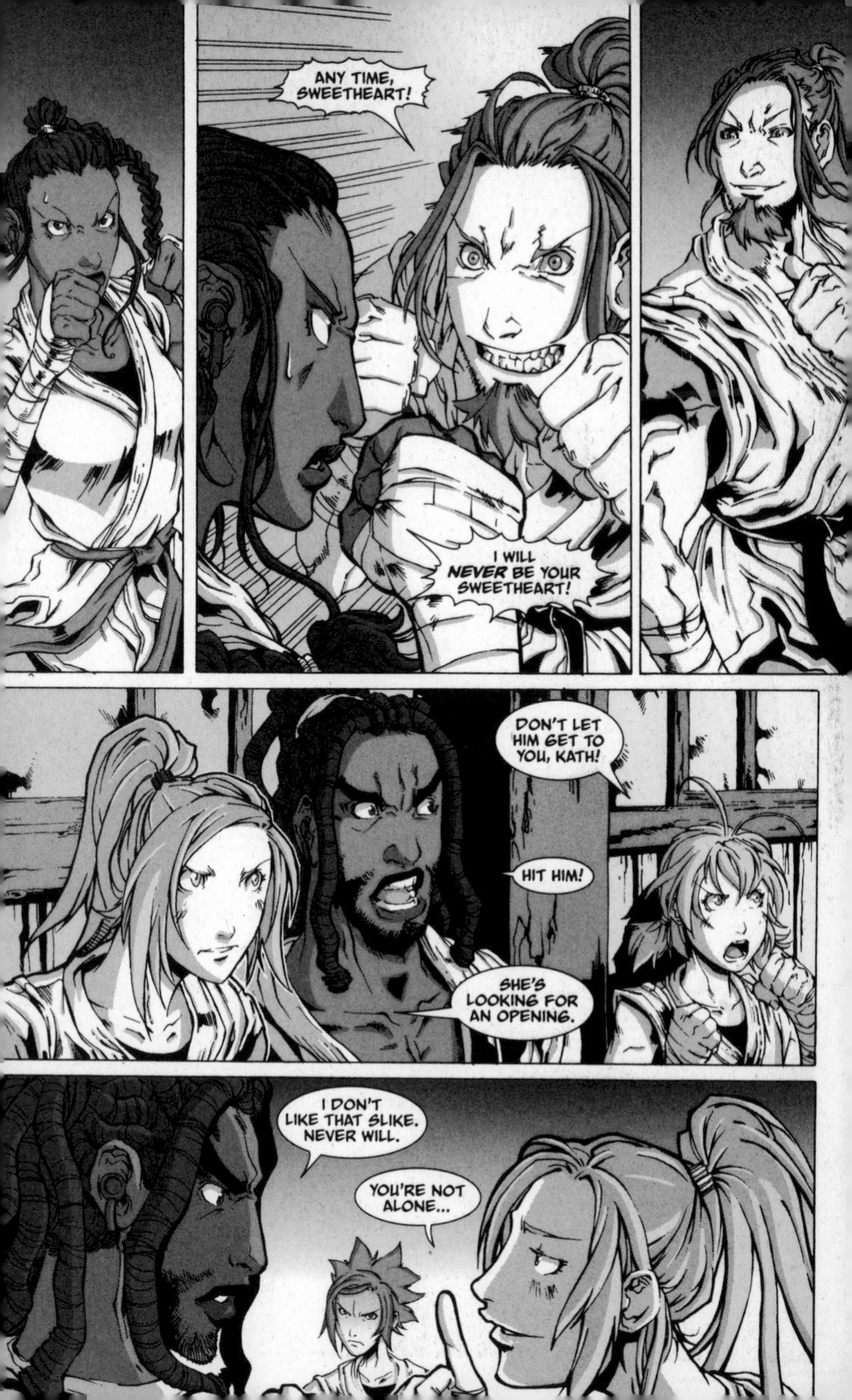
ANY TIME, SWEETHEART!
I WILL NEVER BE YOUR SWEETHEART!
DON'T LET HIM GET TO YOU, KATH!
HIT HIM!
SHE'S LOOKING FOR AN OPENING.
I DON'T LIKE THAT SLIKE. NEVER WILL.
YOU'RE NOT ALONE...

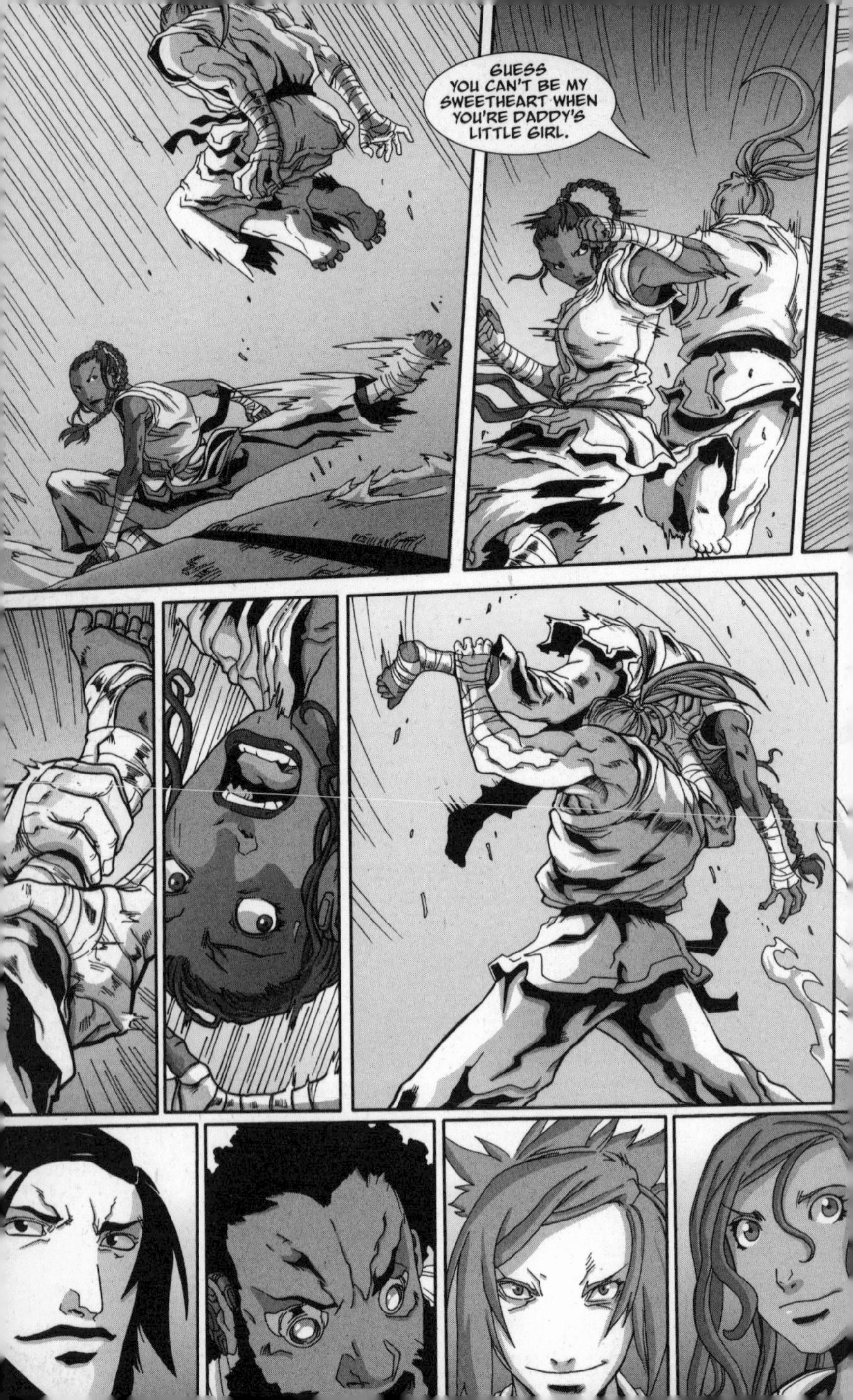
GUESS YOU CAN'T BE MY SWEETHEART WHEN YOU'RE DADDY'S LITTLE GIRL.

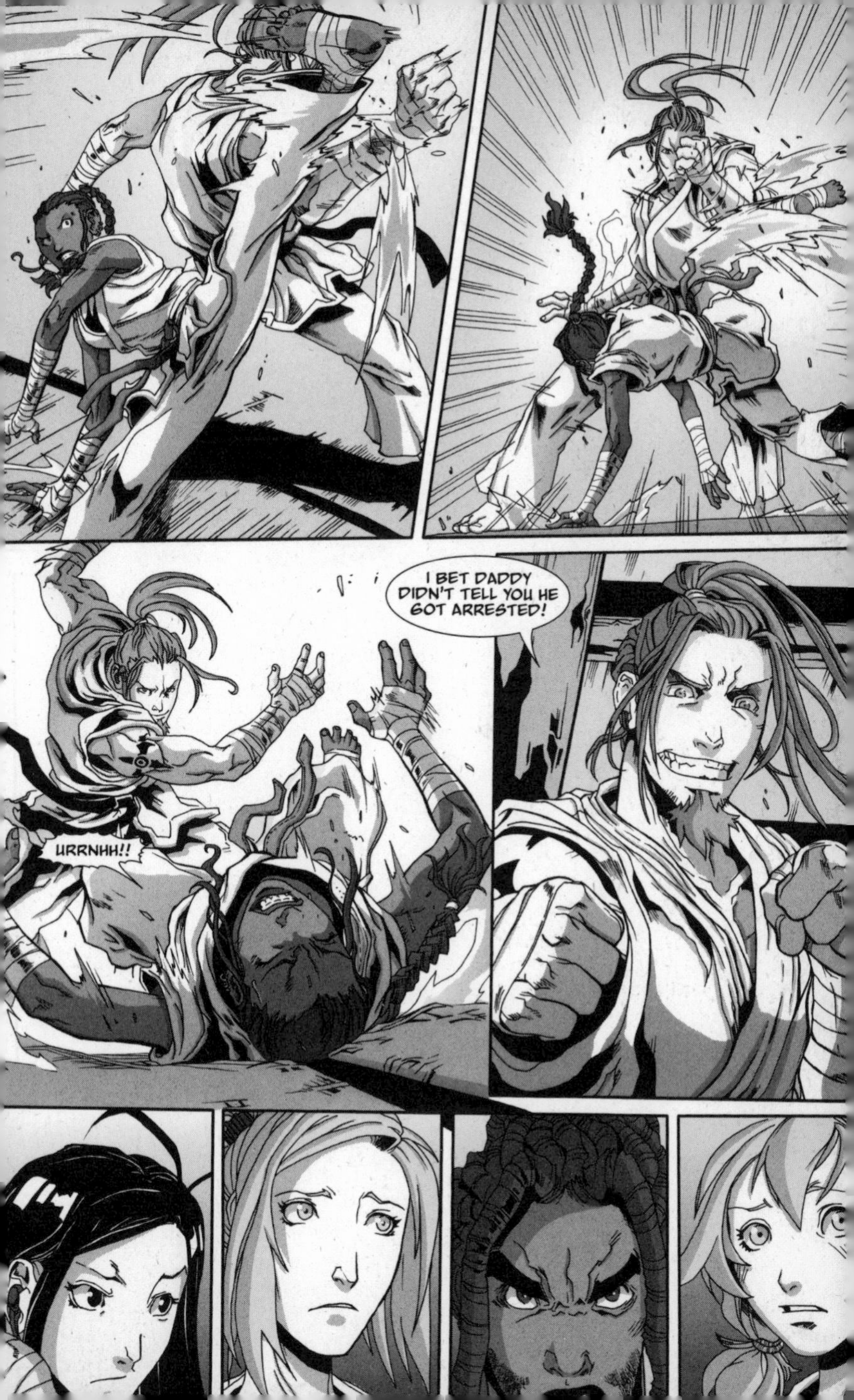
I BET DADDY DIDN'T TELL YOU HE GOT ARRESTED!
URRNHH!!

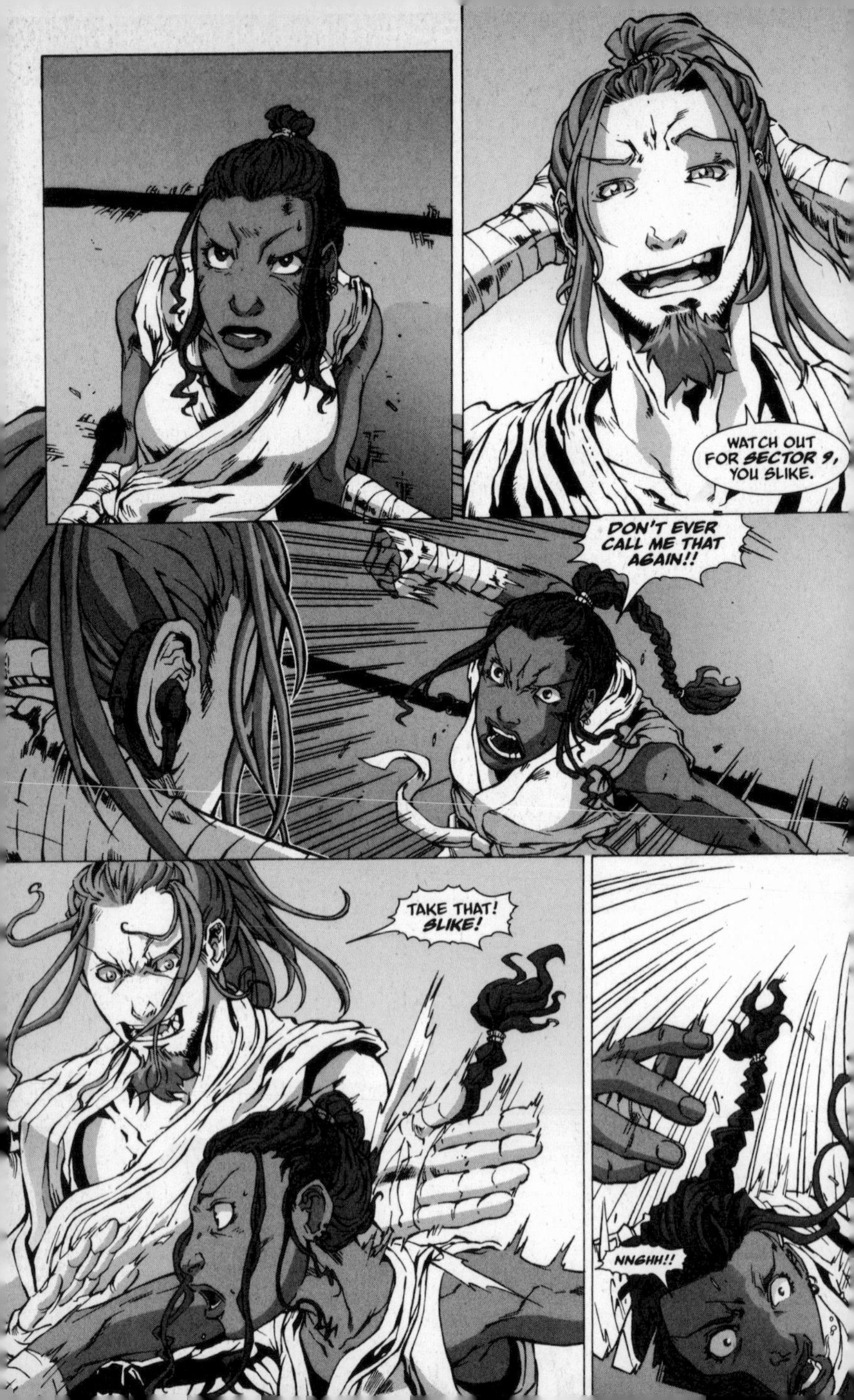
WATCH OUT FOR SECTOR 9, YOU SLIKE.
DON'T EVER CALL ME THAT AGAIN!!
TAKE THAT! SLIKE!
NNGHH!!

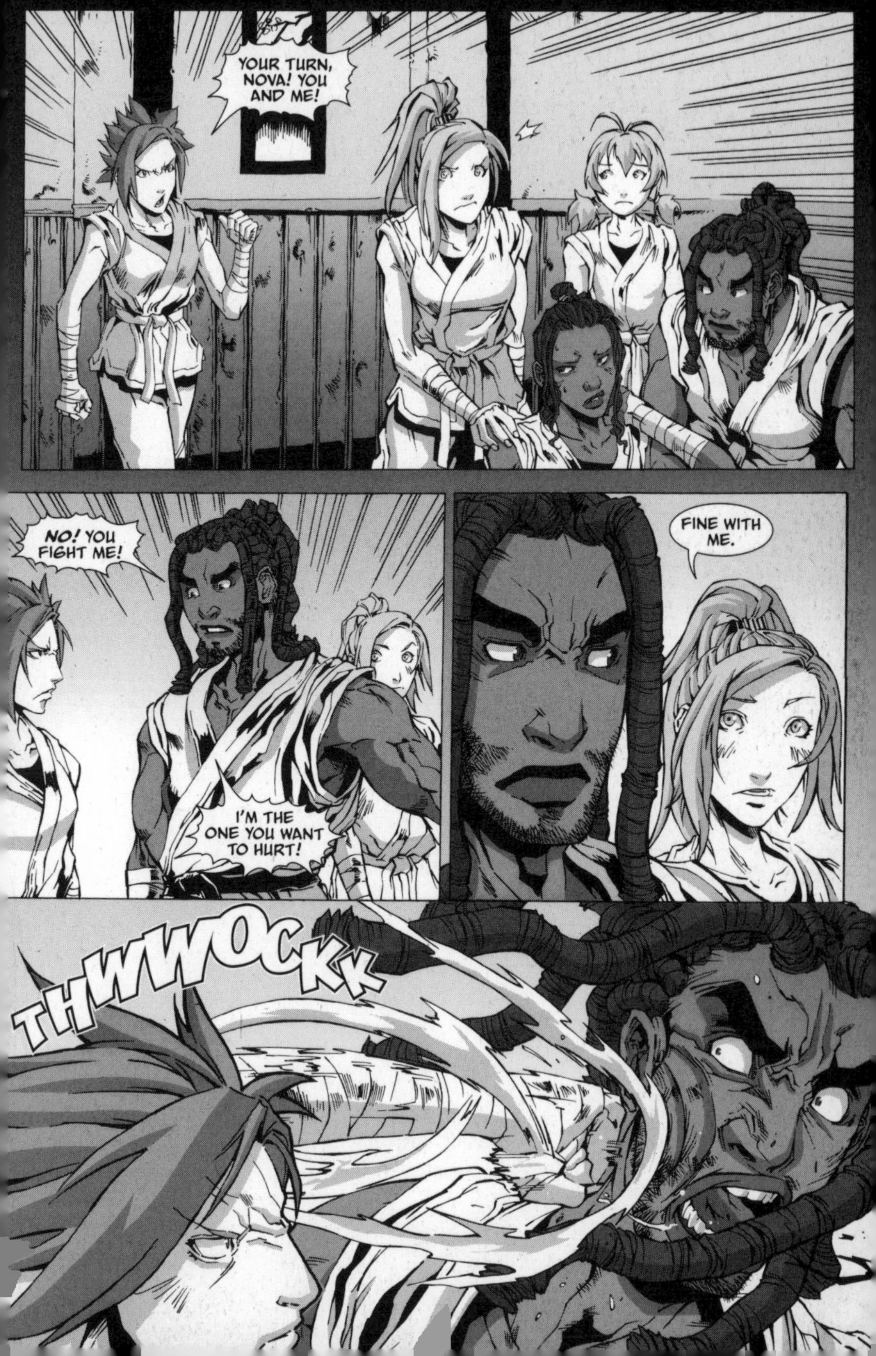
YOUR TURN, NOVA! YOU AND ME!
NO! YOU FIGHT ME!
I'M THE ONE YOU WANT TO HURT!
FINE WITH ME.
THWWOCKK

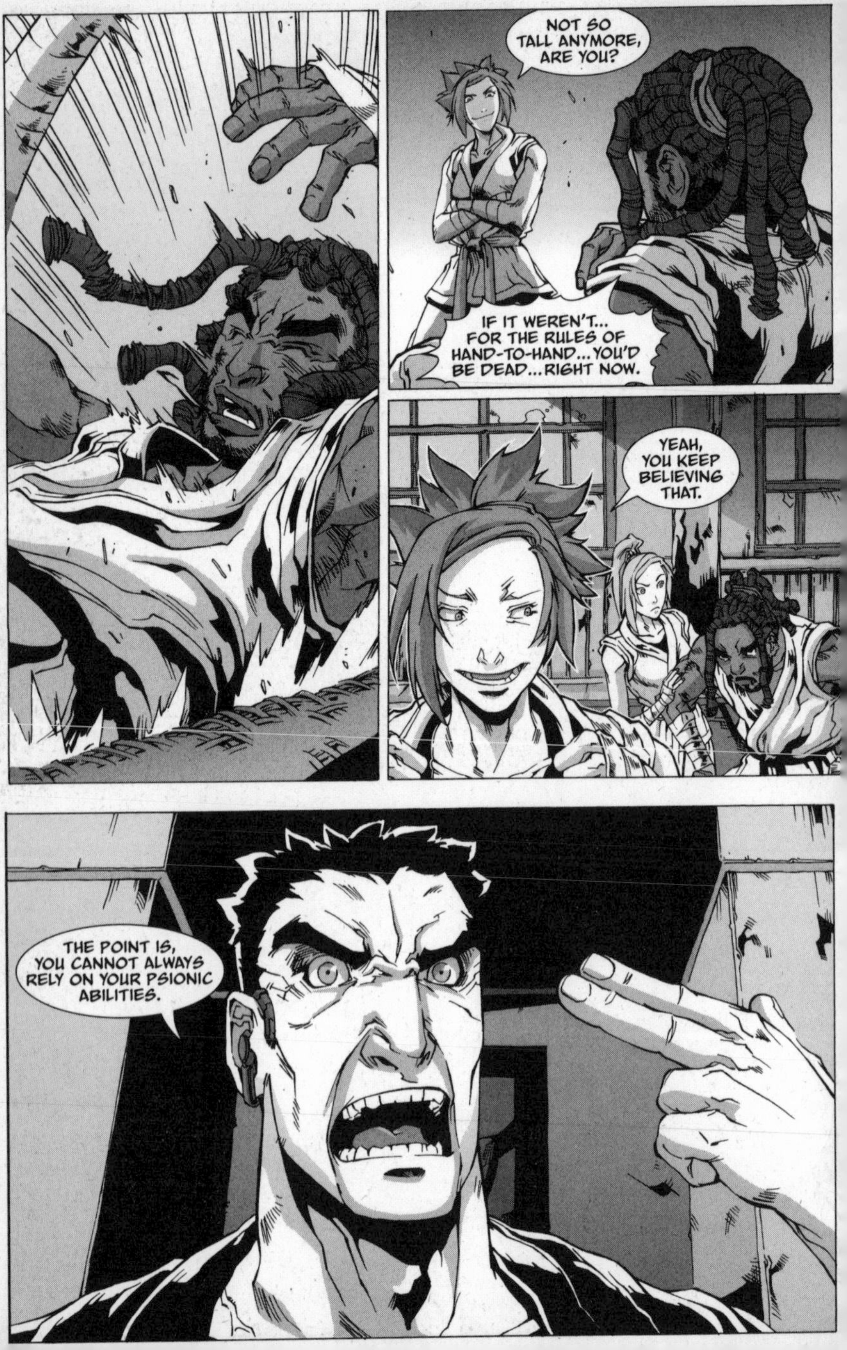
NOT SO TALL ANYMORE, ARE YOU?
IF IT WEREN'T... FOR THE RULES OF HAND-TO-HAND... YOU'D BE DEAD... RIGHT NOW.
YEAH, YOU KEEP BELIEVING THAT.
THE POINT IS, YOU CANNOT ALWAYS RELY ON YOUR PSIONIC ABILITIES.

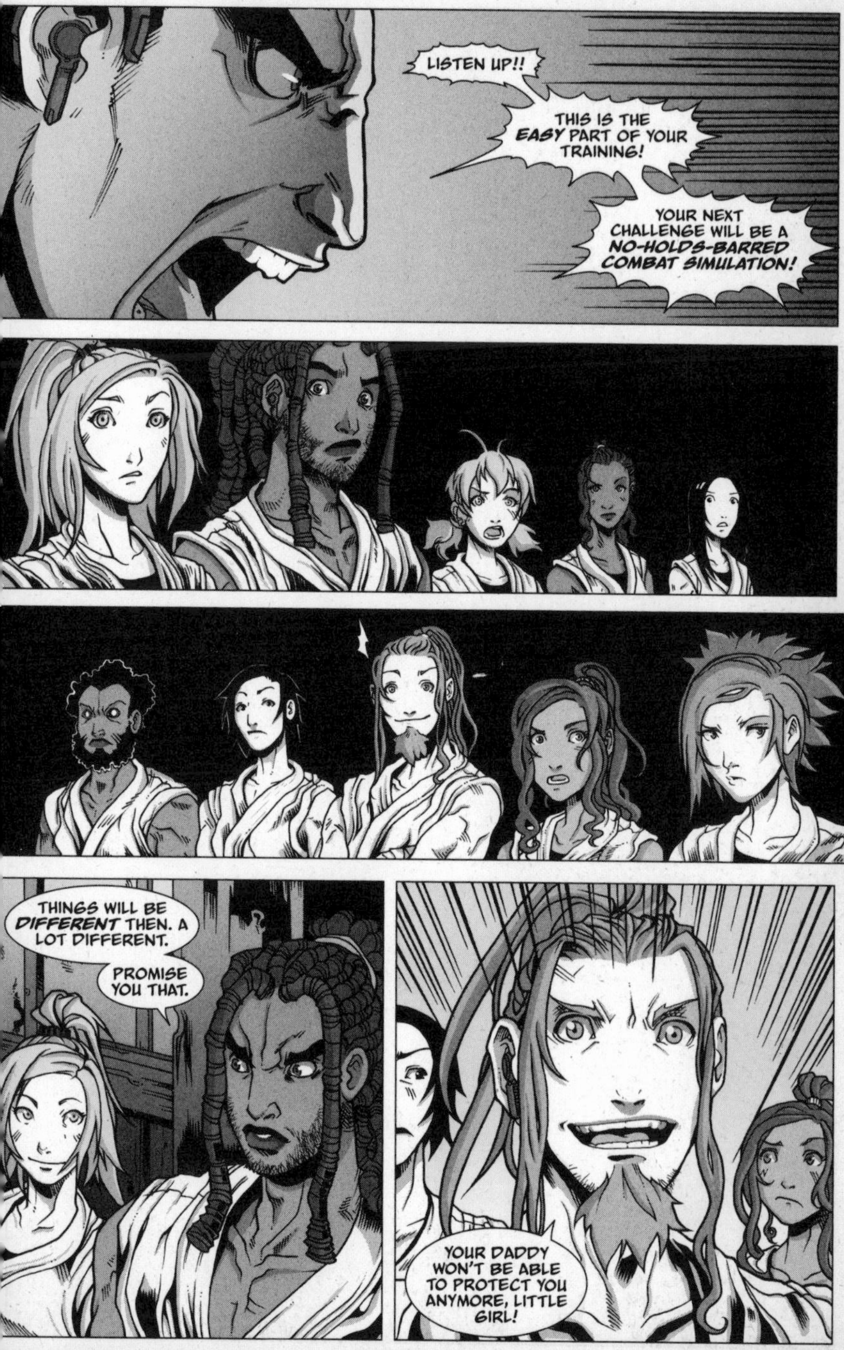
LISTEN UP!!
THIS IS THE EASY PART OF YOUR TRAINING!
YOUR NEXT CHALLENGE WILL BE A NO-HOLDS-BARRED COMBAT SIMULATION!
THINGS WILL BE DIFFERENT THEN. A LOT DIFFERENT.
PROMISE YOU THAT.
YOUR DADDY WON'T BE ABLE TO PROTECT YOU ANYMORE, LITTLE GIRL!

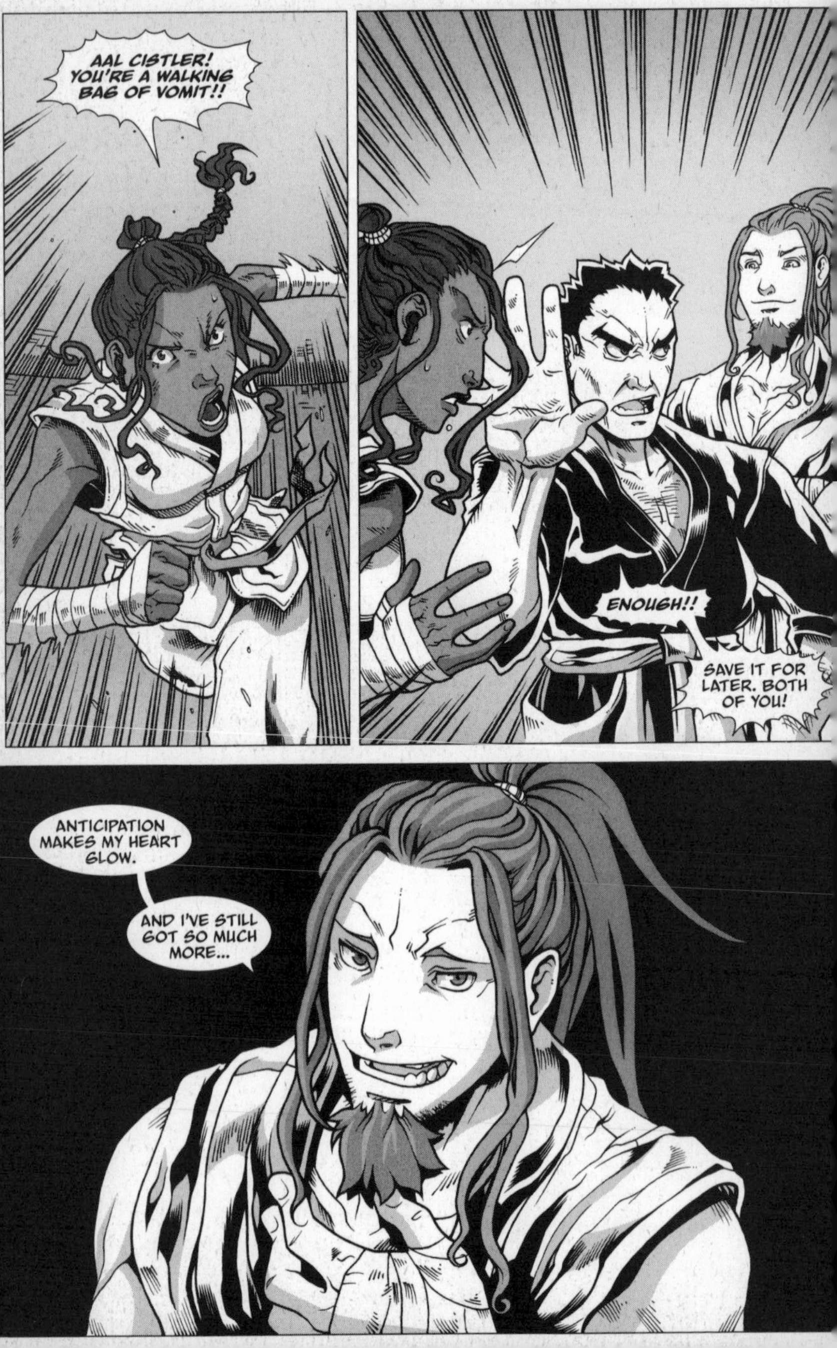
AAL CISTLER! YOU'RE A WALKING BAG OF VOMIT!!
ENOUGH!!
SAVE IT FOR LATER. BOTH OF YOU!
ANTICIPATION MAKES MY HEART GLOW.
AND I'VE STILL GOT SO MUCH MORE...

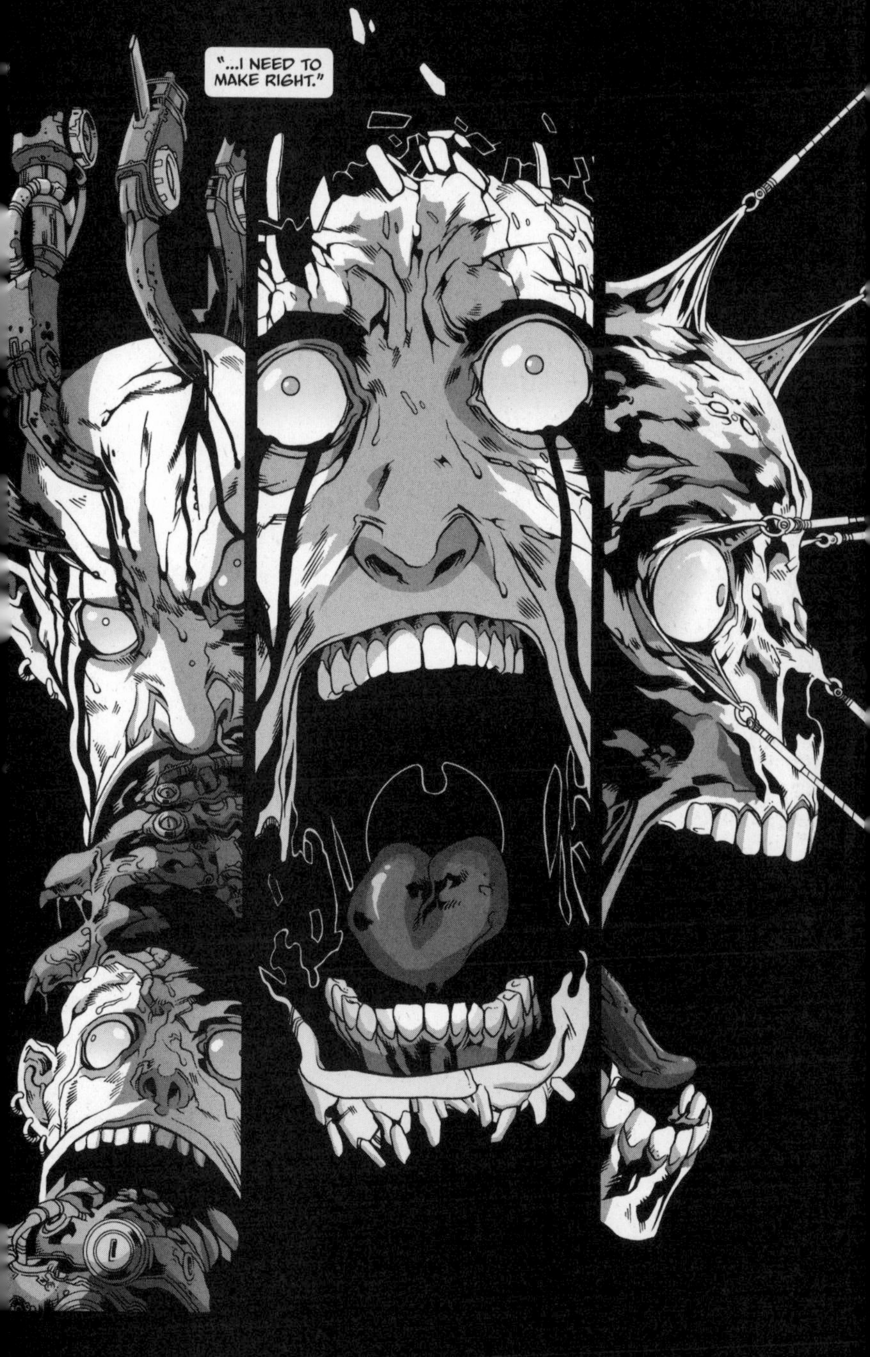
"...I NEED TO MAKE RIGHT."

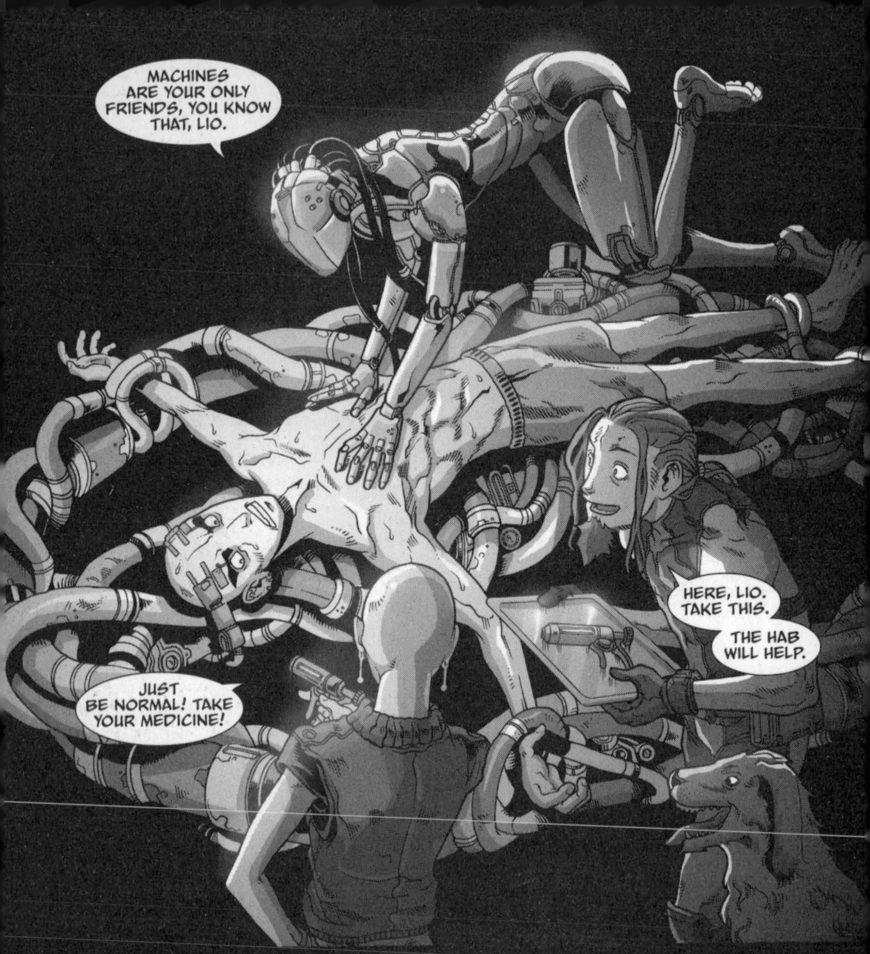
MACHINES ARE YOUR ONLY FRIENDS, YOU KNOW THAT, LIO.
HERE, LIO. TAKE THIS.
THE HAB WILL HELP.
JUST BE NORMAL! TAKE YOUR MEDICINE!

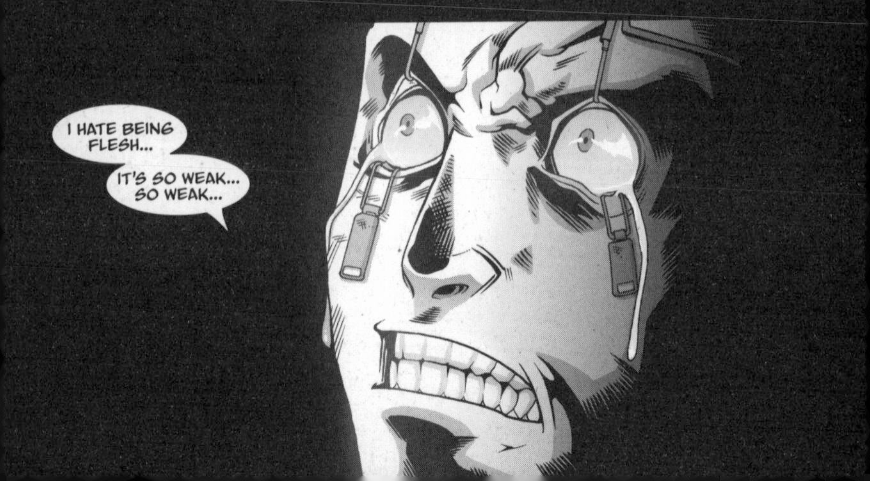
I HATE BEING FLESH...
IT'S SO WEAK... SO WEAK...

# CHAPTER 4
## DANCE OF THE HORRORS

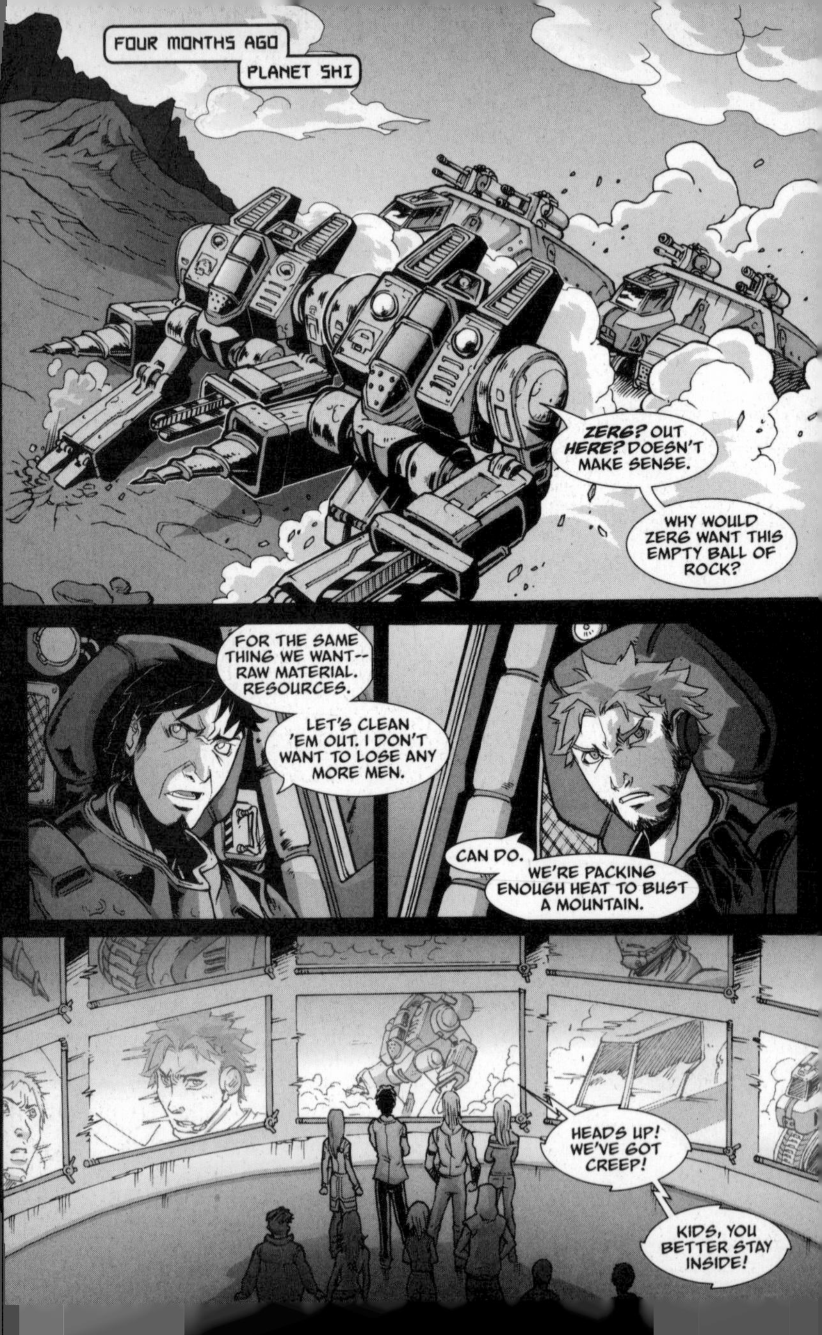
FOUR MONTHS AGO
PLANET SHI
ZERG? OUT HERE? DOESN'T MAKE SENSE.
WHY WOULD ZERG WANT THIS EMPTY BALL OF ROCK?
FOR THE SAME THING WE WANT--RAW MATERIAL. RESOURCES.
LET'S CLEAN 'EM OUT. I DON'T WANT TO LOSE ANY MORE MEN.
CAN DO.
WE'RE PACKING ENOUGH HEAT TO BUST A MOUNTAIN.
HEADS UP! WE'VE GOT CREEP!
KIDS, YOU BETTER STAY INSIDE!

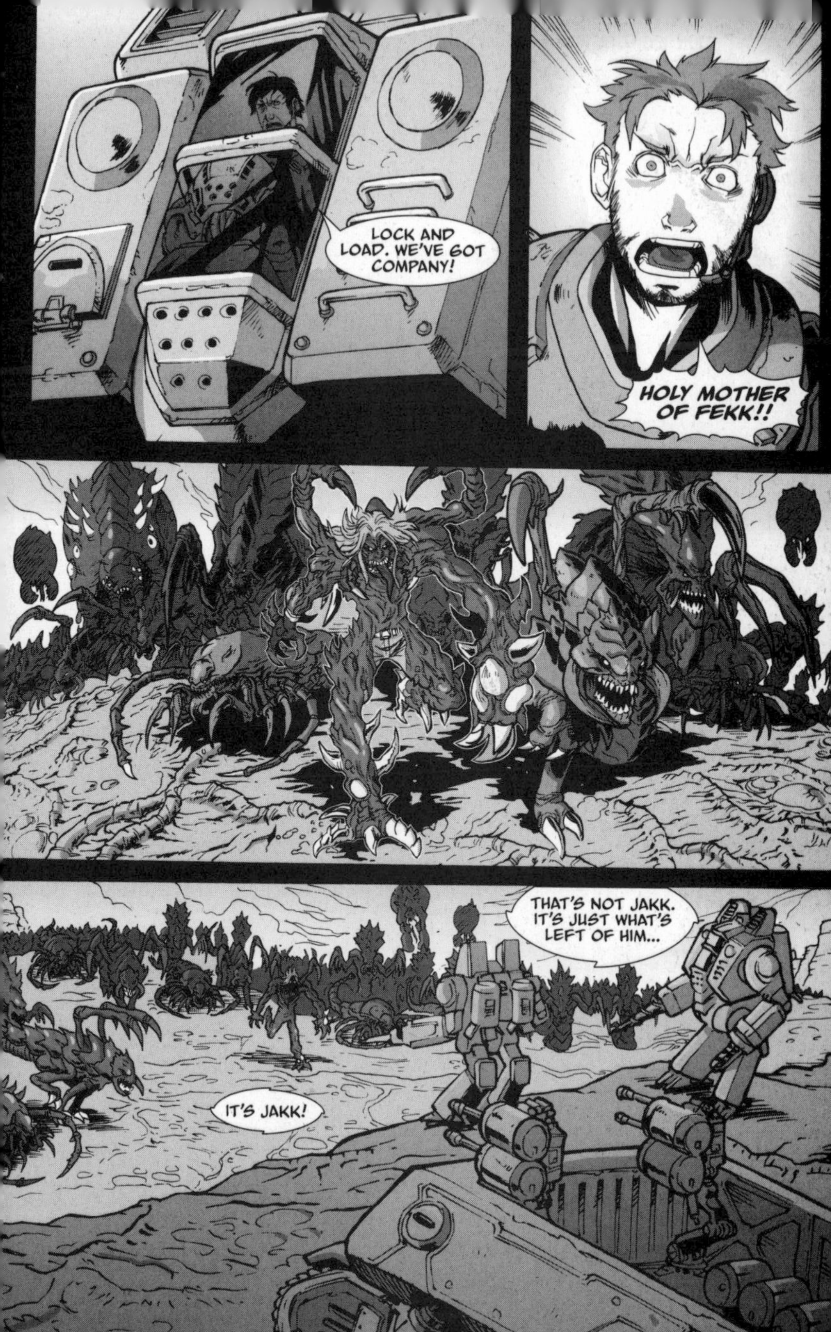
LOCK AND LOAD. WE'VE GOT COMPANY!
HOLY MOTHER OF FEKK!!
IT'S JAKK!
THAT'S NOT JAKK. IT'S JUST WHAT'S LEFT OF HIM...

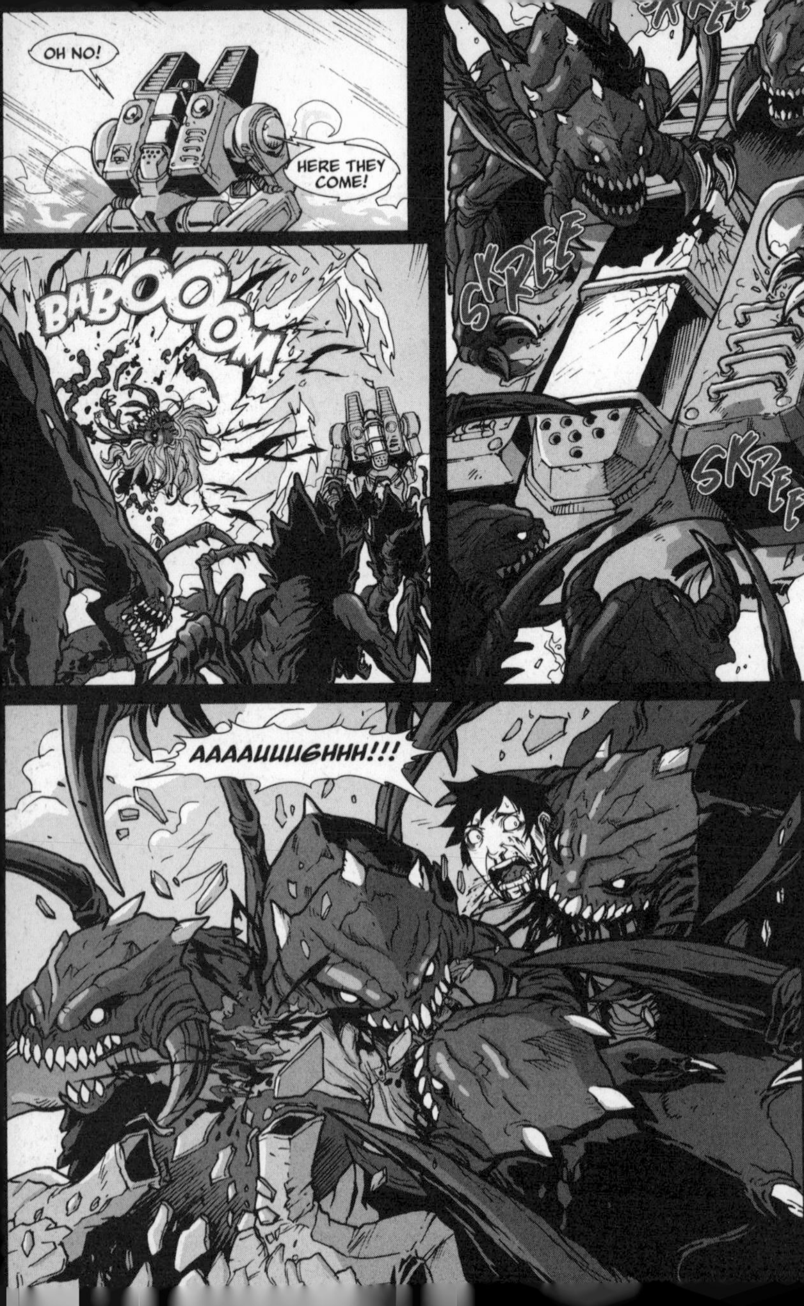
OH NO!
HERE THEY COME!
BABOOOOM
SKREE
SKREE
AAAAUUUGHHH!!!

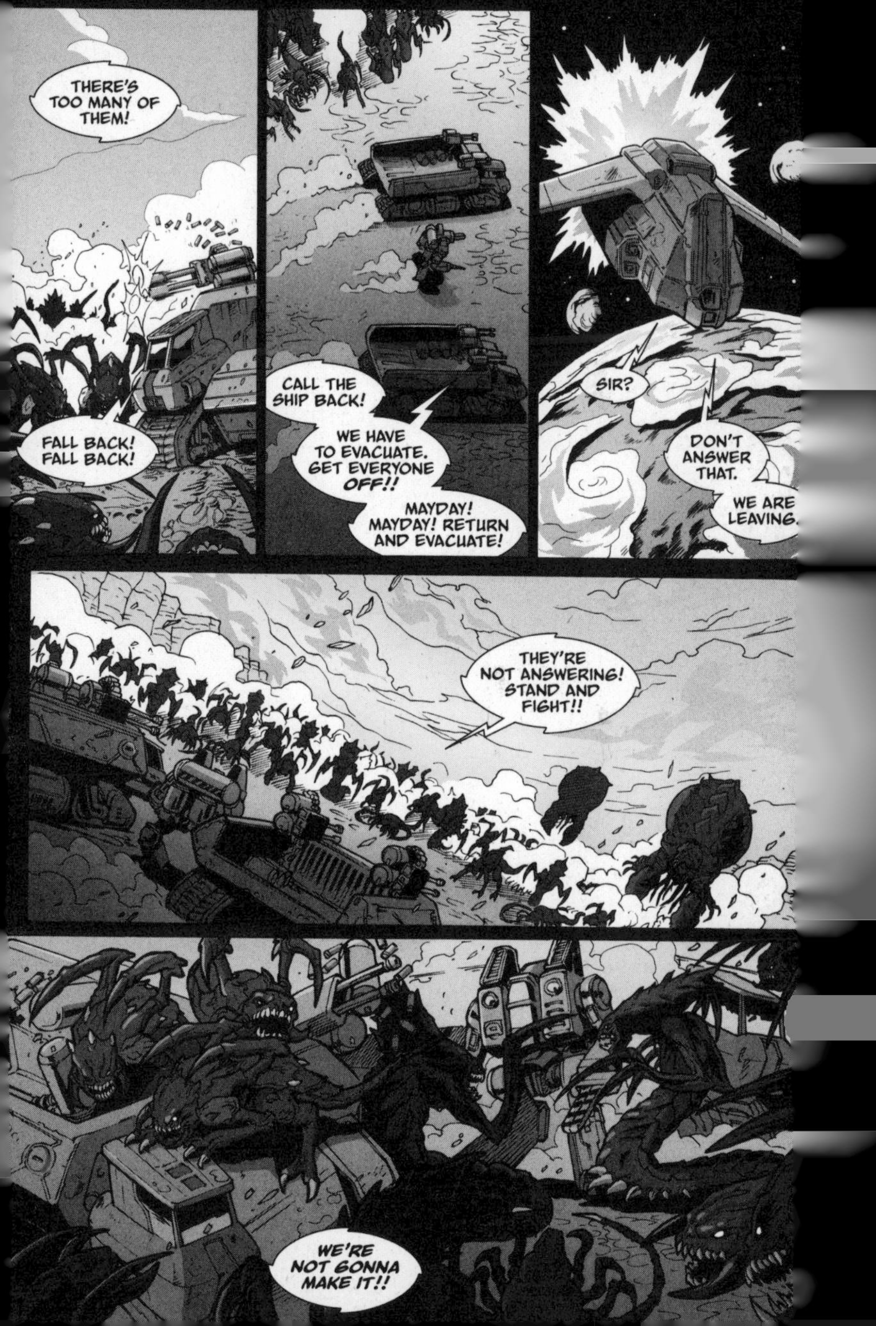
THERE'S TOO MANY OF THEM!
FALL BACK! FALL BACK!
CALL THE SHIP BACK!
WE HAVE TO EVACUATE. GET EVERYONE OFF!!
MAYDAY! MAYDAY! RETURN AND EVACUATE!
SIR?
DON'T ANSWER THAT.
WE ARE LEAVING.
THEY'RE NOT ANSWERING! STAND AND FIGHT!!
WE'RE NOT GONNA MAKE IT!!

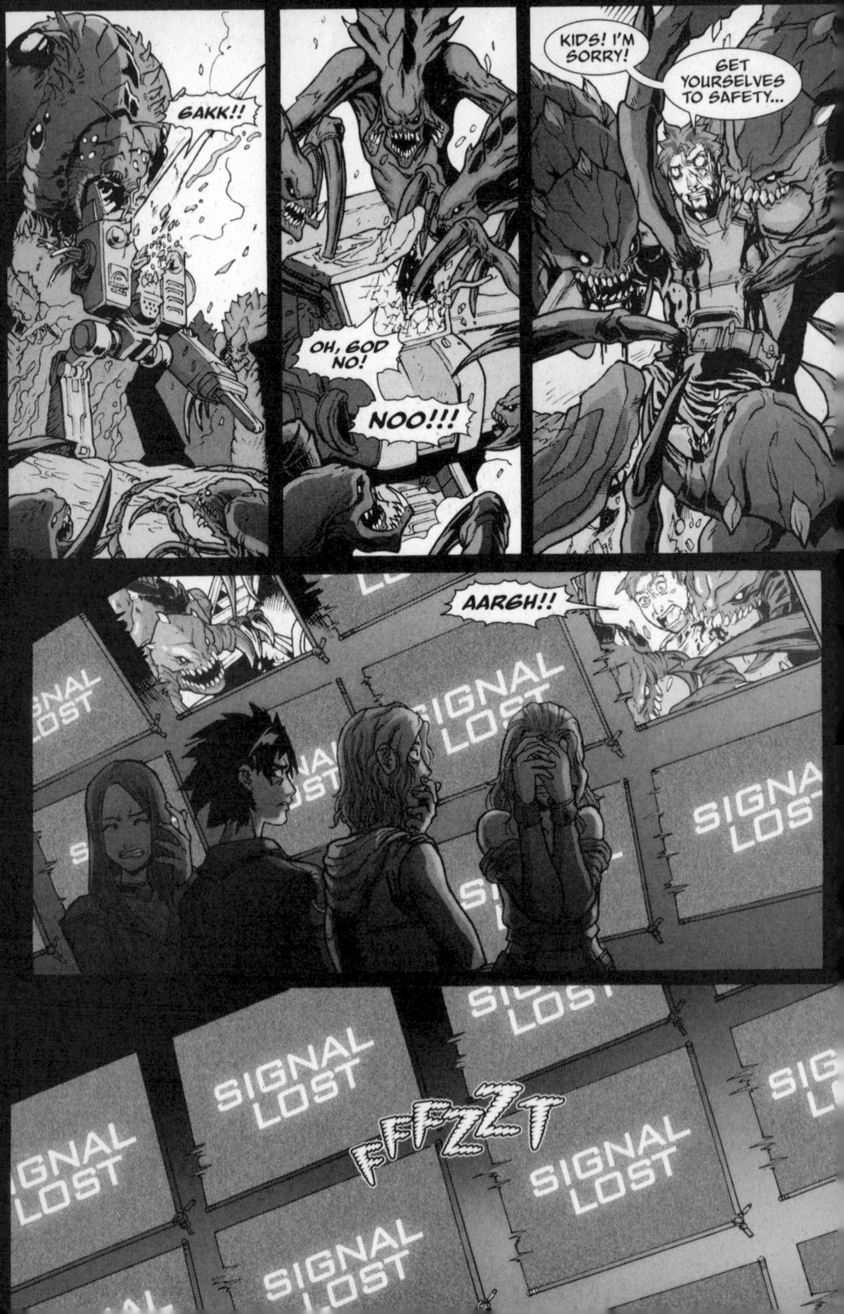
GAKK!!
OH, GOD NO!
NOO!!!
KIDS! I'M SORRY!
GET YOURSELVES TO SAFETY...
AARGH!!
SIGNAL LOST
SIGNAL LOST
SIGNAL LOST
SIGNAL LOST
SIGNAL LOST
FFFZZT
SIGNAL LOST

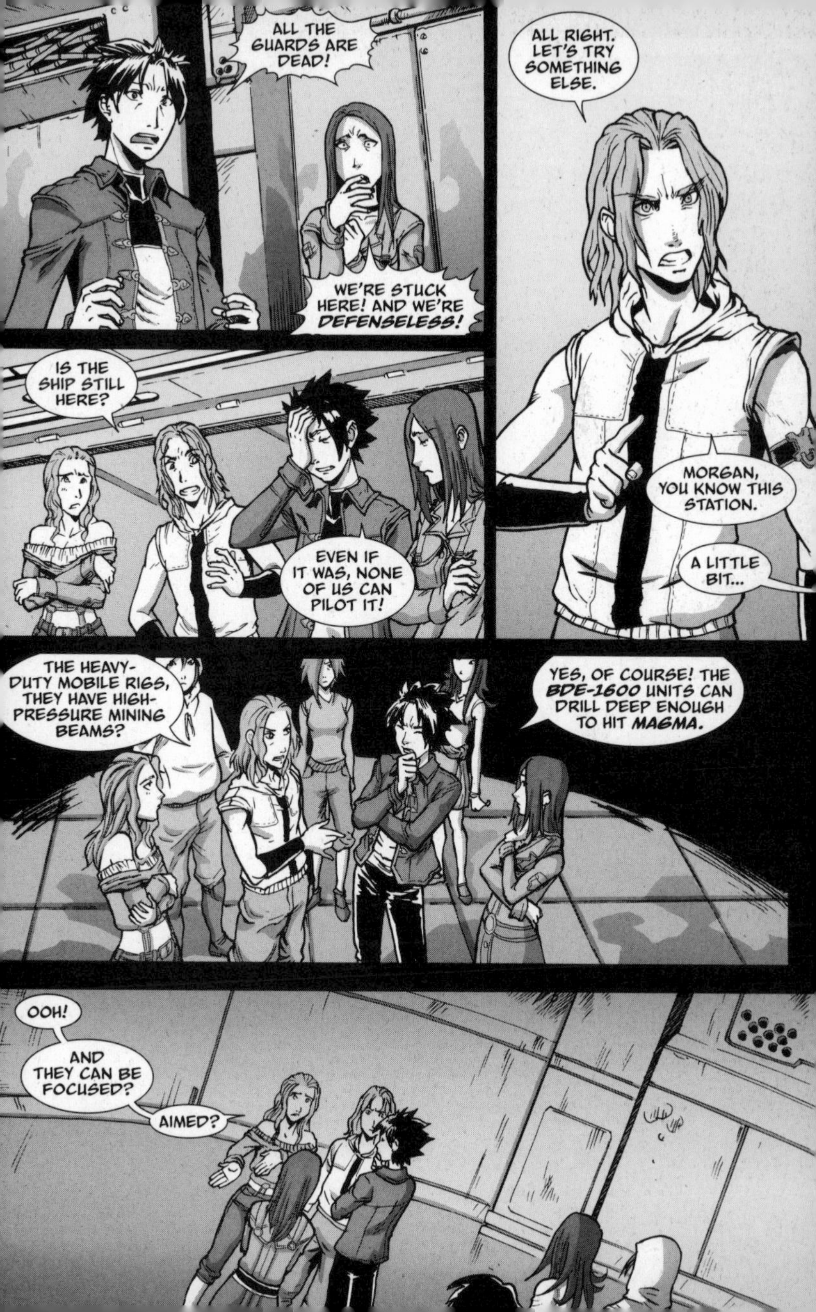
ALL THE GUARDS ARE DEAD!
WE'RE STUCK HERE! AND WE'RE DEFENSELESS!
ALL RIGHT. LET'S TRY SOMETHING ELSE.
IS THE SHIP STILL HERE?
EVEN IF IT WAS, NONE OF US CAN PILOT IT!
MORGAN, YOU KNOW THIS STATION.
A LITTLE BIT...
THE HEAVY-DUTY MOBILE RIGS, THEY HAVE HIGH-PRESSURE MINING BEAMS?
YES, OF COURSE! THE BDE-1600 UNITS CAN DRILL DEEP ENOUGH TO HIT MAGMA.
OOH!
AND THEY CAN BE FOCUSED?
AIMED?

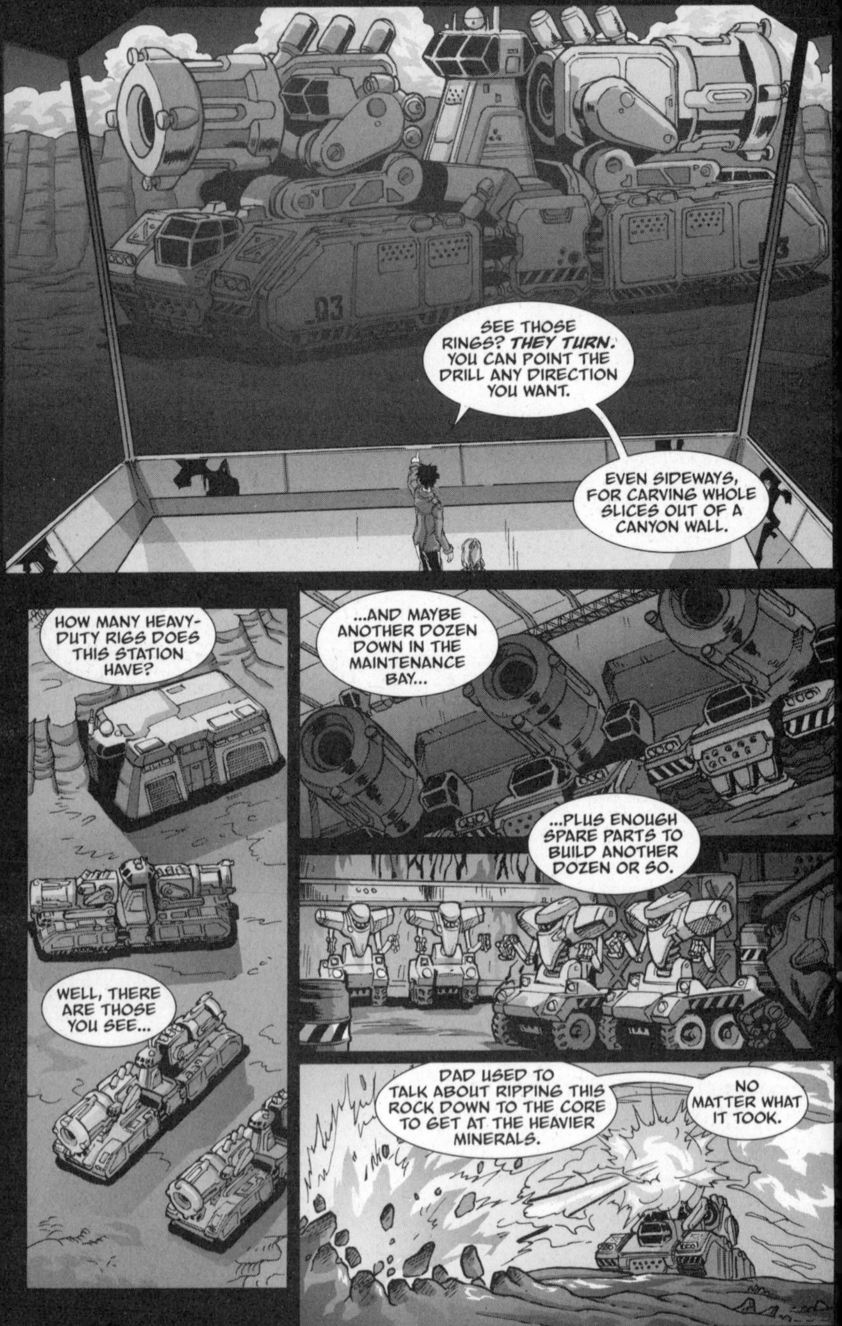
SEE THOSE RINGS? THEY TURN. YOU CAN POINT THE DRILL ANY DIRECTION YOU WANT.
EVEN SIDEWAYS, FOR CARVING WHOLE SLICES OUT OF A CANYON WALL.
HOW MANY HEAVY-DUTY RIGS DOES THIS STATION HAVE?
WELL, THERE ARE THOSE YOU SEE...
...AND MAYBE ANOTHER DOZEN DOWN IN THE MAINTENANCE BAY...
...PLUS ENOUGH SPARE PARTS TO BUILD ANOTHER DOZEN OR SO.
DAD USED TO TALK ABOUT RIPPING THIS ROCK DOWN TO THE CORE TO GET AT THE HEAVIER MINERALS.
NO MATTER WHAT IT TOOK.

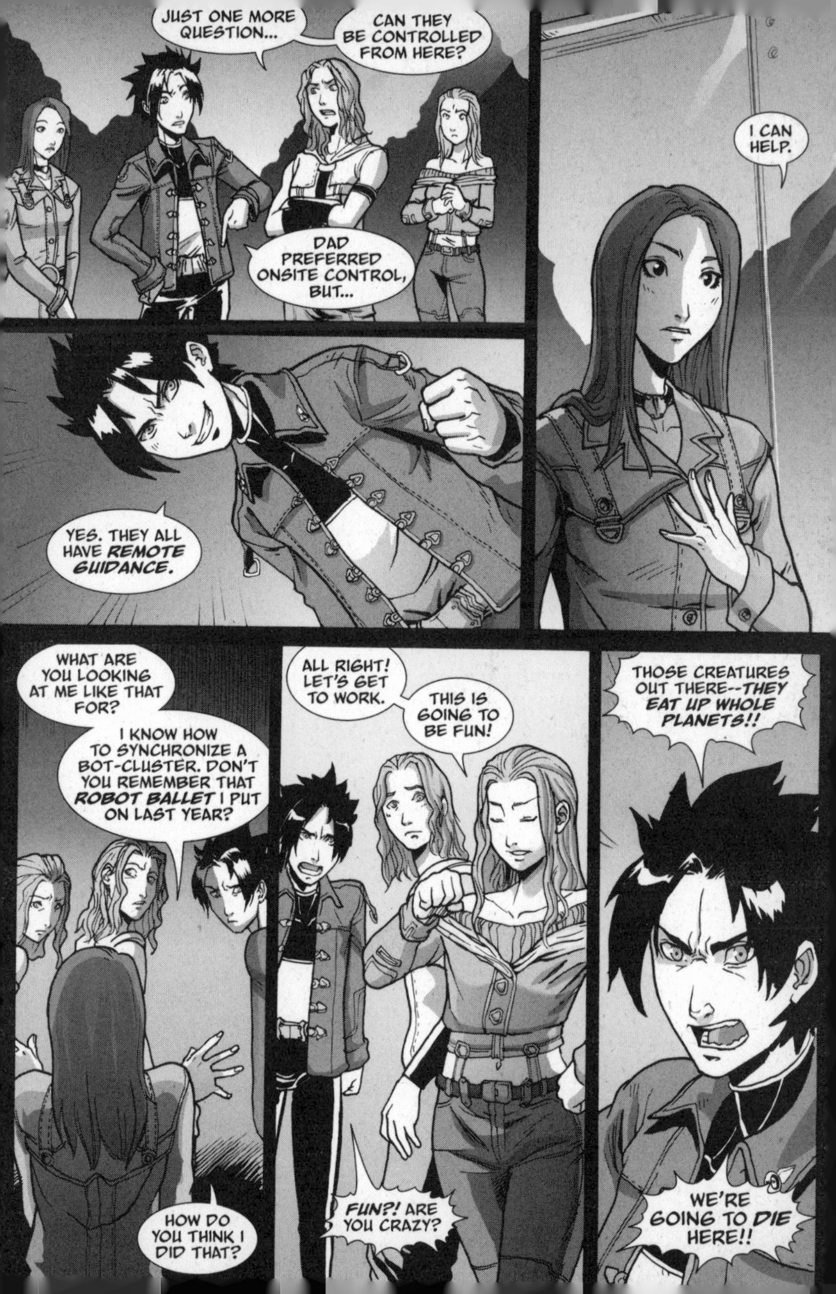
JUST ONE MORE QUESTION...
CAN THEY BE CONTROLLED FROM HERE?
DAD PREFERRED ONSITE CONTROL, BUT...
I CAN HELP.
YES. THEY ALL HAVE *REMOTE GUIDANCE.*
WHAT ARE YOU LOOKING AT ME LIKE THAT FOR?
I KNOW HOW TO SYNCHRONIZE A BOT-CLUSTER. DON'T YOU REMEMBER THAT *ROBOT BALLET* I PUT ON LAST YEAR?
HOW DO YOU THINK I DID THAT?
ALL RIGHT! LET'S GET TO WORK.
THIS IS GOING TO BE FUN!
*FUN?!* ARE YOU CRAZY?
THOSE CREATURES OUT THERE--*THEY EAT UP WHOLE PLANETS!!*
WE'RE GOING TO *DIE* HERE!!

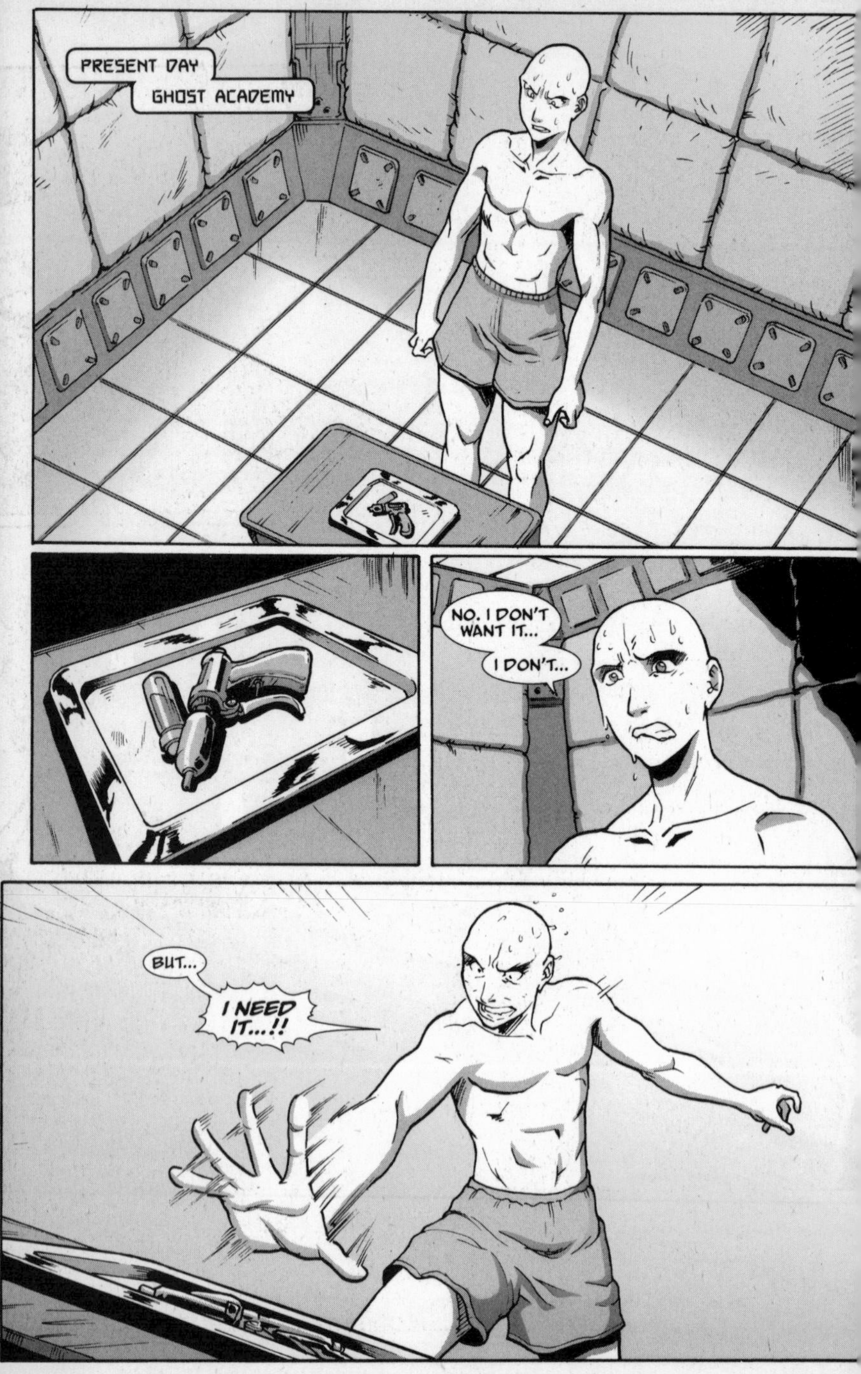
PRESENT DAY
GHOST ACADEMY
NO. I DON'T WANT IT...
I DON'T...
BUT...
I NEED IT...!!

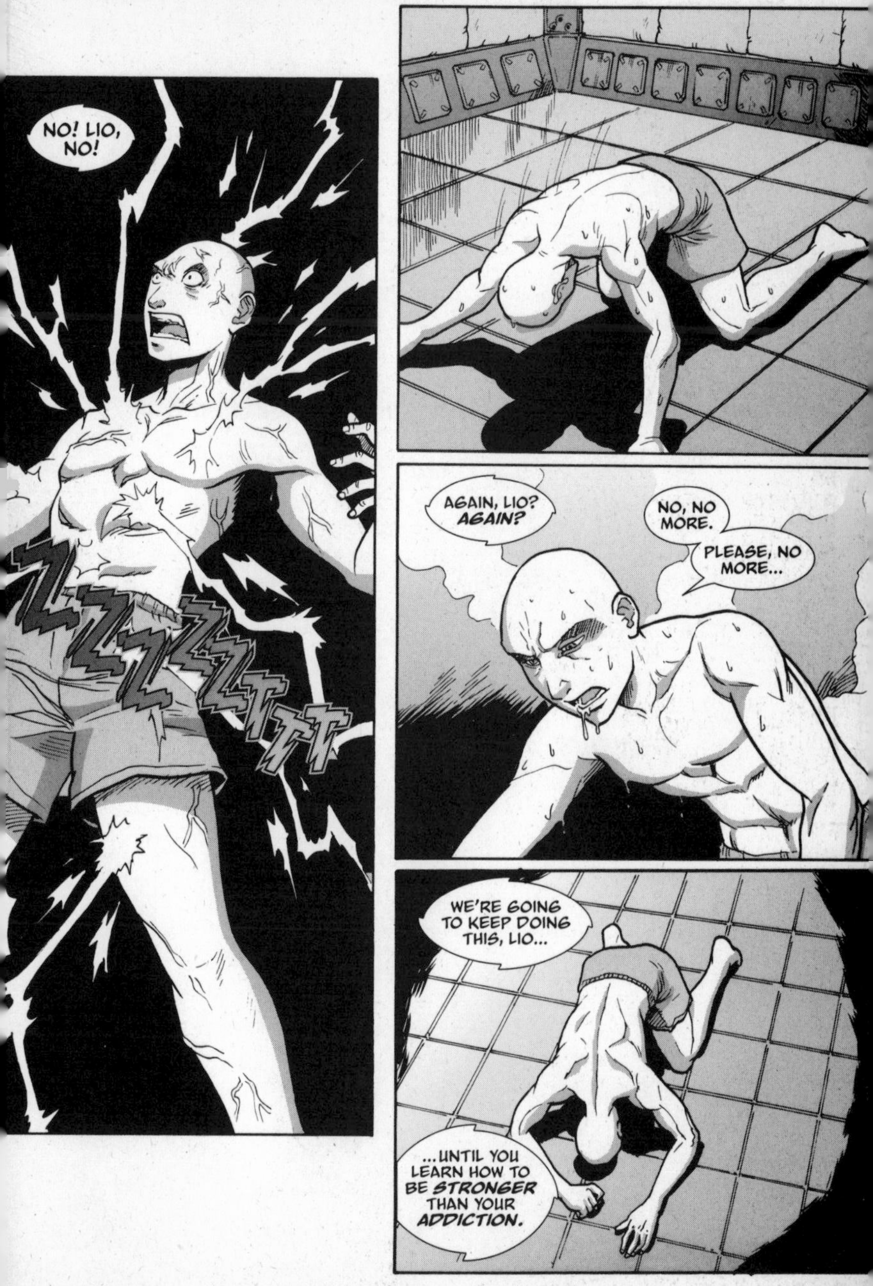
NO! LIO, NO!
ZZZZZZZTTT
AGAIN, LIO? AGAIN?
NO, NO MORE.
PLEASE, NO MORE...
WE'RE GOING TO KEEP DOING THIS, LIO...
...UNTIL YOU LEARN HOW TO BE STRONGER THAN YOUR ADDICTION.

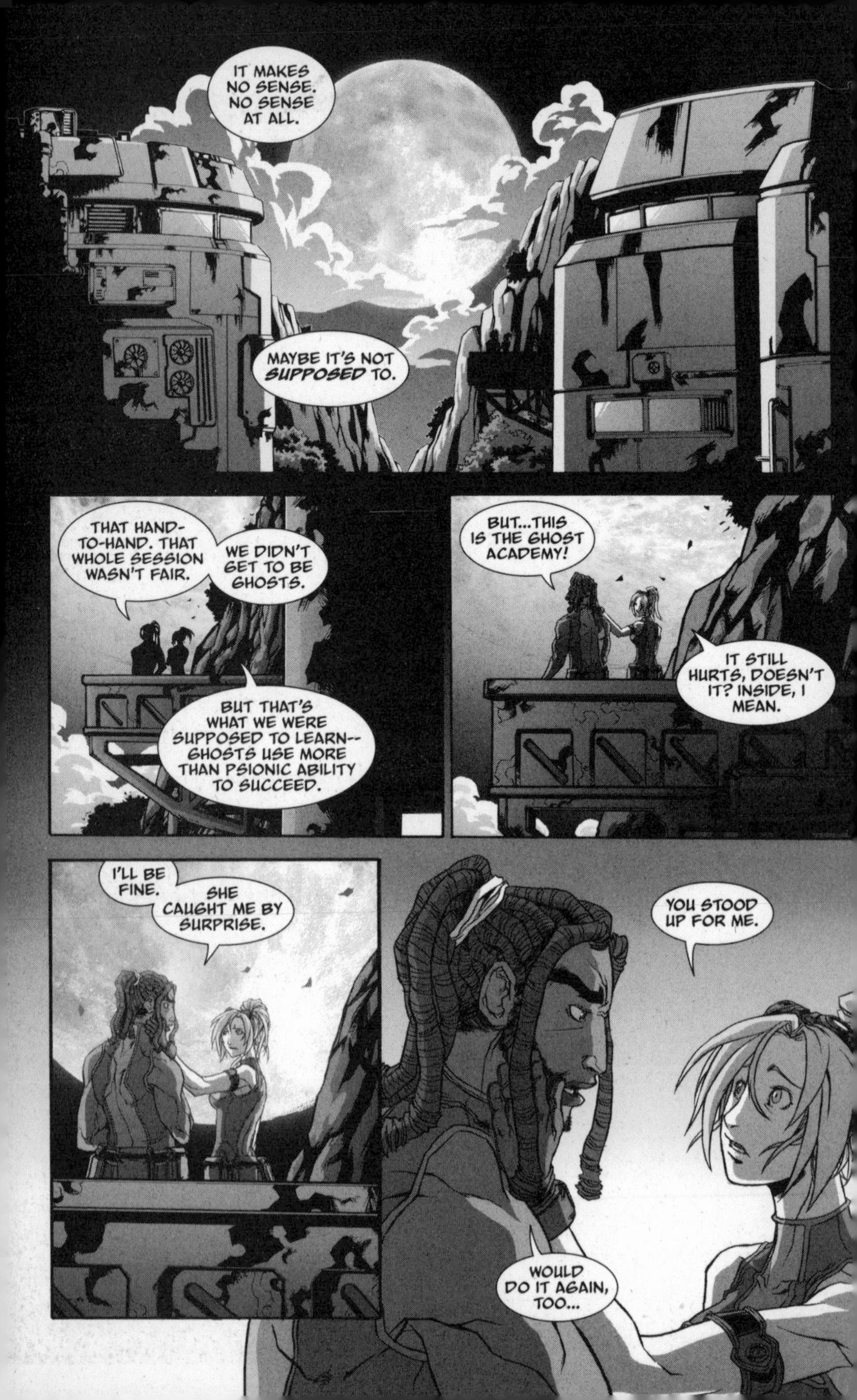
IT MAKES NO SENSE. NO SENSE AT ALL.
MAYBE IT'S NOT *SUPPOSED* TO.
THAT HAND-TO-HAND. THAT WHOLE SESSION WASN'T FAIR.
WE DIDN'T GET TO BE GHOSTS.
BUT THAT'S WHAT WE WERE SUPPOSED TO LEARN-- GHOSTS USE MORE THAN PSIONIC ABILITY TO SUCCEED.
BUT...THIS IS THE GHOST ACADEMY!
IT STILL HURTS, DOESN'T IT? INSIDE, I MEAN.
I'LL BE FINE.
SHE CAUGHT ME BY SURPRISE.
YOU STOOD UP FOR ME.
WOULD DO IT AGAIN, TOO...

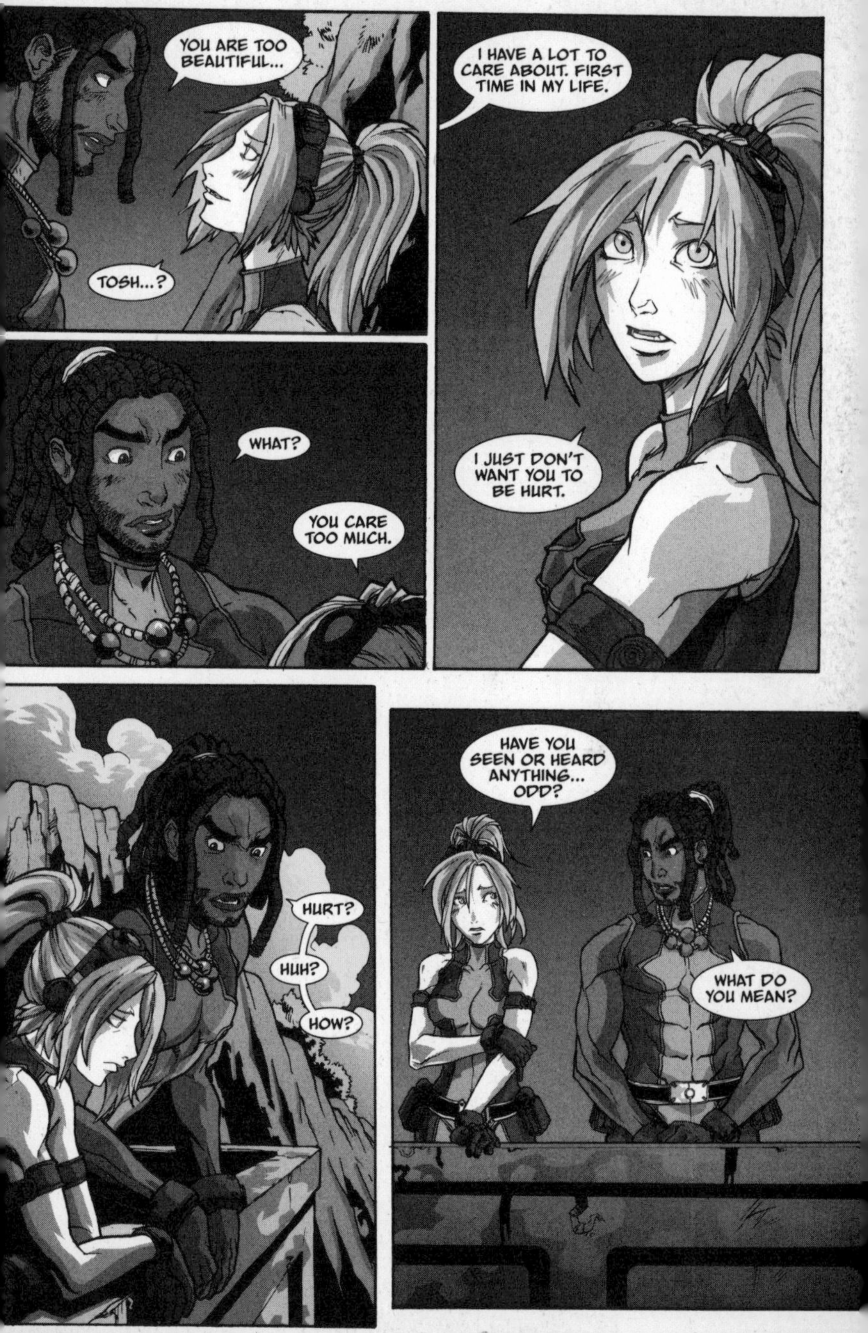
YOU ARE TOO BEAUTIFUL...
TOSH...?
I HAVE A LOT TO CARE ABOUT. FIRST TIME IN MY LIFE.
WHAT?
YOU CARE TOO MUCH.
I JUST DON'T WANT YOU TO BE HURT.
HURT?
HUH?
HOW?
HAVE YOU SEEN OR HEARD ANYTHING... ODD?
WHAT DO YOU MEAN?

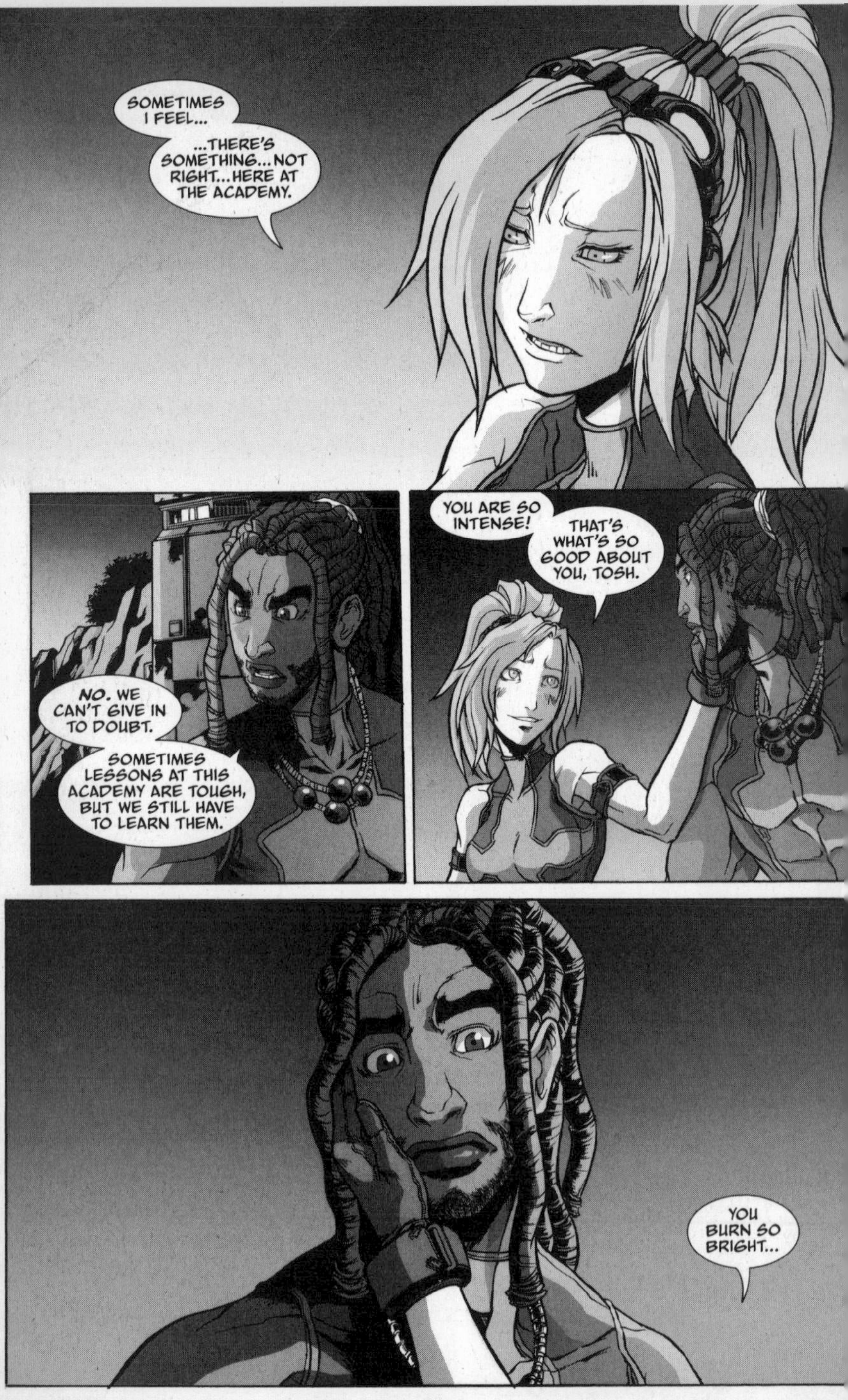
SOMETIMES I FEEL...
...THERE'S SOMETHING...NOT RIGHT...HERE AT THE ACADEMY.
NO. WE CAN'T GIVE IN TO DOUBT.
SOMETIMES LESSONS AT THIS ACADEMY ARE TOUGH, BUT WE STILL HAVE TO LEARN THEM.
YOU ARE SO INTENSE!
THAT'S WHAT'S SO GOOD ABOUT YOU, TOSH.
YOU BURN SO BRIGHT...

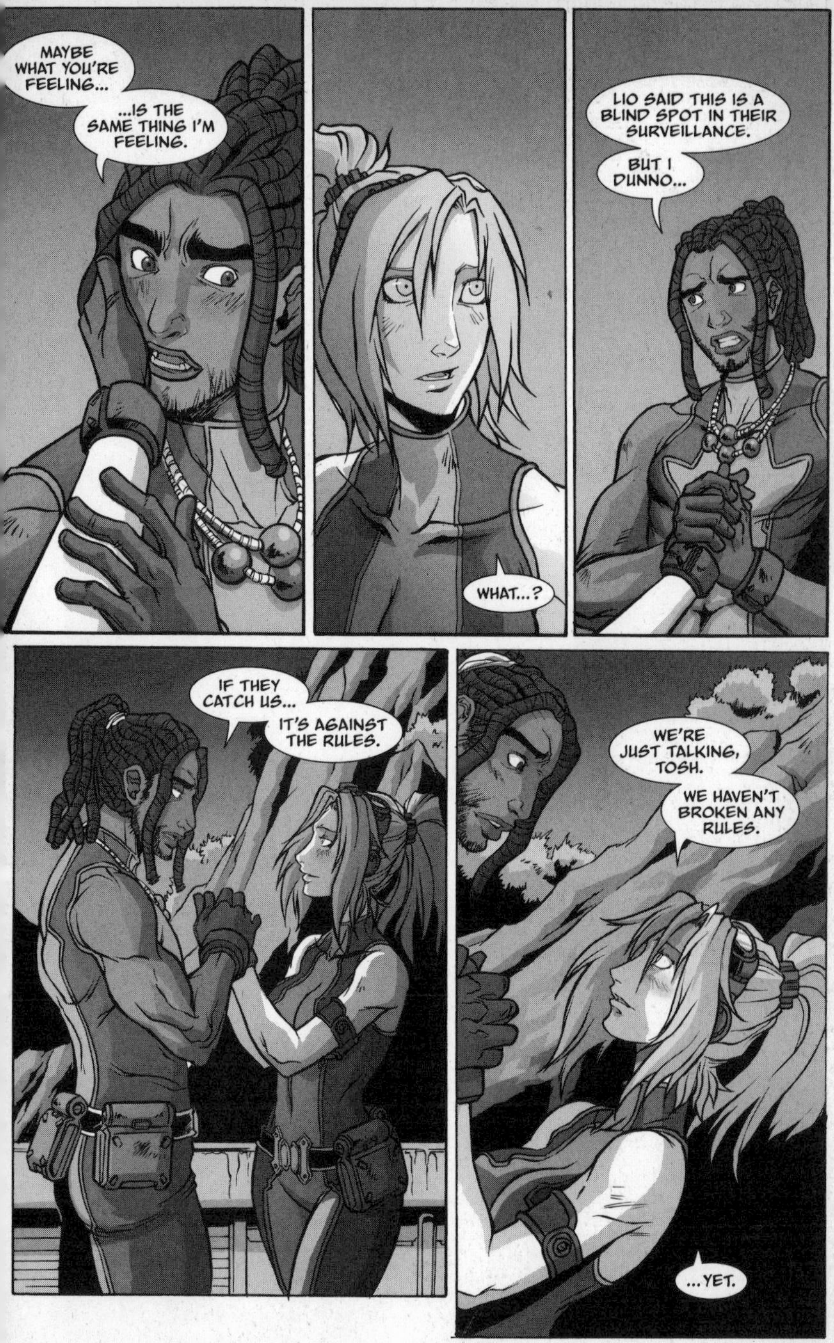
MAYBE WHAT YOU'RE FEELING...
...IS THE SAME THING I'M FEELING.
WHAT...?
LIO SAID THIS IS A BLIND SPOT IN THEIR SURVEILLANCE.
BUT I DUNNO...
IF THEY CATCH US...
IT'S AGAINST THE RULES.
WE'RE JUST TALKING, TOSH.
WE HAVEN'T BROKEN ANY RULES.
...YET.

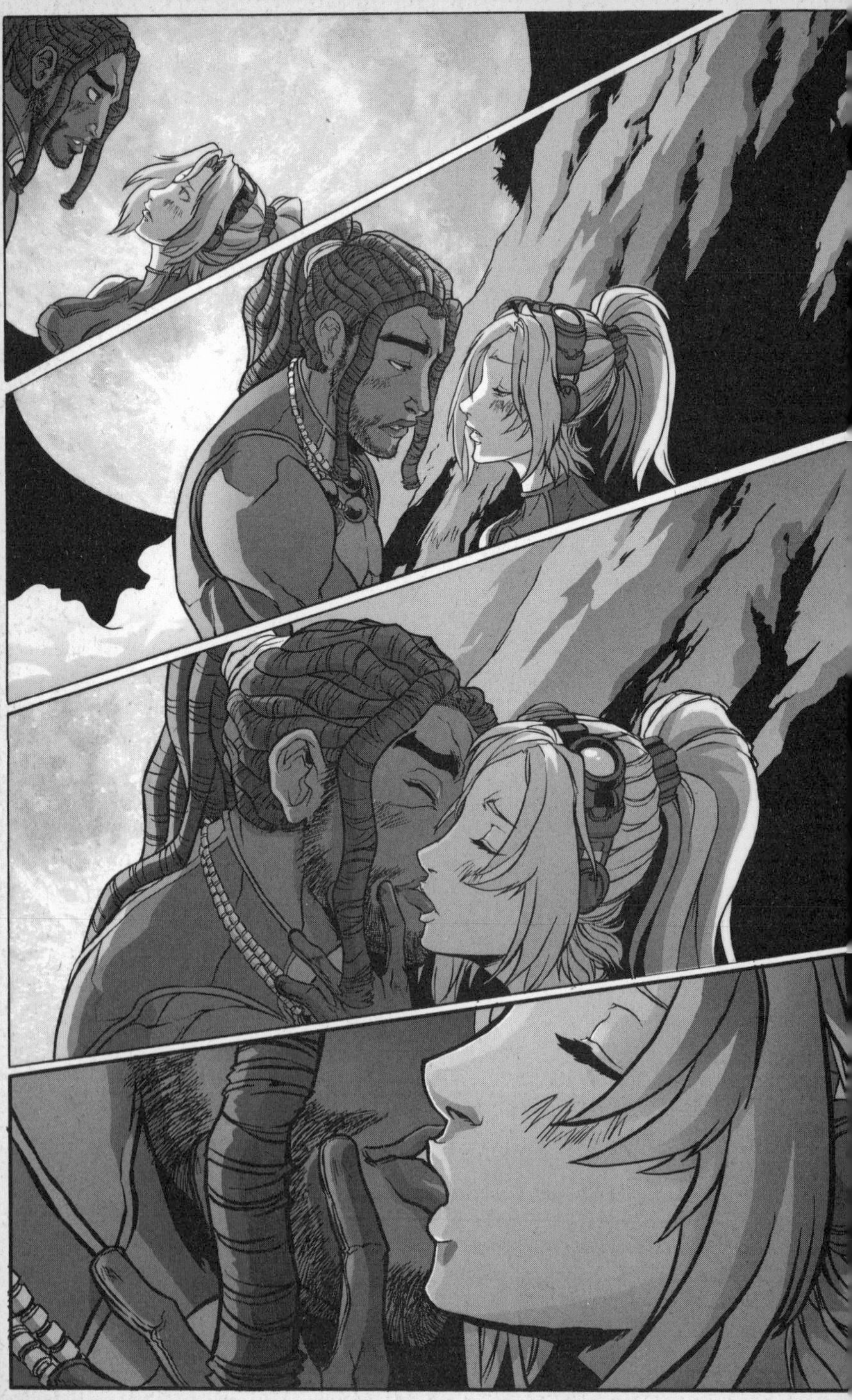

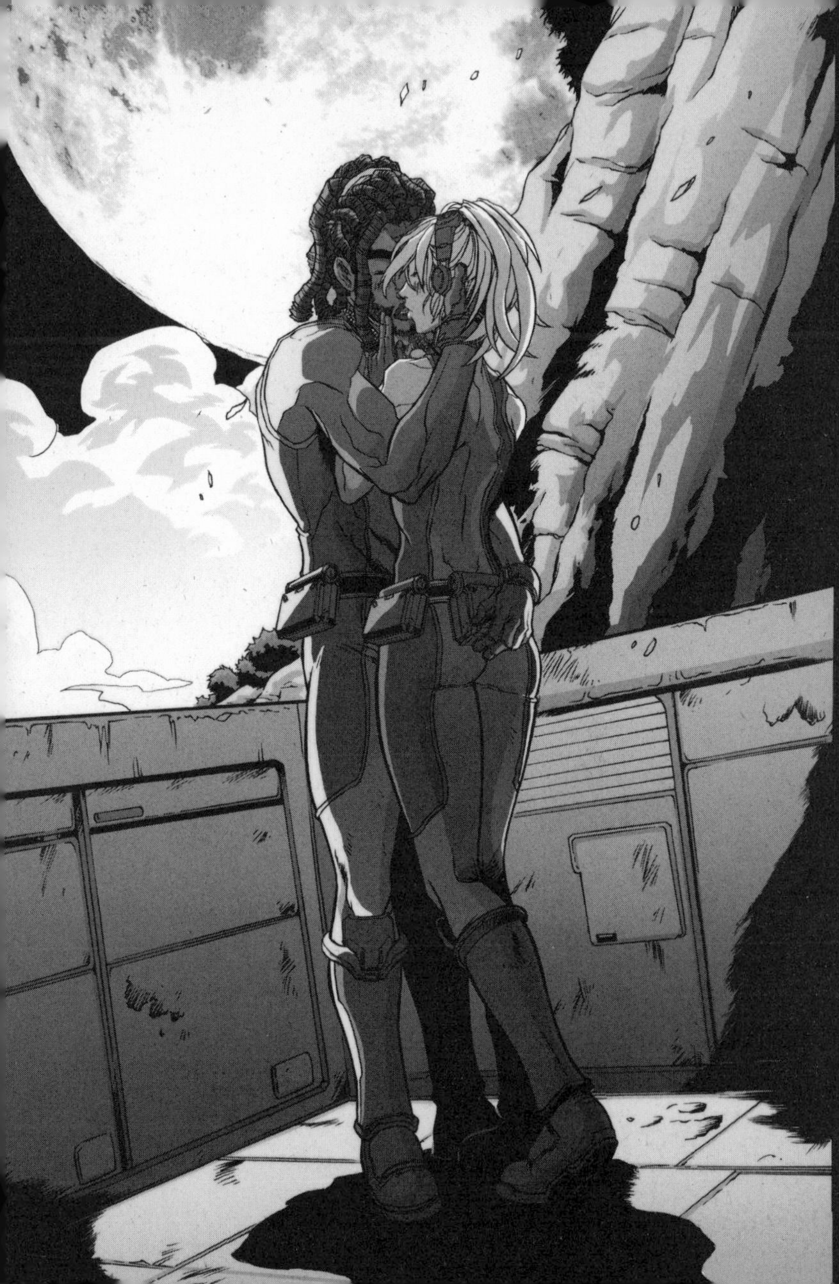

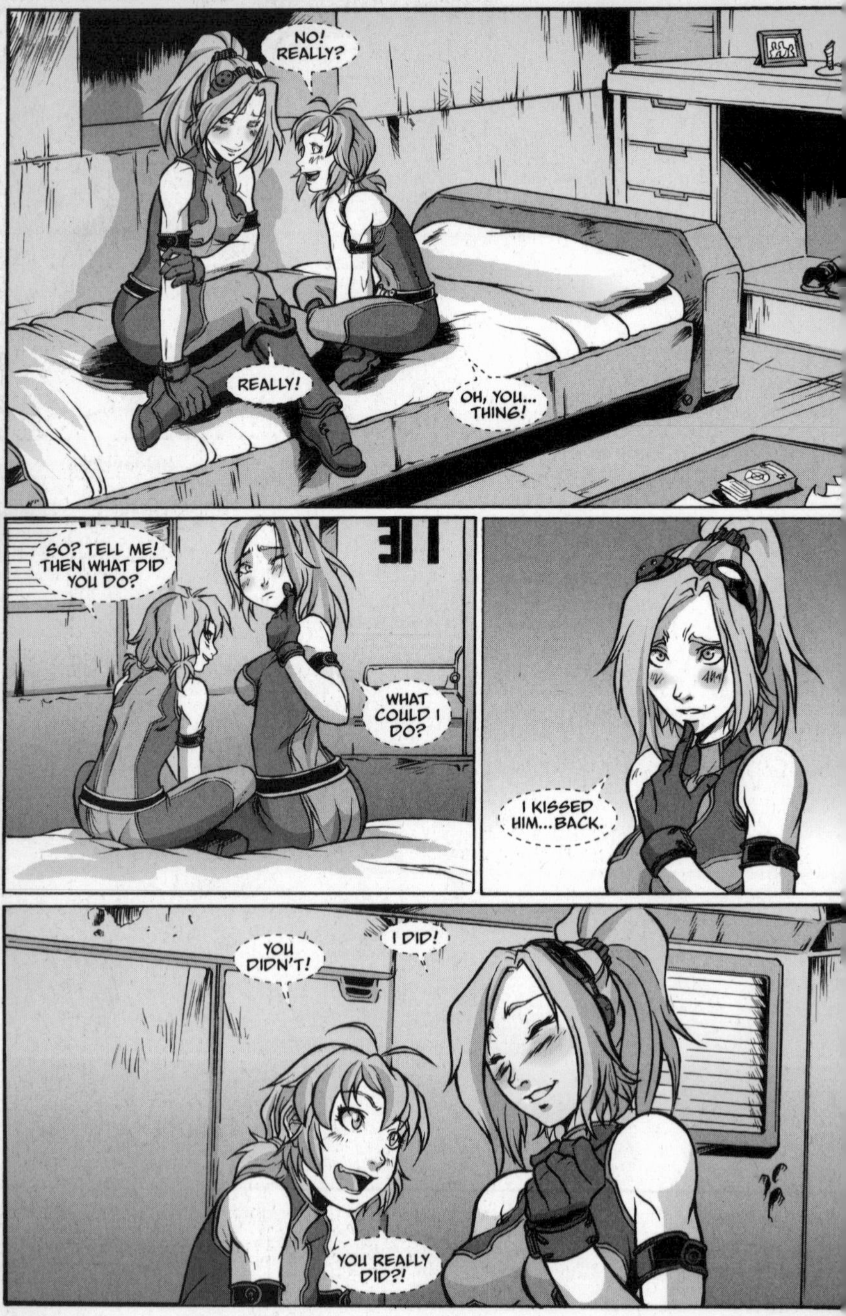
NO! REALLY?
REALLY!
OH, YOU... THING!
SO? TELL ME! THEN WHAT DID YOU DO?
WHAT COULD I DO?
I KISSED HIM...BACK.
YOU DIDN'T!
I DID!
YOU REALLY DID?!

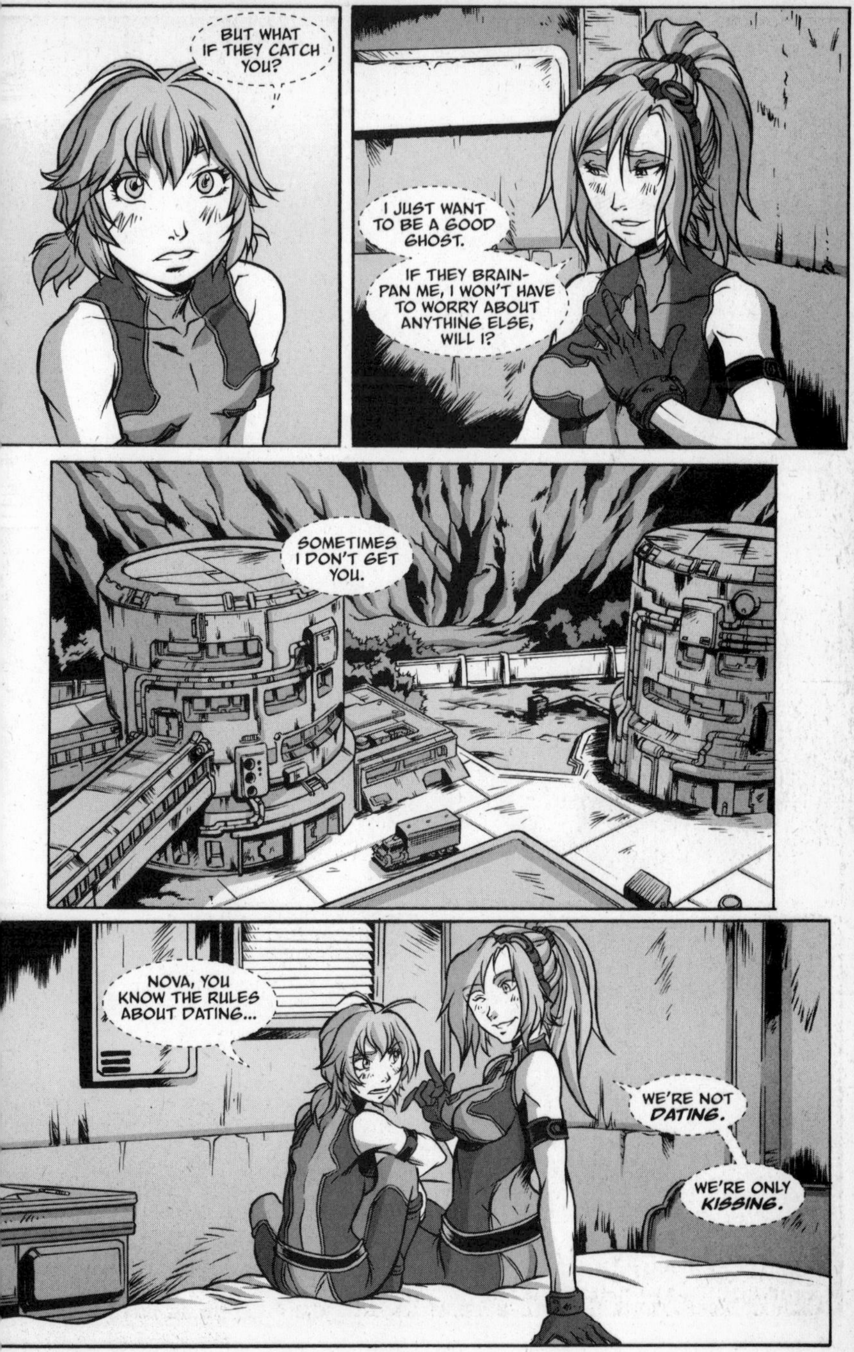
BUT WHAT IF THEY CATCH YOU?
I JUST WANT TO BE A GOOD GHOST.
IF THEY BRAIN-PAN ME, I WON'T HAVE TO WORRY ABOUT ANYTHING ELSE, WILL I?
SOMETIMES I DON'T GET YOU.
NOVA, YOU KNOW THE RULES ABOUT DATING...
WE'RE NOT *DATING*.
WE'RE ONLY *KISSING*.

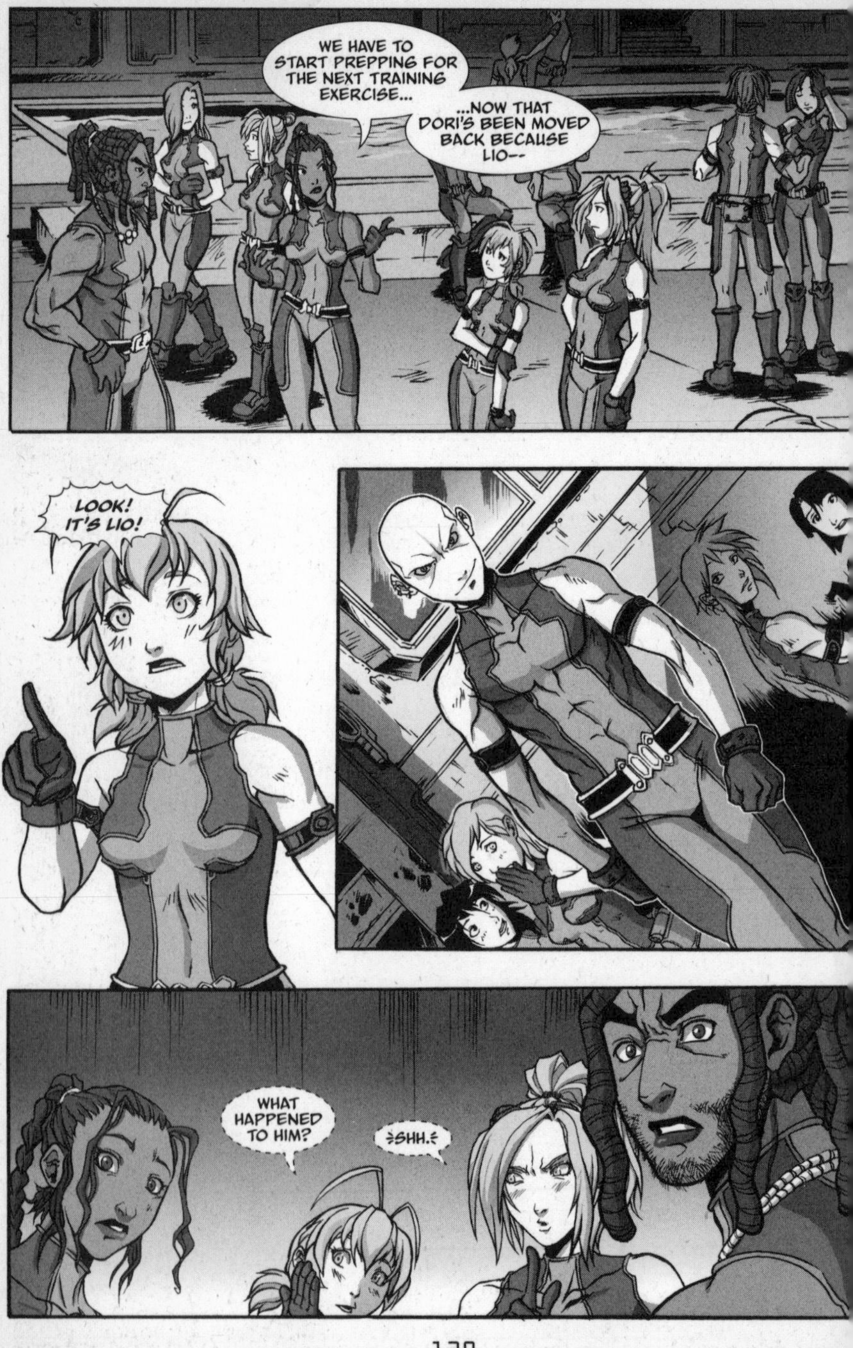
WE HAVE TO START PREPPING FOR THE NEXT TRAINING EXERCISE...
...NOW THAT DORI'S BEEN MOVED BACK BECAUSE LIO--
LOOK! IT'S LIO!
WHAT HAPPENED TO HIM?
SHH.

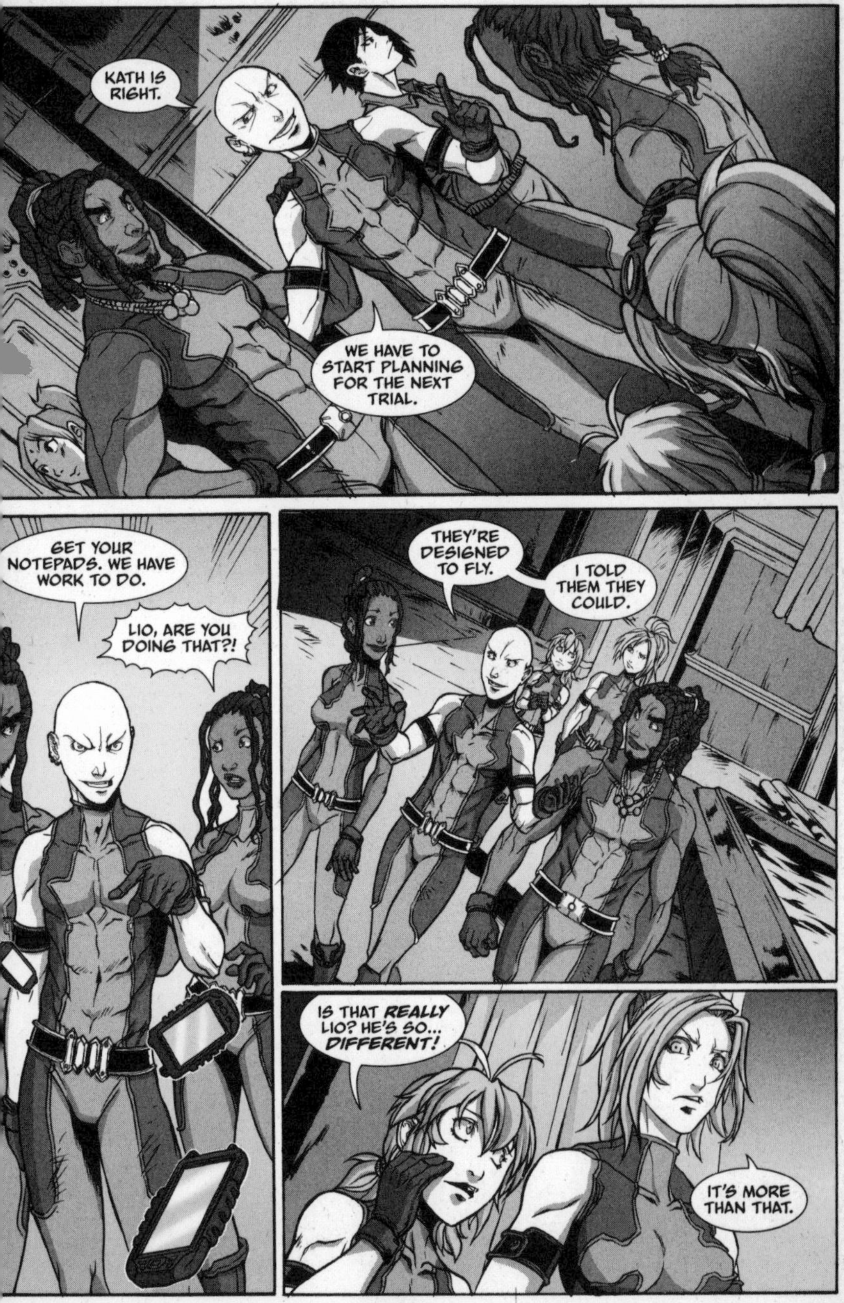
KATH IS RIGHT.
WE HAVE TO START PLANNING FOR THE NEXT TRIAL.
GET YOUR NOTEPADS. WE HAVE WORK TO DO.
LIO, ARE YOU DOING THAT?!
THEY'RE DESIGNED TO FLY.
I TOLD THEM THEY COULD.
IS THAT *REALLY* LIO? HE'S SO... *DIFFERENT!*
IT'S MORE THAN THAT.

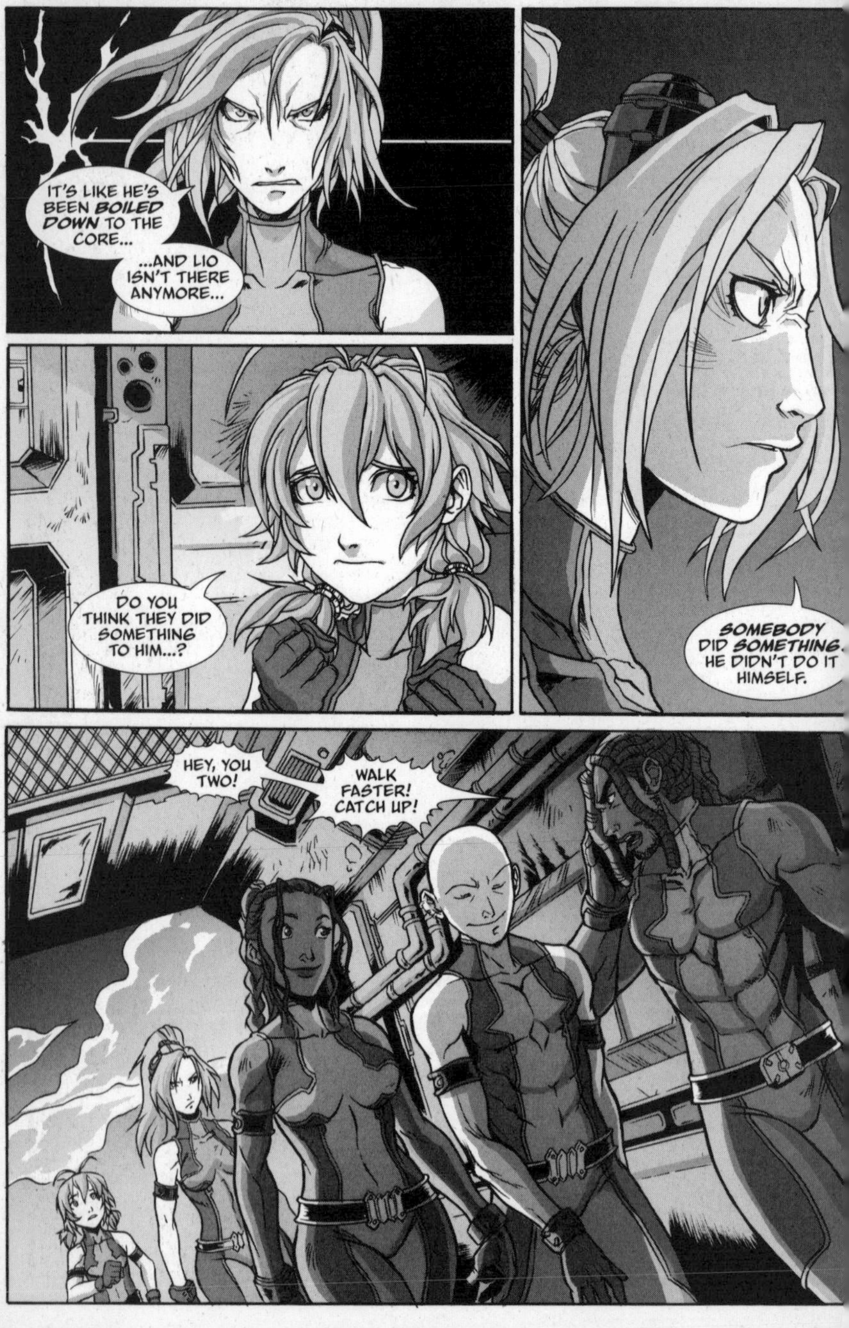

IT'S LIKE HE'S BEEN BOILED DOWN TO THE CORE...
...AND LIO ISN'T THERE ANYMORE...
DO YOU THINK THEY DID SOMETHING TO HIM...?
SOMEBODY DID SOMETHING. HE DIDN'T DO IT HIMSELF.
HEY, YOU TWO!
WALK FASTER! CATCH UP!

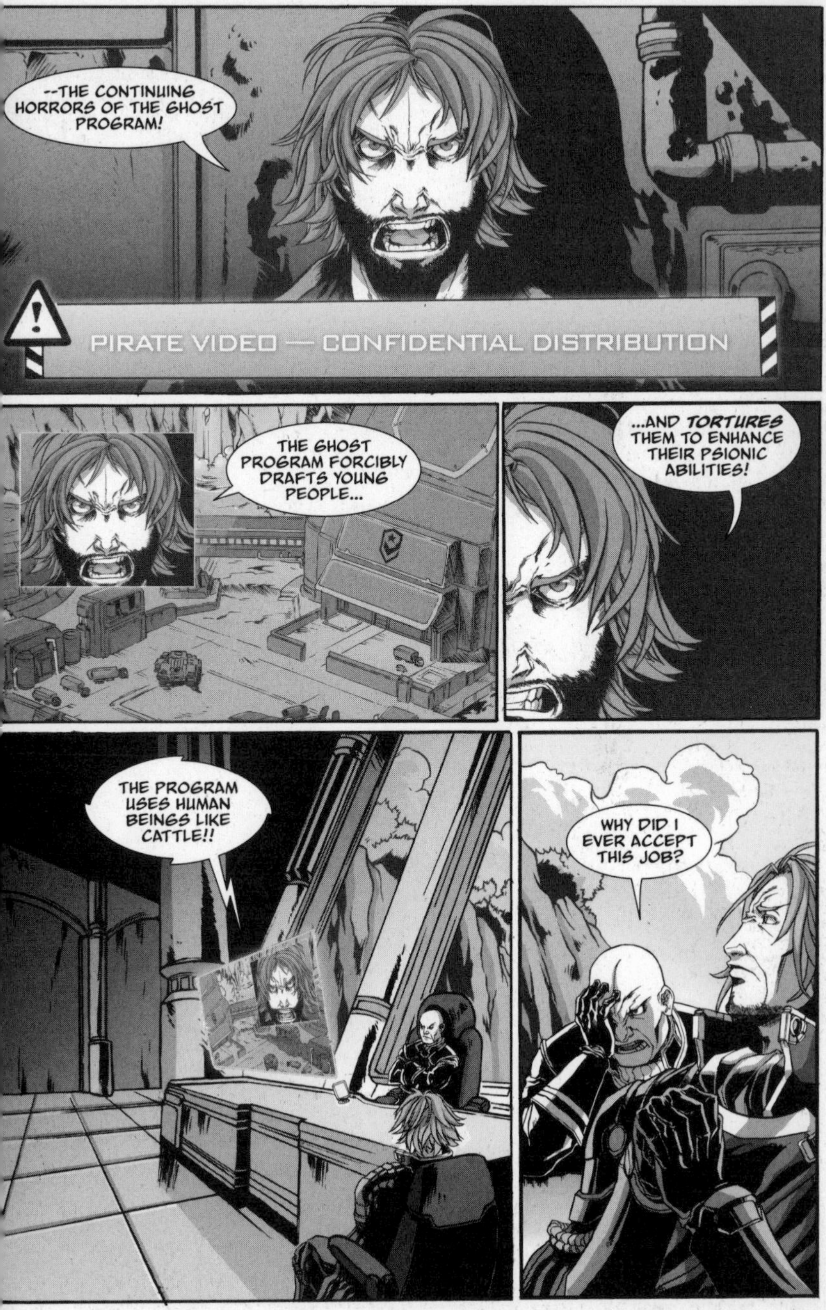
--THE CONTINUING HORRORS OF THE GHOST PROGRAM!
PIRATE VIDEO — CONFIDENTIAL DISTRIBUTION
THE GHOST PROGRAM FORCIBLY DRAFTS YOUNG PEOPLE...
...AND TORTURES THEM TO ENHANCE THEIR PSIONIC ABILITIES!
THE PROGRAM USES HUMAN BEINGS LIKE CATTLE!!
WHY DID I EVER ACCEPT THIS JOB?

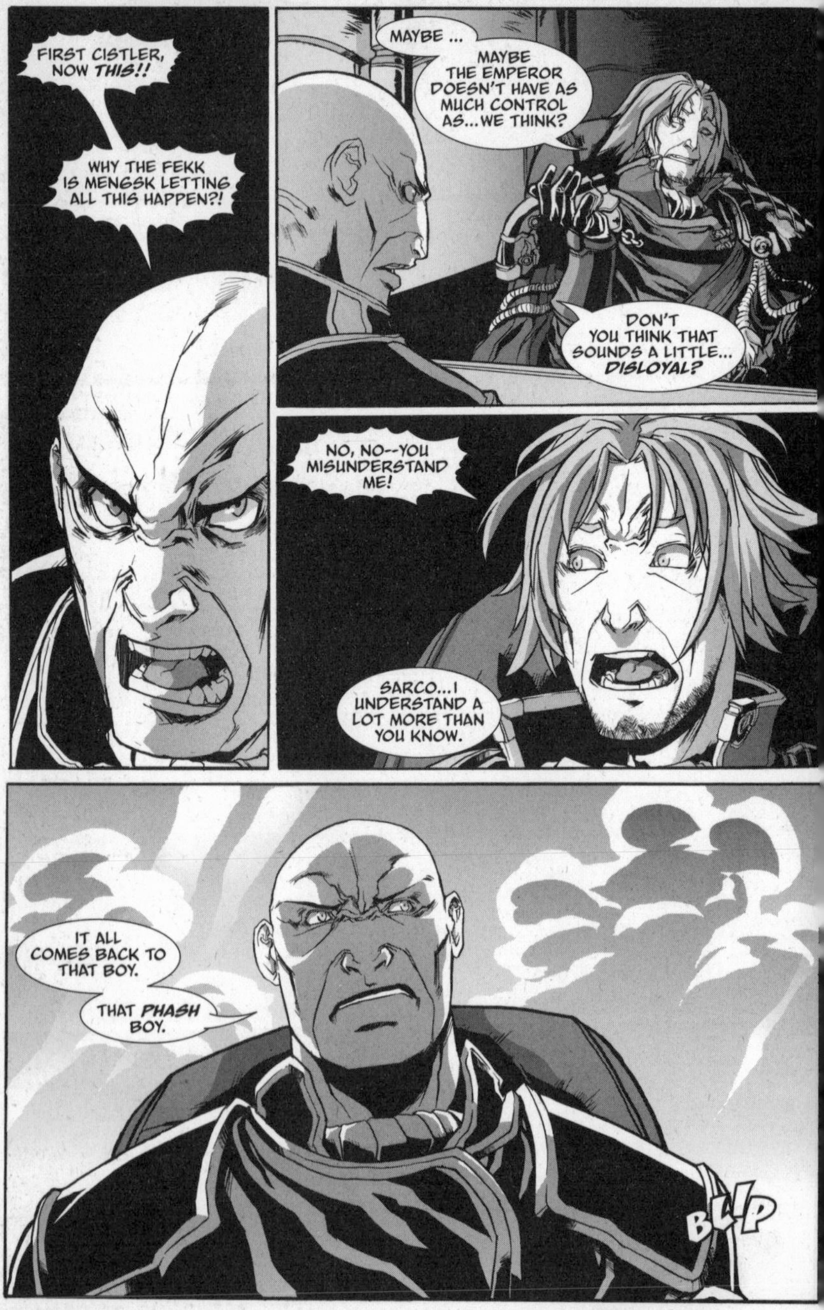
FIRST CISTLER, NOW *THIS!!*
WHY THE FEKK IS MENGSK LETTING ALL THIS HAPPEN?!
MAYBE ...
MAYBE THE EMPEROR DOESN'T HAVE AS MUCH CONTROL AS...WE THINK?
DON'T YOU THINK THAT SOUNDS A LITTLE... *DISLOYAL?*
NO, NO--YOU MISUNDERSTAND ME!
SARCO...I UNDERSTAND A LOT MORE THAN YOU KNOW.
IT ALL COMES BACK TO THAT BOY.
THAT *PHASH* BOY.
BLIP

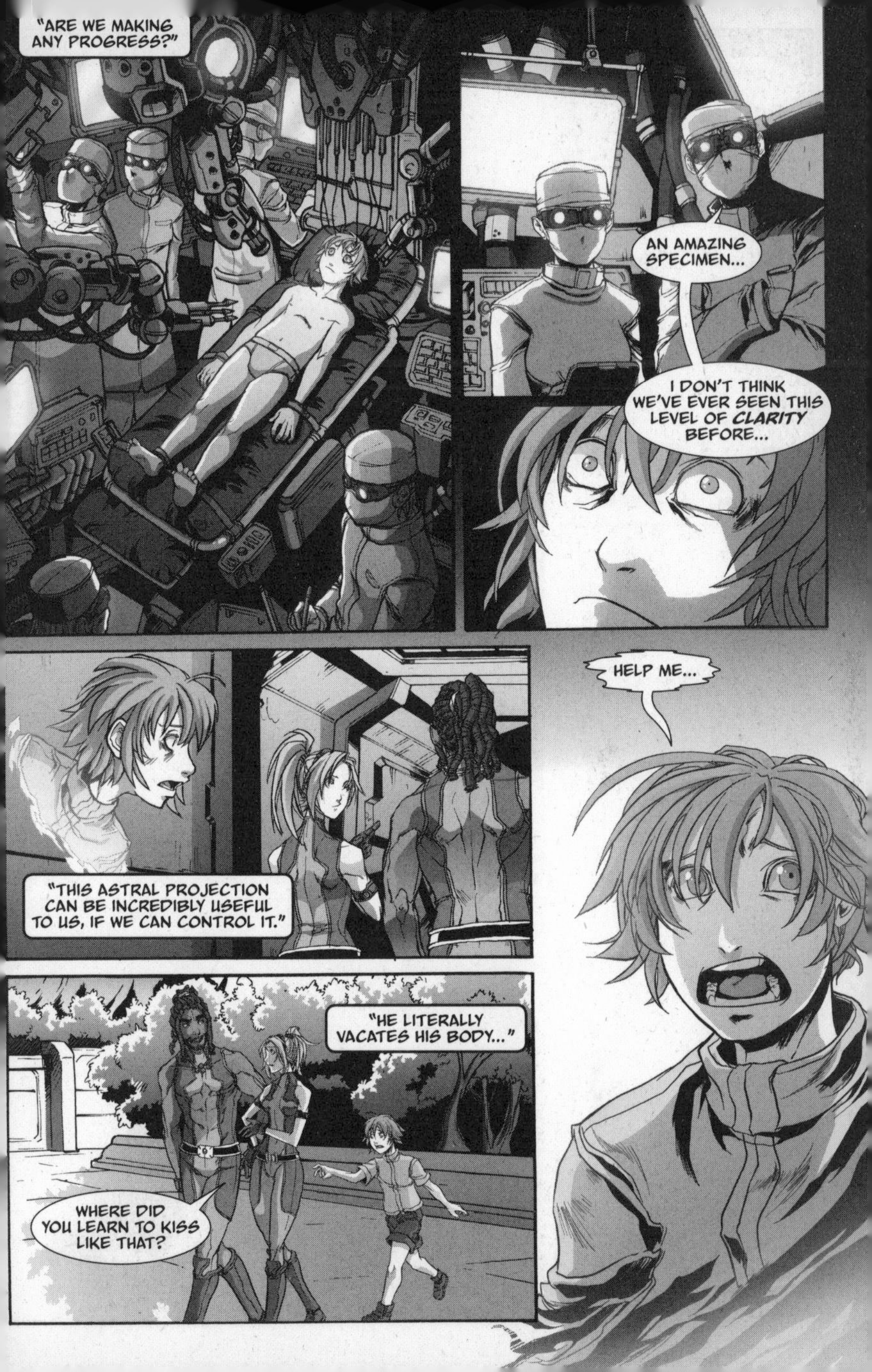
"ARE WE MAKING ANY PROGRESS?"
AN AMAZING SPECIMEN...
I DON'T THINK WE'VE EVER SEEN THIS LEVEL OF CLARITY BEFORE...
HELP ME...
"THIS ASTRAL PROJECTION CAN BE INCREDIBLY USEFUL TO US, IF WE CAN CONTROL IT."
"HE LITERALLY VACATES HIS BODY..."
WHERE DID YOU LEARN TO KISS LIKE THAT?

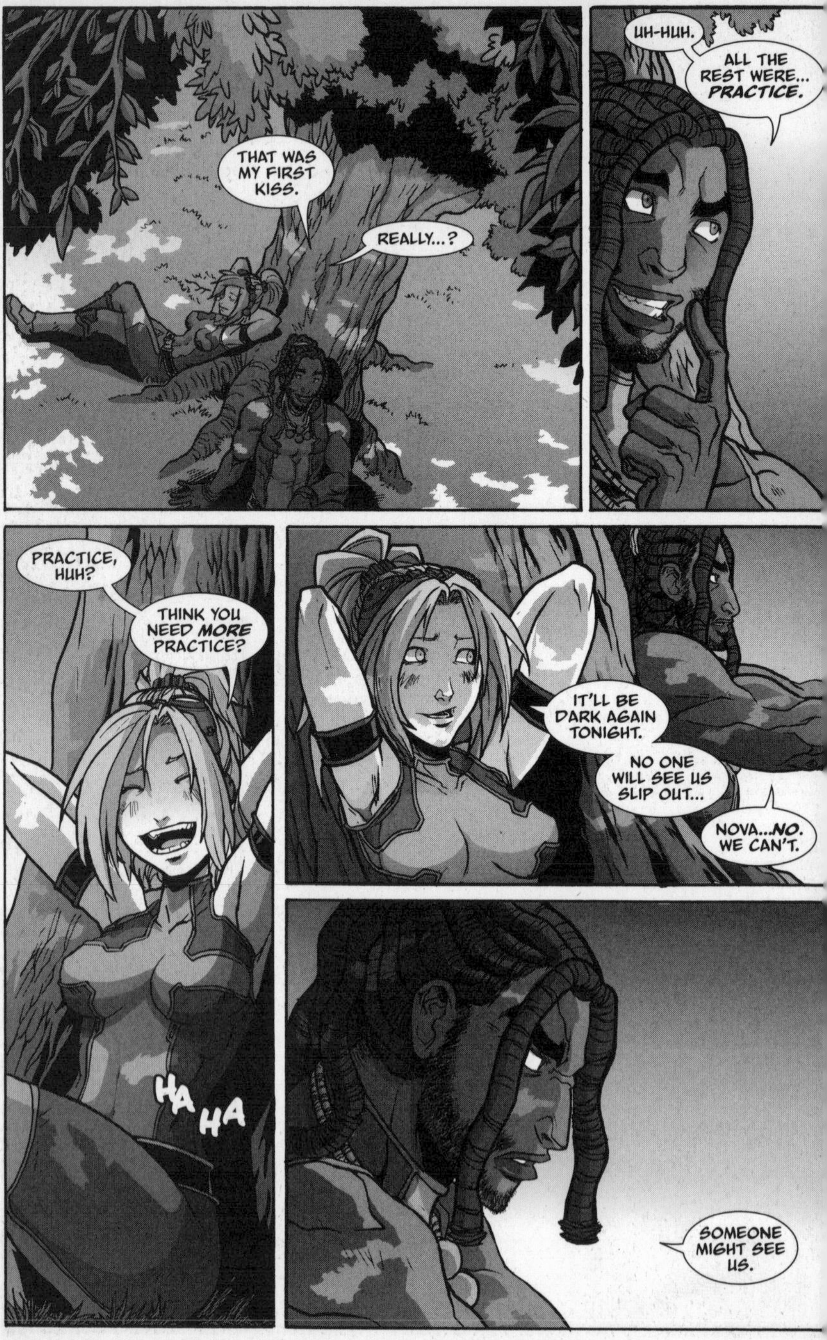
THAT WAS MY FIRST KISS.
REALLY...?
UH-HUH.
ALL THE REST WERE... PRACTICE.
PRACTICE, HUH?
THINK YOU NEED MORE PRACTICE?
HA HA
IT'LL BE DARK AGAIN TONIGHT.
NO ONE WILL SEE US SLIP OUT...
NOVA...NO. WE CAN'T.
SOMEONE MIGHT SEE US.

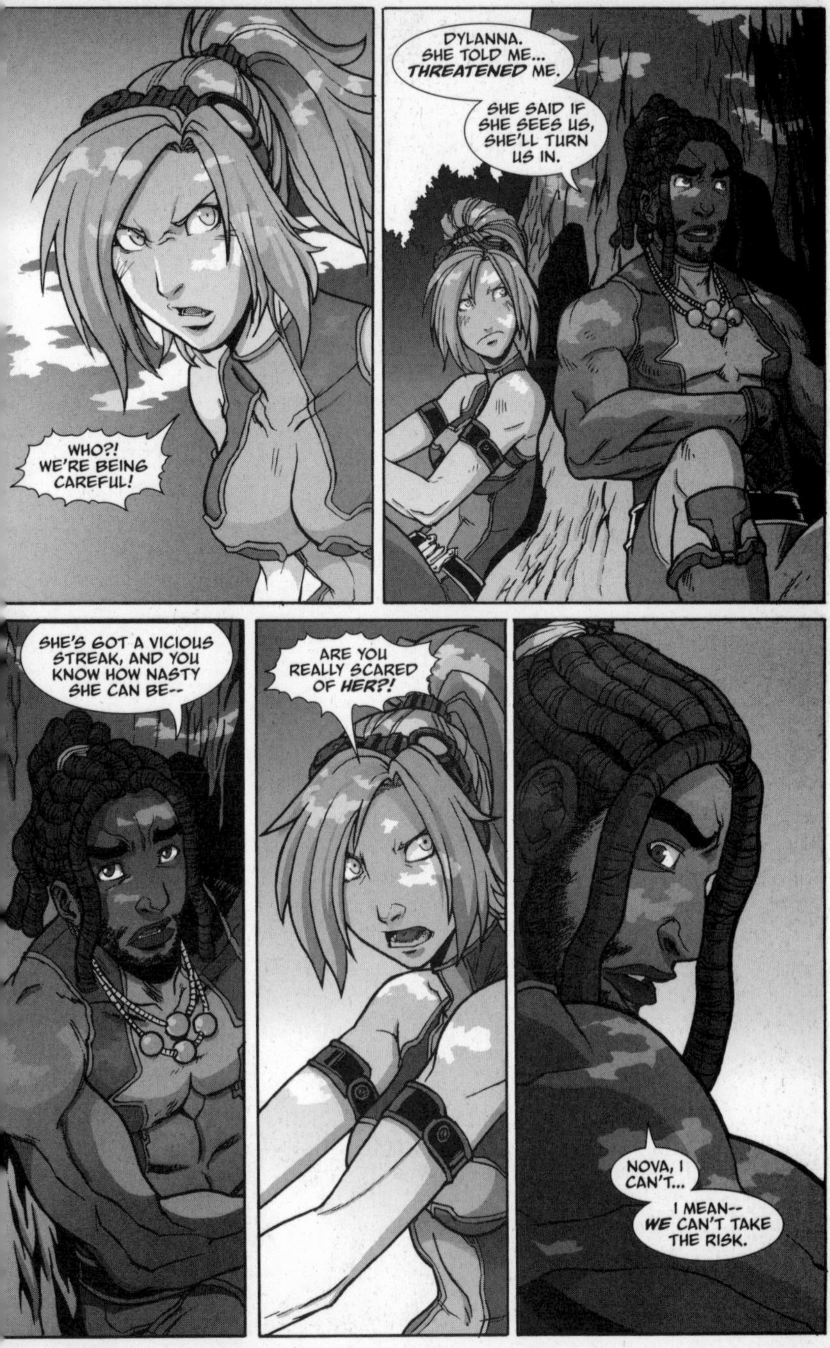
WHO?! WE'RE BEING CAREFUL!
DYLANNA. SHE TOLD ME... THREATENED ME.
SHE SAID IF SHE SEES US, SHE'LL TURN US IN.
SHE'S GOT A VICIOUS STREAK, AND YOU KNOW HOW NASTY SHE CAN BE--
ARE YOU REALLY SCARED OF HER?!
NOVA, I CAN'T...
I MEAN-- WE CAN'T TAKE THE RISK.

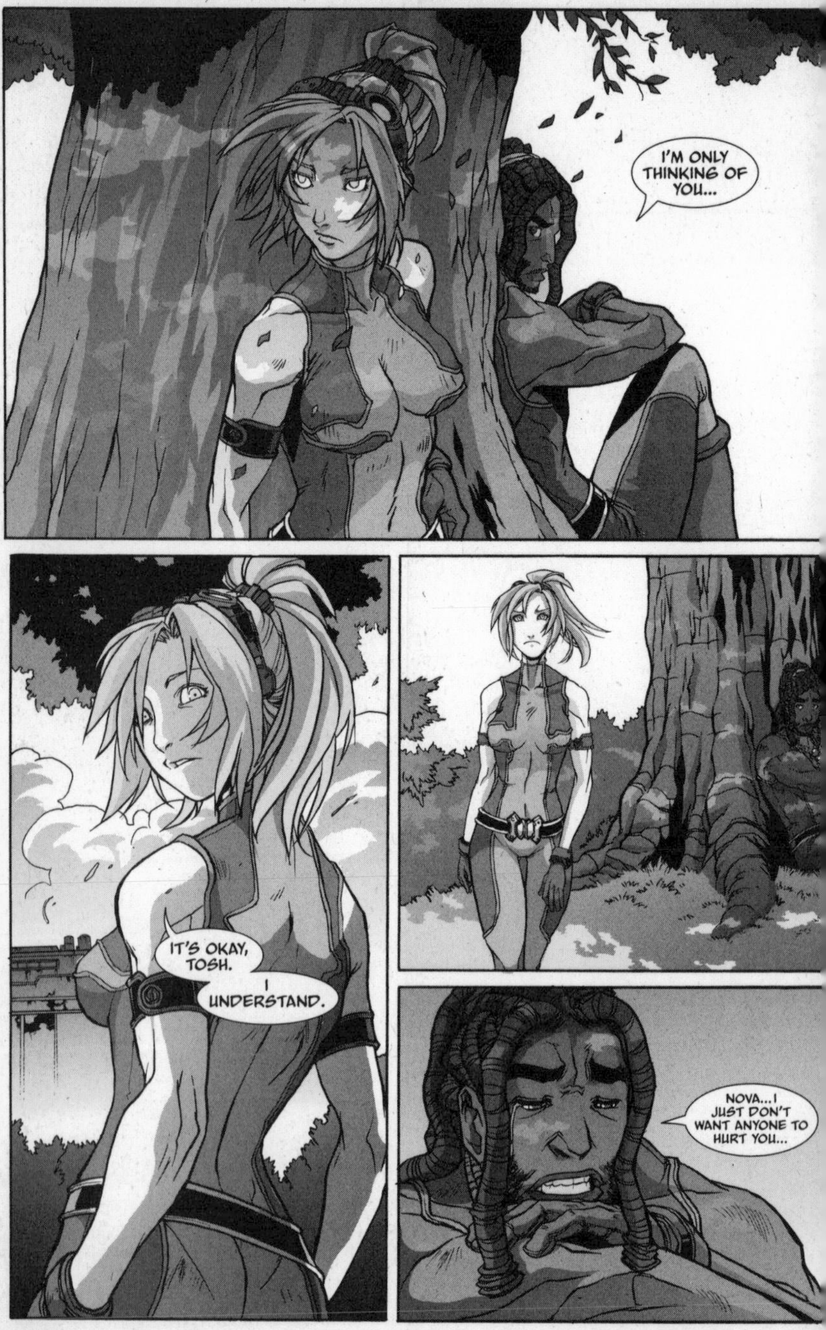
I'M ONLY THINKING OF YOU...
IT'S OKAY, TOSH.
I UNDERSTAND.
NOVA...I JUST DON'T WANT ANYONE TO HURT YOU...

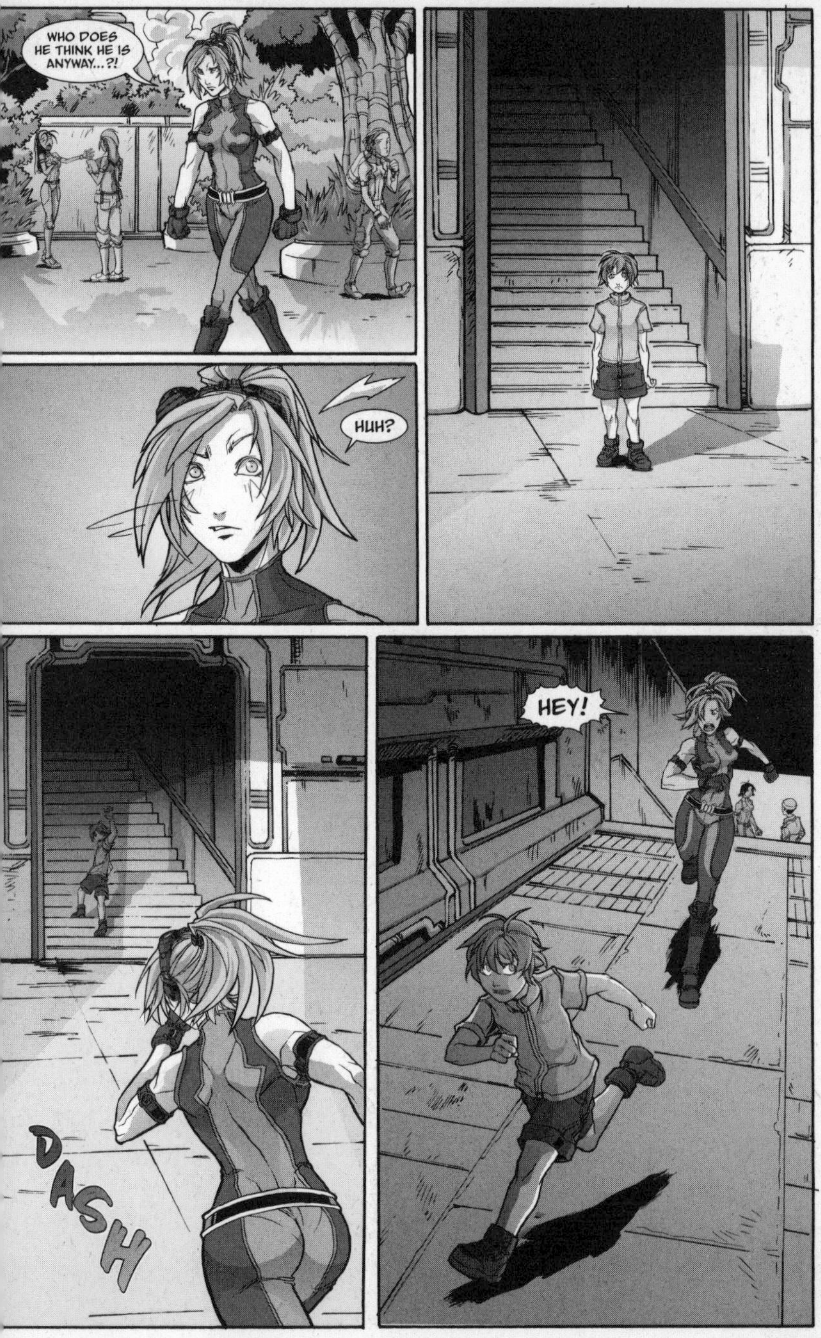
WHO DOES HE THINK HE IS ANYWAY...?!
HUH?
HEY!
DASH

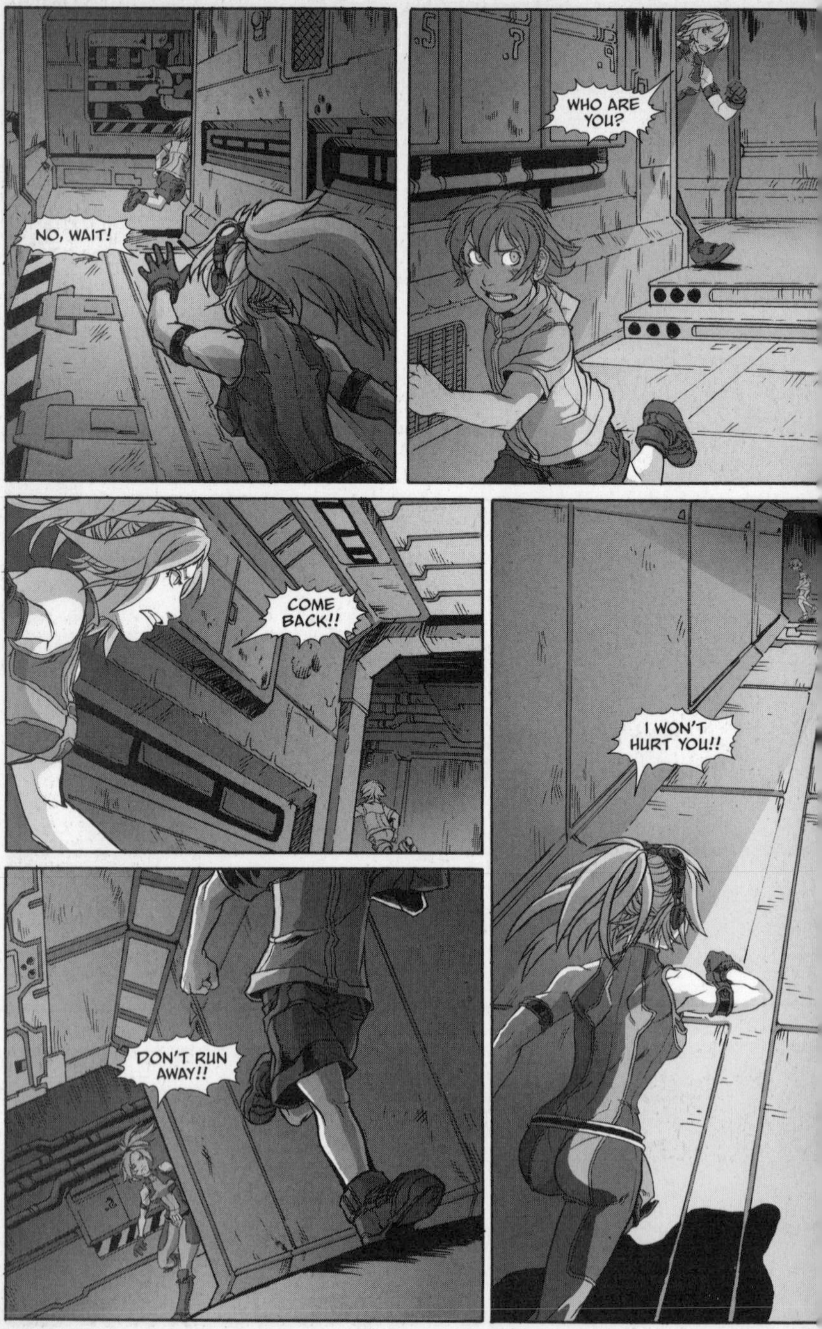
NO, WAIT!
WHO ARE YOU?
COME BACK!!
I WON'T HURT YOU!!
DON'T RUN AWAY!!

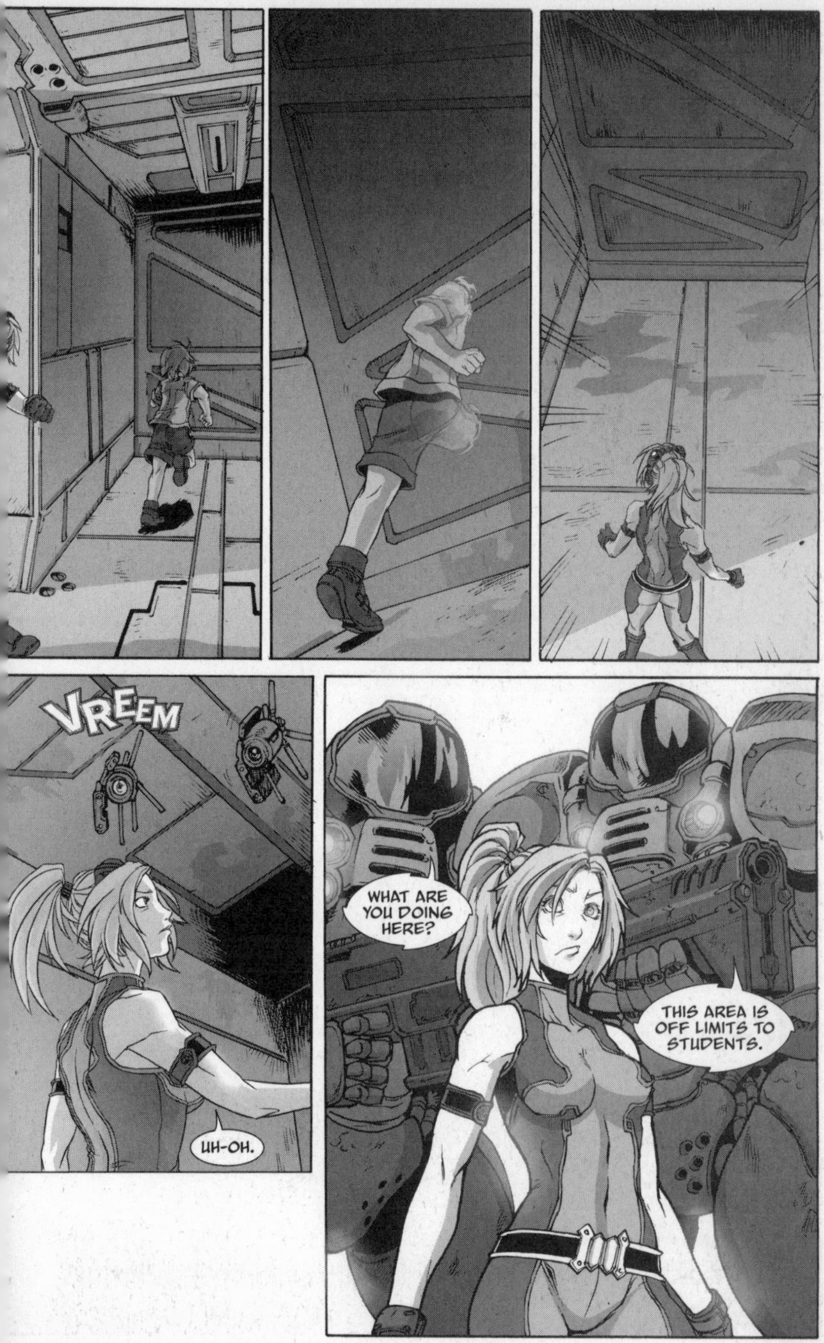
VREEM
UH-OH.
WHAT ARE YOU DOING HERE?
THIS AREA IS OFF LIMITS TO STUDENTS.

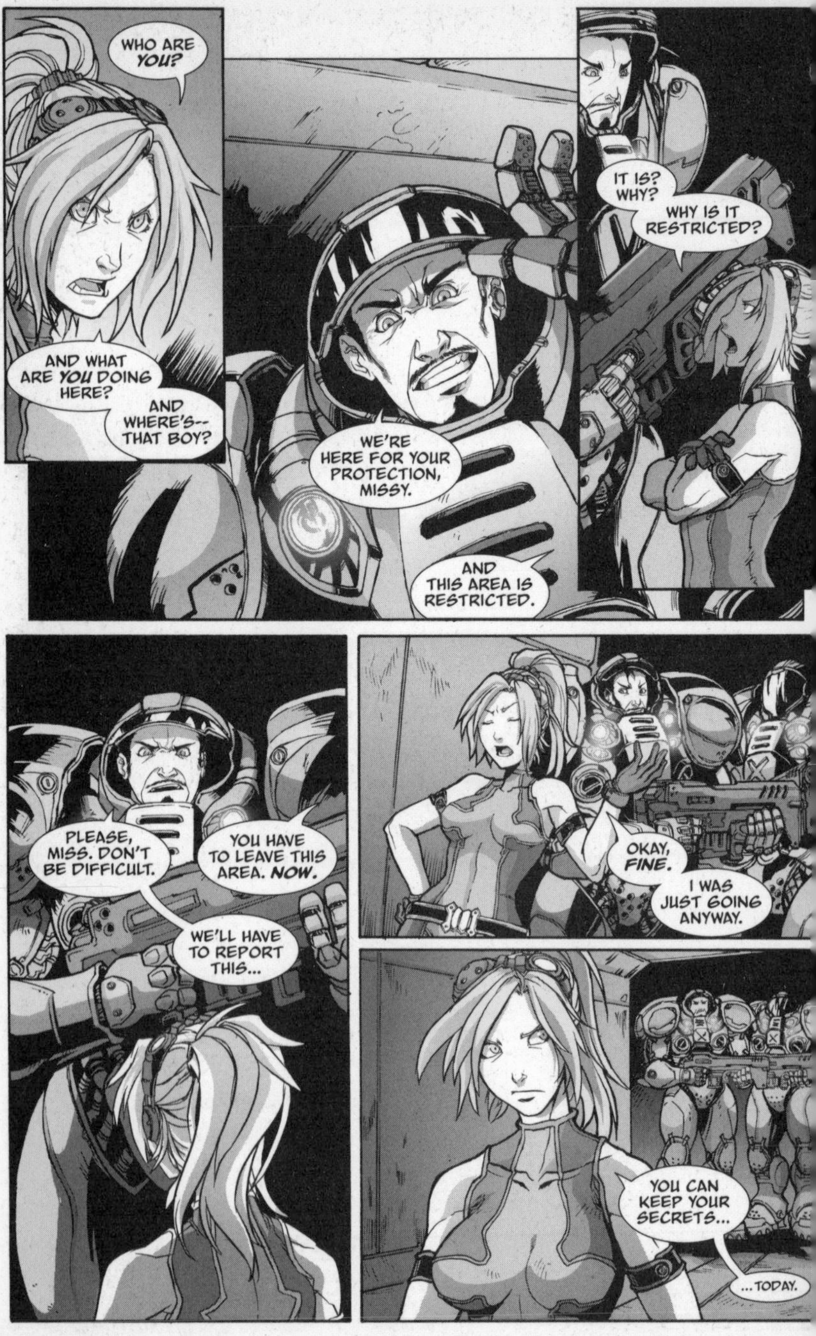
WHO ARE YOU?
AND WHAT ARE YOU DOING HERE?
AND WHERE'S-- THAT BOY?
WE'RE HERE FOR YOUR PROTECTION, MISSY.
AND THIS AREA IS RESTRICTED.
IT IS? WHY?
WHY IS IT RESTRICTED?
PLEASE, MISS. DON'T BE DIFFICULT.
YOU HAVE TO LEAVE THIS AREA. NOW.
WE'LL HAVE TO REPORT THIS...
OKAY, FINE.
I WAS JUST GOING ANYWAY.
YOU CAN KEEP YOUR SECRETS...
...TODAY.

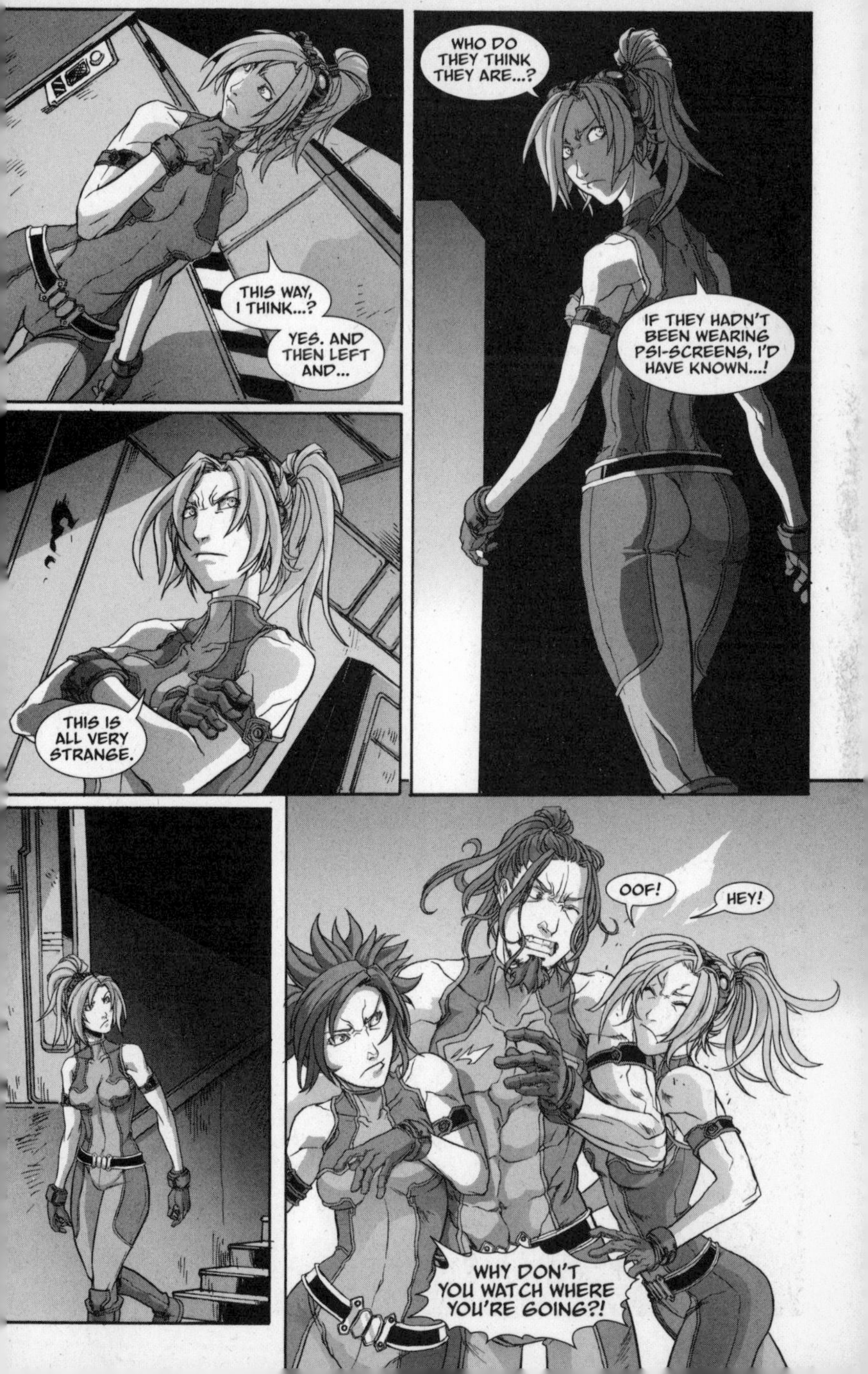
THIS WAY, I THINK...?
YES. AND THEN LEFT AND...
WHO DO THEY THINK THEY ARE...?
IF THEY HADN'T BEEN WEARING PSI-SCREENS, I'D HAVE KNOWN...!
THIS IS ALL VERY STRANGE.
OOF!
HEY!
WHY DON'T YOU WATCH WHERE YOU'RE GOING?!

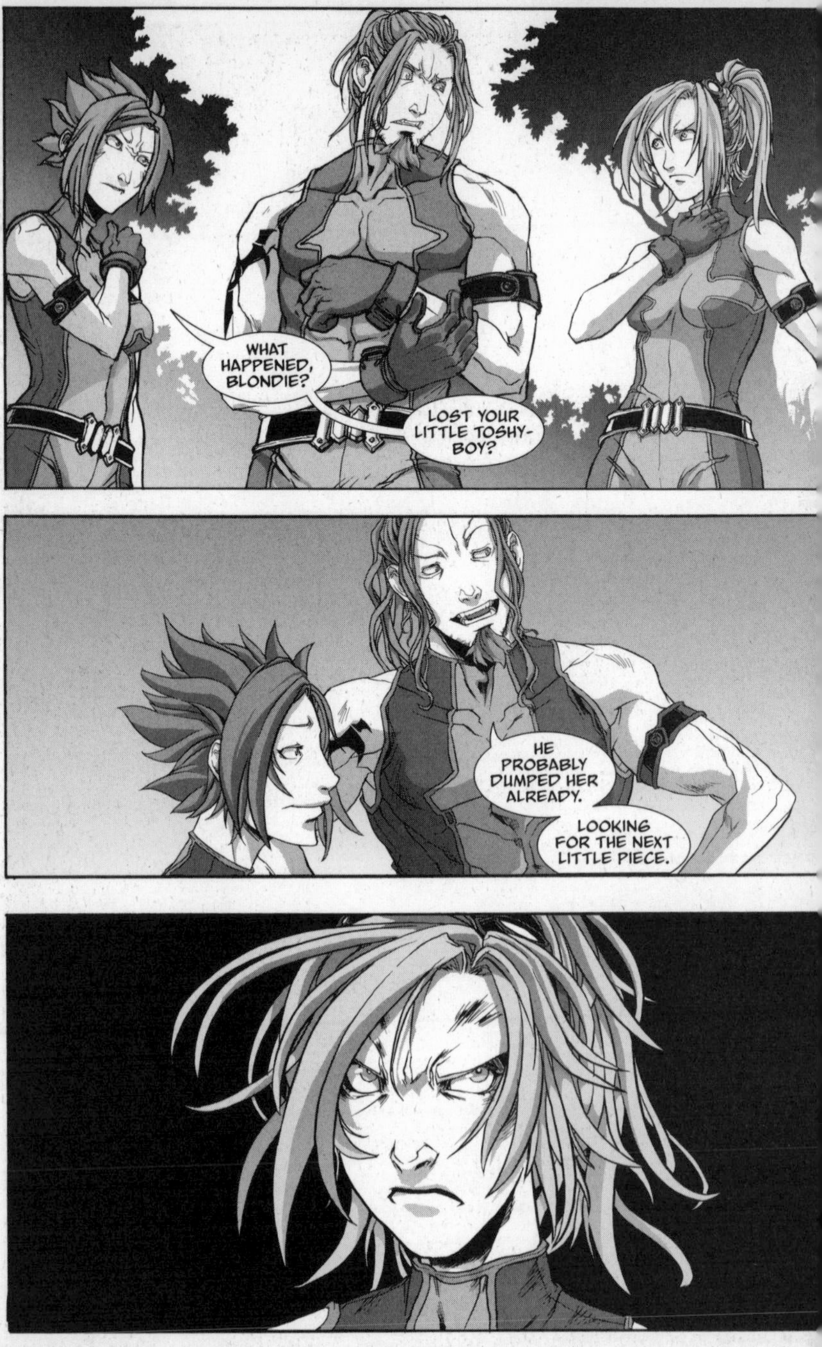
WHAT HAPPENED, BLONDIE?
LOST YOUR LITTLE TOSHY-BOY?
HE PROBABLY DUMPED HER ALREADY.
LOOKING FOR THE NEXT LITTLE PIECE.

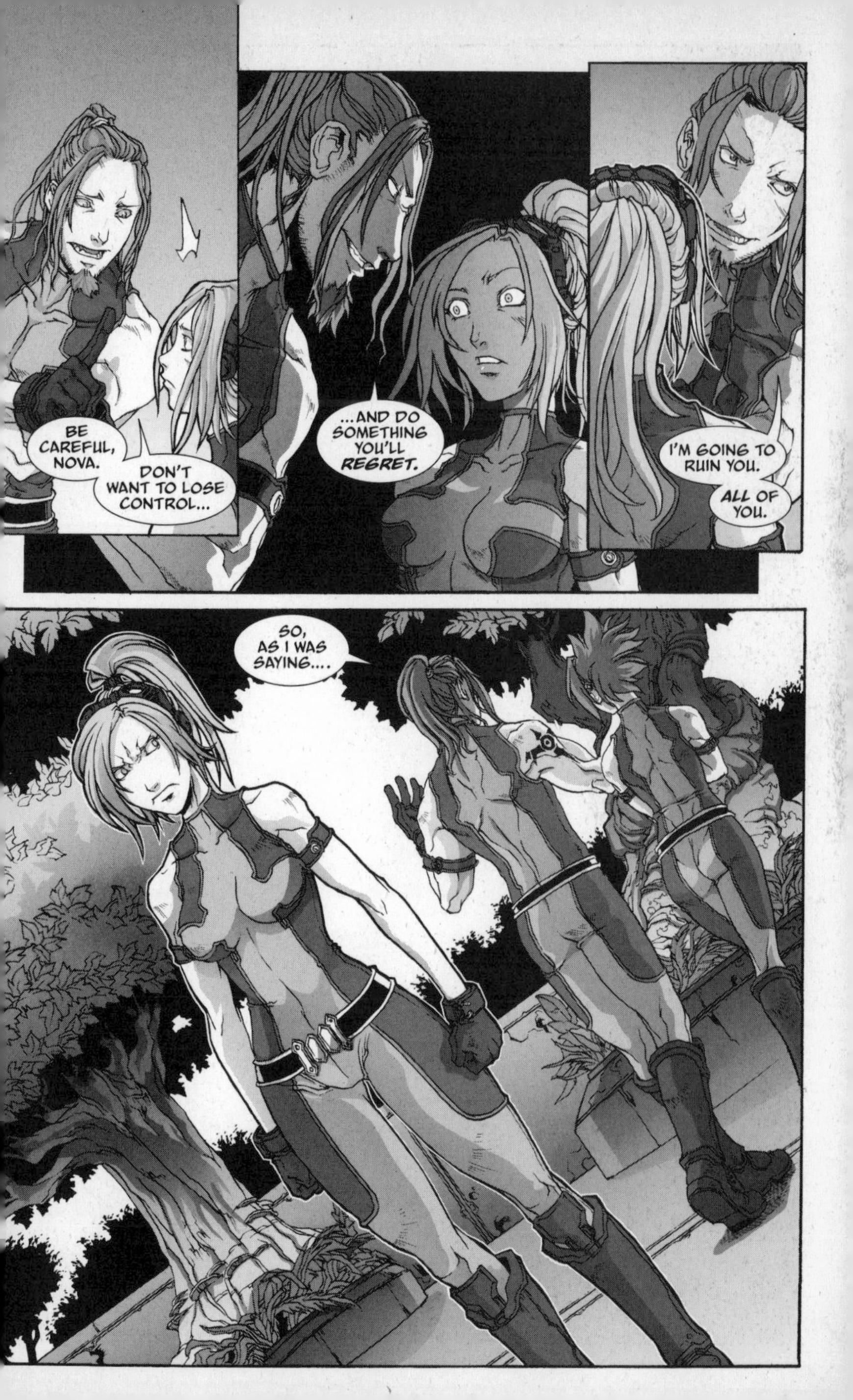
BE CAREFUL, NOVA.
DON'T WANT TO LOSE CONTROL...
...AND DO SOMETHING YOU'LL REGRET.
I'M GOING TO RUIN YOU.
ALL OF YOU.
SO, AS I WAS SAYING....

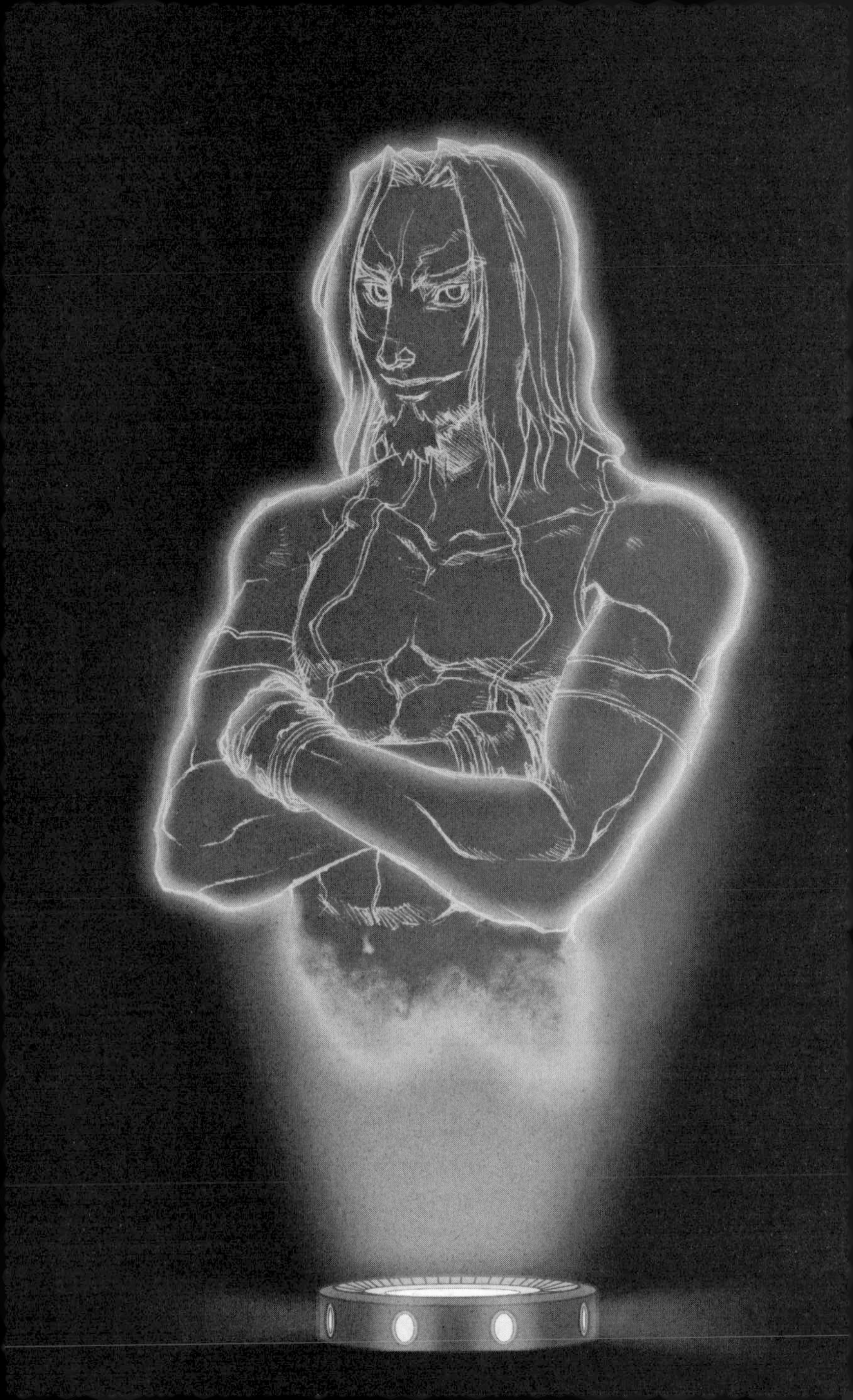

# CHAPTER 5
## DAWN OF THE DREAD

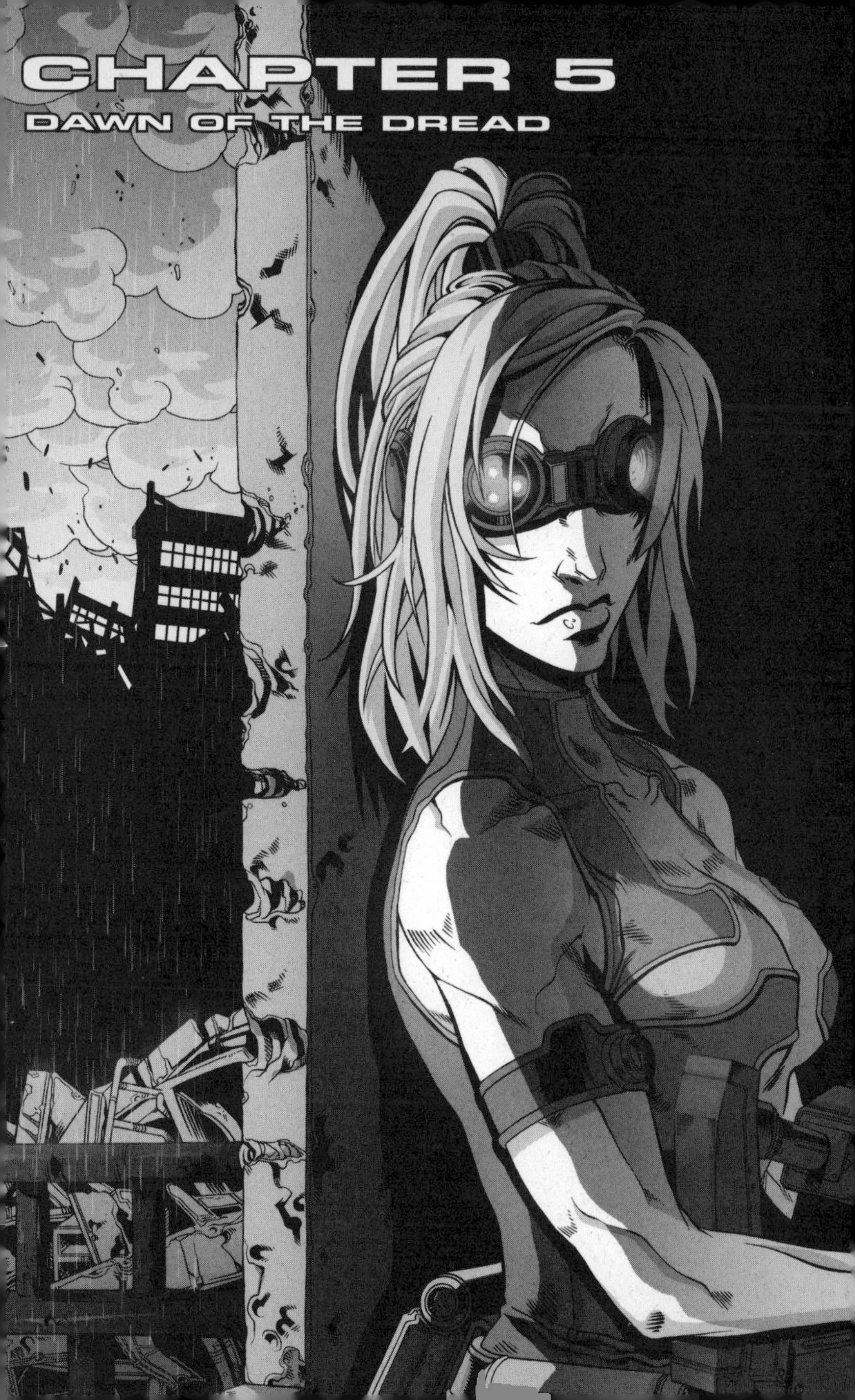

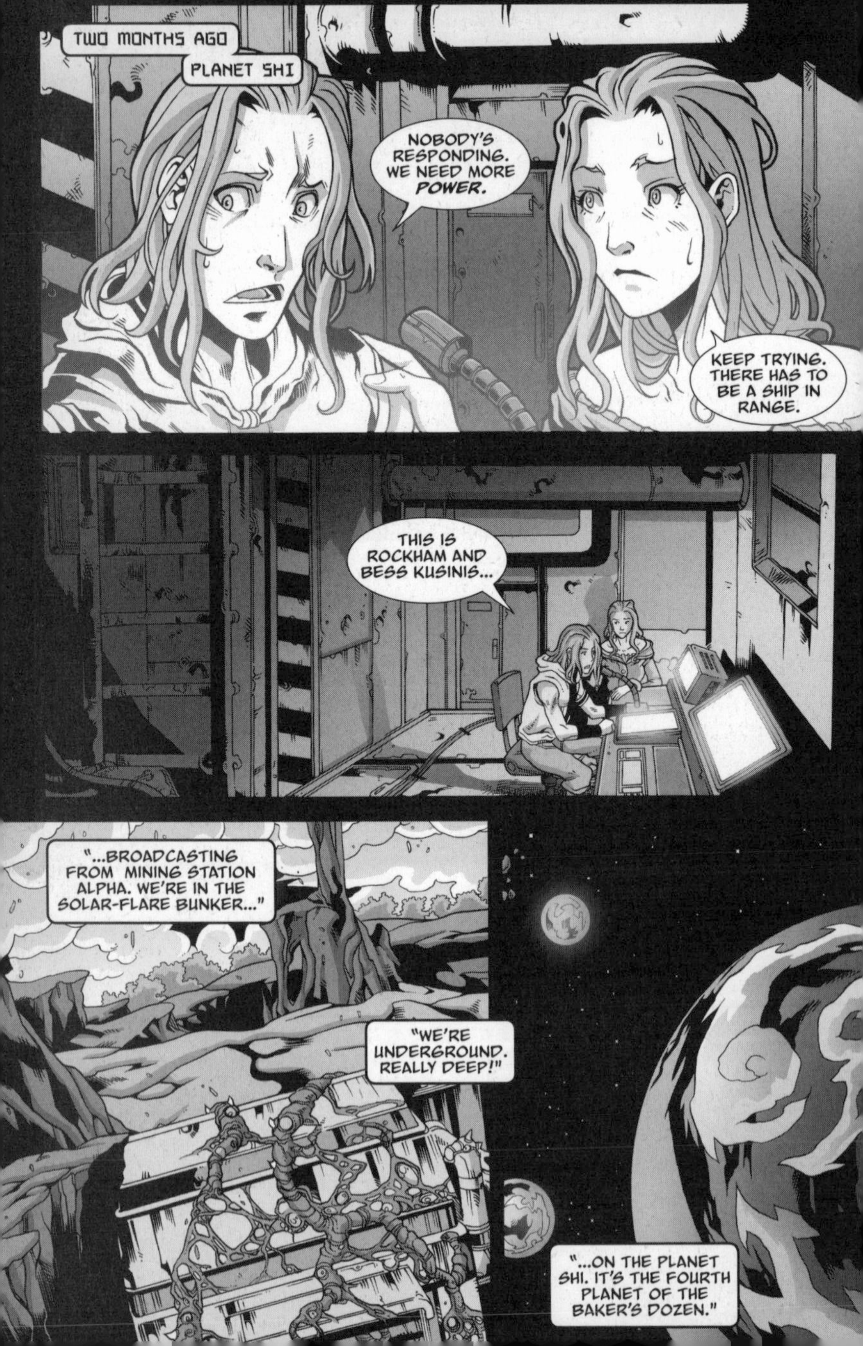
TWO MONTHS AGO
PLANET SHI
NOBODY'S RESPONDING. WE NEED MORE POWER.
KEEP TRYING. THERE HAS TO BE A SHIP IN RANGE.
THIS IS ROCKHAM AND BESS KUSINIS...
"...BROADCASTING FROM MINING STATION ALPHA. WE'RE IN THE SOLAR-FLARE BUNKER..."
"WE'RE UNDERGROUND. REALLY DEEP!"
"...ON THE PLANET SHI. IT'S THE FOURTH PLANET OF THE BAKER'S DOZEN."

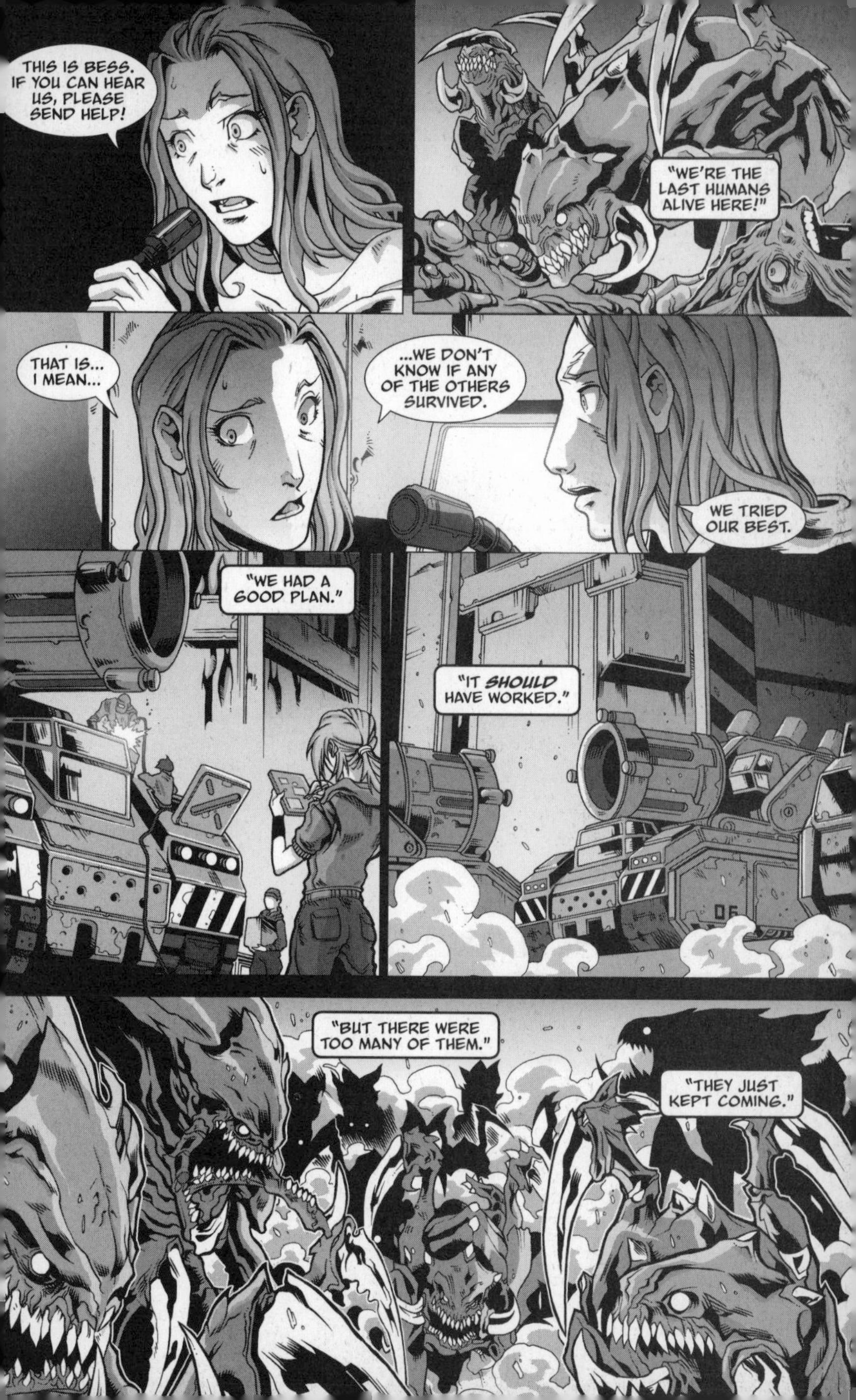
THIS IS BESS. IF YOU CAN HEAR US, PLEASE SEND HELP!
"WE'RE THE LAST HUMANS ALIVE HERE!"
THAT IS... I MEAN...
...WE DON'T KNOW IF ANY OF THE OTHERS SURVIVED.
WE TRIED OUR BEST.
"WE HAD A GOOD PLAN."
"IT SHOULD HAVE WORKED."
"BUT THERE WERE TOO MANY OF THEM."
"THEY JUST KEPT COMING."

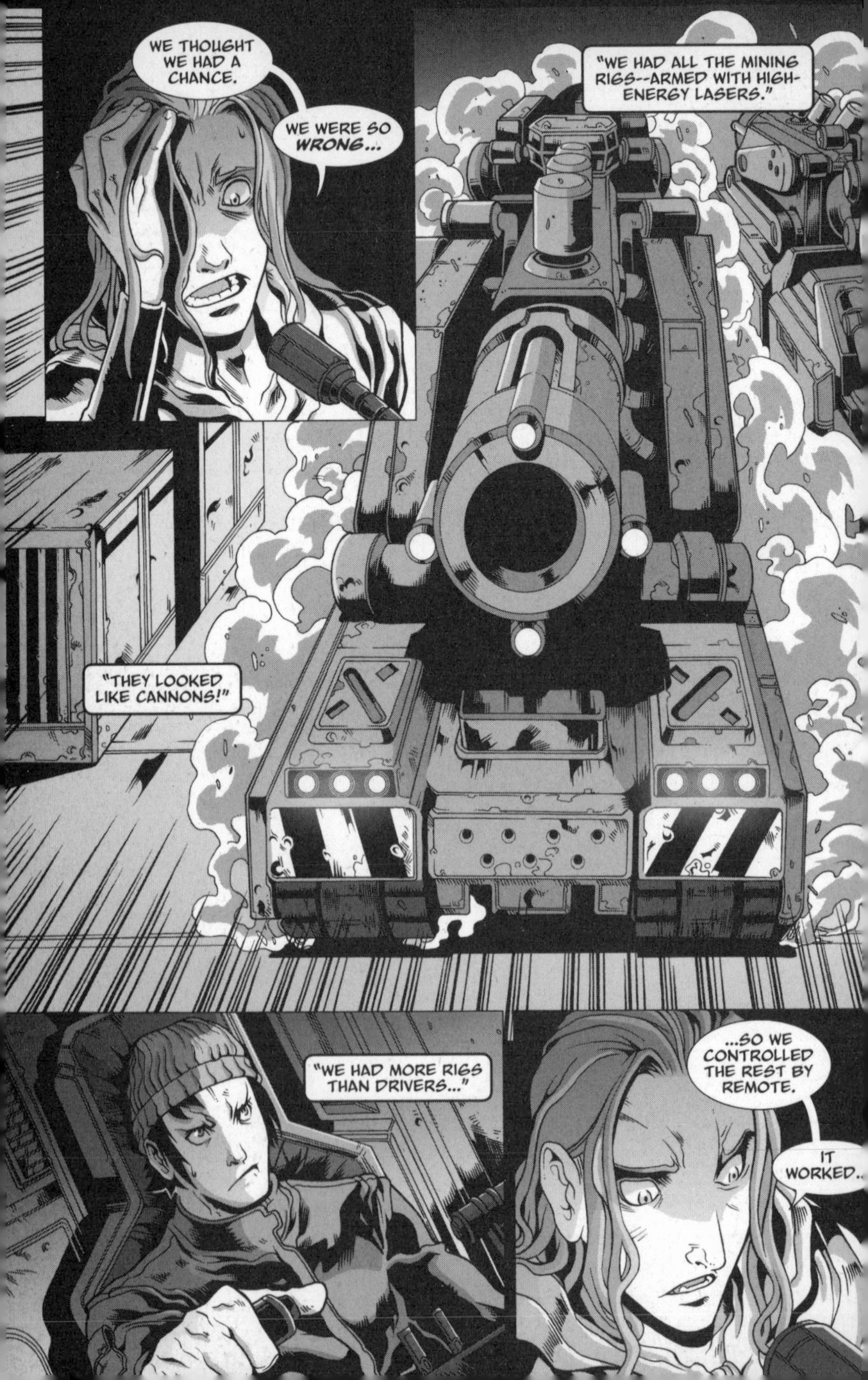
WE THOUGHT WE HAD A CHANCE.
WE WERE SO *WRONG...*
"WE HAD ALL THE MINING RIGS--ARMED WITH HIGH-ENERGY LASERS."
"THEY LOOKED LIKE CANNONS!"
"WE HAD MORE RIGS THAN DRIVERS..."
...SO WE CONTROLLED THE REST BY REMOTE.
IT WORKED...

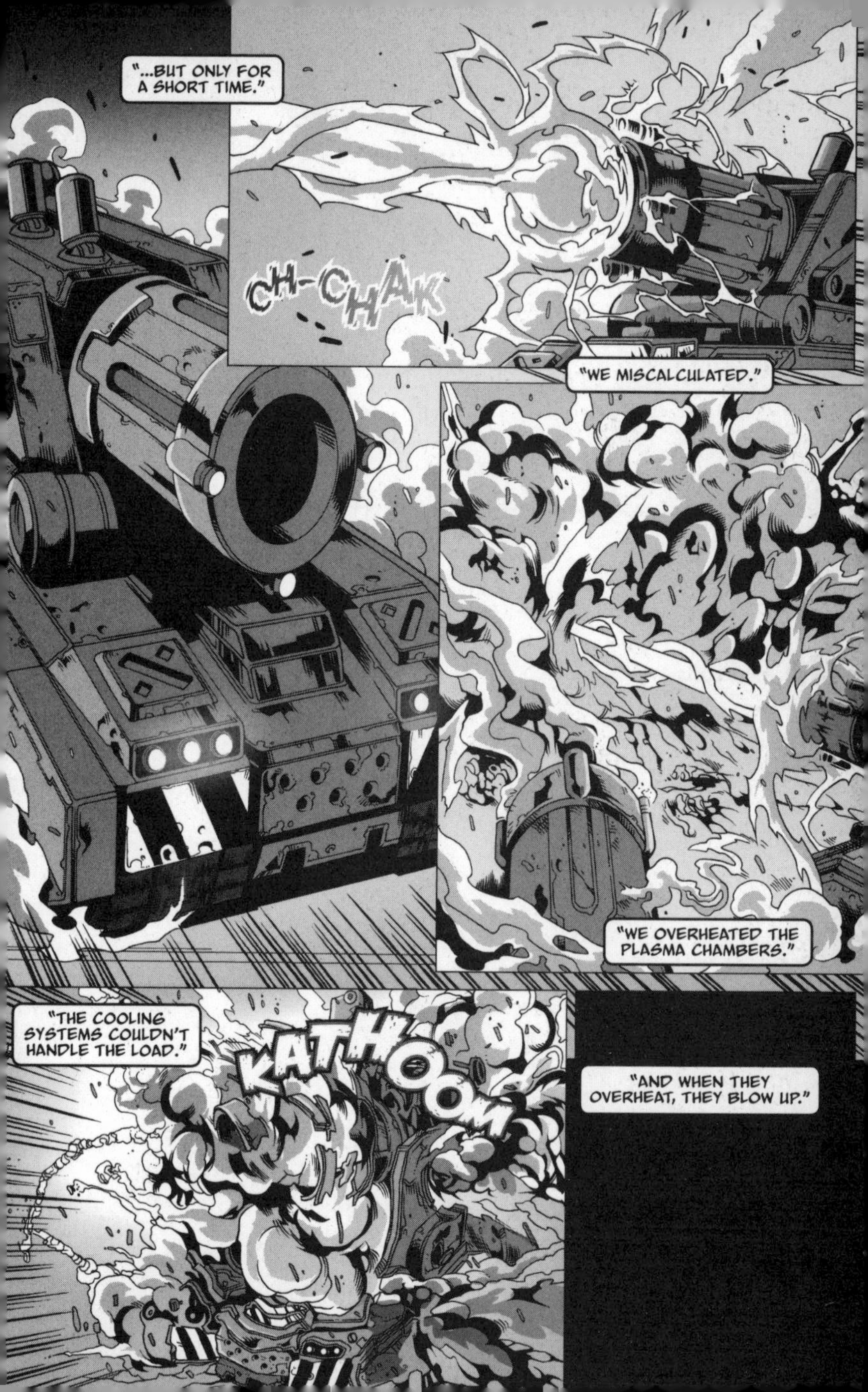
"...BUT ONLY FOR A SHORT TIME."
CH-CHAK
"WE MISCALCULATED."
"WE OVERHEATED THE PLASMA CHAMBERS."
"THE COOLING SYSTEMS COULDN'T HANDLE THE LOAD."
KATHOOOM
"AND WHEN THEY OVERHEAT, THEY BLOW UP."

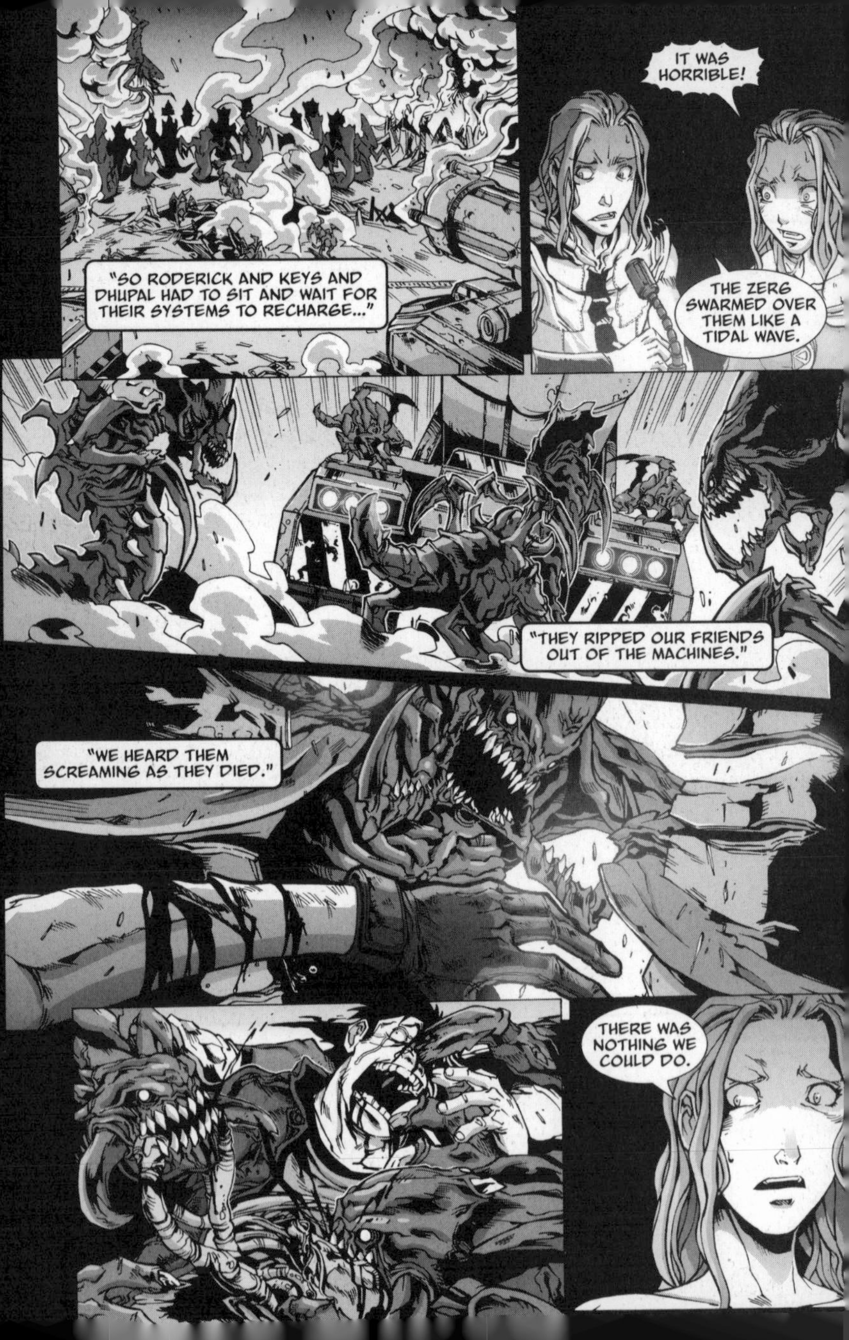
"SO RODERICK AND KEYS AND DHUPAL HAD TO SIT AND WAIT FOR THEIR SYSTEMS TO RECHARGE..."
IT WAS HORRIBLE!
THE ZERG SWARMED OVER THEM LIKE A TIDAL WAVE.
"THEY RIPPED OUR FRIENDS OUT OF THE MACHINES."
"WE HEARD THEM SCREAMING AS THEY DIED."
THERE WAS NOTHING WE COULD DO.

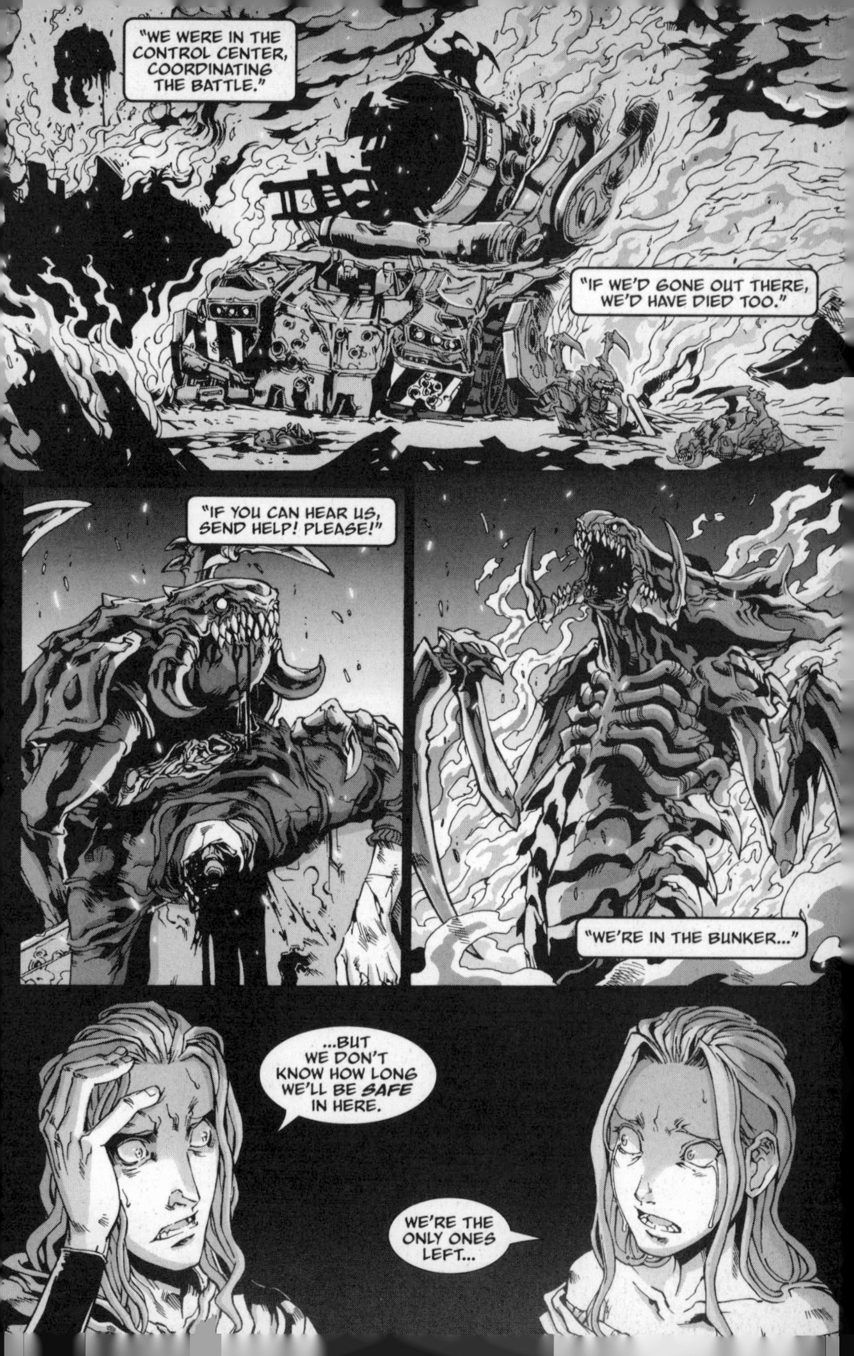
"WE WERE IN THE CONTROL CENTER, COORDINATING THE BATTLE."
"IF WE'D GONE OUT THERE, WE'D HAVE DIED TOO."
"IF YOU CAN HEAR US, SEND HELP! PLEASE!"
"WE'RE IN THE BUNKER..."
...BUT WE DON'T KNOW HOW LONG WE'LL BE *SAFE* IN HERE.
WE'RE THE ONLY ONES LEFT...

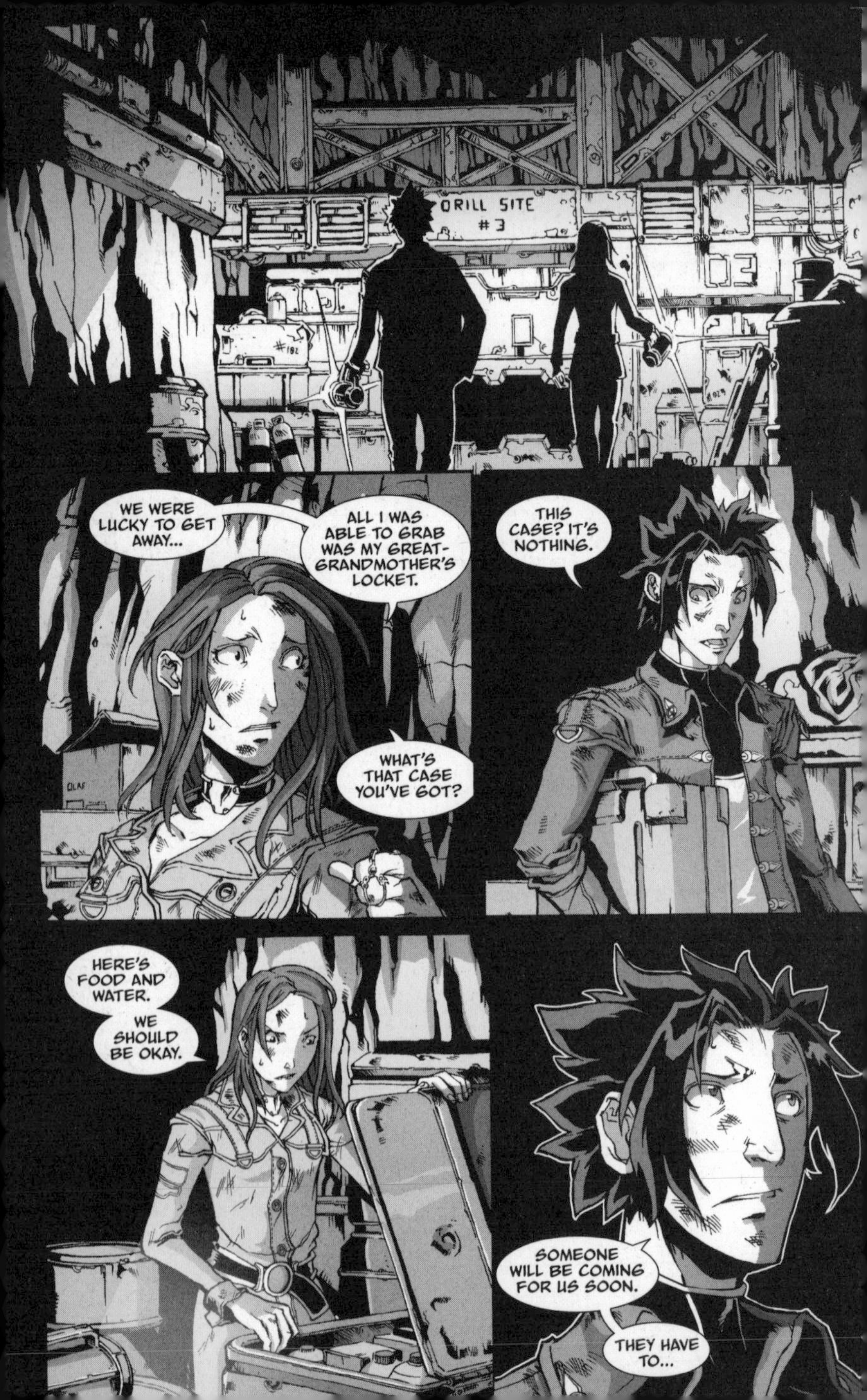
DRILL SITE
#3
03
WE WERE LUCKY TO GET AWAY...
ALL I WAS ABLE TO GRAB WAS MY GREAT-GRANDMOTHER'S LOCKET.
WHAT'S THAT CASE YOU'VE GOT?
THIS CASE? IT'S NOTHING.
HERE'S FOOD AND WATER.
WE SHOULD BE OKAY.
SOMEONE WILL BE COMING FOR US SOON.
THEY HAVE TO...

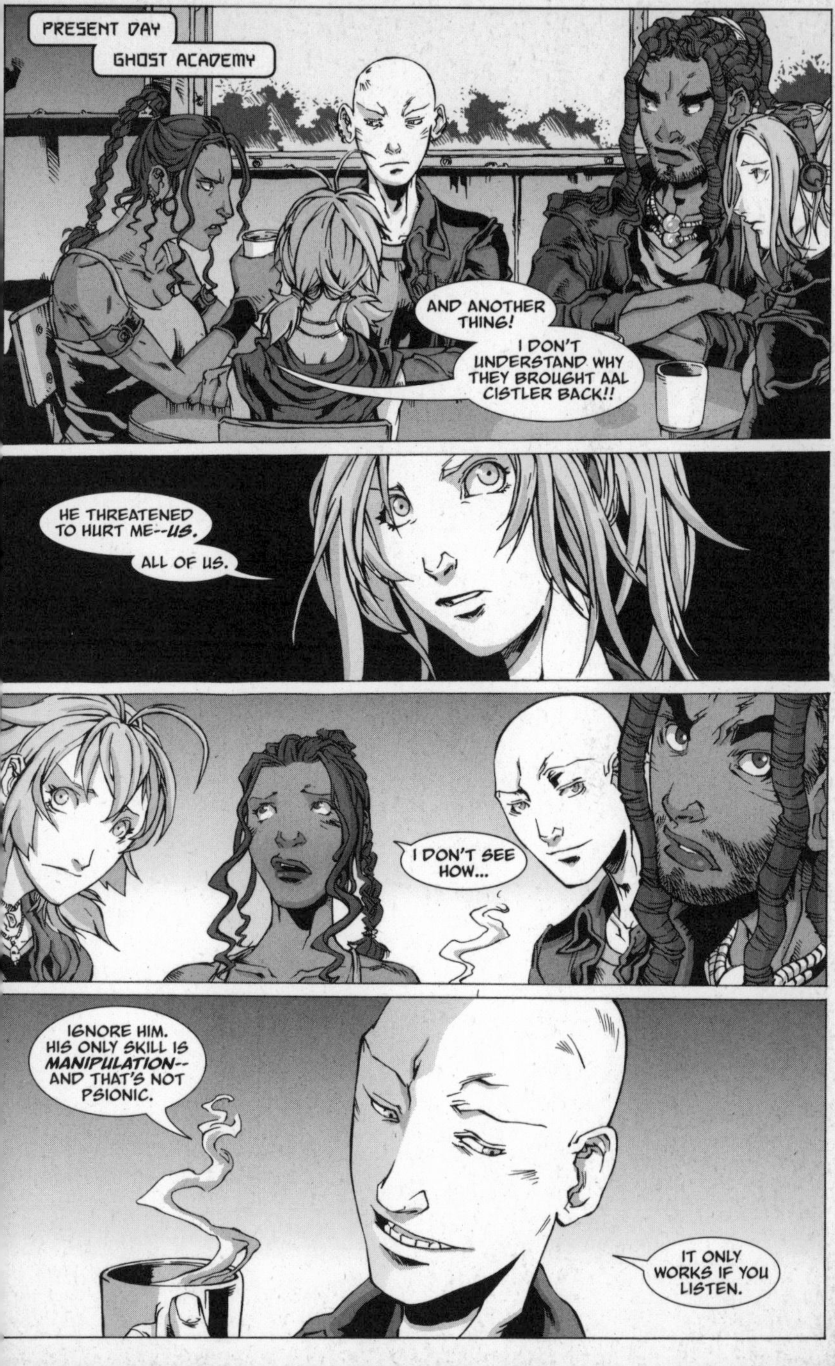
PRESENT DAY
GHOST ACADEMY
AND ANOTHER THING!
I DON'T UNDERSTAND WHY THEY BROUGHT AAL CISTLER BACK!!
HE THREATENED TO HURT ME--*US*.
ALL OF US.
I DON'T SEE HOW...
IGNORE HIM. HIS ONLY SKILL IS *MANIPULATION*--AND THAT'S NOT PSIONIC.
IT ONLY WORKS IF YOU LISTEN.

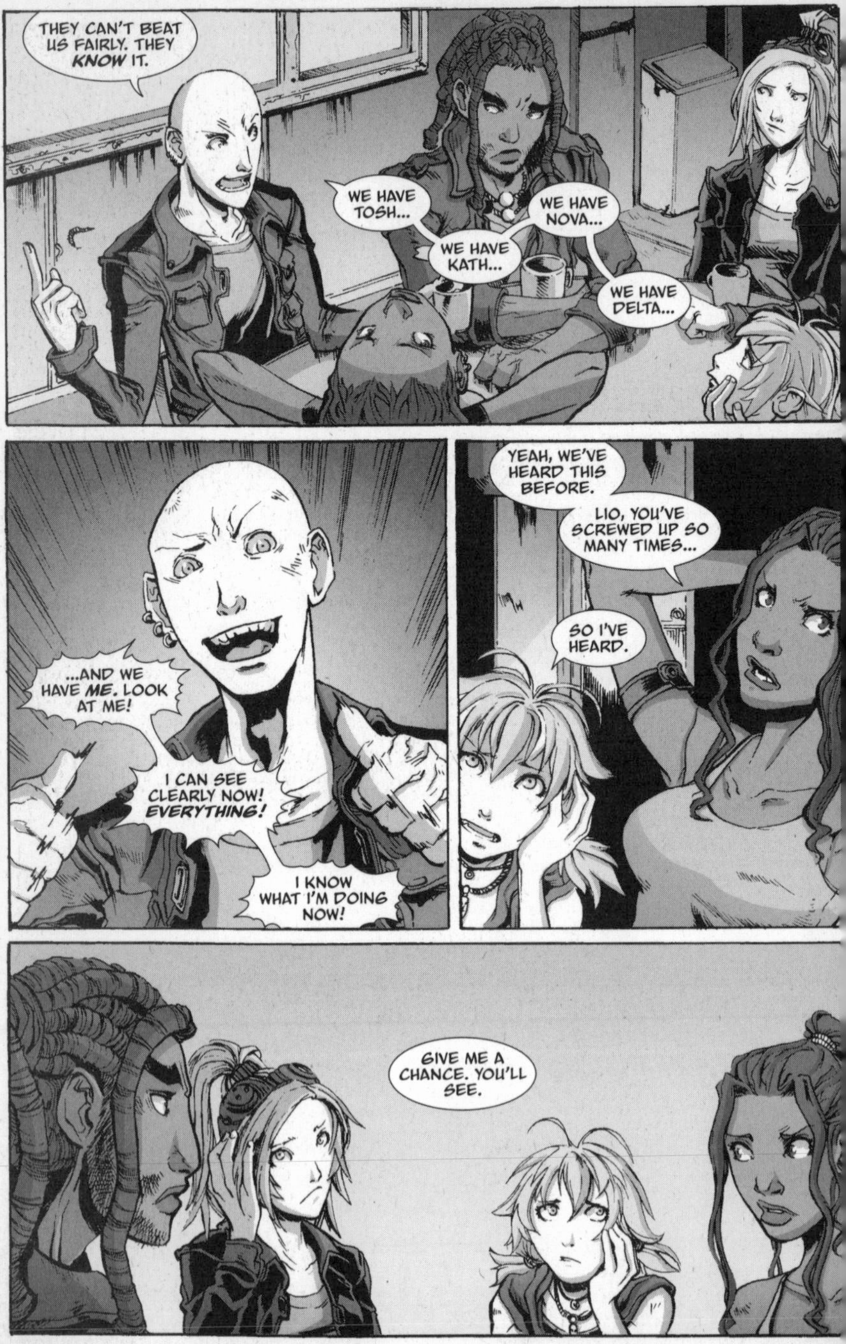
THEY CAN'T BEAT US FAIRLY. THEY *KNOW* IT.
WE HAVE TOSH...
WE HAVE KATH...
WE HAVE NOVA...
WE HAVE DELTA...
...AND WE HAVE *ME*. LOOK AT ME!
I CAN SEE CLEARLY NOW! *EVERYTHING!*
I KNOW WHAT I'M DOING NOW!
YEAH, WE'VE HEARD THIS BEFORE.
LIO, YOU'VE SCREWED UP SO MANY TIMES...
SO I'VE HEARD.
GIVE ME A CHANCE. YOU'LL SEE.

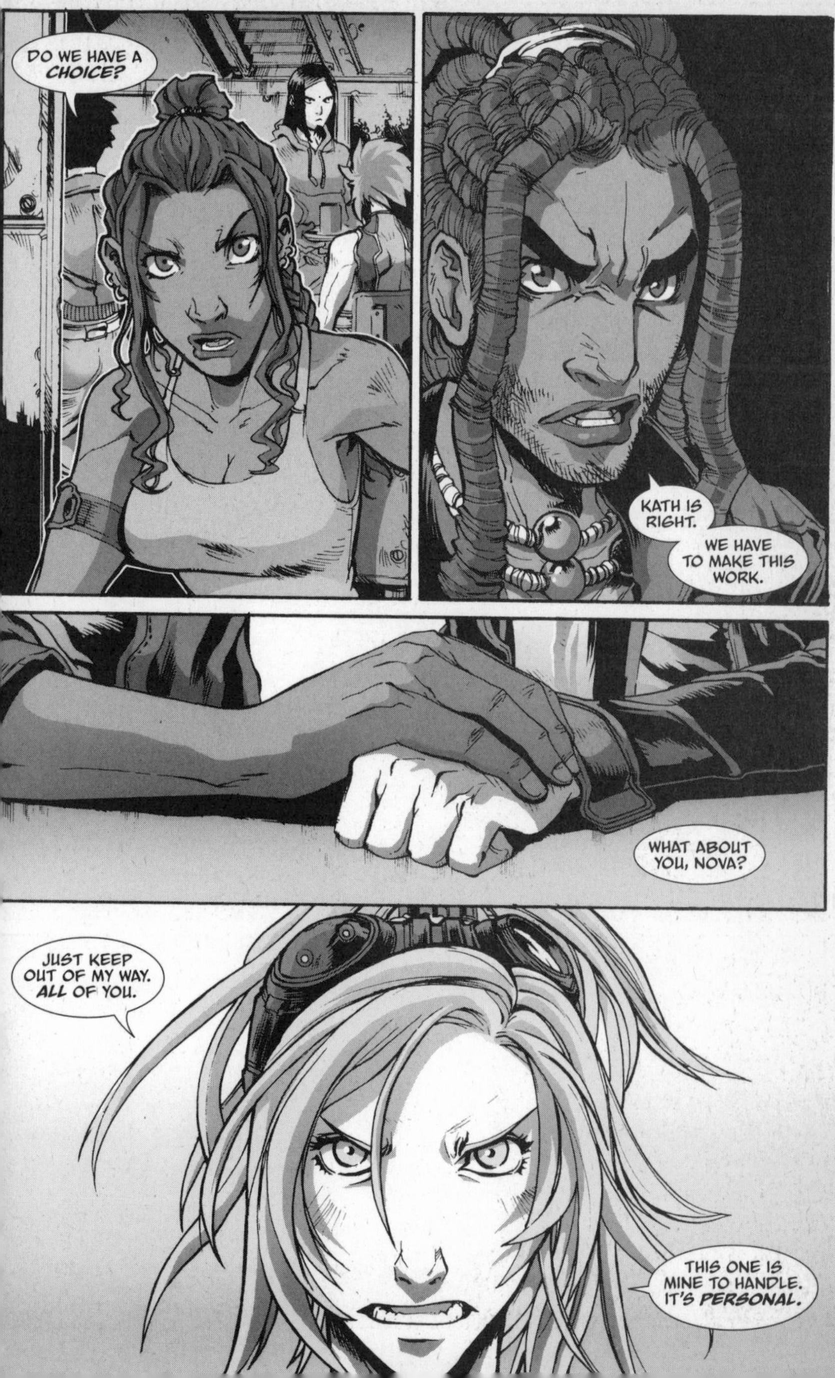
DO WE HAVE A *CHOICE?*
KATH IS RIGHT.
WE HAVE TO MAKE THIS WORK.
WHAT ABOUT YOU, NOVA?
JUST KEEP OUT OF MY WAY. ***ALL*** OF YOU.
THIS ONE IS MINE TO HANDLE. IT'S ***PERSONAL.***

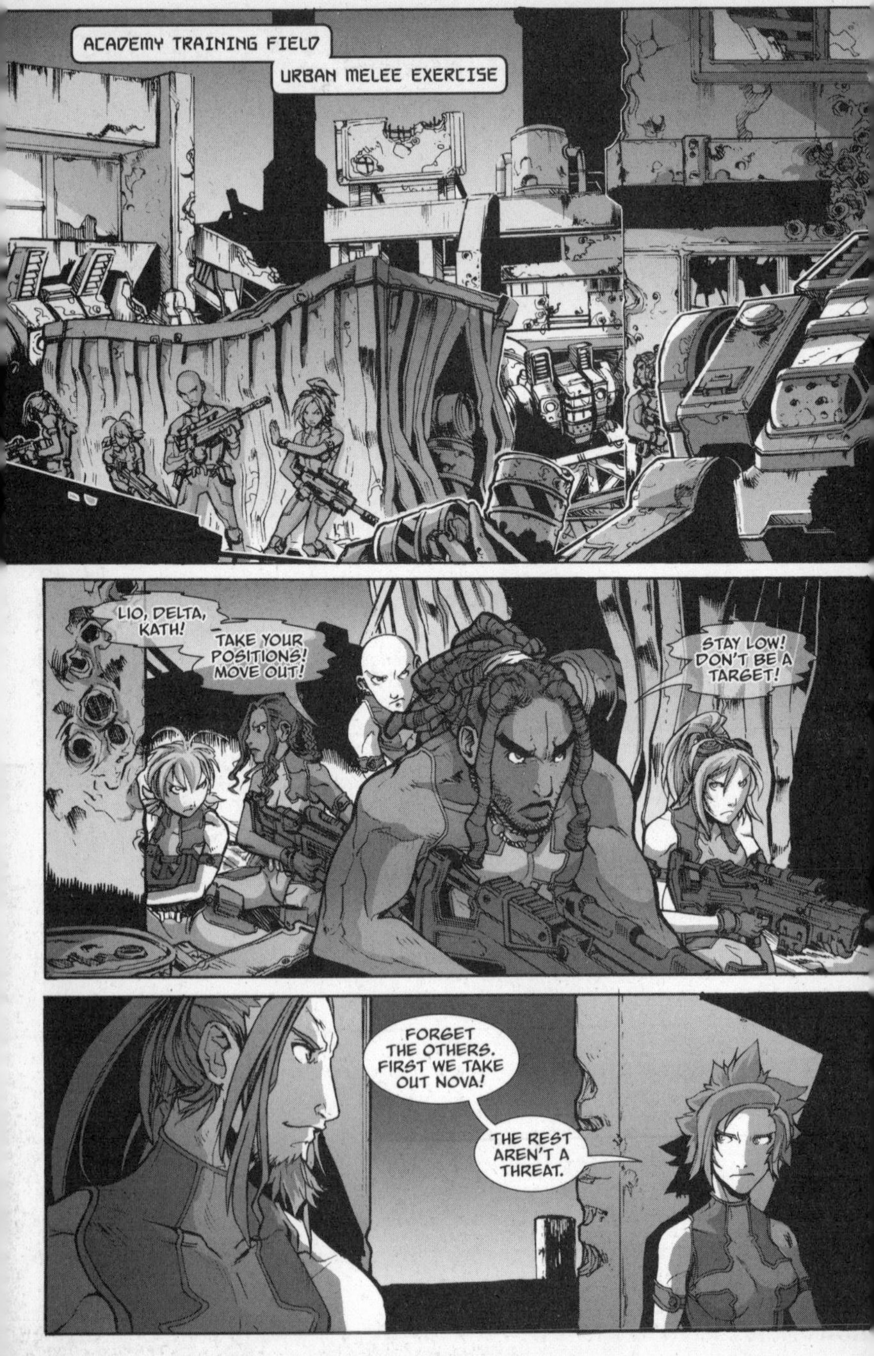
ACADEMY TRAINING FIELD
URBAN MELEE EXERCISE
LIO, DELTA, KATH!
TAKE YOUR POSITIONS! MOVE OUT!
STAY LOW! DON'T BE A TARGET!
FORGET THE OTHERS. FIRST WE TAKE OUT NOVA!
THE REST AREN'T A THREAT.

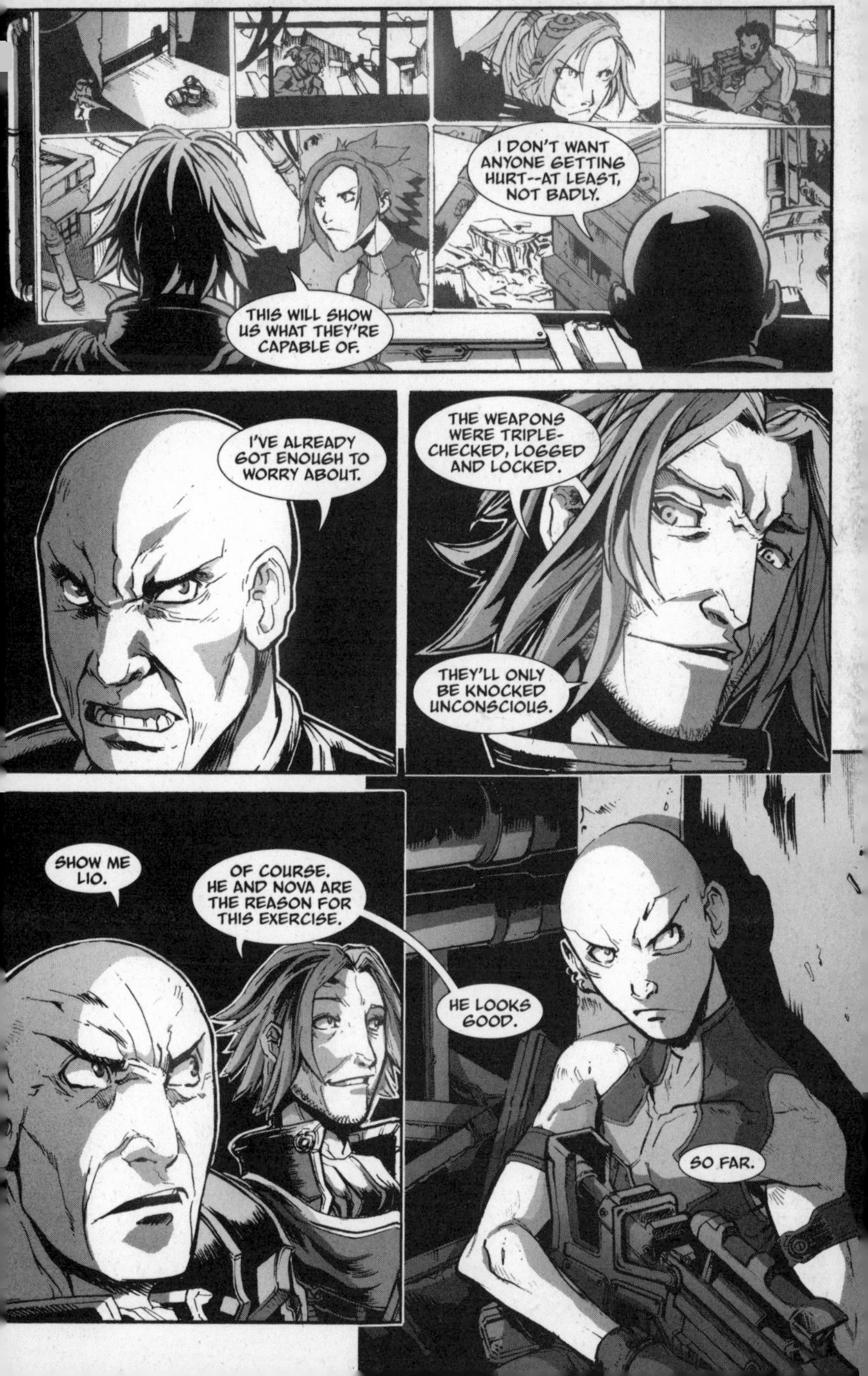
I DON'T WANT ANYONE GETTING HURT--AT LEAST, NOT BADLY.
THIS WILL SHOW US WHAT THEY'RE CAPABLE OF.
I'VE ALREADY GOT ENOUGH TO WORRY ABOUT.
THE WEAPONS WERE TRIPLE-CHECKED, LOGGED AND LOCKED.
THEY'LL ONLY BE KNOCKED UNCONSCIOUS.
SHOW ME LIO.
OF COURSE. HE AND NOVA ARE THE REASON FOR THIS EXERCISE.
HE LOOKS GOOD.
SO FAR.

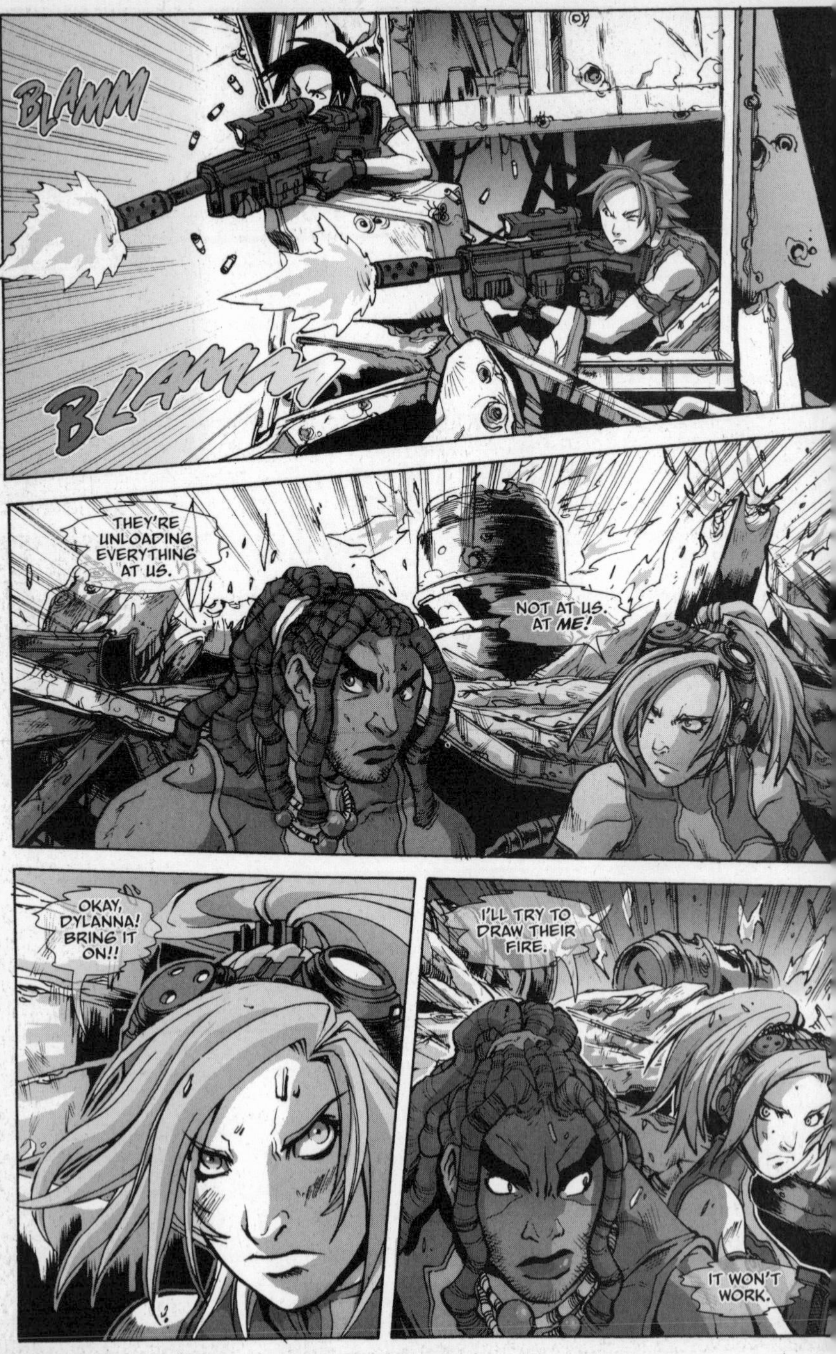
BLAMM
BLAMM
THEY'RE UNLOADING EVERYTHING AT US.
NOT AT US. AT ME!
OKAY, DYLANNA! BRING IT ON!!
I'LL TRY TO DRAW THEIR FIRE.
IT WON'T WORK.

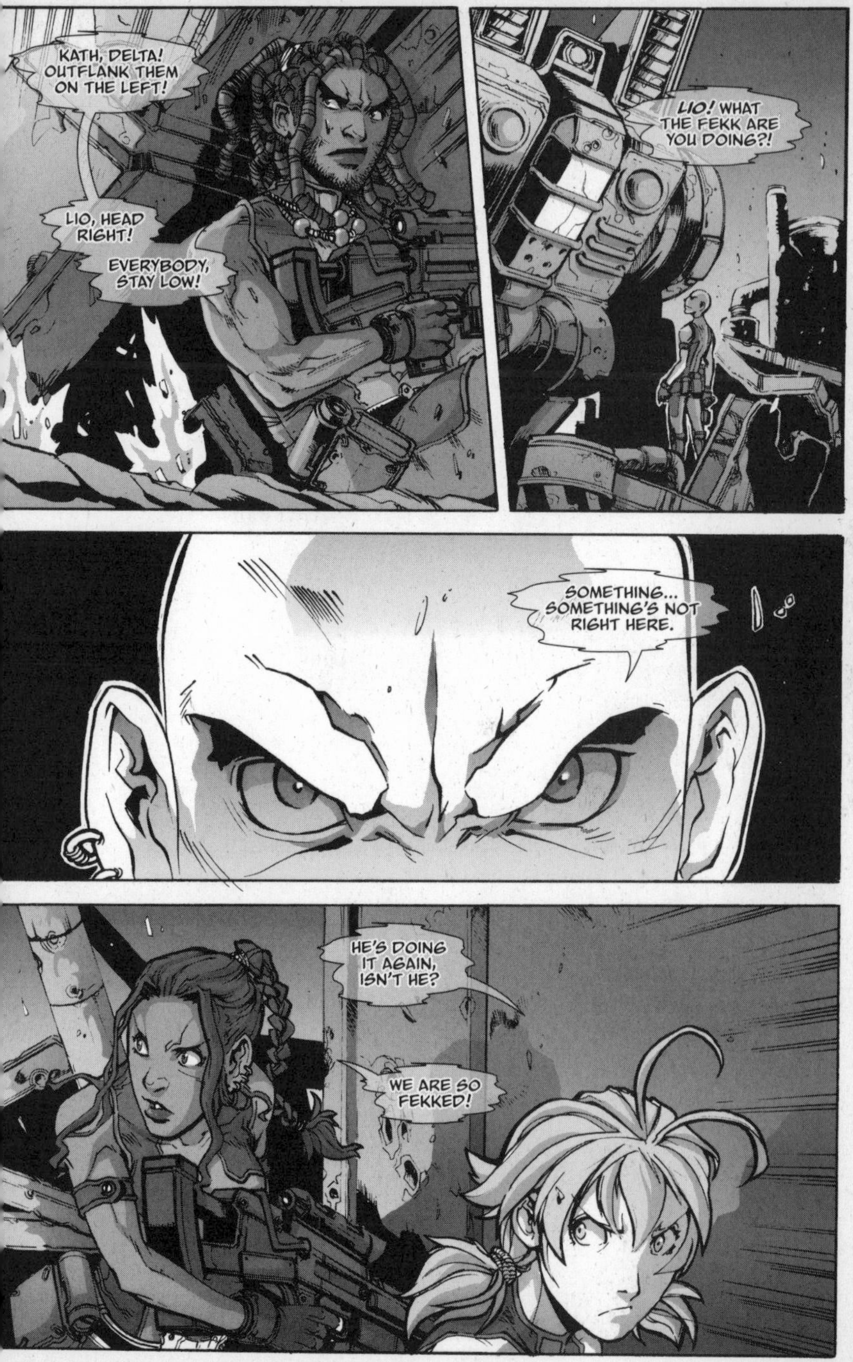
KATH, DELTA! OUTFLANK THEM ON THE LEFT!
LIO, HEAD RIGHT!
EVERYBODY, STAY LOW!
LIO! WHAT THE FEKK ARE YOU DOING?!
SOMETHING... SOMETHING'S NOT RIGHT HERE.
HE'S DOING IT AGAIN, ISN'T HE?
WE ARE SO FEKKED!

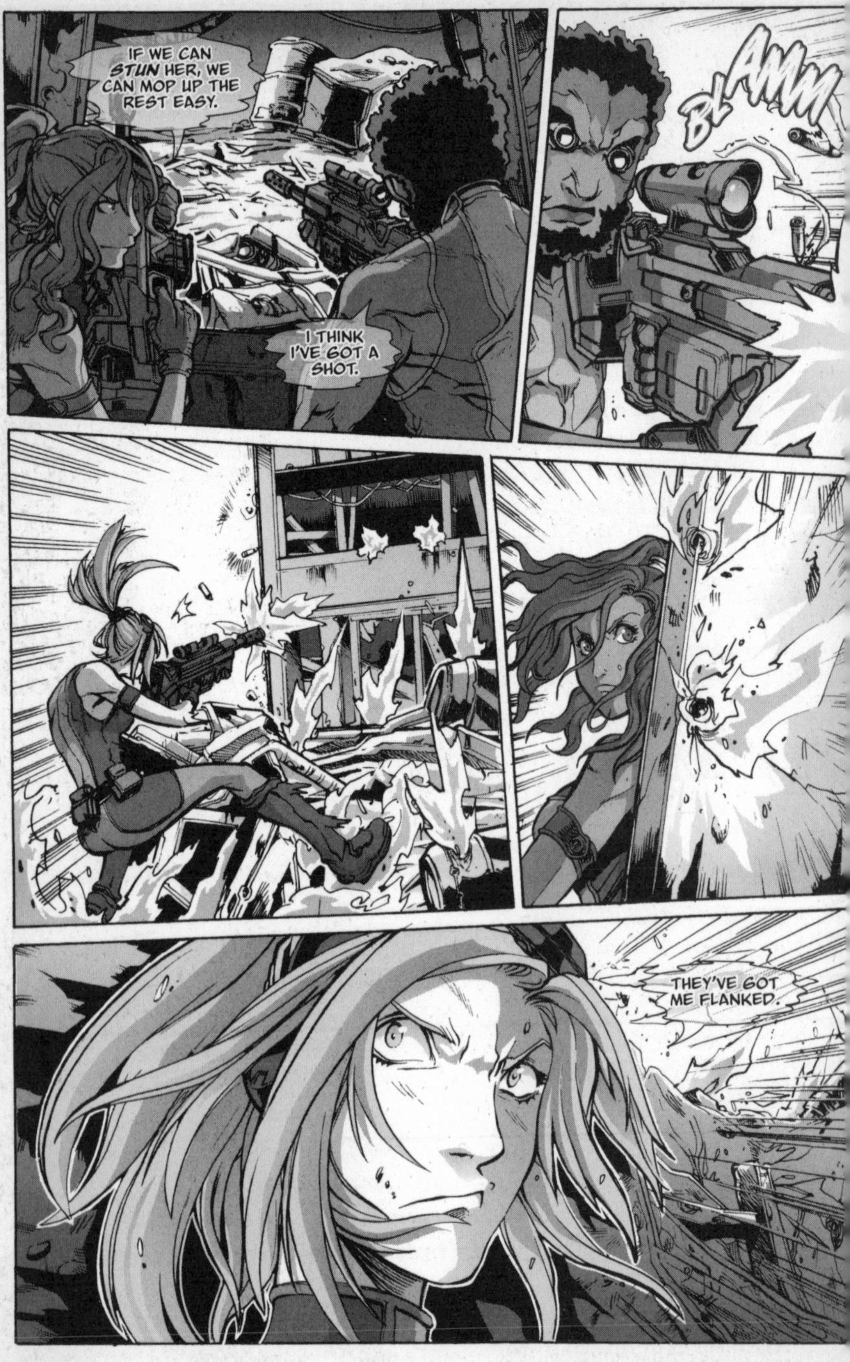
IF WE CAN STUN HER, WE CAN MOP UP THE REST EASY.
I THINK I'VE GOT A SHOT.
BLAMM
THEY'VE GOT ME FLANKED.

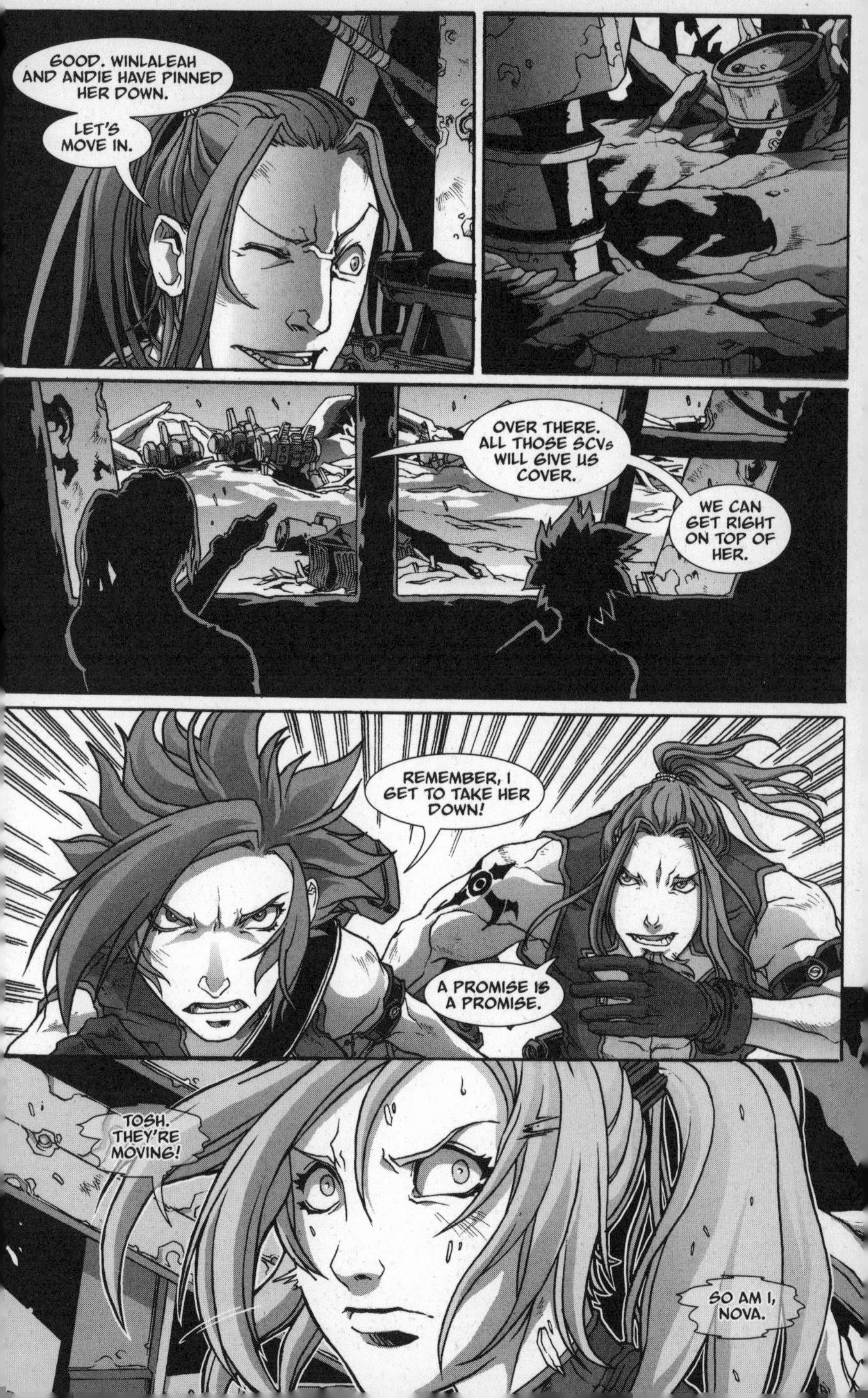
GOOD. WINLALEAH AND ANDIE HAVE PINNED HER DOWN.
LET'S MOVE IN.
OVER THERE. ALL THOSE SCVs WILL GIVE US COVER.
WE CAN GET RIGHT ON TOP OF HER.
REMEMBER, I GET TO TAKE HER DOWN!
A PROMISE IS A PROMISE.
TOSH. THEY'RE MOVING!
SO AM I, NOVA.

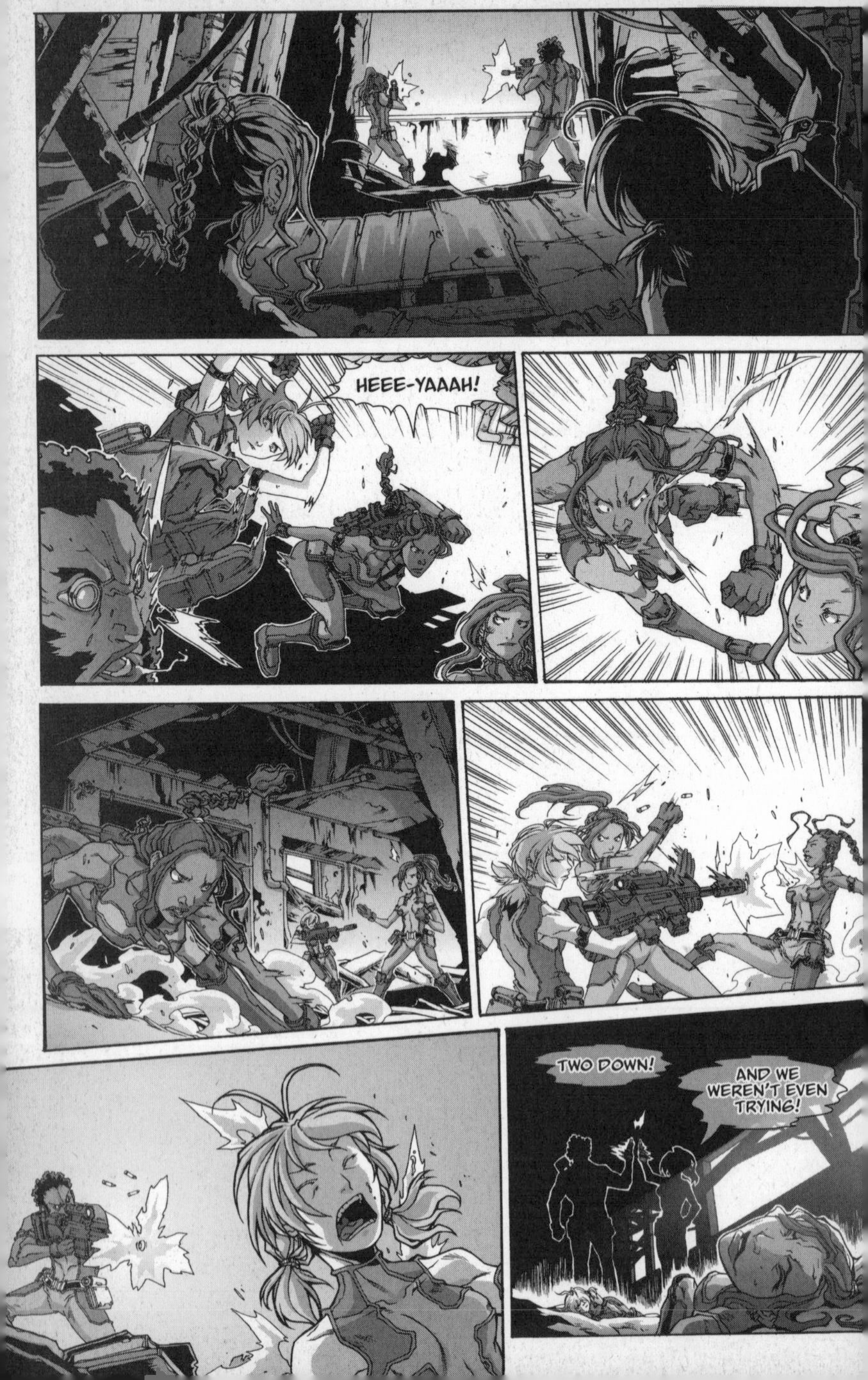
HEEE-YAAAH!
TWO DOWN!
AND WE WEREN'T EVEN TRYING!

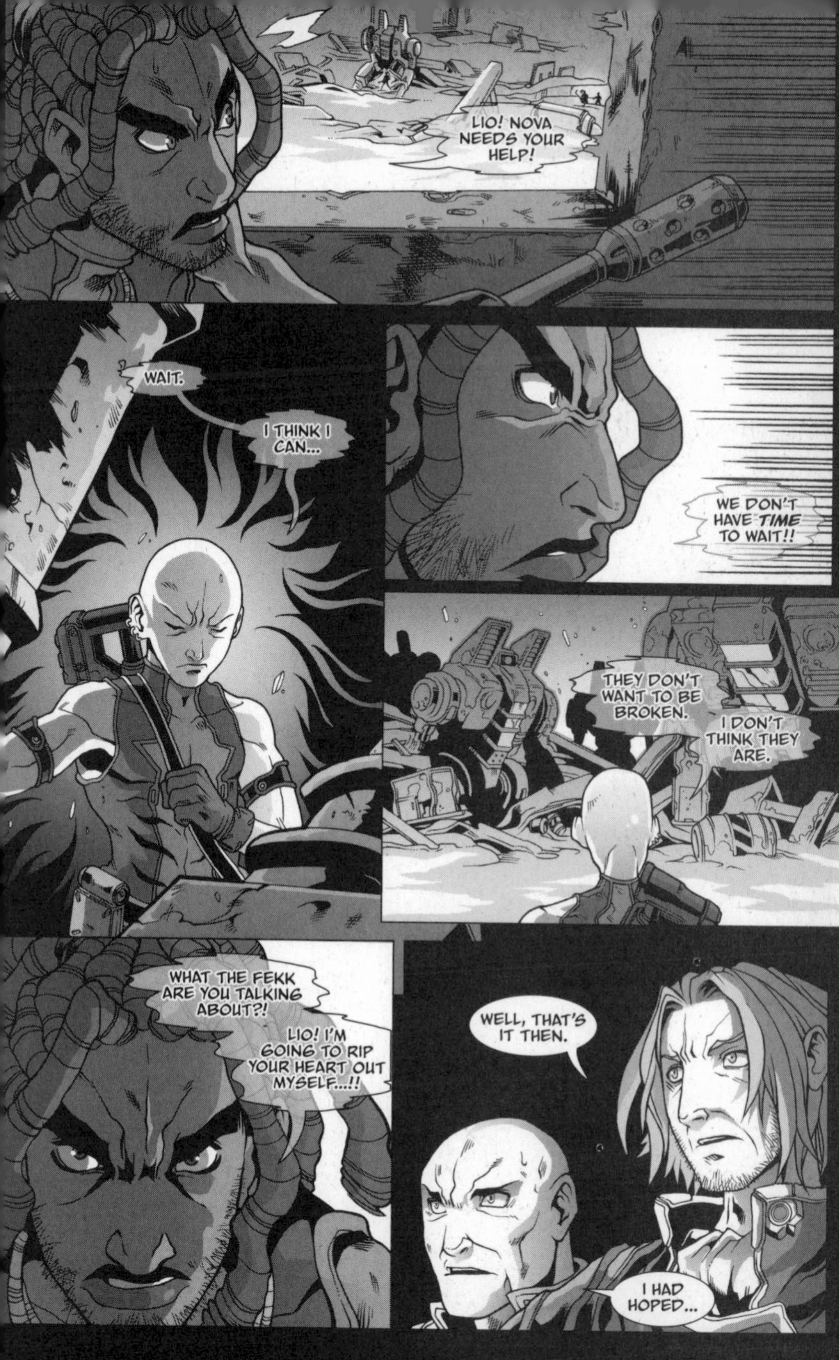
LIO! NOVA NEEDS YOUR HELP!
WAIT.
I THINK I CAN...
WE DON'T HAVE TIME TO WAIT!!
THEY DON'T WANT TO BE BROKEN.
I DON'T THINK THEY ARE.
WHAT THE FEKK ARE YOU TALKING ABOUT?!
LIO! I'M GOING TO RIP YOUR HEART OUT MYSELF...!!
WELL, THAT'S IT THEN.
I HAD HOPED...

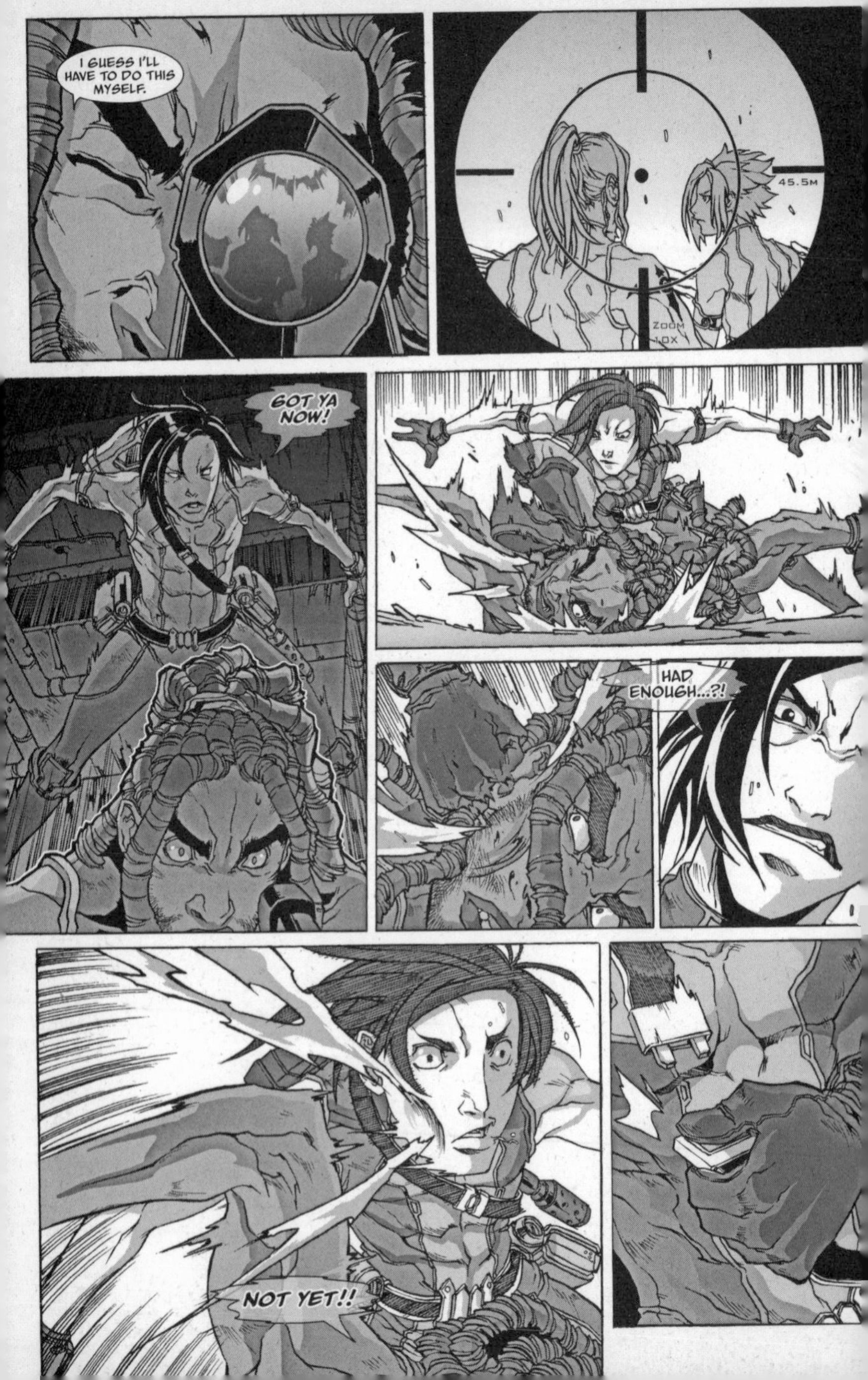
I GUESS I'LL HAVE TO DO THIS MYSELF.
45.5M
ZOOM 10X
GOT YA NOW!
HAD ENOUGH...?!
NOT YET!!

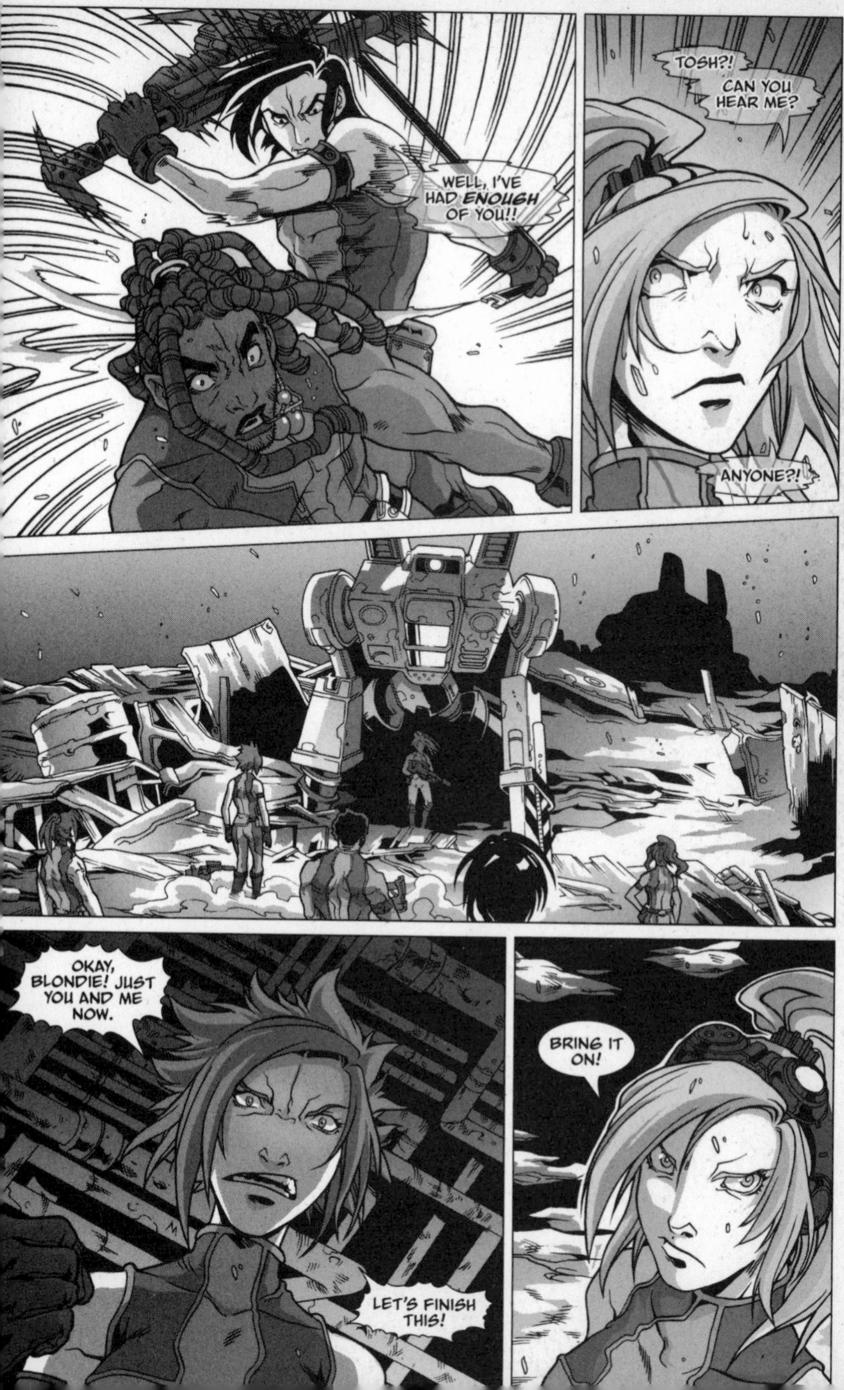
WELL, I'VE HAD ENOUGH OF YOU!!
TOSH?!
CAN YOU HEAR ME?
ANYONE?!
OKAY, BLONDIE! JUST YOU AND ME NOW.
LET'S FINISH THIS!
BRING IT ON!

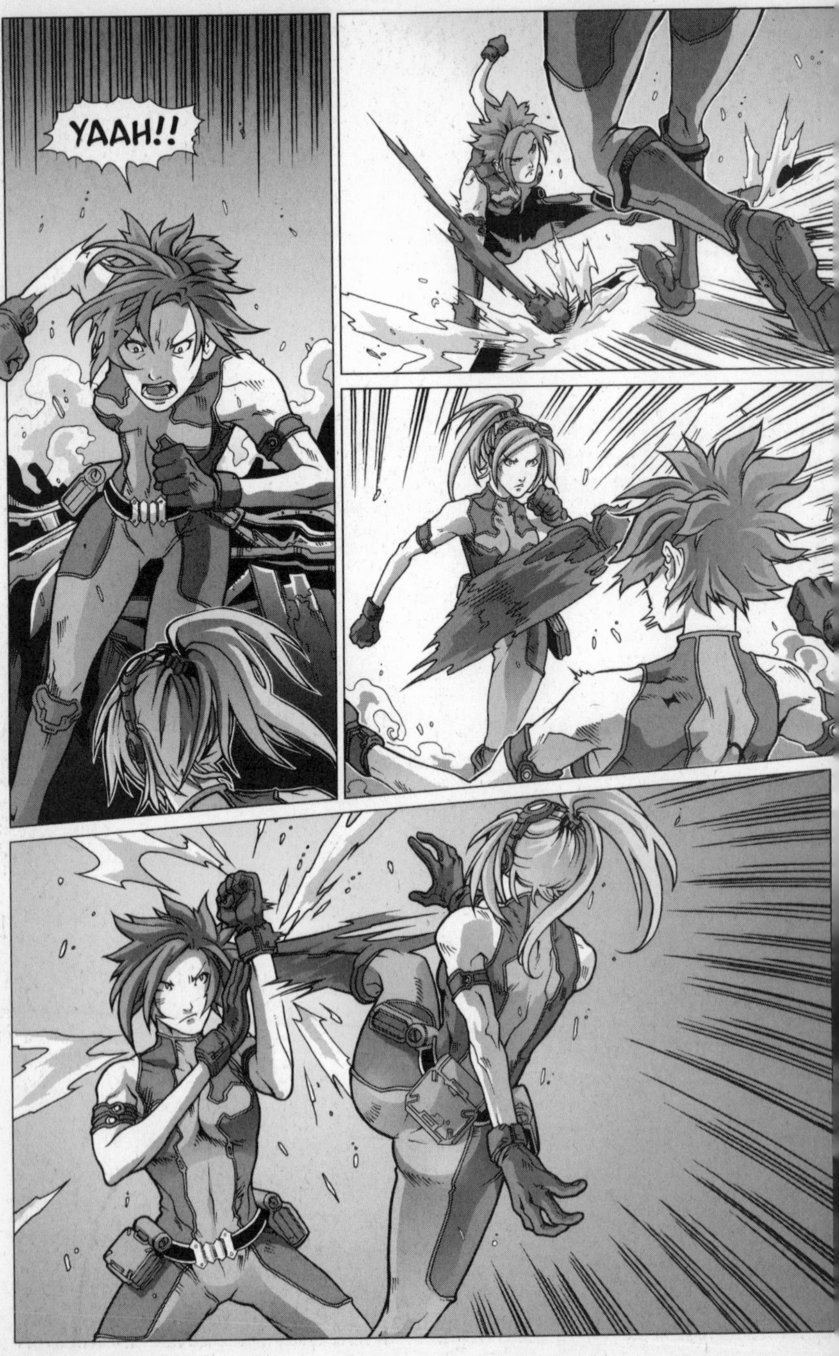
YAAH!!

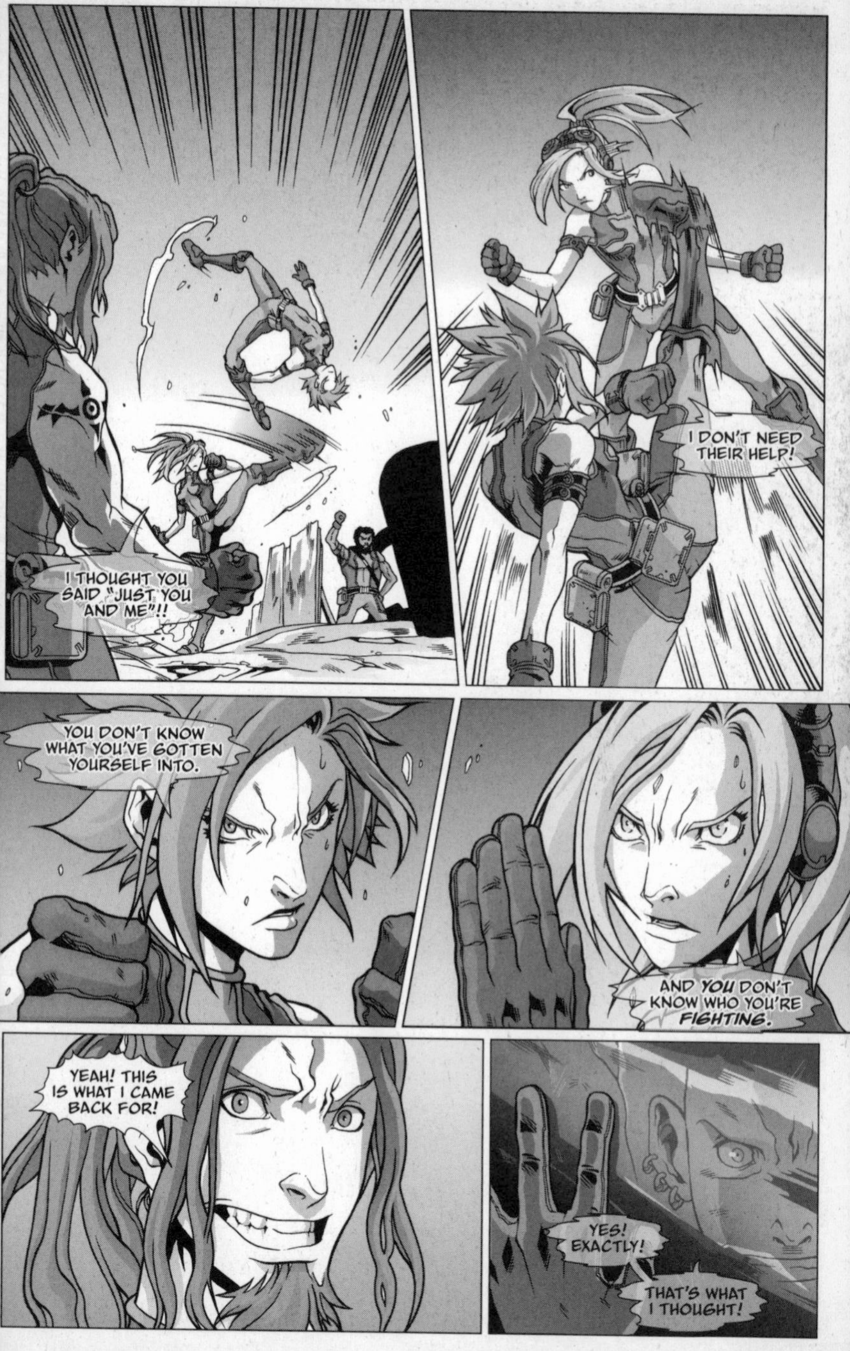
I THOUGHT YOU SAID "JUST YOU AND ME"!!
I DON'T NEED THEIR HELP!
YOU DON'T KNOW WHAT YOU'VE GOTTEN YOURSELF INTO.
AND *YOU* DON'T KNOW WHO YOU'RE *FIGHTING*.
YEAH! THIS IS WHAT I CAME BACK FOR!
YES! EXACTLY!
THAT'S WHAT I THOUGHT!

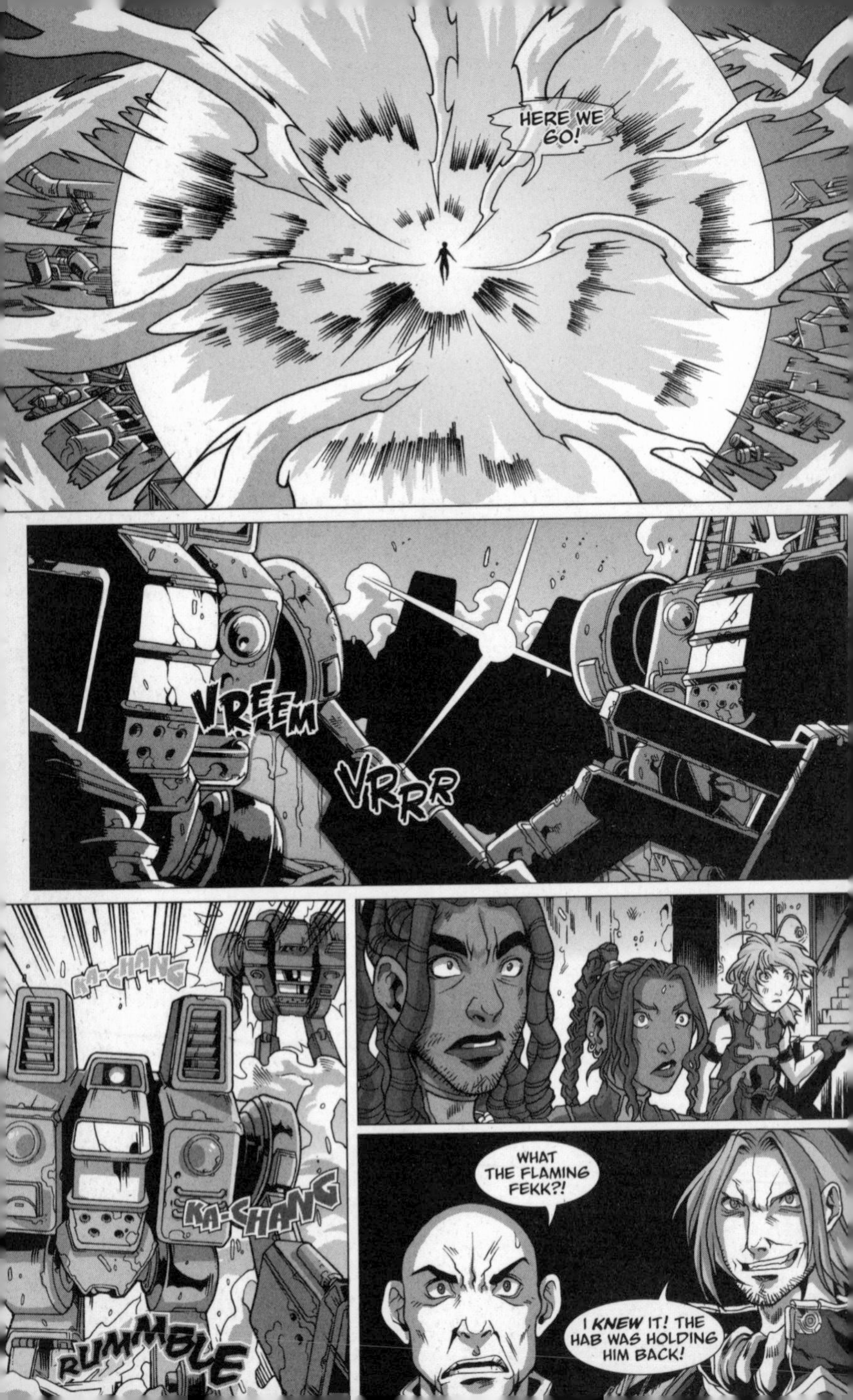
HERE WE GO!
VREEM
VRRR
KA-CHANG
KA-CHANG
RUMMBLE
WHAT THE FLAMING FEKK?!
I KNEW IT! THE HAB WAS HOLDING HIM BACK!

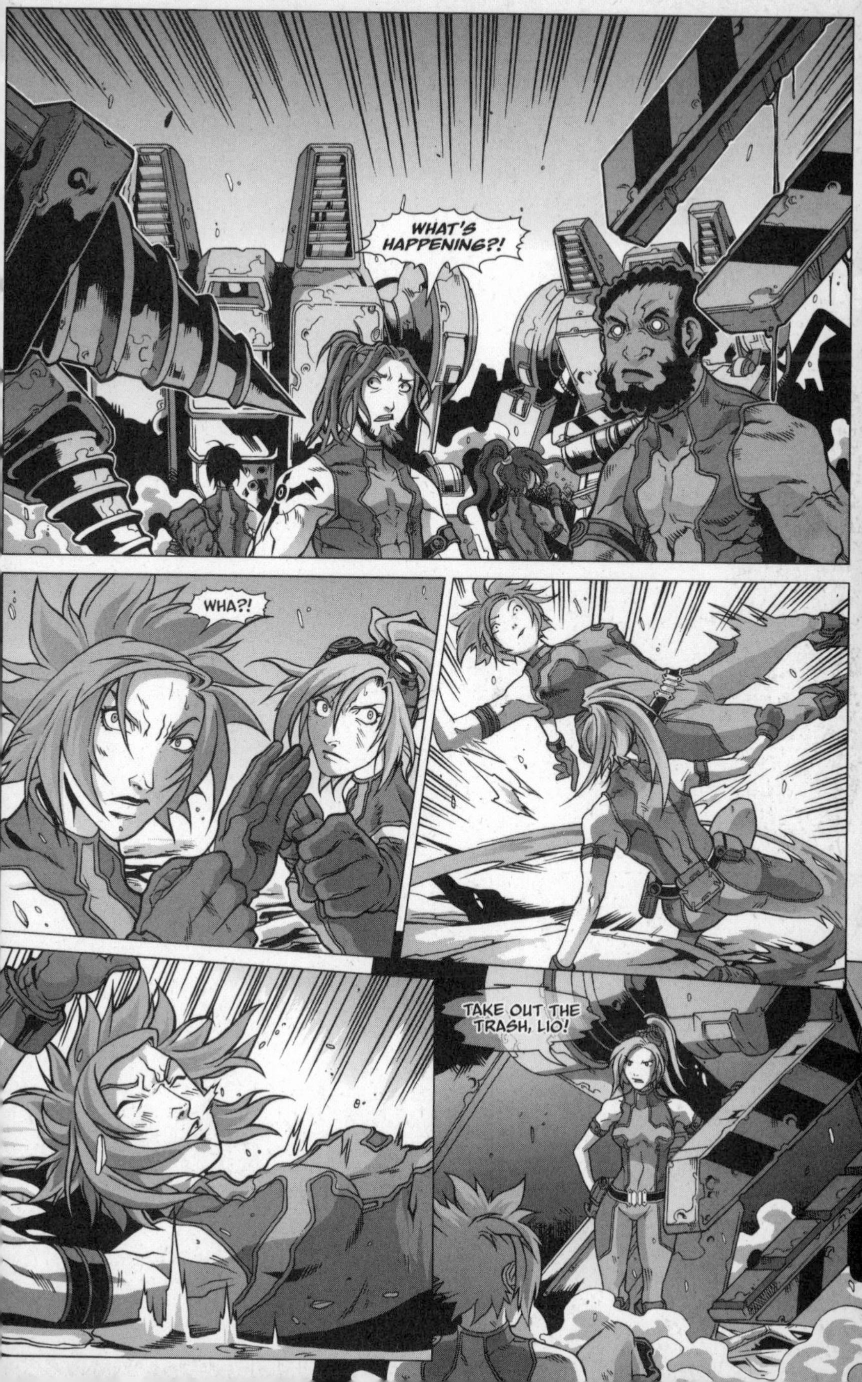
WHAT'S HAPPENING?!
WHA?!
TAKE OUT THE TRASH, LIO!

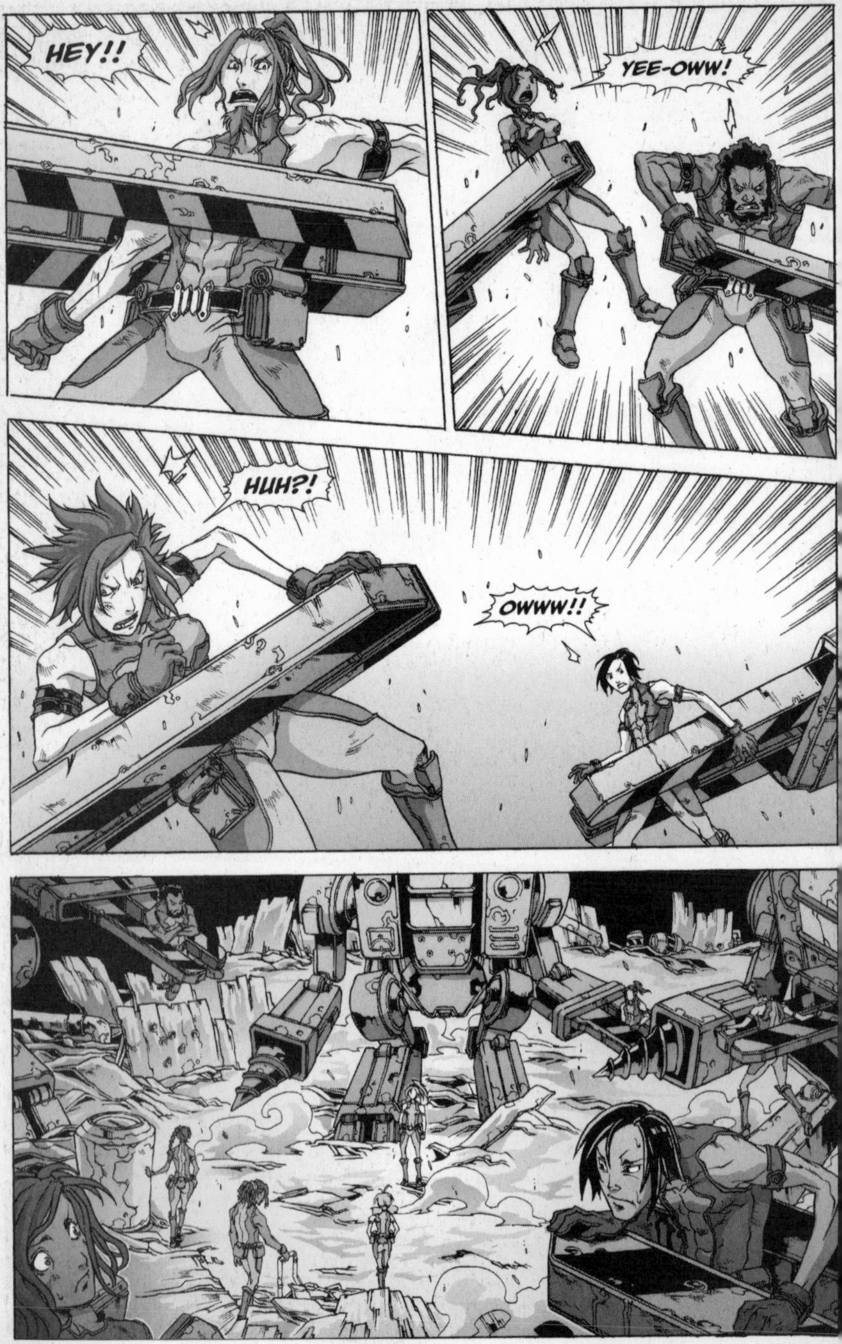
HEY!!
YEE-OWW!
HUH?!
OWWW!!

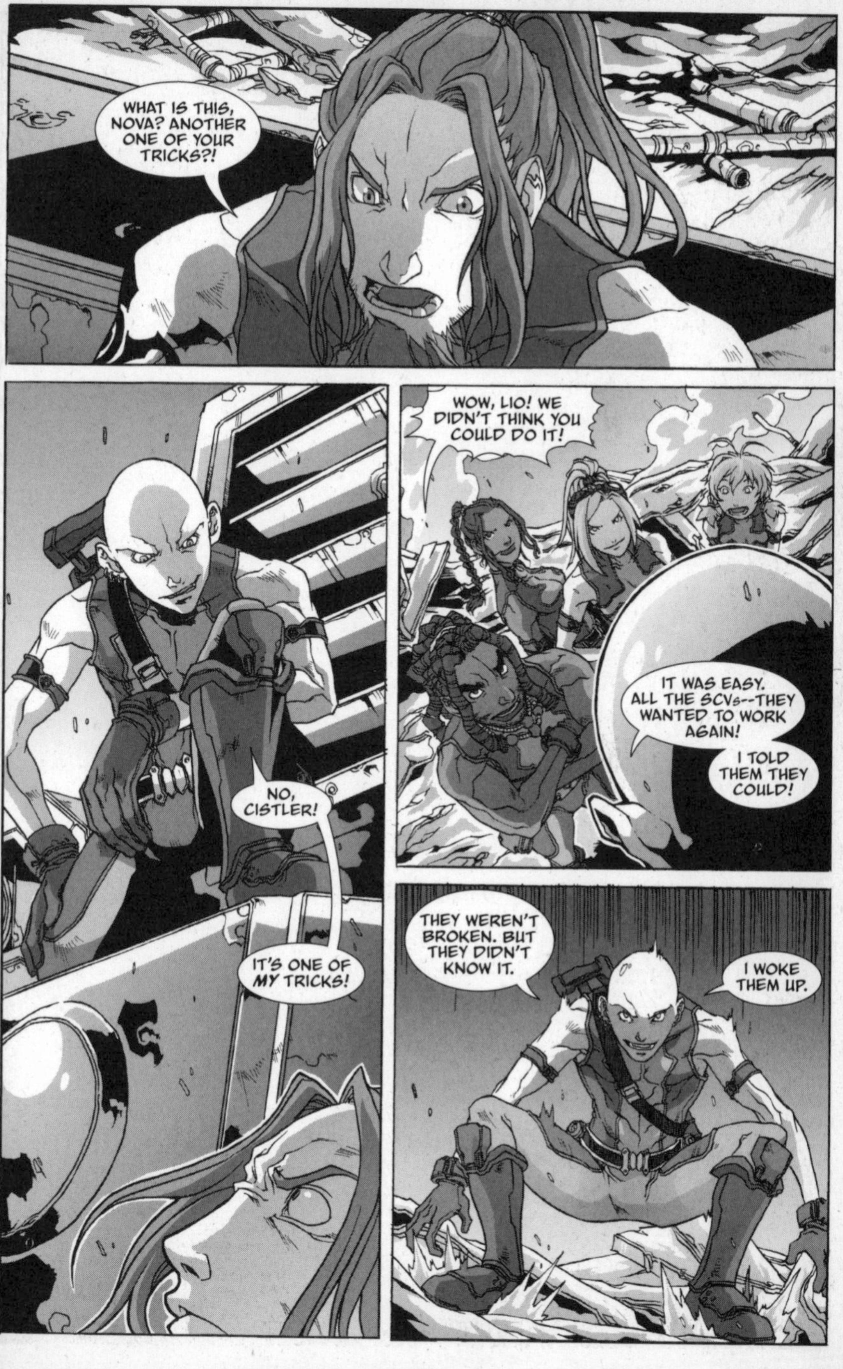
WHAT IS THIS, NOVA? ANOTHER ONE OF YOUR TRICKS?!
NO, CISTLER!
IT'S ONE OF *MY* TRICKS!
WOW, LIO! WE DIDN'T THINK YOU COULD DO IT!
IT WAS EASY. ALL THE SCVs--THEY WANTED TO WORK AGAIN!
I TOLD THEM THEY COULD!
THEY WEREN'T BROKEN. BUT THEY DIDN'T KNOW IT.
I WOKE THEM UP.

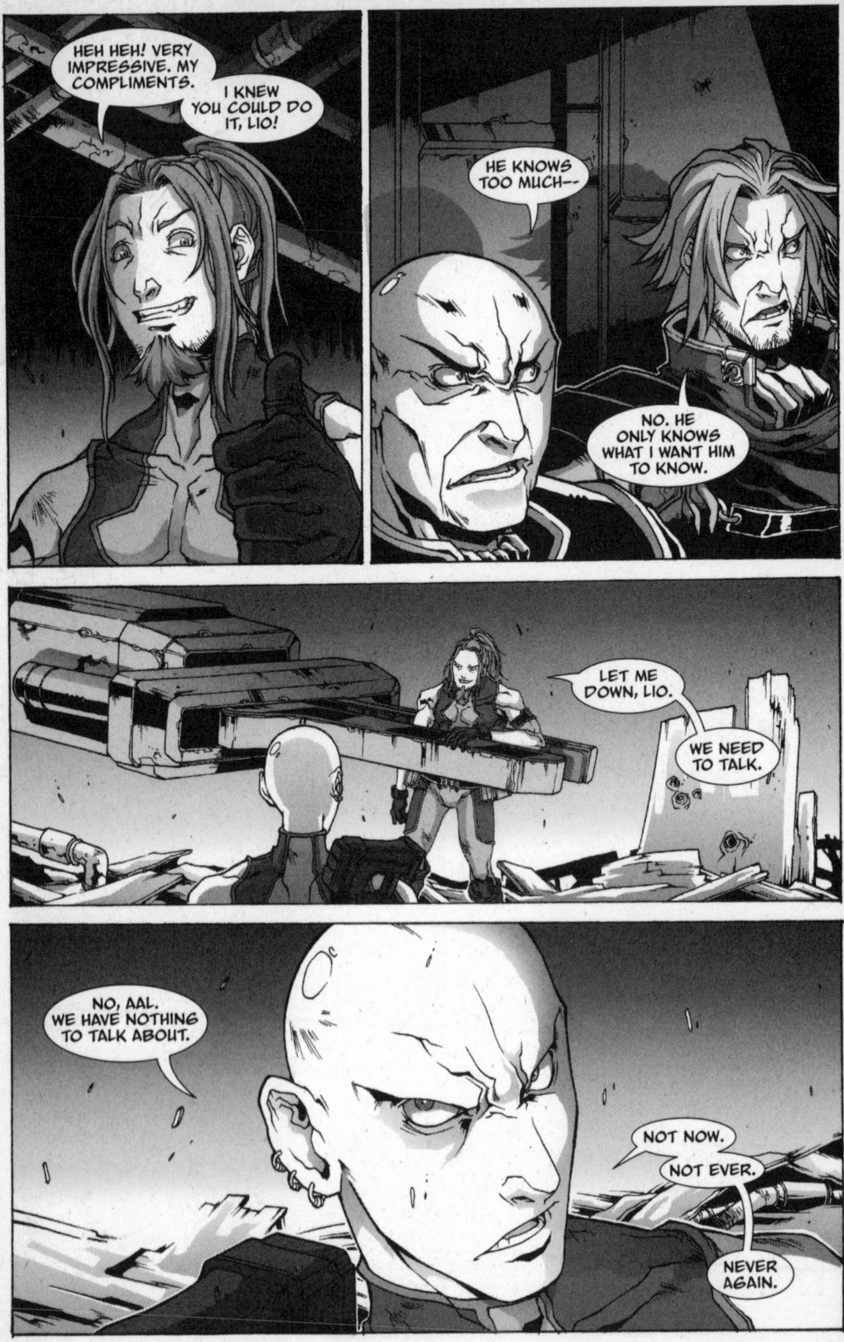
HEH HEH! VERY IMPRESSIVE. MY COMPLIMENTS.
I KNEW YOU COULD DO IT, LIO!
HE KNOWS TOO MUCH--
NO. HE ONLY KNOWS WHAT I WANT HIM TO KNOW.
LET ME DOWN, LIO.
WE NEED TO TALK.
NO, AAL. WE HAVE NOTHING TO TALK ABOUT.
NOT NOW.
NOT EVER.
NEVER AGAIN.

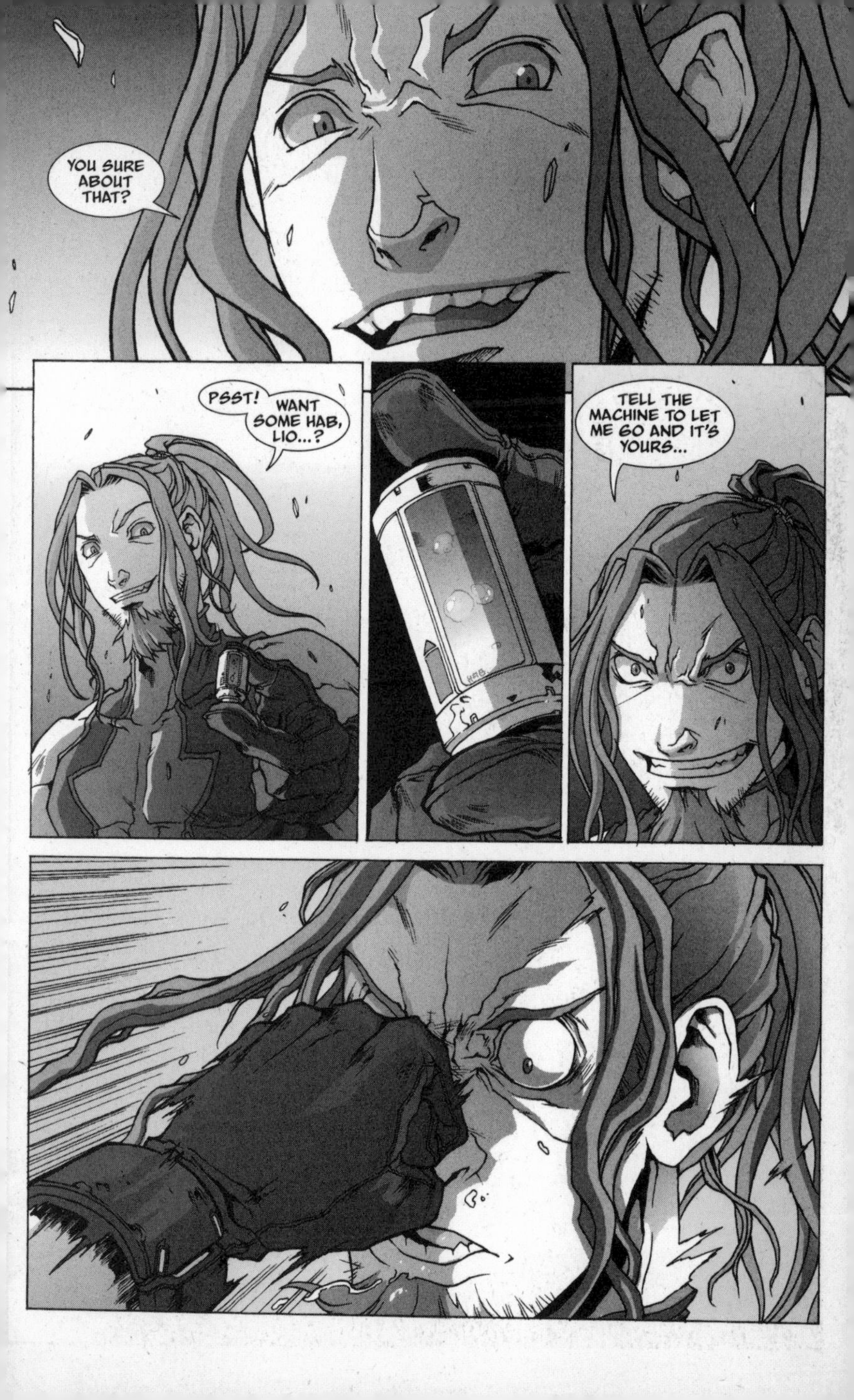
YOU SURE ABOUT THAT?
PSST!
WANT SOME HAB, LIO...?
TELL THE MACHINE TO LET ME GO AND IT'S YOURS...

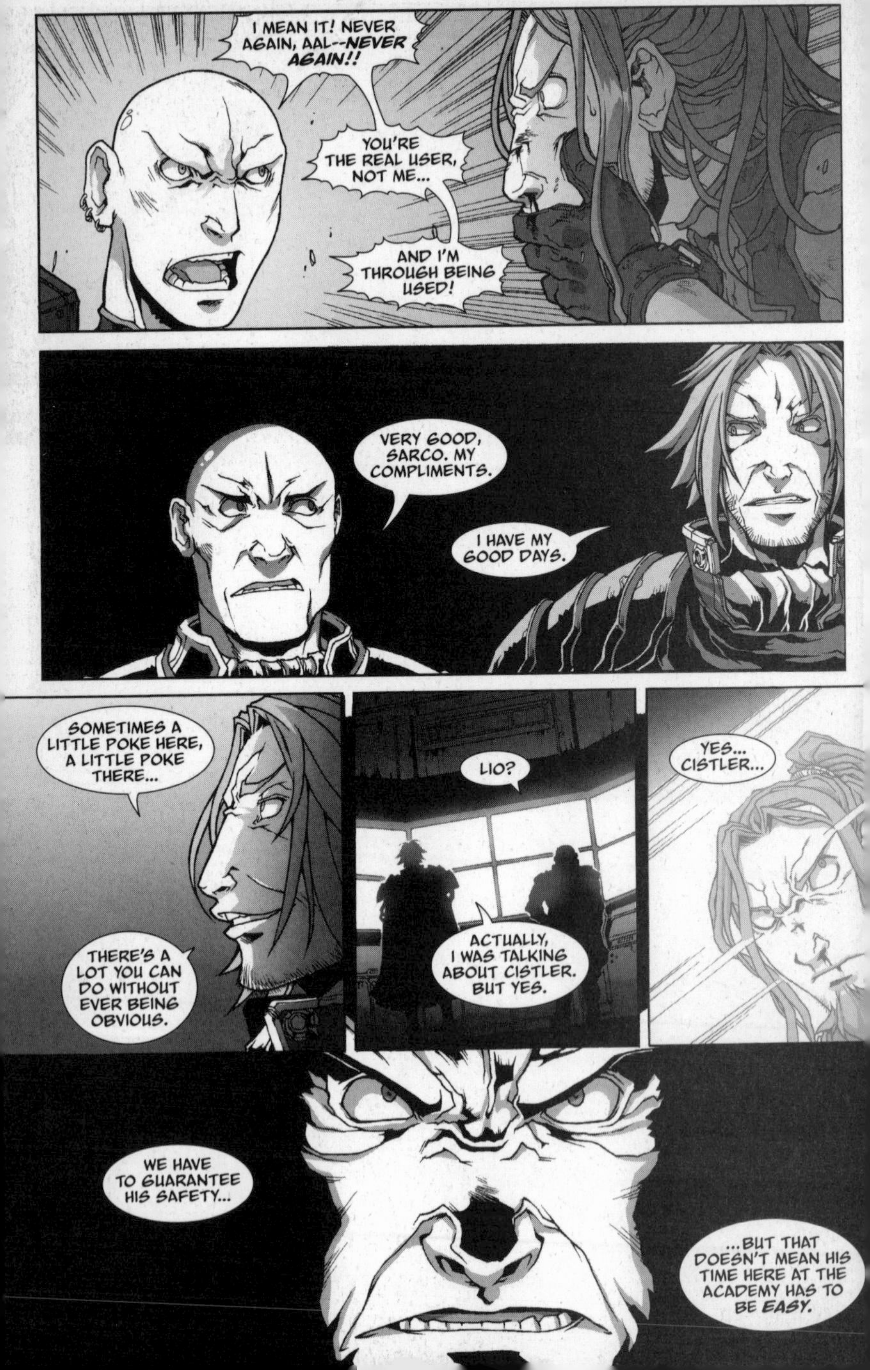
I MEAN IT! NEVER AGAIN, AAL--NEVER AGAIN!!
YOU'RE THE REAL USER, NOT ME...
AND I'M THROUGH BEING USED!
VERY GOOD, SARCO. MY COMPLIMENTS.
I HAVE MY GOOD DAYS.
SOMETIMES A LITTLE POKE HERE, A LITTLE POKE THERE...
THERE'S A LOT YOU CAN DO WITHOUT EVER BEING OBVIOUS.
LIO?
ACTUALLY, I WAS TALKING ABOUT CISTLER. BUT YES.
YES... CISTLER...
WE HAVE TO GUARANTEE HIS SAFETY...
...BUT THAT DOESN'T MEAN HIS TIME HERE AT THE ACADEMY HAS TO BE EASY.

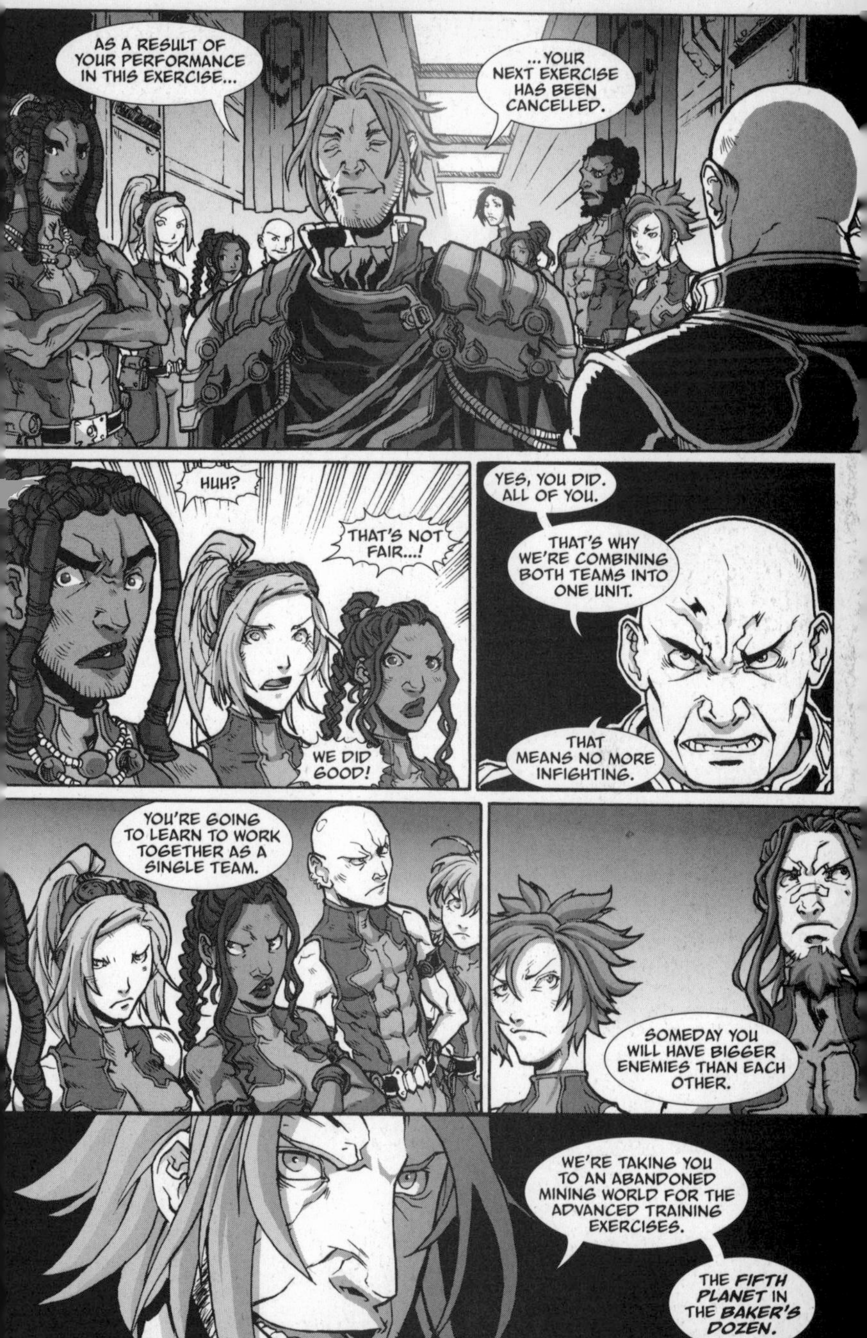
AS A RESULT OF YOUR PERFORMANCE IN THIS EXERCISE...
...YOUR NEXT EXERCISE HAS BEEN CANCELLED.
HUH?
THAT'S NOT FAIR...!
WE DID GOOD!
YES, YOU DID. ALL OF YOU.
THAT'S WHY WE'RE COMBINING BOTH TEAMS INTO ONE UNIT.
THAT MEANS NO MORE INFIGHTING.
YOU'RE GOING TO LEARN TO WORK TOGETHER AS A SINGLE TEAM.
SOMEDAY YOU WILL HAVE BIGGER ENEMIES THAN EACH OTHER.
WE'RE TAKING YOU TO AN ABANDONED MINING WORLD FOR THE ADVANCED TRAINING EXERCISES.
THE *FIFTH PLANET* IN THE *BAKER'S DOZEN*.

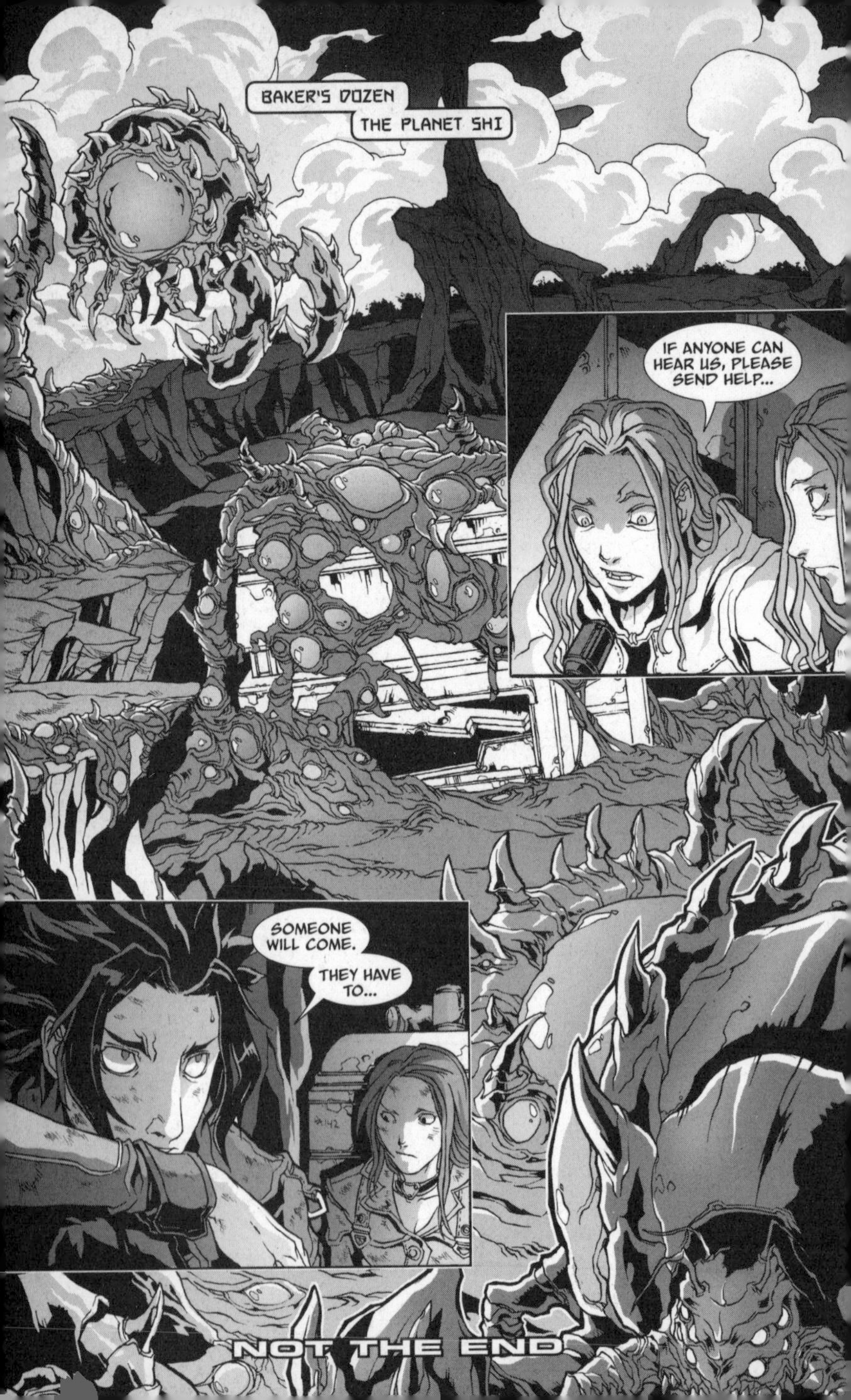
BAKER'S DOZEN
THE PLANET SHI
IF ANYONE CAN HEAR US, PLEASE SEND HELP...
SOMEONE WILL COME.
THEY HAVE TO...
NOT THE END

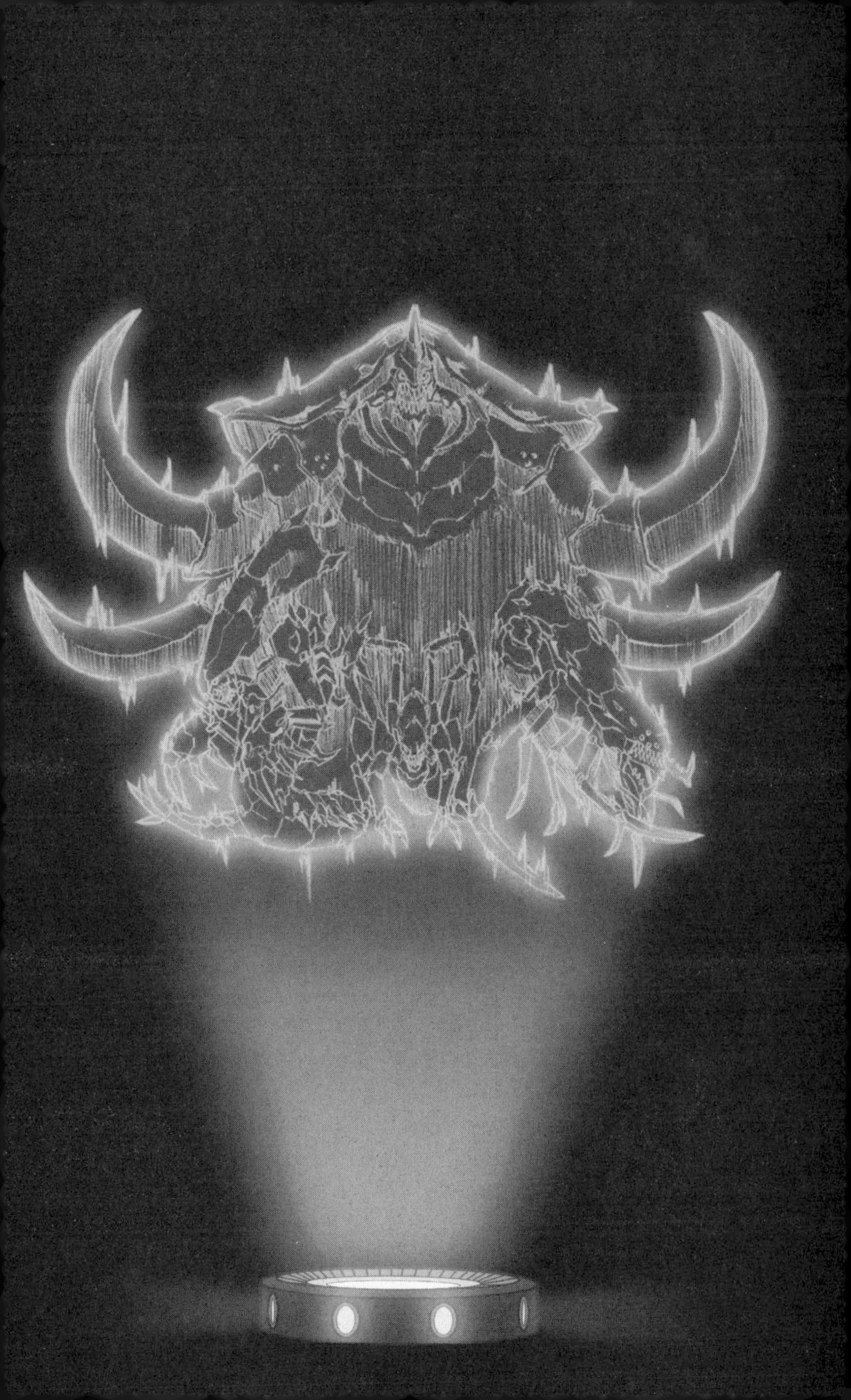

# The Administrative Office of the Ghost Academy

Dear Ghost Academy Educators and Staff,

In light of recent progress by Team Red and Team Blue, both teams will be combined into one unit. This group of trainees will be headed to a mining planet in the Baker's Dozen on an advanced training mission. Please give these trainees encouragement as their departure date rapidly approaches.

As we all know, the anniversary of Mengsk's inauguration will be marked in the coming weeks. For those of you interested, I'll be appearing to celebrate the occasion on a *Dominion and You* holocast, during a program on the missing children of the deposed Old Families.

On this anniversary, remember who we all owe our jobs to: Arcturus Mengsk.

Sincerely,

*Director Kevin Bick*

# THANKS FOR PICKING UP
# STARCRAFT: GHOST ACADEMY!

This latest installment of *StarCraft:Ghost Academy* answers more of the burning questions left over from the *StarCraft:Ghost: Nova* novel. What happened after Nova was plucked from the slums of Tarsonis and ushered into the protection of the Ghost Academy? Did she succeed as an "A student"? I think the answer, so far, is yes. But even more will be revealed in the *upcoming volume 3!*

Speaking of success, this project would not be possible without the thorough and considerable contributions of the Blizzard creative team. I'd like to thank our immediate contacts at Blizzard—Jason Bischoff, Micky Neilson, James Waugh, Glenn Rane, Evelyn Fredericksen, Sean Copeland, as well as Senior Vice-President, Creative Development Chris Metzen—for their insightful feedback and excellent suggestions. We're grateful for their input, which represents the creative endeavors of hundreds of other inventive minds at Blizzard.

Next, thanks goes to the writer and artists who lovingly crafted the pages you have just read. I'd be pleased to introduce the extremely talented David Gerrold...except you probably already know him. Maybe you've heard of a show called *Star Trek*? I thought so! Well, Mr. Gerrold might have just written a few of those episodes. Did you enjoy the revenge story "Fear the Reaper" in *StarCraft:Frontline 4?* He might have had a little...okay, everything to do with writing that too.

It is no easy task to illustrate pages of raging zerg, only to switch to scenes of romance and then to telepathic battles. But one man—nay, one godlike man—finds this child's play...and that man is Fernando Heinz Furukawa and his dedicated crew of supporting artists who carry his cloud like so many cherubs. I'd be remiss not to also thank the patron saint of pages, Matias Timarchi, without whom our prayers for awesome tank designs and kickass zergling clashes would fall on deaf ears.

Finally, thanks to my fellow team members at TOKYOPOP: editor extraordinaire Troy Lewter, who sees all, knows all and stresses over all. And Michael Paolilli, a paragon of layout perfection who also happens to know the *StarCraft* universe inside and out. With a team like this, calling down the thunder means you'll reap the whirlwind!

Hope Donovan
Editor

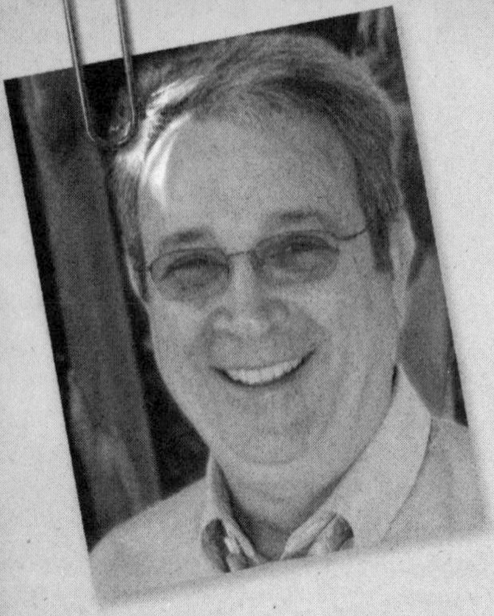

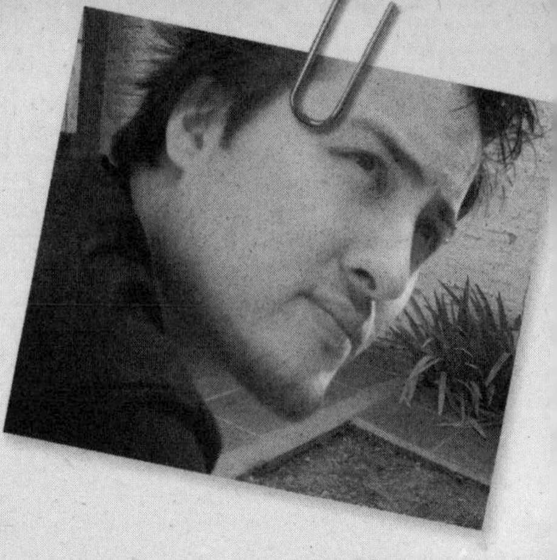

## WRITER:
# DAVID GERROLD

**David Gerrold** is a Hugo and Nebula award-winning author. He has written more than 50 books, including ***The Man Who Folded Himself*** and ***When HARLIE Was One***, as well as hundreds of short stories and articles. His autobiographical story ***The Martian Child*** was the basis of the 2007 movie starring John Cusack and Amanda Peet. He has also written for television, including episodes of ***Star Trek, Babylon 5, Twilight Zone,*** and ***Land Of The Lost***. He is best known for creating tribbles, sleestaks, and Chtorrans. In his spare time, he redesigns his website, www.gerrold.com.

## ARTIST:
# FERNANDO HEINZ FURUKAWA

Born in Argentina, **Fernando Heinz Furukawa** is the son of a German father and a Japanese mother. Fernando has been drawing since he was a small child and furthered his artistic education under the tutelage of local art professors, Pier Brito and Feliciano Garcia Zecchin. He began his professional artist career at age nineteen and was published in several local magazines. This led to him publishing his own series (along with writer Mauro Mantella and artist Rocio Zucchi) ***TIME: 5***. His recent works include his job as lead artist for an online web series, drawing the TOKYOPOP manga ***Tantric Stripfighter Trina***, and drawing two stories for TOKYOPOP's ***Warcraft: Legends*** anthology series, and of course, illustrating the ***StarCraft: Ghost Academy*** series.

# CONTRIBUTING PENCILS:

**Walter Gustavo Gomez** was born in Buenos Aires in 1979 and became interested in a career in art as a child thanks to TV shows like ***Robotech***. After studying sequential art independently, he published his first comic in 1998. Since 2007, he has been a key member of Altercomics Studios, contributing to ***Cats on My Head*** and ***Time: 5***. He pencilled a manga story for the nu metal band P.O.D., and he has also worked on the manga ***Spirit Dancer*** and TOKYOPOP's ***Tantric Stripfighter Trina***. He has recently contributed to a number of ***WarCraft*** and ***StarCraft*** books for TOKYOPOP, including inks on ***StarCraft: Ghost Academy*** volume 1. In his spare time, he draws the humor webcomic ***Spinerette***.

**Rocio Zucchi** is no stranger to Blizzard and TOKYOPOP. She illustrated the full-length ***World of Warcraft: Death Knight,*** and inked the story "Crusader's Blood" (***Warcraft: Legends*** volume 3). Born in Buenos Aires, Argentina, daughter of an Italian mother and an Argentinian father, she began to draw at a very young age. When she was 13, she met Fernando Heinz Furukawa (her fiancé) who helped her develop her artistic abilities. Rocio has also contributed to ***Time: 5*** (written by Mauro Mantella, featuring art by Fernando H.F., which will soon be published in the U.S.), ***Tantric Stripfighter Trina*** (also with Fernando, through TOKYOPOP), the ***Street Fighter*** and ***Darkstalkers*** Tribute books from Udon Studios, the webcomic "Heist," and a series of illustrations for a ***Wizard of Oz*** book. She is also a colorist and one of the key members of Altercomics Studios. She also contributed to the inks and tones in this book.

# INKS:

**Perla Pilucki** was born in Buenos Aires and has studied art since she was a child. She has taken her passion for art into children's book illustrations, concept art and fantasy art—for publishers all over the world. She has worked as a background artist and inker for E. Villagran, and recently joined Altercomics Studios.

**Pablo Churin** was born in Pergamino, Argentina. When he learned that he had the chance to tell stories with his drawings, he started to learn the basics of comic art with a professional working in Europe. Along with some of his fellow artists, they self-published several fanzines. Following that, he decided to make the leap to professional comic artist. After his first professional job at Publisher Studio-407 on the horror miniseries ***Hybrid***, he joined up with Altercomics Studios and has been busy ever since!

**Fernando Melek** (chapters 2,5) was born in 1978 in Tandil, Argentina. He began his professional artistic career in 2004, and has since worked as an illustrator, penciler, colorist and toner in the fields of comics, web comics, covers, calendar illustration, character design, and more. Fernando Melek works for local, national and international publishers. He works well by himself and plays well with others. He's recently contributed to several of TOKYOPOP's ***Warcraft*** manga, and currently inks TOKYOPOP's ***Priest: Purgatory***.

# CONTRIBUTING INKS:

**Tomas Aira** (chapter 2)
**Leandro Rizzo** (chapter 5)
**Mauro Vargas** (chapter 4)
**Roberto Viacava** (chapter 4)
**Gaston Zubeldia** (chapter 2,3)
**Rocio Zucchi** (chapter 4,5)

# TONES:

**Gonzalo Duarte** was born in Buenos Aires in 1986. In 2003, he studied comic illustration at E.A.H. (Argentine School of Comics) under Professor Mariano Navarro, and digital coloring for comics under Professor Hernan Cabrera in 2006. Since 2007 he has been working as a digital colorist, on works such as ***Triad*** from ECV Press, ***Gangland Avalon*** from Visionary Comics, and ***Primordial Man*** from Altercomics Studios. As a toner, he has contributed to several books in TOKYOPOP's ***Warcraft*** and ***StarCraft*** lines.

**Thanks to Altercomics Studios for contributing such fine artists to *StarCraft: Ghost Academy*!**
**Check out more of their work at www.altercomics.com.ar.**

# WORLD OF WARCRAFT®

# SHADOW WING™

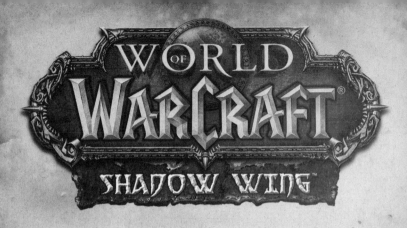

## PREVIEW

TOKYOPOP and BLIZZARD ENTERTAINMENT present ***World of Warcraft: Shadow Wing,*** the thrilling sequel to the international bestseller ***Warcraft: The Sunwell Trilogy!***

In ***Warcraft: The Sunwell Trilogy,*** a good-natured but brash blue dragon, Tyrygosa, and the human Jorad Mace, a paladin struggling to reconnect with the Light, emerged victorious in the Ghostlands after ending the the Undead Scourge's quest to obtain the Sunwell's potent energies, embodied in the form of a young girl, Anveena. Yet as arduous as that task was, Tyri and Jorad's journey is far from over. Both are drawn into the Dark Portal and transported to the shattered world of Outland, where they encounter a group of enigmatic creatures unlike any they have ever seen: the incorporeal nether dragons. But watching from the shadows is the ruthless Ragnok Bloodreaver, one of the original death knights. He has evil plans for the nether dragons that can change Outland and Azeroth forever...

Written by bestselling author Richard A. Knaak and drawn by international superstar Jae-Hwan Kim, ***World of Warcraft: Shadow Wing*** takes readers on an incredible journey through the mysterious regions of Outland. This epic manga also reveals details about the nether dragons' origins and connection to Deathwing, the corrupt Dragon Aspect responsible for the devastating events in the upcoming *World of Warcraft* expansion, ***Cataclysm.***

***Available now!***

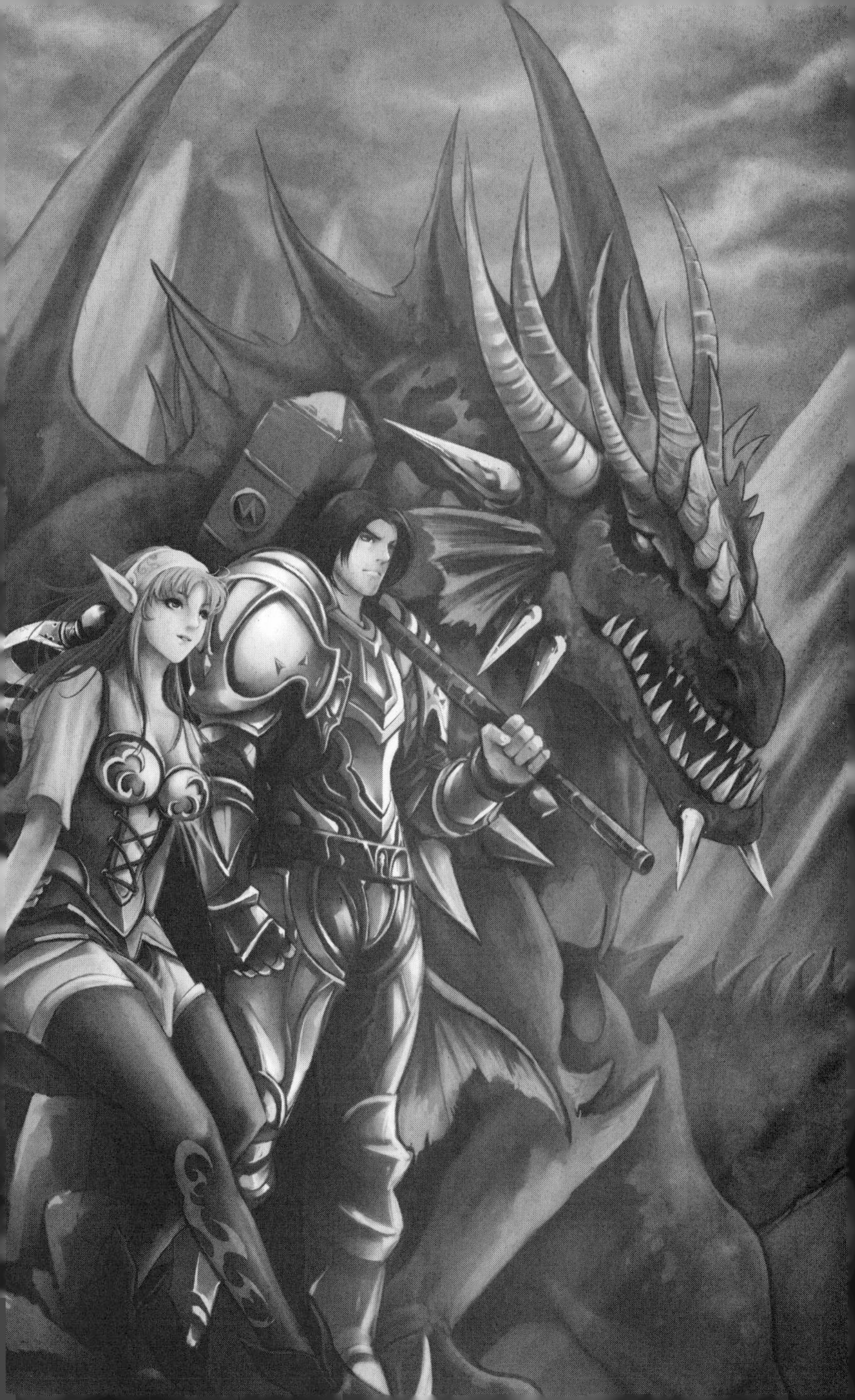

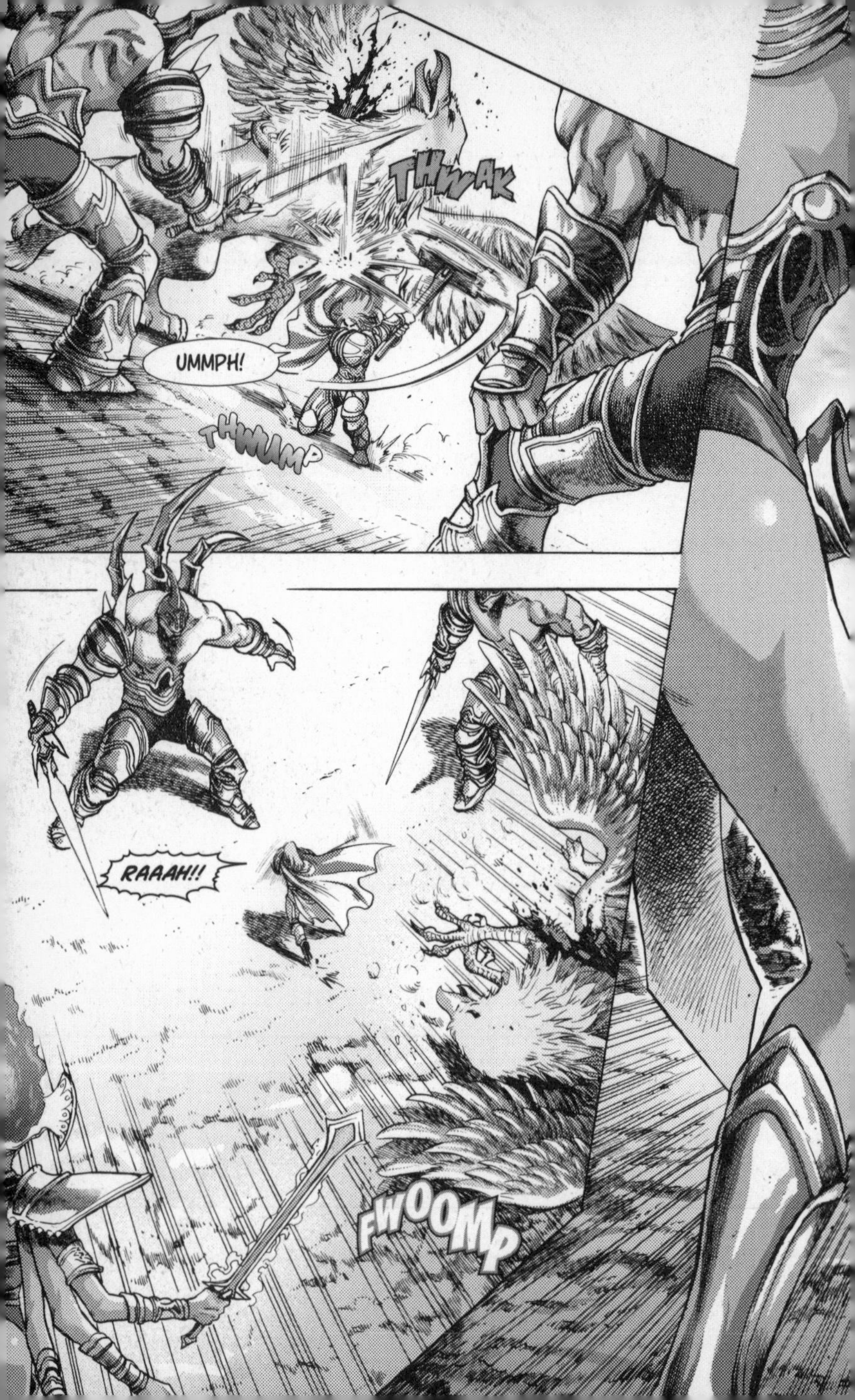
THWAK
UMMPH!
THWUMP
RAAAH!!
FWOOMP

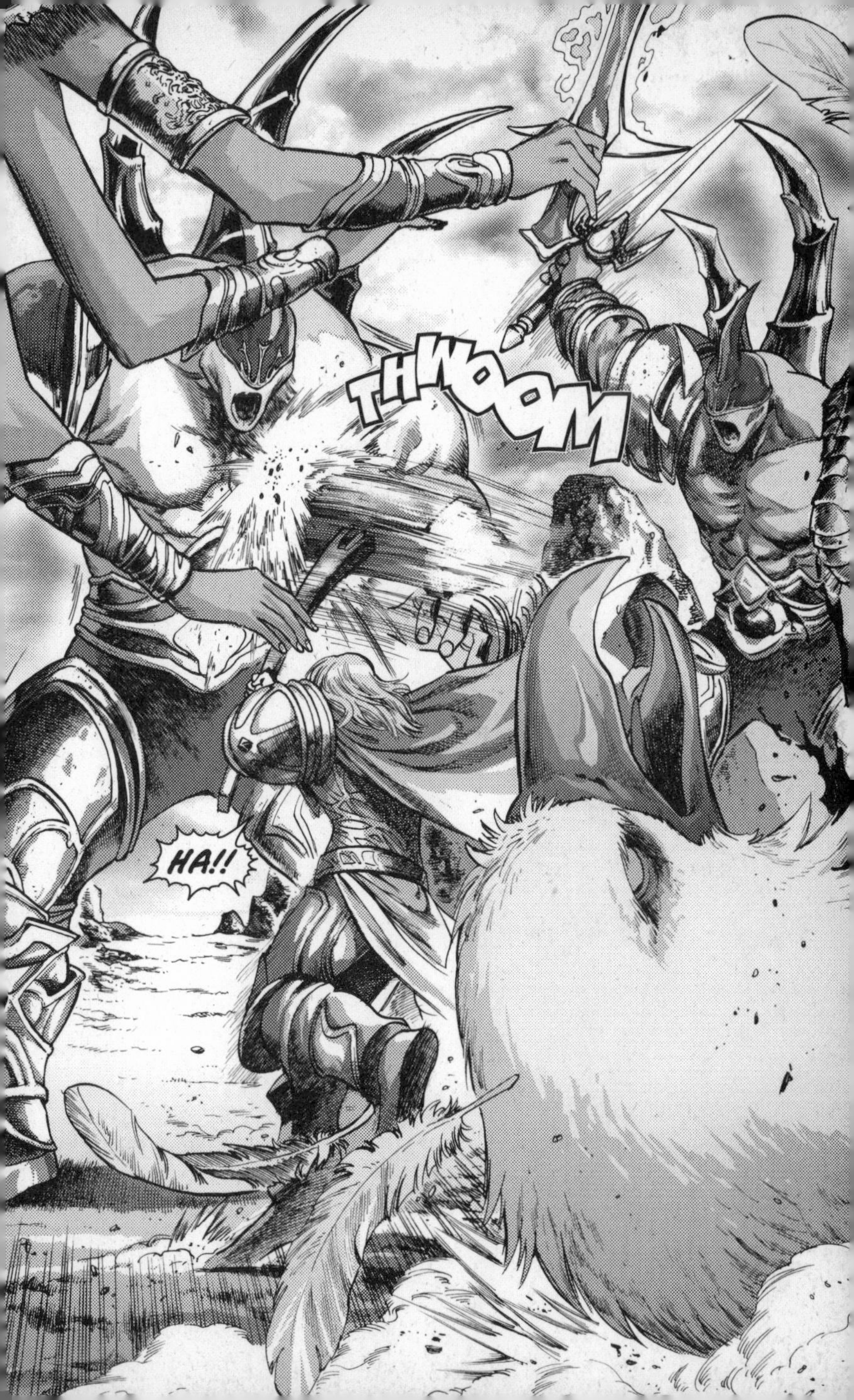
THWOOM
HA!!

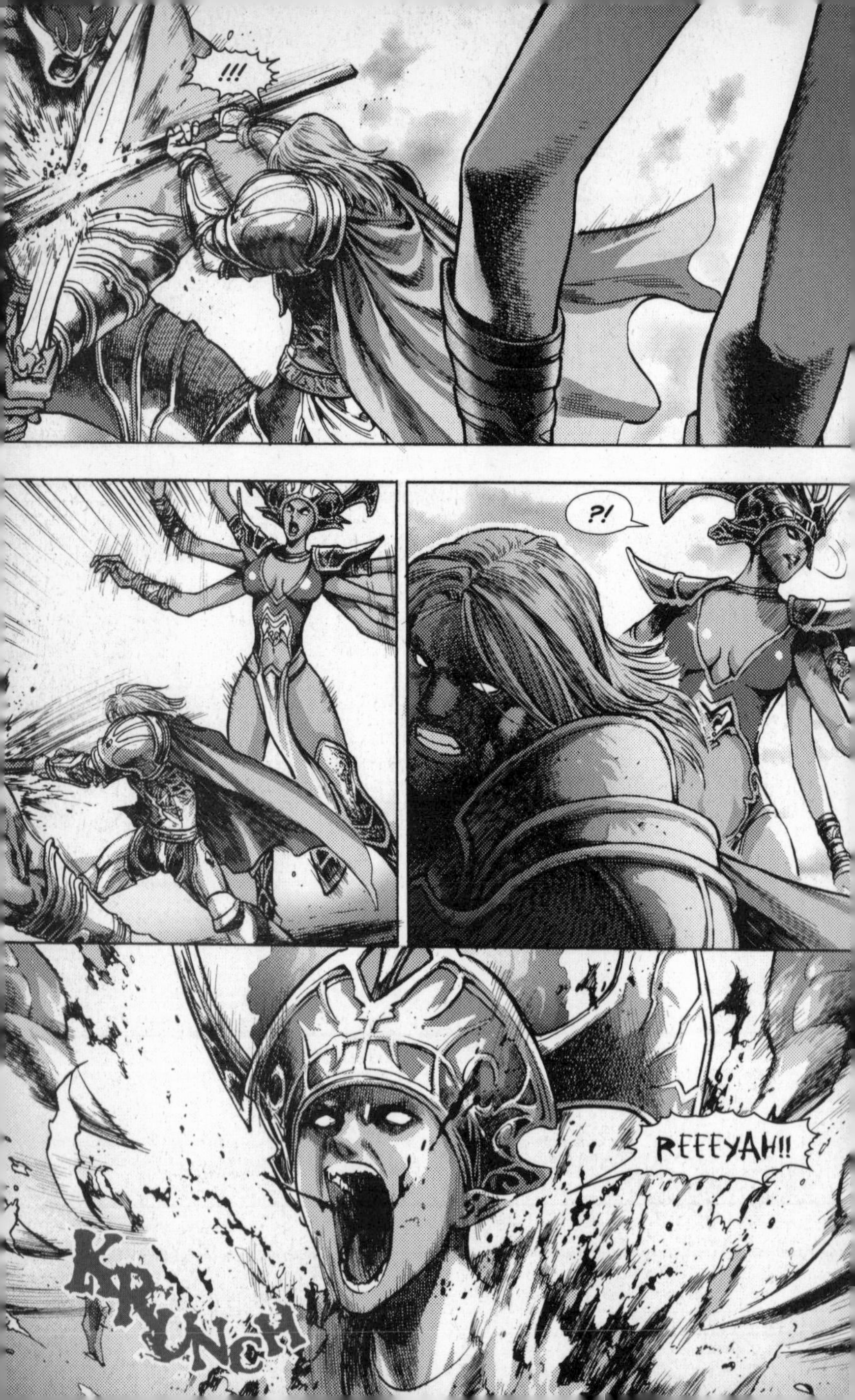
!!!
?!
REEEYAH!!
KRUNCH

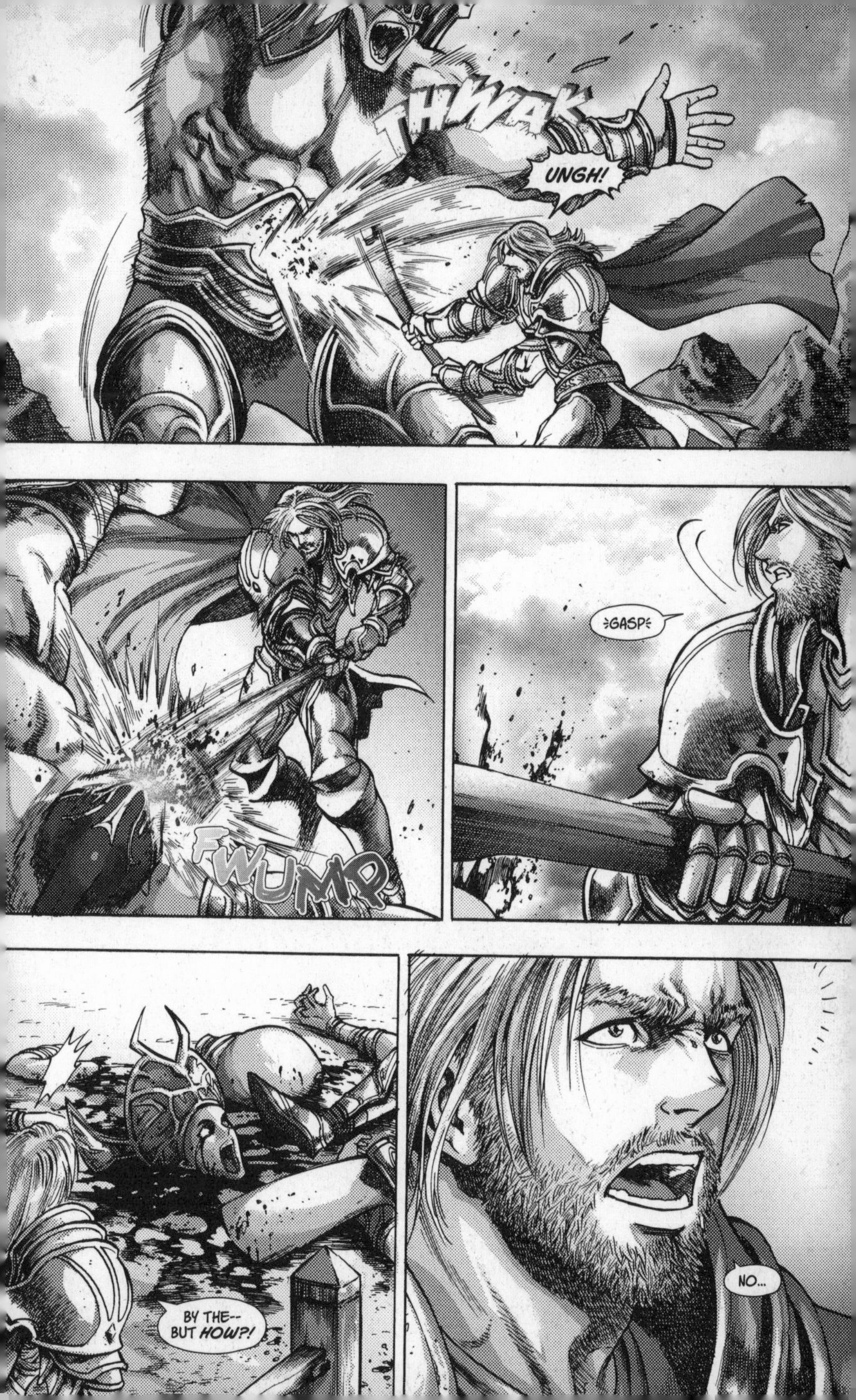
THWAK
UNGH!
FWUMP
GASP
BY THE-- BUT HOW?!
NO...

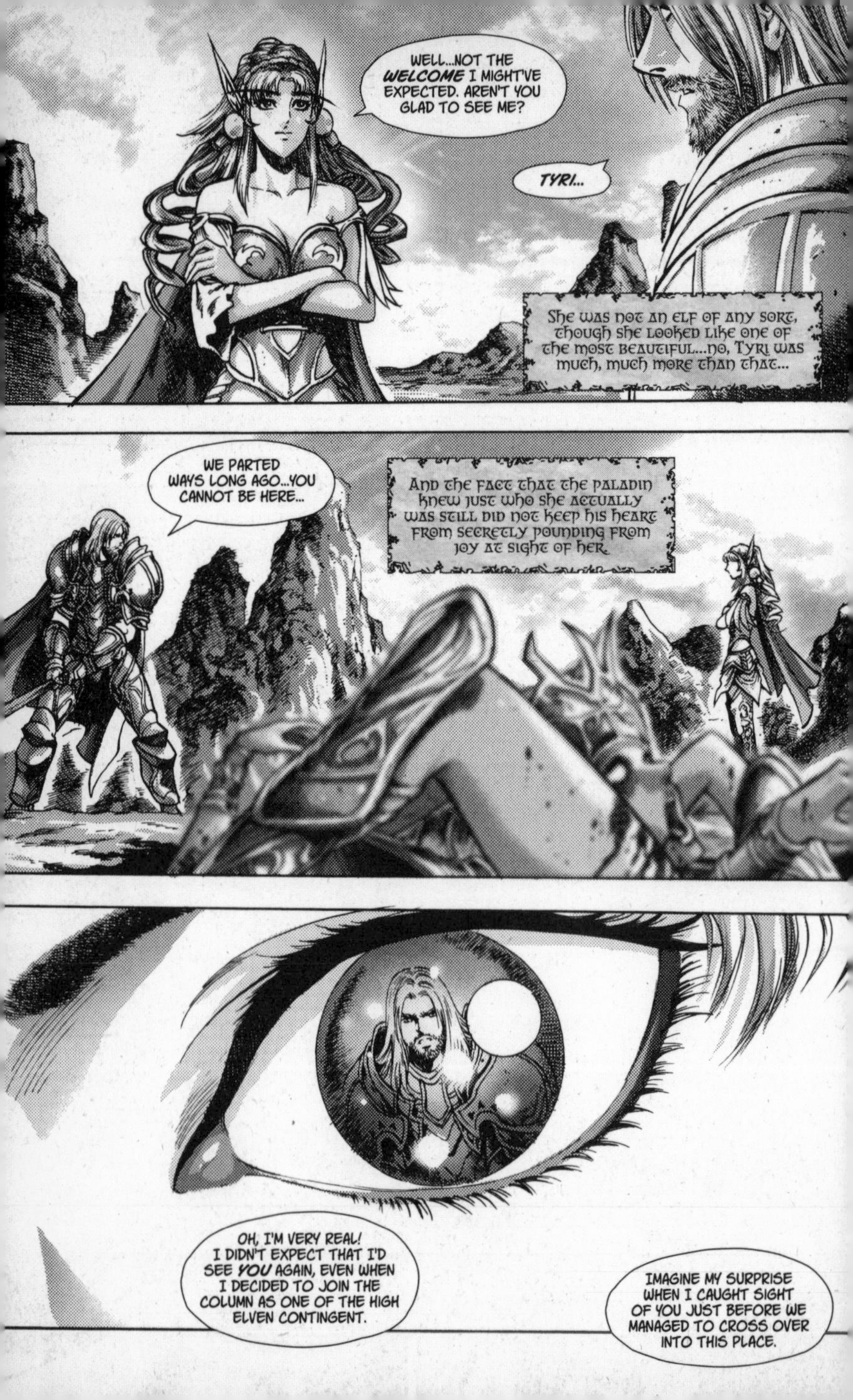
WELL...NOT THE *WELCOME* I MIGHT'VE EXPECTED. AREN'T YOU GLAD TO SEE ME?
TYRI...
She was not an elf of any sort, though she looked like one of the most beautiful...no, Tyri was much, much more than that...
WE PARTED WAYS LONG AGO...YOU CANNOT BE HERE...
And the fact that the paladin knew just who she actually was still did not keep his heart from secretly pounding from joy at sight of her.
OH, I'M VERY REAL! I DIDN'T EXPECT THAT I'D SEE *YOU* AGAIN, EVEN WHEN I DECIDED TO JOIN THE COLUMN AS ONE OF THE HIGH ELVEN CONTINGENT.
IMAGINE MY SURPRISE WHEN I CAUGHT SIGHT OF YOU JUST BEFORE WE MANAGED TO CROSS OVER INTO THIS PLACE.

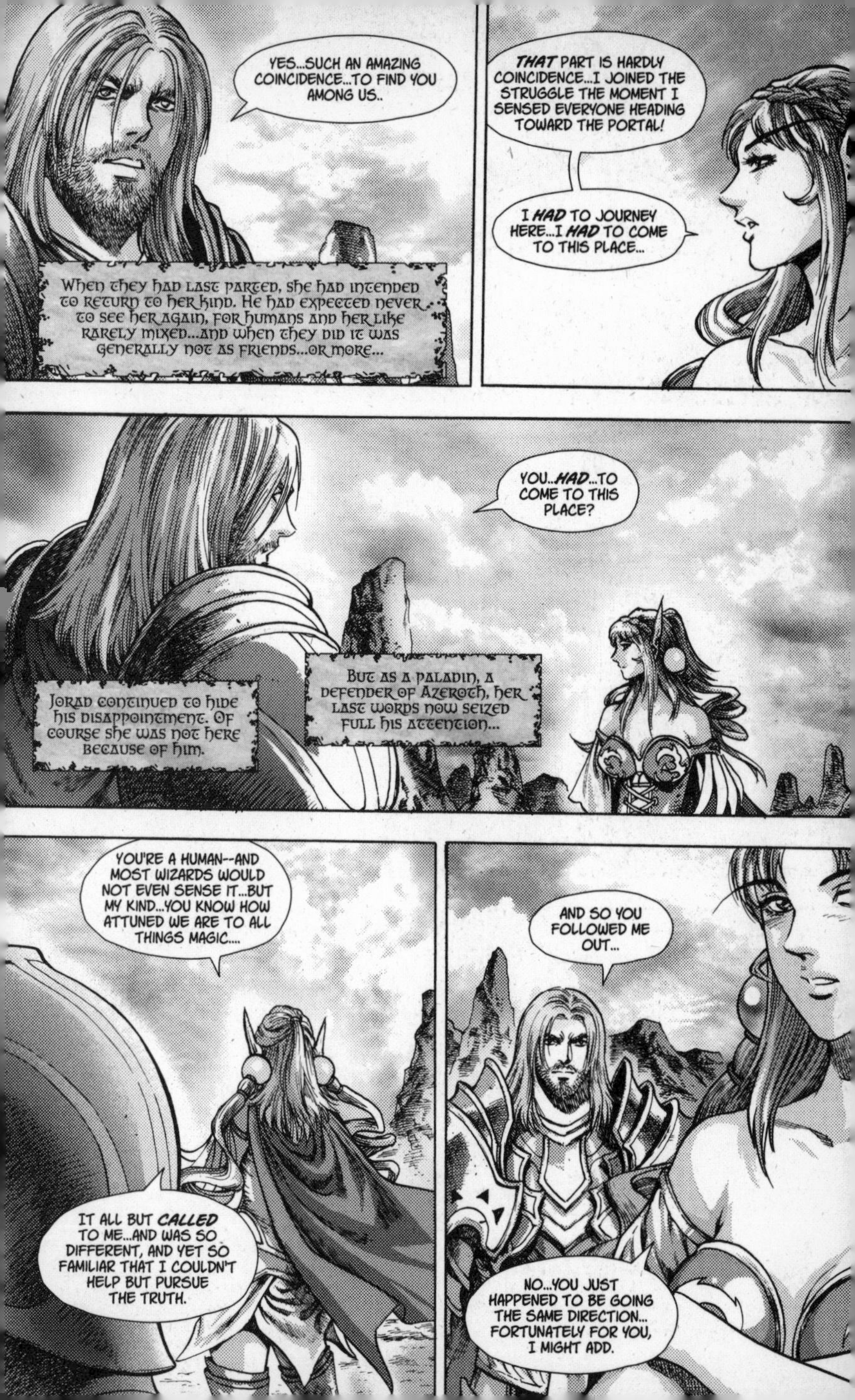
YES...SUCH AN AMAZING COINCIDENCE...TO FIND YOU AMONG US..
When they had last parted, she had intended to return to her kind. He had expected never to see her again, for humans and her like rarely mixed...and when they did it was generally not as friends...or more...
THAT PART IS HARDLY COINCIDENCE...I JOINED THE STRUGGLE THE MOMENT I SENSED EVERYONE HEADING TOWARD THE PORTAL!
I HAD TO JOURNEY HERE...I HAD TO COME TO THIS PLACE...
YOU...HAD...TO COME TO THIS PLACE?
Jorad continued to hide his disappointment. Of course she was not here because of him.
But as a paladin, a defender of Azeroth, her last words now seized full his attention...
YOU'RE A HUMAN--AND MOST WIZARDS WOULD NOT EVEN SENSE IT...BUT MY KIND...YOU KNOW HOW ATTUNED WE ARE TO ALL THINGS MAGIC....
IT ALL BUT CALLED TO ME...AND WAS SO DIFFERENT, AND YET SO FAMILIAR THAT I COULDN'T HELP BUT PURSUE THE TRUTH.
AND SO YOU FOLLOWED ME OUT...
NO...YOU JUST HAPPENED TO BE GOING THE SAME DIRECTION... FORTUNATELY FOR YOU, I MIGHT ADD.

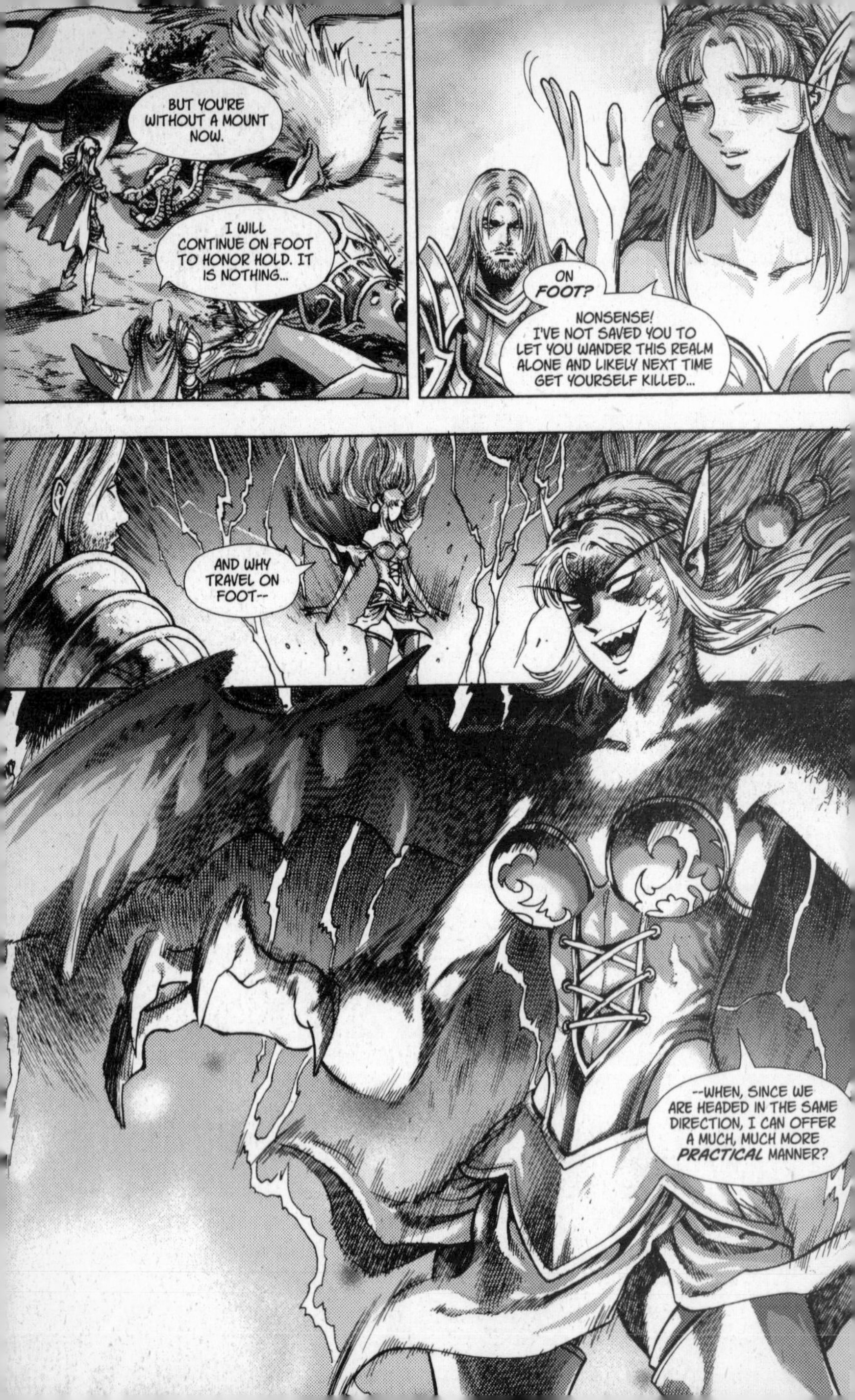
BUT YOU'RE WITHOUT A MOUNT NOW.
I WILL CONTINUE ON FOOT TO HONOR HOLD. IT IS NOTHING...
ON *FOOT?*
NONSENSE! I'VE NOT SAVED YOU TO LET YOU WANDER THIS REALM ALONE AND LIKELY NEXT TIME GET YOURSELF KILLED...
AND WHY TRAVEL ON FOOT--
--WHEN, SINCE WE ARE HEADED IN THE SAME DIRECTION, I CAN OFFER A MUCH, MUCH MORE *PRACTICAL* MANNER?

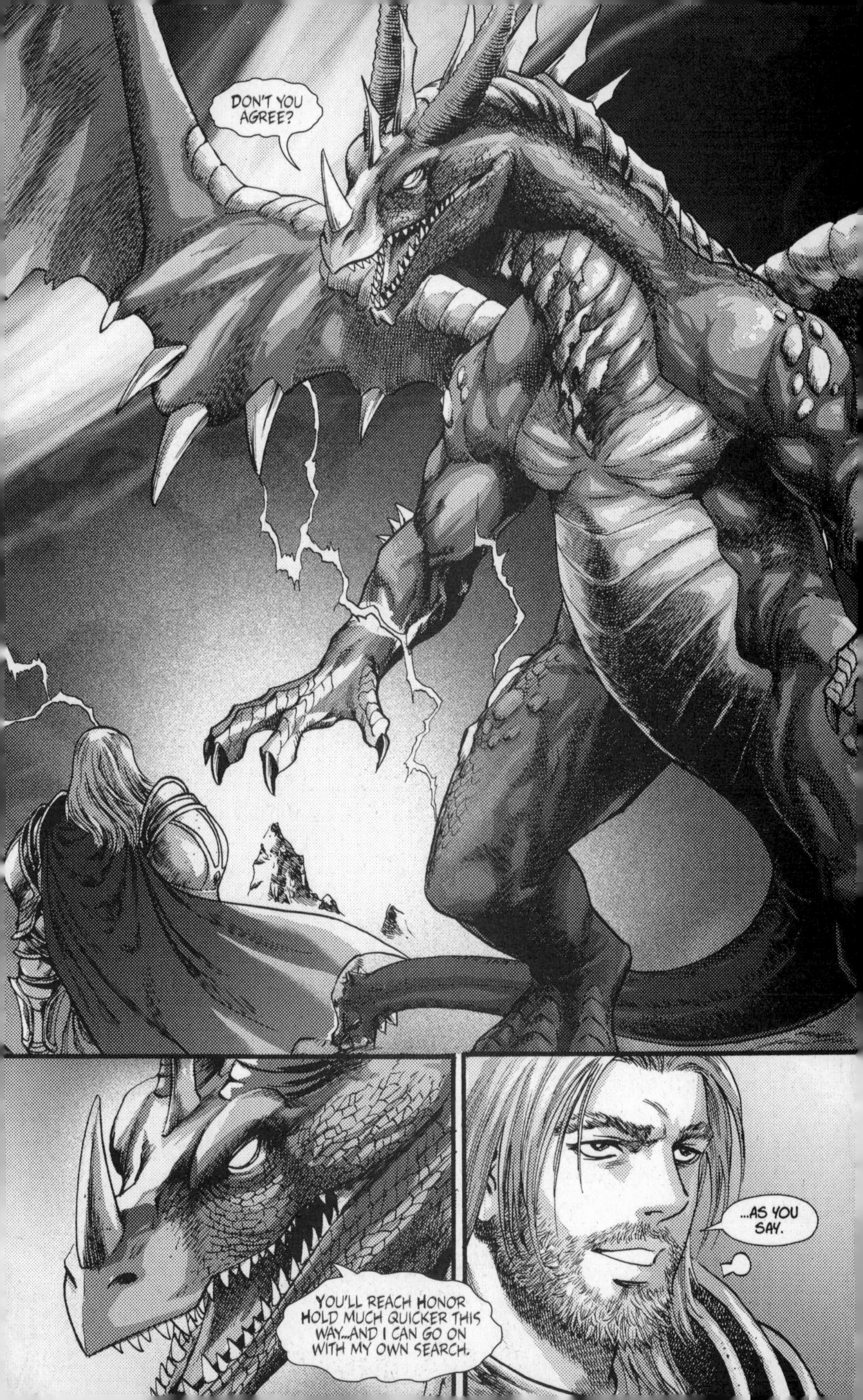
DON'T YOU AGREE?
YOU'LL REACH HONOR HOLD MUCH QUICKER THIS WAY...AND I CAN GO ON WITH MY OWN SEARCH.
...AS YOU SAY.

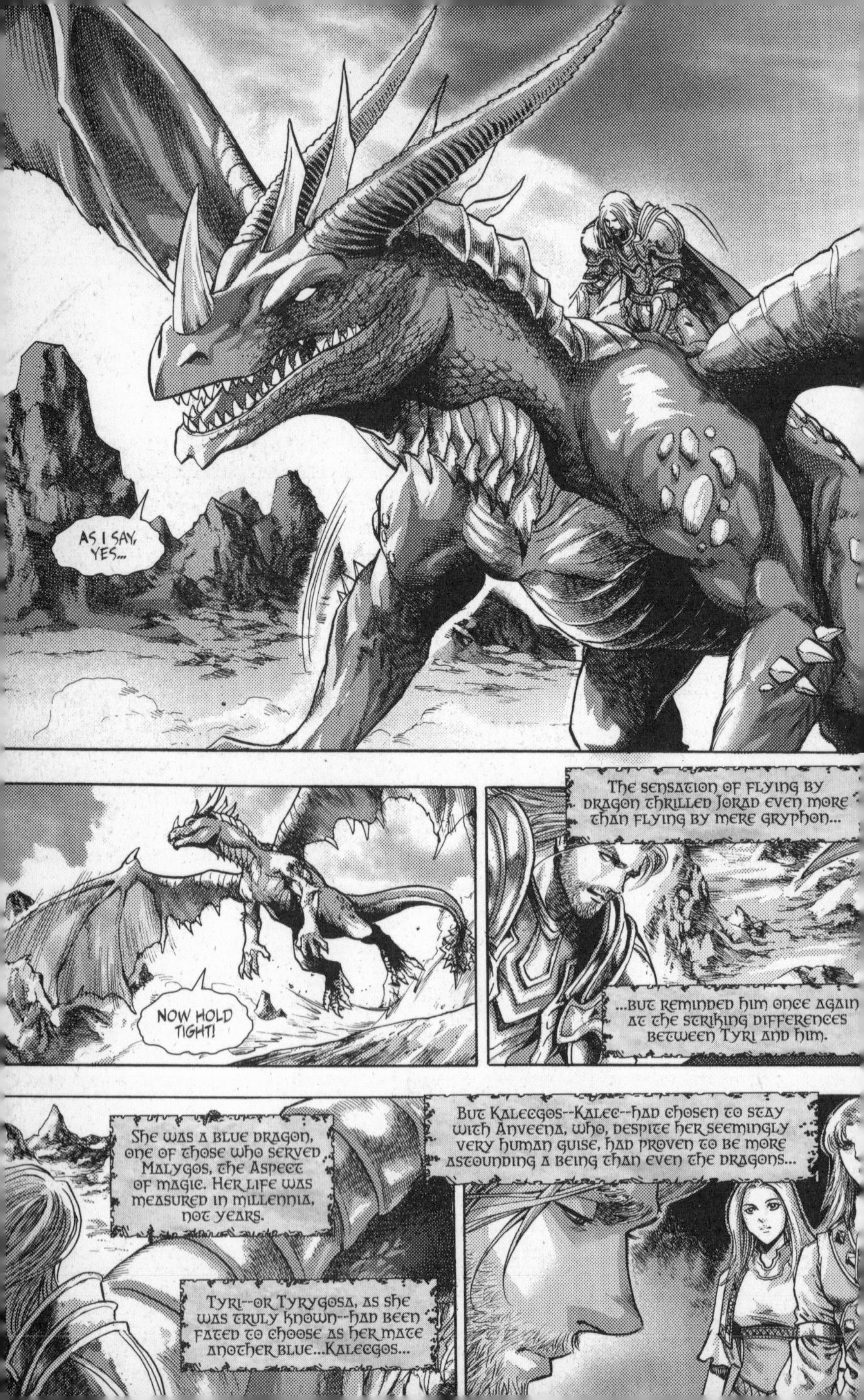
AS I SAY, YES...
NOW HOLD TIGHT!
The sensation of flying by dragon thrilled Jorad even more than flying by mere gryphon...
...but reminded him once again of the striking differences between Tyri and him.
She was a blue dragon, one of those who served Malygos, the Aspect of magic. Her life was measured in millennia, not years.
Tyri--or Tyrygosa, as she was truly known--had been fated to choose as her mate another blue...Kalecgos...
But Kalecgos--Kalec--had chosen to stay with Anveena, who, despite her seemingly very human guise, had proven to be more astounding a being than even the dragons...

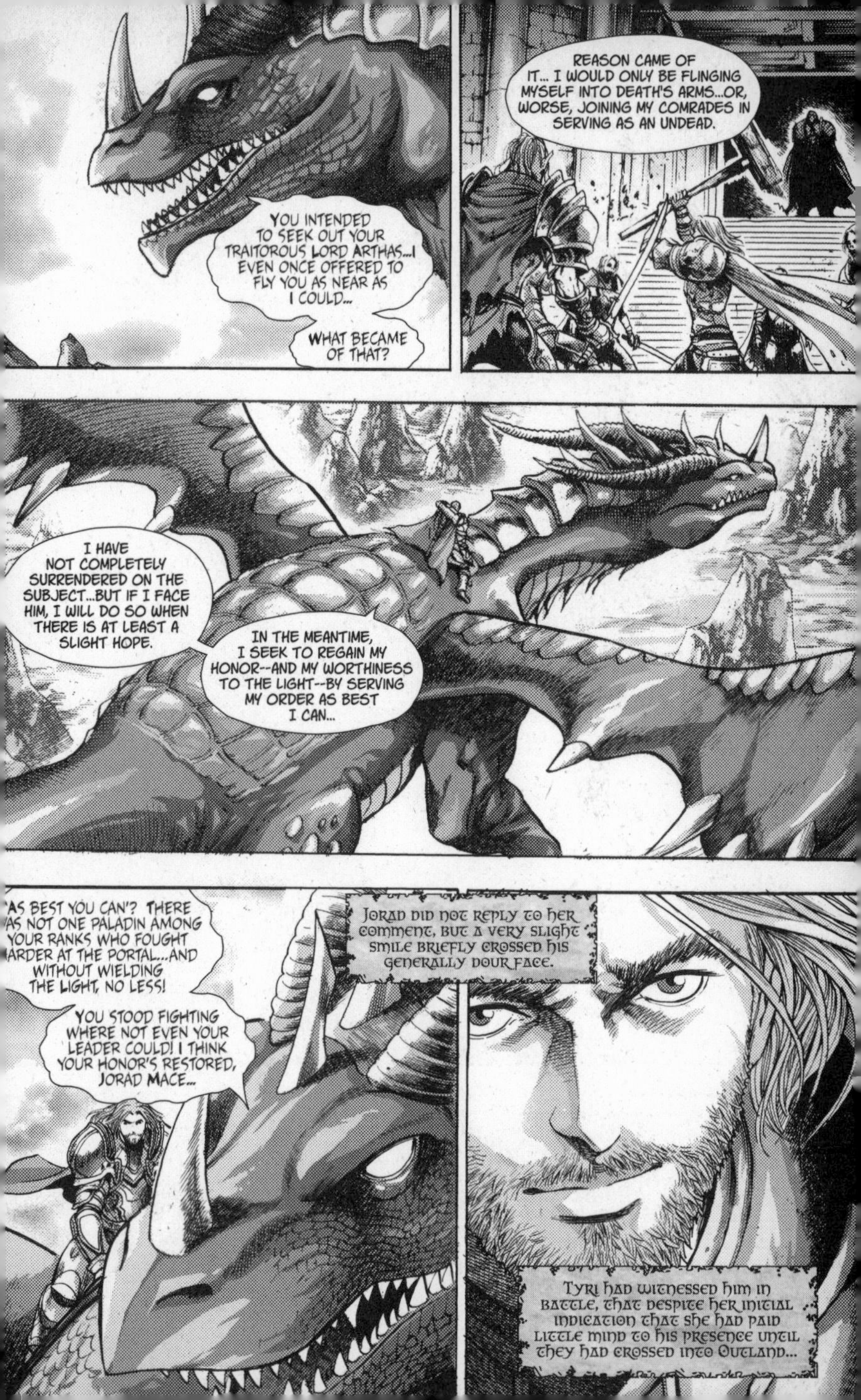
YOU INTENDED TO SEEK OUT YOUR TRAITOROUS LORD ARTHAS...I EVEN ONCE OFFERED TO FLY YOU AS NEAR AS I COULD...
WHAT BECAME OF THAT?
REASON CAME OF IT... I WOULD ONLY BE FLINGING MYSELF INTO DEATH'S ARMS...OR, WORSE, JOINING MY COMRADES IN SERVING AS AN UNDEAD.
I HAVE NOT COMPLETELY SURRENDERED ON THE SUBJECT...BUT IF I FACE HIM, I WILL DO SO WHEN THERE IS AT LEAST A SLIGHT HOPE.
IN THE MEANTIME, I SEEK TO REGAIN MY HONOR--AND MY WORTHINESS TO THE LIGHT--BY SERVING MY ORDER AS BEST I CAN...
'AS BEST YOU CAN'? THERE WAS NOT ONE PALADIN AMONG YOUR RANKS WHO FOUGHT HARDER AT THE PORTAL...AND WITHOUT WIELDING THE LIGHT, NO LESS!
YOU STOOD FIGHTING WHERE NOT EVEN YOUR LEADER COULD! I THINK YOUR HONOR'S RESTORED, JORAD MACE...
JORAD DID NOT REPLY TO HER COMMENT, BUT A VERY SLIGHT SMILE BRIEFLY CROSSED HIS GENERALLY DOUR FACE.
TYRI HAD WITNESSED HIM IN BATTLE, THAT DESPITE HER INITIAL INDICATION THAT SHE HAD PAID LITTLE MIND TO HIS PRESENCE UNTIL THEY HAD CROSSED INTO OUTLAND...

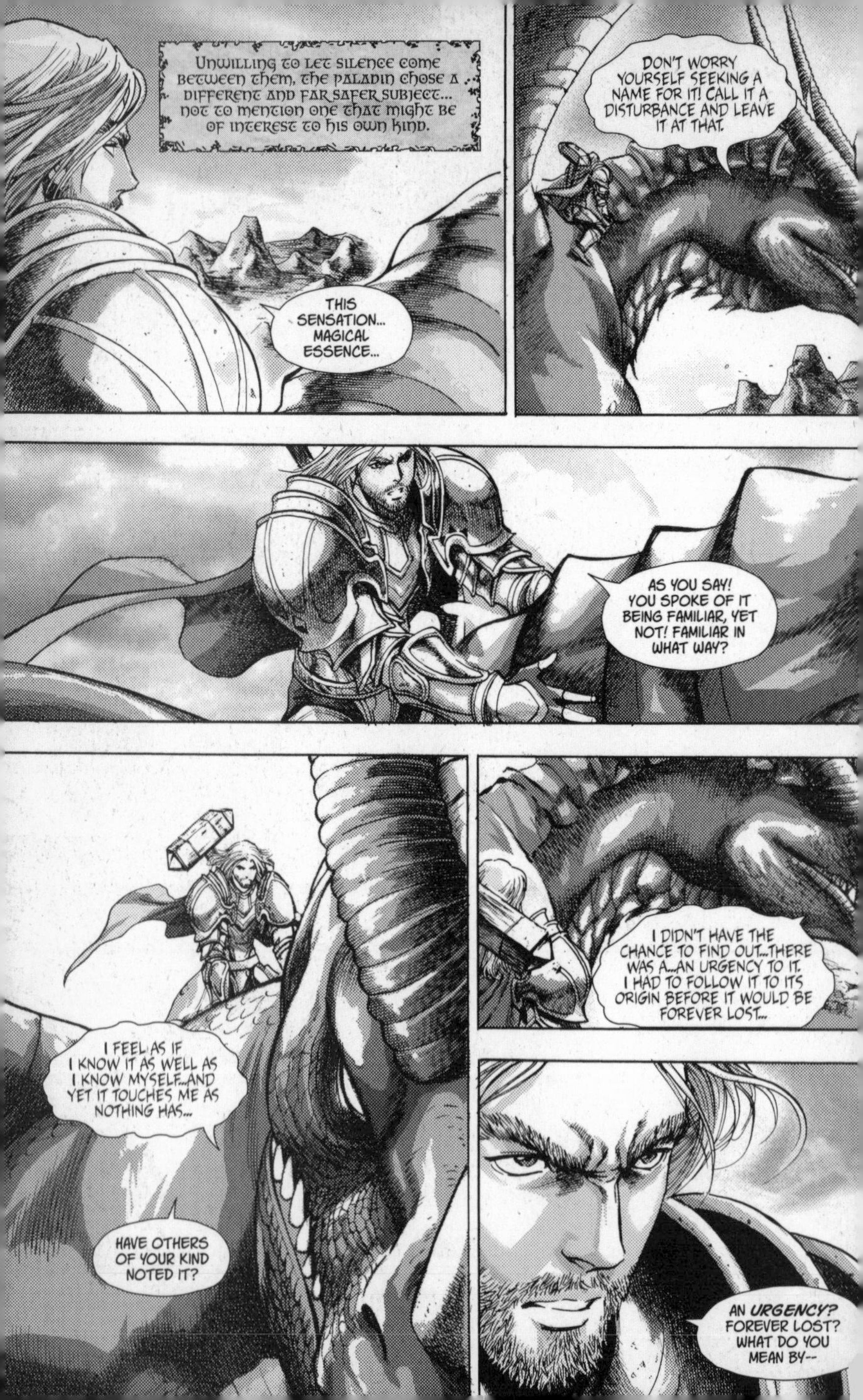
Unwilling to let silence come between them, the paladin chose a different and far safer subject... not to mention one that might be of interest to his own kind.
THIS SENSATION... MAGICAL ESSENCE...
DON'T WORRY YOURSELF SEEKING A NAME FOR IT! CALL IT A DISTURBANCE AND LEAVE IT AT THAT.
AS YOU SAY! YOU SPOKE OF IT BEING FAMILIAR, YET NOT! FAMILIAR IN WHAT WAY?
I FEEL AS IF I KNOW IT AS WELL AS I KNOW MYSELF...AND YET IT TOUCHES ME AS NOTHING HAS...
HAVE OTHERS OF YOUR KIND NOTED IT?
I DIDN'T HAVE THE CHANCE TO FIND OUT...THERE WAS A...AN URGENCY TO IT. I HAD TO FOLLOW IT TO ITS ORIGIN BEFORE IT WOULD BE FOREVER LOST...
AN *URGENCY?* FOREVER LOST? WHAT DO YOU MEAN BY--

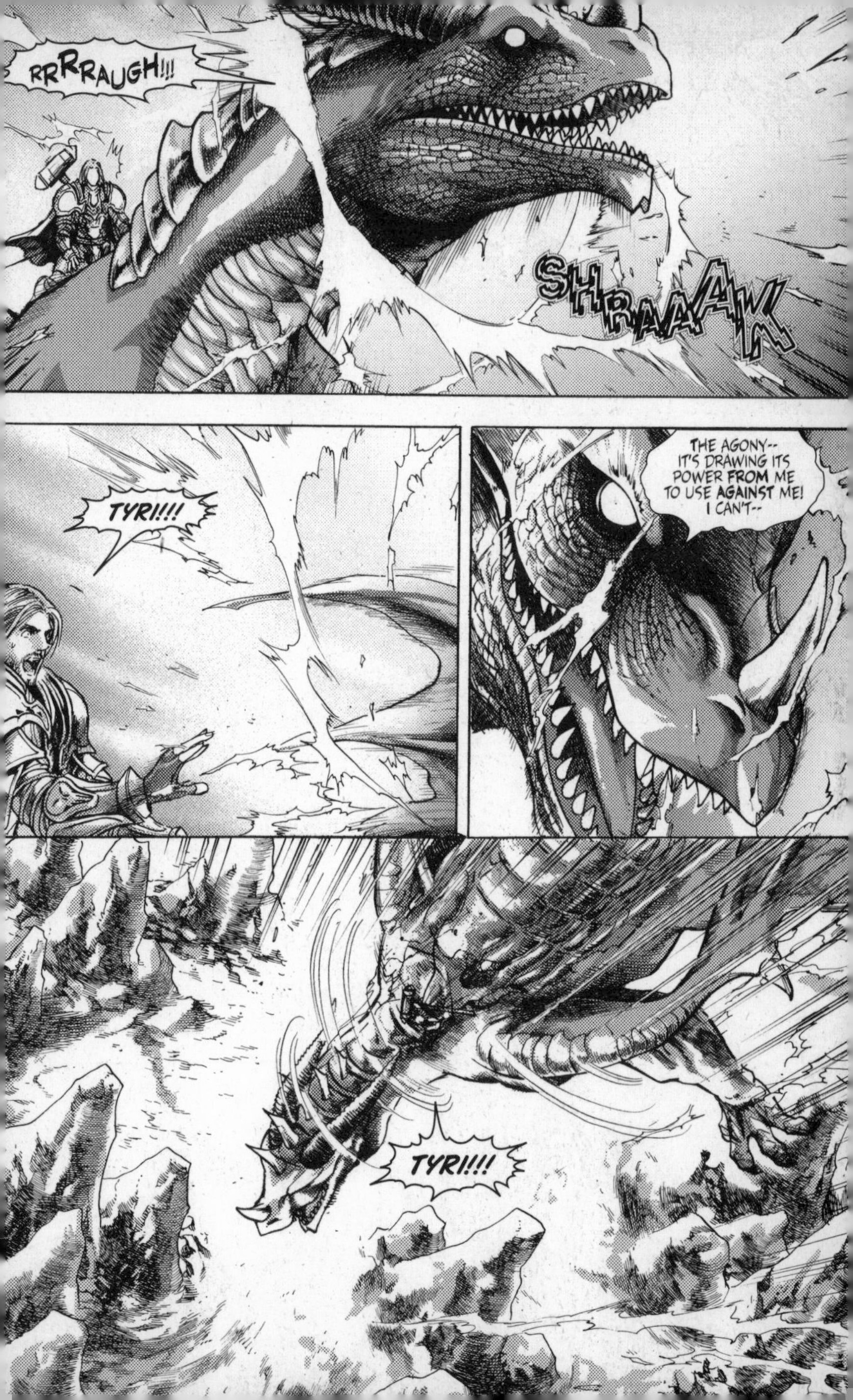
RRRRAUGH!!!
SHRAAAK
TYRI!!!!
THE AGONY--
IT'S DRAWING ITS
POWER FROM ME
TO USE AGAINST ME!
I CAN'T--
TYRI!!!!

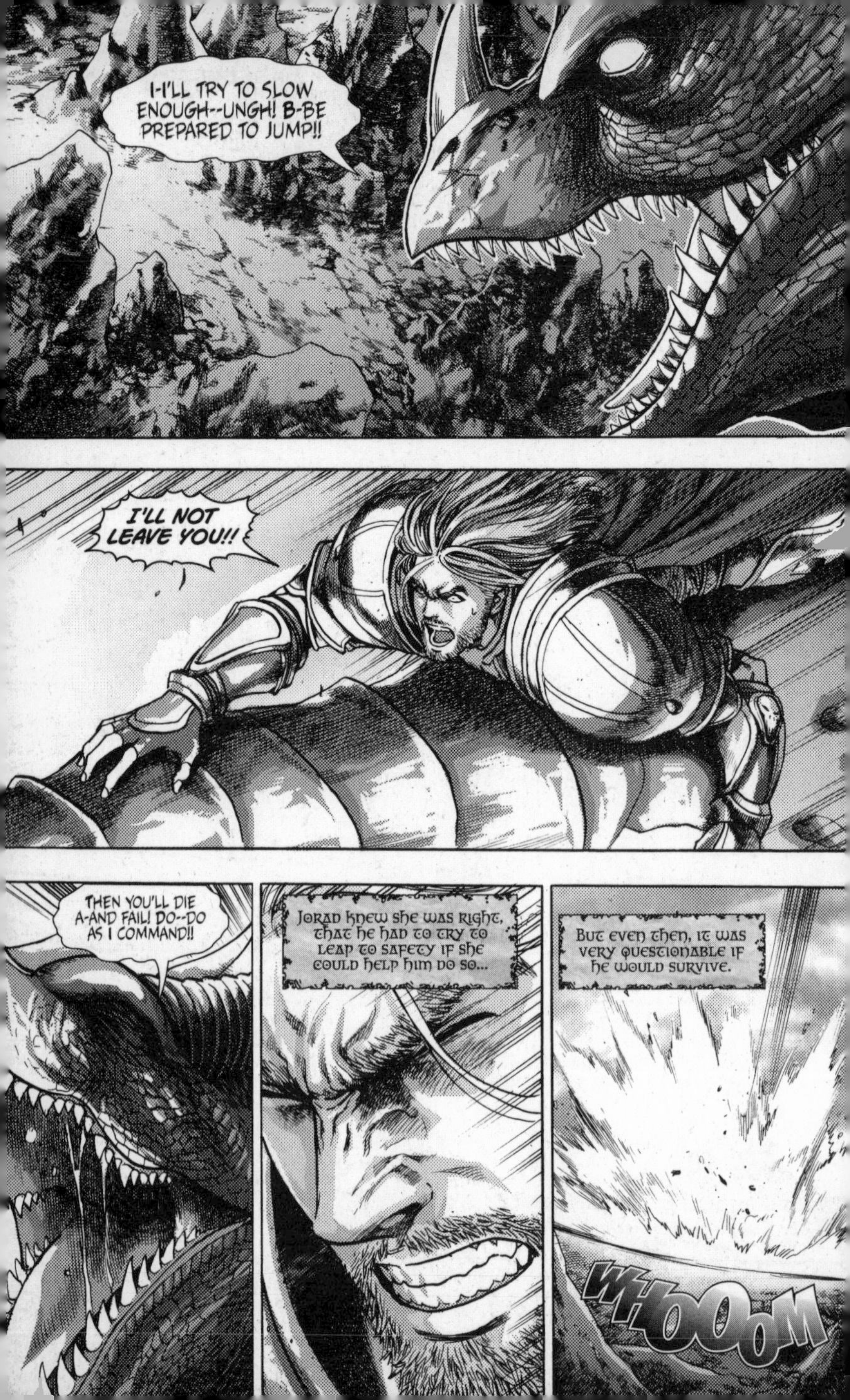
I-I'LL TRY TO SLOW ENOUGH--UNGH! B-BE PREPARED TO JUMP!!
I'LL NOT LEAVE YOU!!
THEN YOU'LL DIE A-AND FAIL! DO--DO AS I COMMAND!!
Jorad knew she was right, that he had to try to leap to safety if she could help him do so...
But even then, it was very questionable if he would survive.
WHOOOM

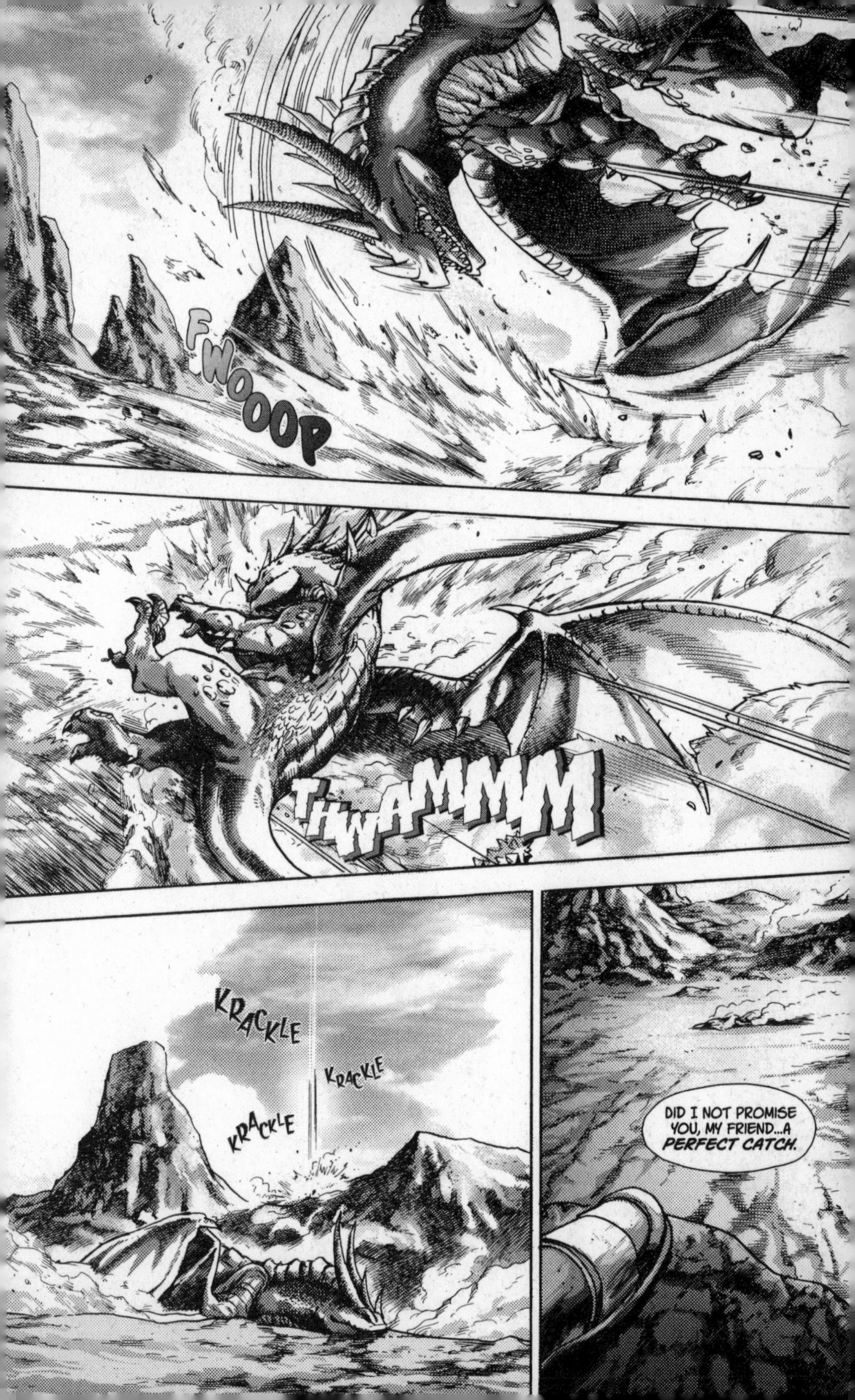
FWOOOP
THWAMMMM
KRACKLE
KRACKLE
KRACKLE
DID I NOT PROMISE YOU, MY FRIEND...A *PERFECT CATCH.*

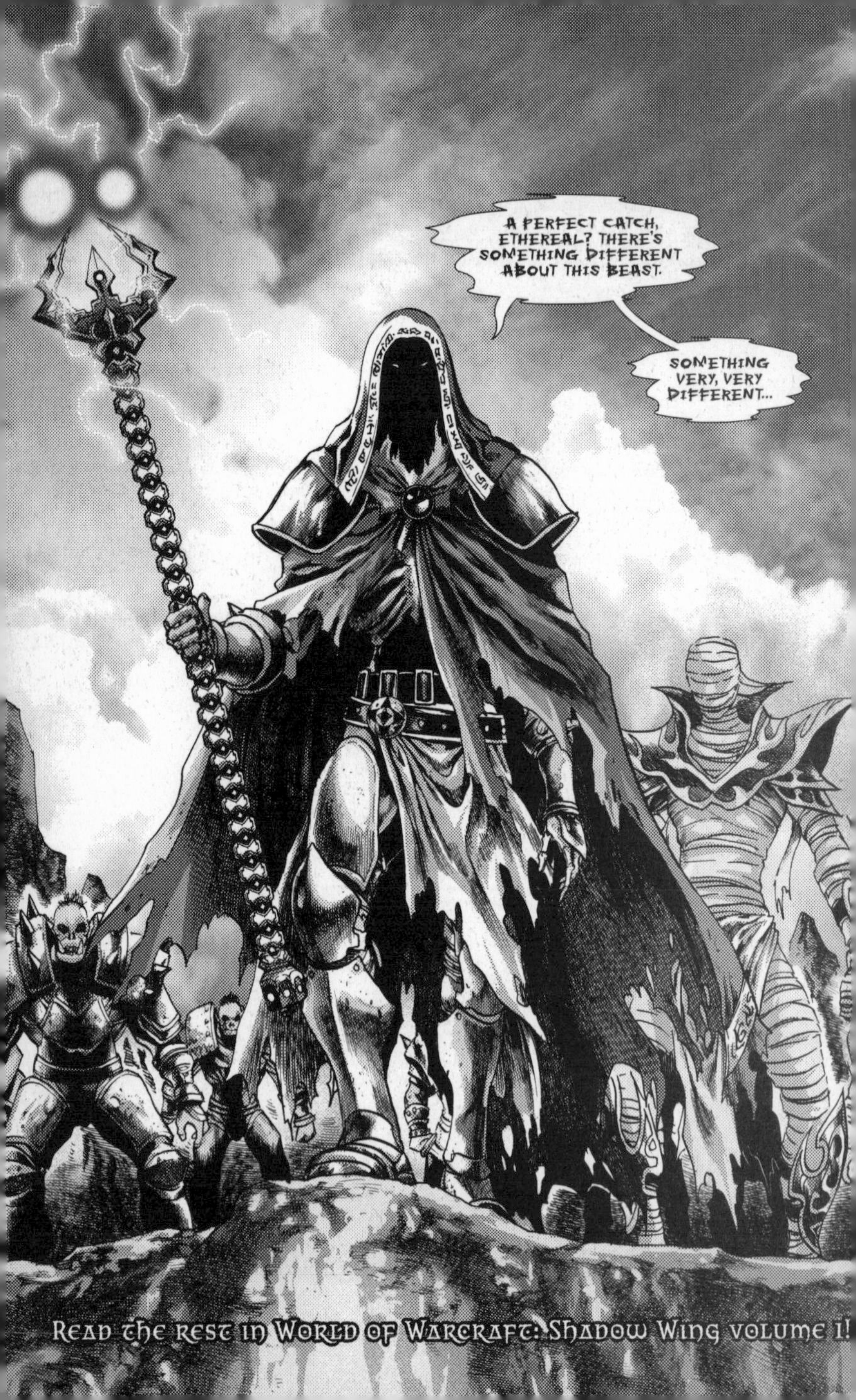
A PERFECT CATCH, ETHEREAL? THERE'S SOMETHING DIFFERENT ABOUT THIS BEAST.
SOMETHING VERY, VERY DIFFERENT...
Read the rest in World of Warcraft: Shadow Wing volume 1!

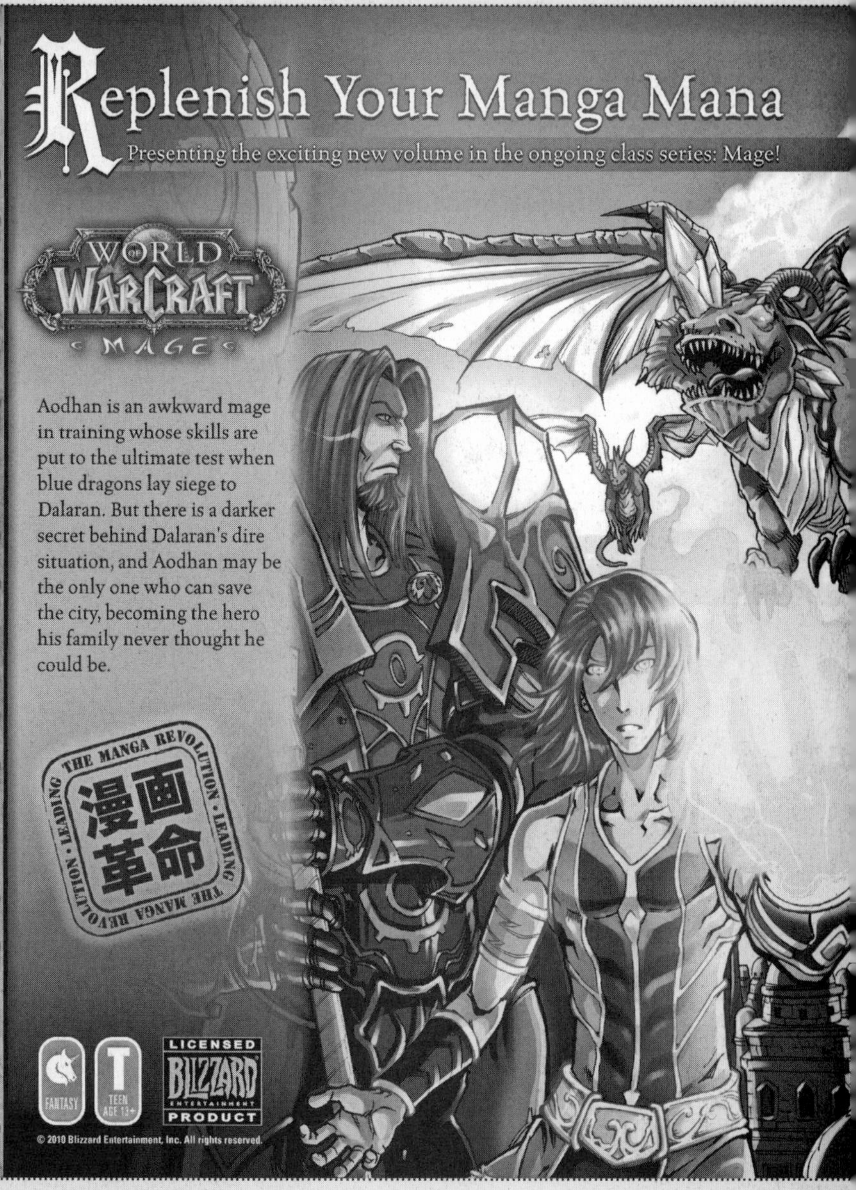
Replenish Your Manga Mana
Presenting the exciting new volume in the ongoing class series: Mage!
WORLD OF WARCRAFT
MAGE
Aodhan is an awkward mage in training whose skills are put to the ultimate test when blue dragons lay siege to Dalaran. But there is a darker secret behind Dalaran's dire situation, and Aodhan may be the only one who can save the city, becoming the hero his family never thought he could be.
THE MANGA REVOLUTION · LEADING THE MANGA REVOLUTION · LEADING
漫画革命
FANTASY
T
TEEN AGE 13+
LICENSED
BLIZZARD ENTERTAINMENT
PRODUCT
© 2010 Blizzard Entertainment, Inc. All rights reserved.

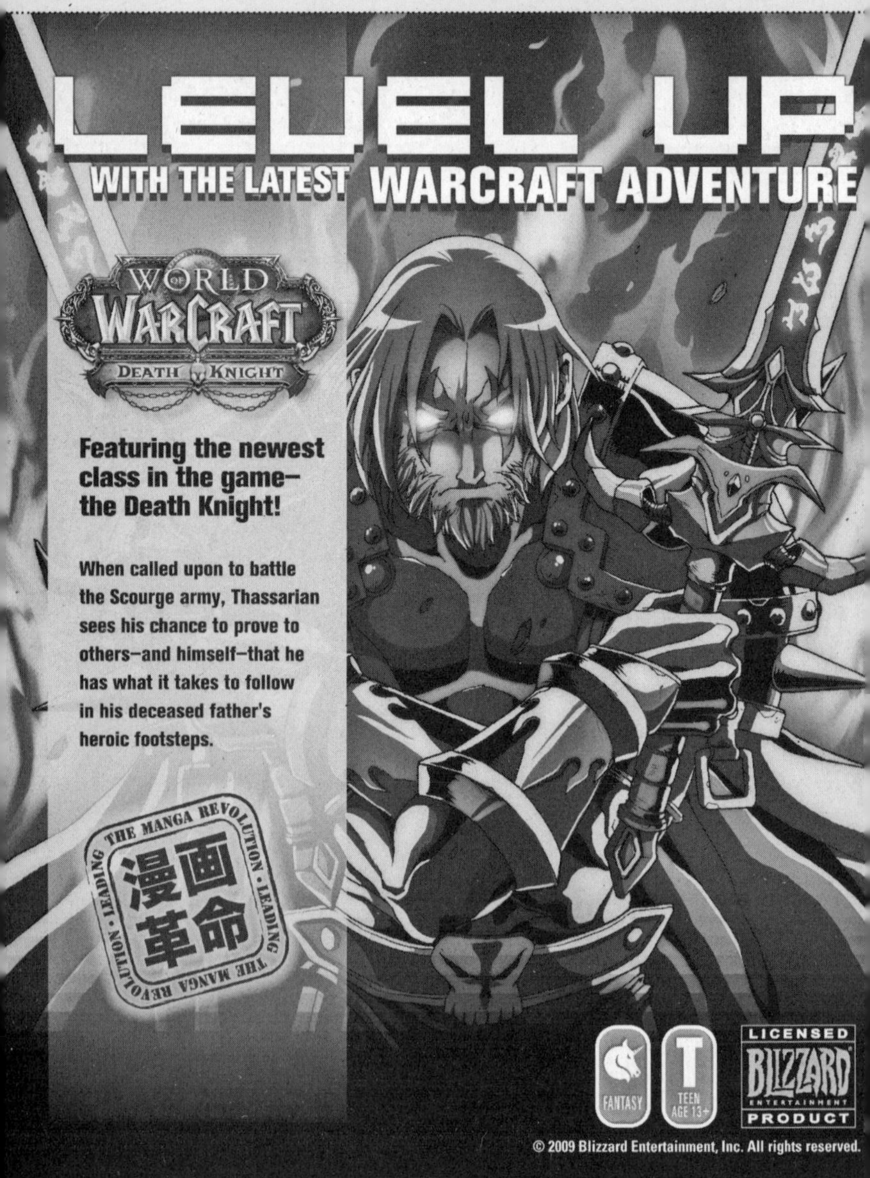
LEVEL UP
WITH THE LATEST WARCRAFT ADVENTURE
WORLD OF WARCRAFT
DEATH KNIGHT
Featuring the newest class in the game—the Death Knight!
When called upon to battle the Scourge army, Thassarian sees his chance to prove to others—and himself—that he has what it takes to follow in his deceased father's heroic footsteps.
THE MANGA REVOLUTION · LEADING THE MANGA REVOLUTION · LEADING
漫画革命
FANTASY
T
TEEN AGE 13+
LICENSED
BLIZZARD
ENTERTAINMENT
PRODUCT
© 2009 Blizzard Entertainment, Inc. All rights reserved.

FOR MORE INFORMATION VISIT: WWW.TOKYOPOP.COM/WARCRAFT